A NEW
PUBLIC
EDUCATION

Educational Policy, Planning, and Theory
SERIES EDITOR: Don Adams, *University of Pittsburgh*

A NEW PUBLIC EDUCATION

Seymour W. Itzkoff
Smith College

DAVID McKAY COMPANY, INC.
NEW YORK

A NEW PUBLIC EDUCATION

Developmental Editor: Edward Artinian
  Editorial and Design Supervisor: Nicole Benevento
  Design: Pencils Portfolio, Inc.
Production and Manufacturing Supervisor: Donald W. Strauss
  Composition: Adroit Graphic Composition, Inc.
  Printing and Binding: Haddon Craftsmen

Library of Congress Cataloging in Publication Data

Itzkoff, Seymour W
  A new public education.

  (Educational policy, planning, and theory)
  Includes bibliographical references and index.
  1. Public schools—United States.
2. Educational planning—United States. I. Title.
LA217.I85   370'.973   75-43802
ISBN 0-679-30303-0

To my mother and sister

Preface

Our nation was conceived in the belief that the institutions of society exist to serve fundamental human needs and values. The creation and life expectancy of institutions are predicated on their successful functioning in fulfilling the purposes of ordinary citizens. The institution of the public school as presently constituted is thus not sacrosanct. Its existence can be rationalized only to the extent that it continues to serve those deepest commitments and values that can be nurtured through the agencies of formal education.

We are all aware of the rising chorus that argues against the public school. This new climate of opinion reflects a great body of evidence that testifies to the failure of public education to meet the value needs of our people. This book does not intend to add another condemnatory ripple to this tide of protest. Rather, its object is to understand how the public schools took on this mantle of national moral authority, and how it has been lost.

Even more important is an attempt to understand the current failure in terms of the changing historical and cultural conditions that now necessitate the rethinking of our educational needs. When we look deeply into our cultural dynamics, look back to history for some perspective, as well as peer hopefully into the future, perhaps certain truths will emerge.

Human beings remain the same, but their social and historical conditions can change radically. If we are to preserve our democratic life as we struggle against ominous challenges that lie before us, we must act quickly to modernize and strengthen all of our social institutions. Rather than less freedom, we will need even more. In the best sense of that term, educational freedom will have to be in the forefront of this demand.

The job of fostering self-determination, individuation, and intellectual power must be returned to the schools. Our confidence in the cultural possibilities of schooling lies in our confidence in the power of the people to make the most of their liberty. The institutional reforms that are set forth here are thus intended for creating a new but more publicly responsive education.

Contents

Part

1

The
Theme

1

Introduction: The Argument

This book is about educational reform. It is not primarily concerned with the particular improvement that can take place in an individual classroom or school. More basically, it is a study of the interaction of the institutions of formal education with our evolving sense of community life and social structure. It constitutes an interpretation of the changing character and direction of American society and education. It also purports to explore the meaning of our present circumstances and the most probable and rational directions for future development.

Two concepts, informal education and formal education, constitute the motifs for studying education in a way that goes beyond common-sense assumptions. Informal education is a subtle concept. It begins in the most homely and ordinary contexts of life. In the family and the community the child is gradually shaped in certain concrete personal and social directions. From an almost infinite spectrum of possibilities, only certain specific values, beliefs, and interpersonal patterns are reinforced to create a unique human personality. Education in this widest human sense serves to inaugurate the individual into his cultural community.

Cultural beliefs, social behaviors, and associations emerge out of a fabric of meanings, a deep, rich tapestry of mutual understanding that binds the members of the community together. Through informal education the sum total of adult teaching, institutional regulation, and emotional commitments produces individuals who can live comfortably with their peers. In this manner informal education serves to perpetuate the society.

Formal education is more specific and concrete in its work. It denotes schools, curricula, the subject matter of knowledge, and the overall patterns by which advanced nations prepare their young for the complexities and dynamics of such societies. Although the surface features of formal education more clearly meet the eye and are more often the subject of comparative discussion, it is especially important to relate the surface institutions to those deep philosophical assumptions that give schools and curricula their meaning and direction.

An educational system as it develops out of a civilized and self-conscious society becomes the institutional actualization of that society's vision of itself and its evolving destiny. A formal educational system becomes the bearer of the society's attempt to shape and order itself to accomplish its corporate ideal. For any nation to bind itself together as an organic cultural and political entity with a viable destiny, a powerful formal educational ideal is a necessity. Schools for the young that incorporate forms of learning and patterns of organization that complement and root these ideals to a structure of knowledge and truth become permanent vehicles for a dynamic social stability.

An analysis of the American tradition (chapters 4, 5, and 6) of formal education reveals several philosophical shifts and their concomitant patterns of schooling. But the most powerful changes began toward the mid-nineteenth century with the coming of industrialization, scientific modernity, and the transformation of an agricultural and immigrant population by the developing public schools. At this point the relative stability and integration of both the informal and formal modes of education were dislocated and began to interact in a rapid dynamic of change.

A society is not merely a political or economic amalgam. It also constitutes a culture wherein are integrated the ideals and values of its people. In the violent displacement of this earlier culture by the enormous physical and attitudinal changes brought about by our commitment to modernity, we can trace our recent concerns. The application of the dual concepts of informal and formal education to the changes that have occurred reveal several interesting factors.

Our educational leaders and planners assumed the inviolability of the informal culture and its implied educational practices by our people. They never understood the significance of the informal domain, or its ultimate fragility. Thus, the expansion of external institutional structure, in education as elsewhere, in the making of the modern ideal, was predicated on the inevitable effacement of traditional values, patterns, and practices in community life and the substitution of an entirely new set of values and social forms.

The speed, efficiency, and far-ranging totality of this new formal ideal has resulted in a significant erosion of intimate community

allegiances, private ethnic and religious commitments, deeply rooted ethical and aesthetic values. Our educational practices have been
complicit in facilitating the development of institutional structures
that in their surge to create a powerful and unified society have
disregarded this important and insistent dimension of human life. In
fact, the practices of formal institutional education today are such
that they effectively bar the spontaneous regeneration of informal
culture and education.

The changing character of our social institutions as they relate to
education emerges in chapters dealing with religion, the teaching
profession, minorities, and the youth problem (chapters 7–11). The
plan here is to show, in the context of these specific issues and areas,
how the original circumstances and concerns that related to the
evolution of the schools have diverged sharply from their original
purposes. What has happened is that the character of these educational institutions and of their specific needs has been altered by the
cumulative response of corporate America; it is a triumph of the
technological and affluent society. The evisceration of the informal
culture and the intoxicating pursuit of wealth and power have con-
spired to puncture our aspirations and ideals.

Survival in late-twentieth-century America has increasingly necessitated the adoption of institutional techniques for the acquisition and use of national political power. Today, control over one's
destiny requires that groups band together into transnational units,
striking, lobbying, penetrating the political power structure so as to
tap the ever-replenishable fount of governmental and corporate
wealth. The growth of this network of gigantic organizations and
institutions, of which formal education is an integral part, has
sharply changed the character of our culture. It has given education
a wholly new face, which now raises questions about the quality of
our lives and the values that motivate us to learn and think.

These questions about the character of our educational institutions are not merely academic. The young, who experience the
living reality of our schools, and the citizenry, who pays for them
through taxation, have also begun to raise questions about the kind
of education that takes place within scholastic walls. In the last
decade evidence has begun to accumulate that those ideals and
goals that were responsible for the dynamic self-assurance of
American society for so many generations have begun to pale on the
young. A wide range of intellectual and institutional solutions that
have worked so successfully in the last one hundred and fifty years

show symptoms of exhaustion. Today each so-called advance in economic expansion or growth dredges up unabsorbable antithetical dislocations and costs.

Psychological factors are also involved. An important segment of our population, restricted to neither young nor old, is alienated from old ways of doing and thinking. The unprecedented turmoil into which our secondary and collegiate educational institutions have been thrown recently is evidence of this predicament. Our problems with the youth of today point most poignantly to the stagnancy of our educational values.

What has developed in our contemporary life is the coinciding of two new historical factors. Affluence and plenty have come to a majority of people. The children of this middle class are not as easily driven to covet that which has already been attained by their parents, many of whom climbed to middle-class status from the lower depths through intelligence, will, and education.

The young, in addition, see the warts of their society as few generations in the past have been able to. Earlier, our social and cultural abuses were buffered by intellectual ideals of a scientifically inspired democratic life of high cultural values, if and when the masses of society could attain to their rightful place. The realization of this hope in the economic and social domains has left much to be desired in the quality of our culture. The price of middle-class status has been the dissociation of the traditional bonds, disciplines, and values of the informal culture and the substitution of dependence on impersonal governmental or corporate structures.

The other new historical element that has severed the old relationships is associated with the unprecedented problems arising from the ideal of economic growth and expansion. Pollution, ecological balance, overpopulation, and the scarcity of natural resources have further tarnished the dreams of affluence. Traditional motifs no longer inspire enthusiasm and commitment among the young. The institutions themselves are tired; their potential for idealism is exhausted. The old reasons "why" no longer prompt the young to take their rightful generational place.

What has happened to our educational situation and most especially to the young who are forced to undergo its discipline is unique. The formal ideals that previously gave it great force and élan have weakened in their efficacy. The values that helped to drive this vision of modernization forward have been found to be corrupt and mean-spirited. And no philosophical alternative has been found to take its place. To parallel this emptiness in the superstructure of education, there is a vacuum in the informal culture.

Life in the small social units of family, neighborhood, religious, and ethnic community has lost its center, opposed as it is by the force of government. There are few social supports that would give substance to initiative and creative effort to herald new living alternatives. The culture that is left is either politicized and controlled from Washington or commercialized and perverted for profit; it does not grow freely. It is difficult for a young person to discover those pregnant symbols and meanings in his environment that might function as a focus for his creative energies. These last decades of the twentieth century seem increasingly sterile in terms of educational possibilities.

Our responsibilities demand more than the intellectual interment of the present. We need to accept the present for what it is, but need also to look forward. The attempt to understand the process and meaning of our involvement in the contemporary predicament is a first step. We cannot retreat from the current realities of technology, institutionalism, an interdependent world, and the necessary rational discipline through which we might confront our social responsibilities.

In pivotal sections of the book (chapters 12, 13, and 14) an attempt is made to build out of the present by following several threads that are intellectually suggestive today and to outline a perspective of a social and educational future that appears to be gaining in plausibility and consensus. Toward this end two new concepts are presented: the equilibrium society and the cultural community.

The equilibrium society is that society that is being gradually but irresistibly created by the cumulative press of contemporary circumstances. This concept exemplifies the overall meaning of what is today occurring and its consequences in terms of social organization and policy. How are the tensions of economic, ecological, and political events changing our everyday expectations as compared to those of the past? These expectations in their impact on our attitudes and behavior result in what I call the equilibrium society.

Unless the world goes up in smoke, we can expect to see the continued growth of an international polity, regulated at first through bilateral and multilateral agreements, eventually through world law. We can expect to see the enunciation of principles such as ecological interdependence, universal distribution of the natural resources of the world, demographic responsibility, e.g., balance and stability, cultivation and valuing of discipline, work, economy, and intelligence in making the most out of the world's finite resources. The developed nations will be called on to account for their exploitation and degradation of the environment and their self-indulgent wasting of the resources of the earth. These belong today to the strong. But they are also rightfully for the weak, ultimately for all of humankind's descendents.

Nations will be forced to live within their own means as well as the capabilities of the world system. Underdeveloped nations will have to take upon themselves a rigorous program of education and social development, to master the skills and discipline necessary to produce and distribute their own resources. The largesse of the world will be carefully distributed not only to those who have but to the competent who can produce.

There has rarely been an era when human beings have not lived with scarcity. The question to come is not one of the application of philanthropy. It will be a matter of just distribution in a world where law will replace the fang and the claw. One wonders if we will be able to avoid those irresistible pressures that may bring some of the world's people into our scientific-technological system and relegate others to oblivion.

The equilibrium society will undoubtedly lead to a more egalitarian world as the demands of competency and functionality are strictly accounted for. Inevitably we will measure each citizen's contributions to society against the rewards that he or she takes away from our limited treasury. We may judge both those at the top and at the bottom of our economic scale whether they give less to humanity than they carry away as compensation.

Equilibrium does not connote an absolute end to all forms of growth or change. The concept is used to underscore the fact of human bio-ecological limitations, of dependence on nature. Undisciplined economic or population growth can cause vast social upheavals. It can result in concomitant contractions in other facets of life—in cultural, intellectual, and ecological values.

The equilibrium society will be a disciplined and regulated society, hopefully democratically and rationally sanctioned, one that will avoid precipitous social, economic, and technological decisions. In this way the possibility of potentially calamitous miscalculation will be neutralized. The world will proceed at a much slower pace of social and technological change. One wonders if there exist physical, material, and economic relationships between people that are not subject to potential public intervention and regulation, given the proven existence of such public consequences resulting from heretofore purportedly private initiatives.

We argue that a life worth living cannot be achieved in any institutionalized setting, even one so philosophically beneficent as an equilibrium society. The legal and institutional structure of such a social framework constitutes no more than an organizational means toward a deeper and richer domain of social life. The cultural community constitutes a setting where more intrinsic satisfaction can be fulfilled. It is in a context of families and neighbors, a community of value and belief in the cultural, ethnic, and religious sense that human beings are first educated. The individual, in such a setting, becomes a valuing creature, one who feels and empathizes, who learns to muster internal discipline in terms of a sense of identity, belief, and commitment. The cultural community becomes a primary context within which the powerful and passionate internal fires of the person are directed outward into socially productive creative efforts.

In short, the cultural community is the natural educational context. It is the framework within which the young learn about people as whole persons, where a commitment to work for one's loved ones and friends is preparatory for labor in the wider world of abstract institutions and relationships. One labors for and in the international society so that one can maintain those fundamental liberties of thought, action, and expression in the intimate community. The cultural community is also a context where one can return to experience the fullness of life and the totality of human relationships and personalities. Here, roles, titles, classes, and status are largely irrelevant. Experience becomes intrinsic and consummatory.

In two chapters (13 and 14) dealing with the cultural community, these themes are amplified. "The Depths of Thought" probes the sources of cultural behavior in the dynamics of symbolic thought and action. It attempts to relate these powerful and deeply rooted personal drives to the shaping educational role of the community. The major implication of this argument is that the human being, the generator of new meanings, values, and material artifacts, needs a social environment for the expression of these deepest inclinations that is flexible and personal, that can receive the blows of innovation and bend with its individuality.

Mass society, in which human life is desiccated by formalistic institutional regulation, is argued to be a perversion of the natural contexts and needs of people. In catering to physical needs, these societies sometimes endure for long periods. But the insistence of individual expression and community autonomy against mechanical institutions and power inevitably results in the destruction of society by the powerful and in this case subversive innovative energies.

The chapter on "Historical Sources" documents more typical and traditional contexts for the cultural community. A long and productive tradition of so-called neolithic communities has represented the most typical social context of humanity over many thousands of years. Those neolithic communities that have in the past coexisted with the great civilizations have also been the source and consequence of unique and complex cultural settings. With the subsequent collapse of the various great societies, this prototypical structure of simple community life has repeatedly been the inheritor of civilizational disintegration.

At various moments in the development of civilizational styles, however, a balance has been found between structure, size, and the internal character of the society such that it has unleashed unprecedented creative power in its constituents. Ancient Greece, the Italian Renaissance, and the early modern era in Europe are examples of cultural communities that have in some manner balanced the various dynamic factors to bring forth a set of human values admired by all.

Enormous energies were released in these areas to produce a flowering of humanity's deepest intellectual and aesthetic capacities. Both formal and informal educational modes seem to have worked together to generate these unself-conscious patterns of behavior. These communities constitute a challenge to our contemporary ingenuity. How do we re-create the social structure and environment that would liberate the educational imagination that is latent in us all?

We have attempted to understand some of the factors that enter into the educational process. The historical development of American education has been traced in the light of this analysis. The problems we have recently encountered are due to the transformation of our educational efforts from the exhilarating utopian vistas of the past to the cold reality of today. A new set of possibilities has been offered as a working antithesis.

The general model has been suggested. But we cannot assert that the models of the equilibrium society or the cultural community have to be realized by one method or conclude in a specific content. We need the freedom to reach for a variety of social and cultural ends. Our claim to this right practically depends upon our obtaining the requisite educational freedoms today.

Toward that end, the final chapters (15, 16, 17) set forth a simple and specific proposal. The American educational system can be liberated from its present institutional paralysis without revolutionizing the existing social and political structure. Liberation need not connote the dissolution of a structure of education that respects the intellectual challenges of the modern world. There is no need for new centralized bureaucratic "reforms" which only act further to regulate and manipulate the schools. Nor do we acquiesce to the Pied Pipers of the "heart" who would lead the children out of school away from disciplined reason and into the byways of "social relevance."

Reform is as simple as the gradual establishment of voluntarism, wherein parents and children can exercise some initiative in deciding which schools best reflect their own values. There is no suggestion here to eradicate state supervision and regulation which ensure that the public interest is secured. What is opposed is the monopoly of state operation, especially as it is joined to compulsory attendance and the confiscatory taxation that gives only the rich the opportunity to exercise choice. At first, partial reimbursement for students attending independent secular institutions would allow us to evaluate our needs and trends. Eventually a full voucher equivalent would in all likelihood be a stimulating boost to educational innovation and progress.

The expected opposition of traditional liberal opinion is confronted. Hostility to private and sectarian education arose from historical conditions that, reasonably, reflected the existing advantages of secular public schooling over the conservative parochial religious systems or elitist private schools for the privileged. New historical circumstances oblige us to face the real and present dangers to our freedom and not harken back to phantoms of the past.

A new American public exists today. It is largely middle class and increasingly college educated. It is beginning to resent its treatment as an educational ward, to resent being manipulated as the political and social winds blow. The political enmeshing of the school is compounded by the deadening bureaucracy and the mechanistic and meritocratic orientation of these state institutions. Underneath the sound and fury that surround education today exists a creeping public unease.

The centralization of power and the increasing pervasiveness of controls and regulations seem to call for the cultivation of privacy, community autonomy, and voluntary action. The possibilities for educational choice lie at the heart of any program to serve such areas of freedom.

People need to be alerted to the reality that even such vaunted institutions as the public schools, as they are presently constituted, can become historically dated. They must be educated to the fact that institutions are created by the people to secure important human needs. Each generation, therefore, must reshape these institutions to the most appropriate contemporary function.

Both formal and informal education are central supports of civilized life. When they interact and flourish, freedom and culture thrive. When they are constrained by artificial impediments, society withers.

2 | Informal Education

He walked along towards home without attending to paths. If anyone knew the heath well, it was Clym. He was permeated with its scenes, with its substance, and with its odors. He might be said to be its product. His eyes had first opened thereon; with its appearance all the first images of his memory were mingled; his estimate of life had been colored by it; his toys had been the flint knives and arrowheads which he found there, wondering why stones should "grow" to such odd shapes; his flowers, the purple bells and yellow gorse; his animal kingdom, the snakes and croppers; his society, its human haunters. Take all the varying hates felt by Eustacia Vye towards the heath, and translate them into loves, and you have the heart of Clym. He gazed upon the wide prospect as he walked, and was glad.

—Hardy, The Return of the Native

Generally, informal education connotes patterns of education taking place within the family or neighborhood, or even within the school, under special situations such as field trips or extracurricular projects, where the usual forms of structured classroom instructions are not operative. This is a perfectly useful and ad hoc use for this concept, but it bypasses another important and basic aspect of informal education. Informal education as used here is far more than a relaxed adjunct of traditional forms of schooling.

Rather, I argue that seen against the backdrop of human learning, culture, and society, informal education acts as the most fundamental step in the induction of the individual into the human community. Further, I claim that out of the frenetic dynamics of recent social and educational change in America, this aspect of existence and learning has been subject to enormous attrition that has produced a lamentable gap in our contemporary life. This fact is at least partially at the root of our current cultural travail.

LEARNING

In order to place informal education in its proper perspective we must draw aside a fairly remote conceptual curtain. *Education* is a term we generally reserve for *Homo sapiens.* It is a semantic variant on the more generic word *learning.* The latter word usually refers to a wide variety of animal behavior, not excluding human. Indeed, we often speak as though all living things—at the least, all animals—learn: "the acquisition of new behavioral patterns as a result of life experiences."

The range of learning is immense. From the amoeba to the bison, animals gain something from their generational exposure to life on earth. In spite of the gross variation in what and how, the purposes of learning for all animals are similar. They learn to meet the test of adaptation and natural selection, in short, to survive as a species. If they bring their young to reproductive maturity generation after generation, then they have fulfilled their learning obligations to nature.

To be sure, porpoises and chimpanzees are clever; they can be taught to perform certain humanlike behaviors, even to engage in elaborate "communication." Essentially, the dynamics and intentions of their learning are practical and reflexive. Their state of awareness is probably reducible to the biological satisfactions that conditioning has led them to expect, the results of what they are trained to learn to perform. They have responded to the stimuli and rewards in their training that triggered certain overt and specific responses on their part. The fish or the banana have to be proffered at some point, or the show will not go on.

In nature the rigid specificity of instinct holds each member of a species within a clearly delimited set of behaviors. The old pass on their genetic map of what to learn and adapt to. Only through the mutation of the species itself can these learnings be altered. The leopard or the eagle is fixed within a specified ecological domain to learn, adapt, and survive as their predecessors had for eons before them or else to disappear from the face of the earth. Human beings, however, have found a new and infinitely flexible mode of learning and adapting. Instead of possessing rigid and specific behavioral drives, humans learn in a more ambiguous manner. Their reactions to external experience are mediated by symbolic responses rather than by signals that elicit concretely adaptive behavior. From the standpoint of several billion years of clearly delineated and coherently survivalistic animal learning and behavior, *Homo sapiens* is indeed a peculiar animal.

True, the domain of symbolic learning, communicating, and behaving, with regard to agreed-upon conventional meanings, is ultimately determined by human genetic structure. Yet the genetic structure opens up a realm of learning that is almost infinite in its capacity for innovation, diversity, complexity, and variation. We can see and note some of the universals of human learning and behavior. Yet we are more taken by its amazing pluralism and the fact that we have as yet been unable to understand the nature of this learning so as to subject it to systematic study and predict the outcome of even the most mundane human events.

SCHOOL AND CULTURE

The symbolic communication we call *language* is enough of a divergence from animal communication to make us pause in our evaluation of the nature of learning. To be sure, there are certain species-wide characteristics. Languages can consist of between two and an infinite number of phonemes (sounds recognized as distinct within a language), yet all languages use between twenty and fifty. The number of possible grammatically distinct patterns of subject and object is six—no language uses more than three of these. Universally, children use language in the same way at different stages in their development.[1]

But these similarities do not sweep away the vast number of languages and the infinite diversity of ideas, emotions, and values that are expressed in the creation of that social domain of symbolic meanings that we call *culture*. Because what people learn in their noninstinctually rooted social environment is so unique in terms of its structure and purpose, it points sharply and clearly to a wholly new realm of learning. This human form of learning we call *education*.

Culture educates people to respond to ideas and meanings. There is little in the biological realm that they cannot be trained to reject—food, sex, even life itself. Humans are the only animals that can say "no." All "lower" forms of life assent to the dictates of their genes and instincts. Throughout the history of *Homo sapiens*, what people have assented to and denied has varied from hour to hour,

1. Frank Smith, *Understanding Reading* (New York: Holt, Rinehart & Winston, 1971), pp. 18–52.

from society to society. Educated to the beliefs and habits of their forebears, they even have the capability of turning their backs on education, its values and truths.

The range of human learning is almost limitless. It progresses from generation to generation and evolves in almost infinite variation without ever encompassing a biological mutation. Human habitat at one time excluded only the Antarctic wastes. Today people survive even that foreboding chill. At the very dawn of human culture, artists religiously evoked and gave tangible if mysterious symbolic significance to their animal rivals as they painted them in the dark recesses of their cavernous homes. With a brain no different in structure than it was fifteen thousand years ago, but with several thousand generations of education accrued, *Homo sapiens* has left the earth and explored the moon in a first contact with the universe.

Informal education then is the stuff from which the most basic patterns of human learning are made. In substituting culture for genetically specific adaptive responses, nature has given human beings a new context within which their primordial, if unknown, nature will be exemplified. We cannot know human nature nor the ultimate patterns of human learning. In this sense, we continuously remake ourselves culturally while remaining the same biologically. There is no human fulfillment without a culture. Here, each individual can absorb the symbols of value and belief that define his or her life expectations.

Without necessarily knowing or understanding this process of education, a person is acculturated to a society. Each individual is endowed with a set of learnings that differs from all other beasts and often, in addition, from other people. In this process of informal education, the first and most fundamental stage of human nature is thus completed.

THE SOCIAL FUNCTION OF LANGUAGE

The human infant born into any society indiscriminately babbles and gurgles, uttering a wide range of sounds which maturation and the social reinforcements of the world will shape into the language of his or her experience. The sounds uttered by an infant three months of age are indistinguishable from one culture to another. At six months, however, the child seems already to be babbling in French, English, Chinese, or whatever the case may be.

One can take an American three-month-old infant to China and raise the child in that substantially different racial and cultural environment. In time the child will naturally respond to the language, culture, and values of the foster society. Language is therefore our first introduction to the web of culture within which our individuality will be shaped. Language will not only condition the external manifestations of one's thoughts; it will act as a filter shaping the content and the feelingness of our contact with the outside world.

The story of the tower of Babel symbolizes this enigmatic fact. Unlike other interbreeding species, whose behavior varies little from one environment to another, every human being creates unique learning environments and superimposes them to a significant extent on the existing natural conditions. We do know that children have similar patterns of language development at each stage of their physical and mental growth, e.g., words at twelve months, two- and three-word sentences at eighteen months.

In spite of these universal characteristics in language and the existence in culture, as claimed by George Murdock, of seventy-three universal characteristics—e.g., incest taboos, technology, dance —the range of variation is still tremendous.[2] The great number of different languages having great systematic as well as phonological (sound) diversity is equaled by the diverse cultural solutions and their varied patterns of learning behavior. Only recently, under the pressure of the forceful expansion of Western technology, has the diversity of cultural solutions to this unique evolutionary predicament been diminished.

The unity and diversity in language points to an interesting question. How is it that a species of animals *(Homo sapiens)* that is freely interbreeding, with only marginal differences of race, can diverge so radically in the variety of languages and dialects? If language has an important role in shaping the character of individuals and cultures, so too is language itself influenced by important internal and external forces. For no language remains unchanged over time, even in societies that are placid, isolated, and relatively unchanging. Here we have a mysterious reflection of the power of human personality and individuality. From generation to generation that amorphous "thing" to which we are so beholden in terms of the shaping of our learning is itself molded and thrust down its special historical road at the very least by the innovative drives that lie deeply within the individual's psyche.

2. George P. Murdock, "The Common Denominator of Culture," in *The Science of Man in the World Of Crisis*, ed. Ralph Linton (New York: Columbia University Press, 1957), chap. 2. Also see *Social Structure* (New York: Macmillan, 1949), p. 124.

CULTURAL DIVERSITY

In *Sex and Temperament in Three Primitive Societies,* Margaret Mead gives a graphic description of the variation in cultural patterns of life and thus of the diversity of values and concerns that people can develop through informal education.[3] Mead describes three New Guinea tribes living less than one hundred miles apart, yet which are eons apart in their style of life. Though they are ethnically similar, geographical variations in their localities lead to certain differences in economic patterns. Ultimately, the mountain-residing Arapesh, the Mundugumor living along the Sepik River, and the Tchambuli on Aibom Lake are too different for us to explain these differences in terms of external and specific causes.

The Arapesh are a peaceful, docile people, almost effeminate in their personalities and cultural orientation. They have an almost hysterical fear of interpersonal conflict; all their relationships are formalized so as to avoid random encounters. The Mundugumors, by contrast, are an overtly emotional, aggressive people; conflict is open and engaged in with gusto. They are ardent headhunters whose aggressive drives do not end when they return to their village. The great conflict at home is between male and female over the wealth that will be passed on from generation to generation in terms of male and female economic prerogatives.

A man's son, rather than being his pride and joy, can be his greatest enemy. The birth of a child is symbolized in the conflict of the parents over the use of the child for their respective economic drives. "And throughout the battle, the woman is regarded as a fit adversary, who is, it is true, handicapped, but never weak." [4]

The Tchambuli likewise veer off in their own unique cultural direction. As Mead points out, sexual differences in personality in this tribe do exist, as contrasted with the passive Arapesh and the antagonistic Mundugumors. The Tchambuli men are the temperamental, artistic members. They act out the old warlike rituals and their associated sexual patterns. Yet, behind the scenes the women control the wealth and dominate the men through a subtle manipulation of the rules that the men supposedly created for their own benefit.

One is struck by the extreme diversity of human behavior that

3. Margaret Mead, *Sex and Temperament in Three Primitive Societies* (New York: William Morrow, 1963).
4. Ibid., p. 224.

each tribe has transmitted to its young as its normal way of life. For a child growing up in any of these cultures, what he learns is standard operating procedure. His personality is shaped to accept those activities and attitudes that each society adopts as its way of life. Informal education in this context constitutes those unquestioned values, behaviors, role determinations by which each individual is shaped to live in a cohesive social environment. Whether in conflict, fear, or ritual exhibitionism, the individuals who lead these various lives are happy, fulfilled humans. Their culture and the process of informal education have given them a coherent structure within which their life tenures and aims will be completed.

UNITY IN CULTURE

It would be wrong to overemphasize the factor of diversity in culture and in the patterns of informal education. For culture, as a unity of symbolic meanings, work habits, rituals, historic memories, visual art forms, music and dance, familial patterns that are absorbed in a synthetic integration, makes life appear whole. Murdock's universals in culture merely reiterate the well-understood fact that we are a species with a biological nature that ultimately lives within each of us.

But this biological nature does not merely come alive with each individual's ontogeny. For culture itself takes a crucial part in this process of making each sapient creature truly a humane being. Thus we can empathize with the problems of our fellow beings because their distinctive social institutions and problems are still part of the human situation. The variety of ways of making a living, from the Eskimo to the Andes Indian, represents naturally enforced diversities of behavior. But underneath, the rhythms, joys, and values of life, yes even of the Arapesh and the Mundugumor, are recognizable.

Friendship, love, leisure, exuberance, all have their particular cultural nuances. In every case they are ordered securely within the cultural fabric of agreed-upon behaviors and beliefs. One can accurately say that for the human being as a biological creature, the primary adaptive level is this intimate culture wherein are experienced directly and ineluctably the joys, tensions, dangers, and fulfillments of those with whom he or she communicates in the most personal nuances of life. The continuity of an individual's adaptation to nature and nature's culture and with other individuals is dependent upon the ease with which these values will be transmitted from one generation to the next. The essence of human survival (consequently which can meet the test of natural selection) is society's capacity to transmit in fairly intact form the entire structure of cultural feeling, thought, and behavior to the next generation.

COMMUNITY

This deep determinedness of culture that contributes to our becoming human beings has another aspect, one which can only underline the primacy in function of this subtle, unquestioning kind of educational experience. As we have reiterated, humans have no specific instinctual pattern of behavior to fall back upon. What is left to them are the contexts and necessities of social life. This is the natural environment into which they are born, from which they must wrest both their economic sustenance and their personal and social identity.

Culture, that spontaneous and universal entity—malleable, variable, and basic—serves also to stabilize human life. Thus, even if it is not universal in its specific forms, it certainly functions to provide a universal ground for human adaptation. Wherever people have accommodated themselves to their natural environment, or extracted a living from nature, there they sink their material roots. Even more fundamentally, however, the roots they put down are deeply emotional and symbolic.

The material and social environment is alive with symbolic significance. Every tree and rock, the holy places where ritual celebrations take place, the male or female cult houses, the marketplace, the hunting or fishing areas, the love spots—all are endowed with deep emotional as well as practical importance. They are familiar haunts that offer a sense of belonging and identification. One can argue that the simple society is static, that it is limiting in terms of individual and social possibilities. But we cannot gainsay the fact that it provides for the basic human satisfactions. In being the primary context within which human learning takes place, this initial cultural community, whether it be the small cluster of homes on stilts of the primitive Manus, a rural village in northern Greece, or the neighborhood community of an ethnic minority in a great city, is where the unique experience of human learning or informal education begins.

Henceforth, an individual will not be able to return to those familiarities without experiencing that odd sense of being "home," where each plant, rock, house, smell, or sound will have a familiar emotional impact. The cold formalities and inexplicable occurrences of life away from home melt away. The sense of security, of appropriateness and stability, return. Every person should someday return to his or her home community.

The Athenians built their famous and beautiful temple to Poseidon, god of the sea, on the high cliffs of Cape Sounion, as a symbolic welcome to those ships returning to Athens from their precarious journeys about the Aegean and the Mediterranean seas. When the sailors caught a glimpse of the sunlit reflections glancing off its lovely white Parian marble columns, it is said that they rose to give a cheer, for beyond were the familiar welcoming hills, valleys, and inlets of their beloved Attica. In a day or two, they would be home.

INDIVIDUALITY AND INFORMAL CULTURE

All these elements of culture shape us into human beings. Yet we are not just passive receivers of an external structure of things. While we have no choice over the culture into which we are born, we still retain the possibilities for individual behavior given by our personality and intelligence. Why, for example, have there been so many thousands of differing cultures over the last several millennia? External conditions in and of themselves do not explain the variation in personality type, religious beliefs, language, and other crucial aspects of culture, else there would be a discernible pattern of differences between cultures distant and close, both geographically and ecologically. The answer to this puzzle may lie in the powerful impact of individual personality.

Every simple culture develops a fairly clearly delineated ideal personality type. If we ask why one type and not another, perhaps the answer is merely that at some critical point in the history of the culture, a strong leader left the imprint of his will upon the society. A host of other behaviors and attitudes that reflected his character may have been stylized as symbolic evocations of both individual or event. We know the impact on our society of a strong personality, for example, John F. Kennedy or Marilyn Monroe, even though the impression may be due to efficient public relations. This hypothesis about the cause of cultural diversity is merely a conjecture set forth to illustrate the issue as well as reflect on its great complexity.

Certainly every society moves along its own path of cultural change. It is difficult to break into it at any one time to discover how current influences are redirecting or perhaps even buttressing the existing trend. But the fact that primitive societies have a way of symbolically isolating extreme deviants into special niches, for example, the medicine man (shaman), and consciously shaping the more malleable majority through informal education into an ideal type indicates the need to take into account this variability in individuality. And it is probably due to this cultural bias that some personalities flower in certain societies while others are stifled, often to become unhappy misfits.

INDIVIDUALITY AND EDUCATIONAL INNOVATION

Another aspect of individuality is displayed in culture. This is illumined by the fact that cultural change takes place constantly and unremittingly. There has never been a society wherein language changes have been unobservable over a period of time or a steady flow of alterations in the aesthetic design of the pottery, the dances and chants, even the basic styles in technology. Now, what is it that generates this innovative trend? We have only to look to our society to witness the impact of the energies of the young as they come crashing into our cultural consciousness. It is difficult to deny the reality of young, enthusiastic, energetic, and creative minds having some effect on even the most stagnant societies.

In those quiet cultural nooks and crannies, for the most part not under the direct scrutiny of the elders, we should find some elasticity. In the spoken language, some of the visual aesthetic styles, perhaps even in the form and content of the rituals, an especially energetic or creative person will produce changes that will endure. But certainly we can state that the primitive and simple society is a poor environment for the development of those latent abilities that lie within each individual. As we have noted above, one cannot estimate the extent of the loss of talent and ability that has taken place because personalities have been labeled misfits on the one hand or have vegetated in the society on the other, their talents thus effectively excluded from the communal gene pool.

The scope of personal differentiation is close to infinite. The number of existent cultures attests to this variability. The range of human creativity, which has constantly produced new cultural dimensions in which people have subsequently contented themselves to live, testifies to the drive of innovation in the human being, the human capacity to adjust one's sights to complexities in culture which primitives could not even have conceived of.

Yet in all of this dynamic differentiation and even progress, creative, individualistic people still have needed a cultural context. When they create they go from what is to what is not. The new builds on the old, but in an integral if subtle and often covert manner. In the informal cultural settings, the individual is the key to innovation and change. Thus informal education as it facilitates the experiencing of the new by the individual supports the formal structure of education. The creative individual, on the other hand, needs the formal educational system to discipline, refine, and structure a vision as yet inchoate.

> The free artist, scientist, or teacher is always, in some degree, involved in the contexts of communication and association. His may be a detached position; he may be the recipient of impulses sent out from a variety of fields; he may live, more than do most of us, toward the periphery of his community and thus be in more sensitive nearness to other communities. But what is crucial to the creator is not release or separation, not inward withdrawal, but imagination feeding upon diverse social and cultural participation.[5]

Informal education, then, is basically a process of introduction and adjustment of the individual personality to the cultural norms of the society. Nowhere is there the vaunted freedom of which the idealists dream. In the first weeks of life, the options for individual expression everywhere begin to be foreclosed. Indeed, one might say that human freedom from instinctual specificity is purchased at the price of a gradual surrender of the unlimited cultural potentialities given genetically. In the development of people and their cultural forms, there has been a constant tension of thrust and counterthrust between the given culture and the individual's perennial sense of innovation and self-expression. Rarely have societies solved that dynamic tension in a satisfactory manner over any extended period of time.

CHANGE AND CONSERVATION

Another tension grows out of the culture-personality dialectic: stability and change. Informal education is obviously the more conservative element in the process of cultural and historical change. Changes that occur in the subliminal manner, such as phonemic and grammatical drifts in language, aesthetic and stylistic

5. Robert Nisbet, *Community and Power* (original title, *The Quest for Community*) (New York: Oxford Galaxy, 1962), p. 236.

changes in clothing or household utensils, and those which do not call into being any overt social or institutional alterations are the easiest to handle educationally. Human experience is suffused with the factors of change. All human beings undergo the cycle of growth, maturity, and decay. Few societies are freed of periodic changes in climate, the sudden intrusion of great natural events, either disastrous or benign.

Most authorities are convinced that, in addition to the natural, external changes, there is a basic thrust for individuation and self-actualization in humans. In more flexible cultures this unabiding thrust for novelty gives the society a steady movement, depending on the kinds of institutions and cultural forms that people can work within. The human being is predatory and aggressive. But in principle it is a basic aggressive hunger for new symbolic meanings, perceptions, and creations. There is no element in human experience, either in terms of interpersonal relations, in dance and in song, dreams and work, or even in the basic economic terms of survival that an individual will not reshape to fit innovative strivings.

As long as the continuity of the culture is seamless—the national integrity of a United States, for example—the innovations can be accommodated within the informal educational techniques. Most societies will impose as an immovable body of tradition certain institutional barriers to the particularly aggressive or imaginative individuals if their new ideas, schemes, and visions threaten the existing web of meanings that constitute their neighbors' intimate, comfortable, recognizable culture. The social techniques of isolation are varied; they extend from placing the individual in a unique role or caste to expelling them, as in the ancient Greek *ostracism*.

Why does informal education have this conservative characteristic? Why does it tend to filter out the most creative individuals, restrict social change to a small set of controllable or wholly uncontrollable subconscious factors? In part the answer is that the function of culture—static or dynamic—is to adapt the human being to society. By this is not necessarily meant physical adaptation. To maintain one's psychological or symbolic equilibrium, one needs the steadiness and security of a consistent cultural system. People are naturally hesitant to venture onto foreign ground (a new way of life) while they are satisfied with the patterns that exist and can still fulfill their basic social, psychic, and material needs.

There is, in addition, a concrete material factor that subdues innovation in most primitive societies. Here the ecological or geographical condition—perhaps an island community or surrounded by enemies—has shaped their culture and disciplined them to live within their means. And unless there is a sharp change that is clearly for the better—such as new technologies of war or a new source of mineral wealth or food supplies—any other changes could be threatening. Thus, out of gross physical necessity, small societies may act (with an educational purpose in mind) to defuse the explosive creative force that lies within each individual.

THE FAILURE OF INFORMAL EDUCATION

We think we know what the inevitable outcome is in retrogressive and conservative cultures. More and more specialized, less able to adapt to any new intrusion into their environment, they gradually decay. Sometimes they are pushed into the recesses of a geographical area, such as is the case with the African Pygmies or the Amazon Indians or even the recently discovered Stone Age people of the Philippines. They steadily degenerate culturally until they become extinct or else are resuscitated artificially from the outside and placed on reservations for their "protection." At other times, the forces of change with which they are suddenly faced are so apocalyptic that they literally explode and disintegrate. Thereupon they either die as cultures or perhaps exist in precarious limbo either to be amalgamated with new cultures or slowly to adapt and begin to assert their identity, albeit under new circumstances.

One can point to the Tasmanian aborigines, made extinct by the English colonizers in the nineteenth century, or the present Australian aborigines, who even after a century have not yet been allowed or caused to adjust to modern existence. Margaret Mead speaks about the powerful personality of Paliau, who caused the Manus tribe of the Admiralty Islands to adjust to a modernity whose intrusion was milder than in Australia or in Tahiti and Samoa.[6]

In Tahiti, a more developed people, with a decidedly specialized island culture, were decimated by a combination of Western technology, alcohol, and religion. The exhilaration that resulted from the first contacts between Western sailing ships and the Tahitians is characteristic of the excitement that newness brings to human beings. In the end the new was too much for these people to absorb over a short period of time. By the middle of the nineteenth century the fabric of their traditional society had been torn asunder, the

6. Margaret Mead, *Continuities in Cultural Evolution* (New Haven: Yale University Press, 1964), pp. 192–234.

people enveloped in lassitude, indifference, and demoralization. Their population was reduced from 40,000 to 6,000.[7]

Fortunately for the Tahitians, other horizons beckoned for the European nations, and their level of intercourse with the outside world was reduced. They now had time to attempt to integrate the new cultural elements into what was by then only a memory of the past. An indigenous culture was reconstituted, the enterprise of the new generation supplanted the apathy and disheartenment of the old, and life was rebuilt. A new informal educational tradition now exists, combining what is possible to be retained from the past with what is necessary for the present.

The simple and isolated society is inherently fragile and unstable. Like a specialized animal, it is well adapted but suitable only to a limited social and ecological environment. Because it has chosen or been forced through circumstance to limit its vision, it has small capabilities of resistance or resiliency. And so often it suffers inordinate shocks, of the kind delineated above. Nevertheless, because most of these cultures are fragile and small-scale, their confrontation with large dynamic cultures does hold out new options. And, as we have seen with the Bantu of South Africa, they can be absorbed into a new way of life, though as submissive and subdued as they are, they are often exploited. Eventually they will either adapt educationally to the new mode completely and be culturally absorbed, or else they will create some balance between the past and the present and gradually strike out in a new cultural direction.

In this respect great and developed cultures do not have as simple a choice. The history of civilization is the history of the rise and fall of people mainly through war and devastation. However, if a culture is strong enough, if it has a well-developed formal system of education and a consciousness of tradition and history articulated through the written word, it will, like the Jews, be able to ward off the initial thrust and the early disasters.

The Japanese, a good example of social resiliency, were first contacted on a continuing basis by Dutch traders and missionaries in the seventeenth century. For two hundred years they eyed the advancing West warily and kept them out. Their geographical isolation aided them. In addition, they were socially strong as a nation and, unlike the great Indian civilizations of the Americas, avoided falling under the heel of the first adventurers. When the time finally came to face the new American challenge from the West, the Japanese were well prepared, intellectually, culturally, and politically, to meet the

7. Alan Moorehead, *The Fatal Impact* (New York: Harper & Row, 1966), p. 88.

West halfway. They would take on Western forms of power, but in their own way, thereby hopefully retaining their cultural integrity. The judgment of history is still to be reckoned.

The Incas and Aztecs were not so fortunate. In one dramatic moment of history they had to confront a small but determined military force whose nature they did not understand. Seemingly powerful, with well-developed institutions, the Incas and Aztecs crumpled. The brutal military extermination of their elite, the perhaps incomplete formal educational and intellectual development of the people gave them no time to reintegrate once the immediate military and religious domination eased; and thus the institutions of their culture suffered a fatal shock from which they were never able to recover. Why they fell probably lies as much in the semideveloped character of the formal structure—religious, political, and social forms, military techniques and technology—as it does in the technical and cultural shock with which the conquistadors overwhelmed them. Today, sadly for their peasant inheritors, life has reverted to the lowest common denominator, even as it was lived five hundred years ago.

CONCLUSION: THE CRISIS OF CULTURE AND COMMUNITY

Beneath the hustle and bustle of our complex and dynamic modern existence lives a world of meanings, symbols, and deep-rooted psychological needs that we often ignore. Two concepts represent this nexus of needs—culture and community. The concept *culture* denotes the tangible values, language, aesthetic images, ideals, and intimacies that bring us together as a group of human beings able to share and communicate with one another. A culture has a limited set of meanings whose boundaries of communication exclude those whom we would call strangers. We cannot share our intimate values with the vast multitude of other human beings living in diverse cultures. Nevertheless, there are universals that bring all people together in the hope for peace and prosperity. These universals in thought and social action contribute to the hope that a world of cultural diversity is compatible with international amity and law.

The concept *community* here connotes a social context. Within this context we think of people sharing certain explicit cultural and social ideals and interests. A community is not a place where one merely sleeps, to leave each day for work elsewhere. It is not a place where one only resides. One must share intimacies of thought and communication, must love what the community stands for and participate in its dreams. Thus the great metropolitan cities are not communities. The lines of control and authority exist too far away; there are just too many people, and the people are either too transient or too anonymous to be able to develop any sense of interpersonal sharing.

In our own lifetime, we have seen both culture and community, as they had historically developed in our society, torn, shredded, and discarded by convulsive social changes that have left the past far behind. Our formal educational system was created in an altruistic attempt to lift the population into the main lines of scientific, urban, and material advance. We wanted to guide the young in adapting to a future that was often obsolescent before it arrived.

We hurtled forward too fast to allow culture and community, with their slow organic rate of response, to adapt to the external social relations being constantly re-created. The result was either the disappearance of previously functioning communities or else their complete disorientation and disfunctioning so as to be useless to us in our new needs. High and low culture itself was an ersatz creation of mass media, rarely reaching or touching the deeper springs of moral or aesthetic commitment. The old culture had been dismembered, the new was made of tinsel.

The roots of our formal educational system established in an earlier cultural and communitarian setting were eventually laid bare. The erosion complete, the schools were helpless in finding a defensible stance for their obligations. For as the social dynamic began to lose some of its forward motion, the emptiness between terra firma and its high-flying impetus was revealed. The contemporary convulsions and travail in the social and educational system are reflective of the gap between the surface structure of life lived in our affluent, ambitious society and the deeper needs of people that have been eroded by change.

The informal culture and its educational means will eventually be revivified; new flesh will be put on those sorry bare bones. But before this can happen, we will have to lift from the current social and educational scene the dispirited anxiety that afflicts us. We will have to recognize the malaise for what it is fundamentally: a crisis of informal education, of culture and community.

3 Formal Education

But if civilization is to be coherent and confident it must be known *in that civilization what its ideals are.*

—Walter Lippmann

Formal education refers to something specific and tangible in American social life: kindergarten, elementary, and secondary school; college and university; technical schools that promote specific vocational skills; and the entire constitutive instutional apparatus—teachers, buildings, students, curricula, diplomas. This chapter argues that this long existing phenomenon of American life is merely one historical embodiment, one solution to persistent problems that indeed may take in other organizational forms.

In the social analysis of education we must whenever possible take a long view. The more we can reflect on our own achievements and difficulties from the standpoint of the broader considerations of history, society, and philosophy, the better we will be able to absorb the periodic crises that afflict all prior social arrangements and the better we can strive for newer solutions. It is not enough to label as formal education only that which is so common-sensically defined in American life. In so doing we limit our ability to make important analytical distinctions between forms of "education" as they exist either in other developed or undeveloped societies.

We have separated education from generalized animal learning as being concerned with the symbols and meaning produced by the particular culture in which the child grows up. Ordinary kinds of cultural behavior are not merely responses to external stimuli; they are not predetermined genetically in a strictly stereotyped manner. Neither are the learned responses—those changes in behavior that occur as a consequence of experience—necessarily those that serve

29

the basic biological survival needs of the species. Human learning or education is a mediated, conventional, symbolic process. Through enculturation, the individual is brought into a social system whose function is not clearly material nor even ideational. Culture and one's education within culture are certainly biologically adaptive in the broadest sense. It is one's first and foremost home, bringing both comfort and warmth. Beyond providing for the existence of the almost subliminal web of meanings that is informal education, culture has no further discernible purpose.

SOURCES OF FORMAL EDUCATION

If informal education were the only end product of the universal acculturative process, we would not need to question the whys and wherefores of our contemporary educational dilemma. We would have in the world a series of simple, slowly evolving societies, maintaining an equilibrium with nature and one another, sometimes culturally converging, in war and peace, sometimes fragmenting, becoming isolated, stagnant, extinct. There has been, however, in those great land masses of Europe and Asia where the interactions between communities have been relatively intense and continuous, a tremendous thrust upward and outward.

The great societies that arose in the river valleys of Asia and North Africa are a widely accepted criterion of what is usually meant by a civilization. Civilization brings about new social arrangements; various specialized functions are taken over by societies within societies. Here we have a context of rapidly evolving skills, technologies, and knowledge, as well as specializations, that cannot be shared by the society as a whole. As a process that takes place universally whenever there is rapid growth in an urban environment, we can well argue that the emergence of this environment as a new locus for such activity is natural and inevitable in human beings. The mason, soldier, priest, scribe, ship builder all have different skills that serve varying interests of the society.

The child born into a simple society would learn informally all that it was necessary to learn to be an acceptable adult male or female in that society. But the child born into a family having a specialized trade will be initiated into a more private and select social group. Instead of one general center, complex societies—civilizations in nutrio—have a diversity of centers and interests. Now a political center is necessary to guide the society as it develops so that it will not fragment into subgroups with conflicting educational and cultural ideals. Political power may assert itself from many points of origin—from scribes, the literary intelligentsia, from the soldier, or from the religious center empowered with ritual and magical potency.

The steady accumulation of information and data that occurs in a complex society gradually leads to abstraction; the use of numerals as a shorthand way of symbolizing large quantities of things; measuring scales both for weights (agriculture, precious metals) and for distances (surveying, architecture); and perhaps at a slower rate than the prior factors, chronology (calendars and astronomical correlations). The most revolutionary mode of abstraction is, of course, the invention of written language. One might say that with this development the temporal horizons of people are extended enormously, the whole process of social complexity and change is made self-conscious and deliberate, and the potential powers of human beings greatly expanded.

With the invention of cuneiform, hieroglyphics, numerical measurements, calendars, astronomical calculators, etc., had we stumbled upon formal education? Certainly, in abstraction, a great advance had been made. Had a qualitative change in thought and attitude been produced?[1] Far more sustained effort is needed to train the young to read and write, compute, organize a large army or civil service than in a simpler society. The question is whether merely "more of" is enough to have made a shift to a level that we could call formal education.

Certainly teachers must be appointed, perhaps buildings set aside for the training of the young in any one of several specialized areas. (This did occur in Sumer.) It is probable, however, that this training was at first primarily vocational; it was certainly not systematized or made the concern of the state or the society as a whole. As we have noted, this development in the training of the young effectively removed them from contact with the concreteness of the whole that is characteristic of small communities, but it did so only as it transferred them to a new context of specialized work in the urban community.

It is important to make the distinction between the kinds of education: (1) holistic vocational (informal education) of the simple society; (2) private, vocational education in a complex society—the

1. The evidence is that in Sumerian, as in the most ancient Greek language, practical or economic interest was of enormous importance in generating written language. Minoan linear B of Michael Ventris fame was apparently exclusively a language of business—of accounts keeping, stock lists, and trading (1500 b.c.).

early civilizations of Eurasia, Africa, and the medieval craft guilds; (3) the educational efforts that issue from the political centers in philosophical, cultural, or religious terms for all the citizens. Only the latter we here call "formal" education.

Claude Lévi-Strauss has expressed amazement that the discovery of writing did not advance the rational development of disinterested learning. His expectations were based on writing's enormous potential for expanding our intellectual horizons.[2] But why should it? Was writing in and of itself anything more than a new symbolic technique in culture for organizing social experience? One would just as well wonder, and many have, as to the ultimate virtue of mass literacy in an era when the people can be even further enslaved by debased forms of written communication—tabloids and slick magazines.

One could ask whether the early educational efforts of the Sumerian or Egyptian civilizations constituted a formal educational system. Skills in the written language were developed under the aegis of the temple. Writing was initially a secret art cultivated by the priests and disseminated to a few favored sons of the upper classes, themselves often destined to be priests.

But as described by Samuel Noah Kramer, the Sumerian school of 2000 B.C., even then having a tradition of several hundred years, was to a large extent secularized and professionalized. Kramer describes the role of the Sumerian scribe:

> Head of the Sumerian school was the umma, "expert," "professor," who was also called "school father," while the pupil was called "school son." The assistant professor was known as "big brother" and some of his duties were to write the new tablets for the pupils to copy, to examine the copies, made by the pupils, and to hear them recite studies from memory. Other members of the faculty were "the man in charge of drawing" and "the man in charge of Sumerian." There were also monitors in charge of attendance and "a man in charge of the whip," who was presumably responsible for discipline. We know nothing of the relative rank of the school personnel, except that the headmaster was the "school father." Nor do we know anything about their sources of income. Probably they were paid by the "school father" from the tuition fees he received.[3]

2. *A World on the Wane* (London: Hutchinson, 1961), pp. 291–92.
3. Samuel Noah Kramer, *History Begins at Sumer* (New York: Doubleday Anchor Books, 1959), pp. 3–4.

The graduates of the school who themselves went on to become scribes or "school fathers" seem to have come from the highest levels of Sumerian society. The "school father" presumably was also a member of this upper class. In addition, he accrued respect and dignity both because he purveyed a special and rare skill and because he preserved an important national heritage. This sacred literature, the stories and myths of the past, once transmitted through oral tradition and now transcribed in written language, constituted the social dimension of schooling.

Whether this combination—the utilization of such technical aspects of writing, reading, and counting in practical life and the preservation of the sacred documents of myth and poetry, the cultural tradition—constitutes what we would today define as formal education is a difficult question. The Sumerians had not as yet transformed their myths and tales, their ritual and lore into a body of philosophical beliefs. Nor had they developed any self-consciousness about their implicit conception of the nature of the universe, the moral problems of men, or the course of social history. What they had created to inculcate into a small proportion of the young was still only an implicit form of education, albeit technically sophisticated and with a rich literature. It had yet to attain to full intellectual self-consciousness.

PHILOSOPHICAL THOUGHT AND FORMAL EDUCATION

Because of its ephemeral nature, it is difficult to define the precise features of formal education and the exact time of its inception. Formal education is not a thing. Rather, it is a state of mind. It is gradually brought into being by a set of social and cultural circumstances. Formal education exemplifies a dimension of man that for long eras had been latent.

In an important sense, formal education is the product of the philosophical mind at work in society. We use "philosophical mind" only in its most generic sense, recognizing that with the first glimmerings of self-consciousness there also developed religious movements whose intellectual focus was essentially philosophic.

The origins of philosophical thought lie in a sense or feeling for the abstract mode. The awareness that an idea or a concept can be held before one and shared with other human beings as a means of organizing the complexity of particular things marks its beginning. An abstract idea holds out the possibility of envisioning relationships that do not yet meet the eye. A wholly new mode of thinking is thus created that would have consequences not heretofore thought possible in human behavior.

One can note the general social factors that must have been critical in the release of the mind for that ultimate abstractive leap of human intelligence into the philosophical mode. In the primary sense, it must always have come about after people had been emancipated from their enslavement to brute labor as a prerequisite for survival. Leisure and the creation of new kinds of individuality to enjoy it—which develop a situation unlike the typical embeded life experienced by the person in the peasant society—now demand choice.

Emancipation from physical drudgery in a complex, evolving society is prelude to the development of one of the most critical elements of this new type of individuality—personal creativity. The locus of innovation in any society is the individual. The person perceives and conceives; personal vision is always expressed in some new pattern of behavior, either in social interaction or in personal action—speech, painting, military activity, storytelling, etc. In the slowly changing peasant society, the social structure is rare that will allow the individual significant innovative impact on the group's life style and behavior.

The group's "cooling down" power over any thrust of personal experience, i.e., individuality and creativity, is not a matter of patent or raw suppression. Rather, from the day a child is born, the informal educational patterns impose a subtle molding effect on personal expression, behavior, etc., so that the child's impulses as translated into adult actions will follow the established channels of behavior. Not only will there be no opportunity for the expression of latent individuality, but there will be no external reference point for innovation.

The growth of civilization is accompanied by the development of techniques that give greater scope for personal initiative in the political, military, and religious realm; they also provide new means—writing, painting, sculpture, and architecture (pyramids, fortifications)—for the enunciation of individuality and the transmission of its import to all who can behold. The suppleness of the written word to set forth the richness in the character and actions of people again allows what was latent and implicit to precipitate itself from the inchoate unity of the simple society into a new dimension of expressiveness. This can take place only in a larger and rapidly evolving society.

As the social and intellectual experiences of the citizens are extended, as literacy and other cultural symbolism become available as means of social expression, the seer, social reformer, religious visionary, and philosopher inevitably come into their own.

HISTORICAL BEGINNINGS

Homo sapiens has been a resident of this earth for over fifty thousand years. In this time, humans slowly but surely made their impact felt on other earth dwellers and on the natural environment. Yet the process was gradual for most of this period, event flowing into event with quiet inevitability. There was, however, a period of about two centuries in which certain intangible intellectual developments occurred and recurred over a wide span of geography, which ultimately transformed the character of human cultural existence. For human beings and nature, the results were unidirectional, both permanent and cumulative. Historically, these two centuries were crucial in our understanding of humanity and formal education.

Historically, we make much of the question as to whether the great material inventions of the past—the wheel, metal smelting, explosives, fire, glass—were independently derived or diffused gradually to different parts of the world. Our remoteness in time from some of these occurrences makes it difficult to decide the issue because, from our standpoint several thousand years later, a century or two, which at that time might have been a sufficient period for invention and diffusion to take place, cannot be distinguished. But because the important intellectual occurrences to be discussed took place separated by such great distance (yet in the context of roughly similar civilizational environments), the weight of evidence speaks for a parallel development of what would turn out to be a new kind of education—*formal education.*

Between the years 750 B.C. and 550 B.C. in various parts of the civilized world, i.e., in those parts of the world in which the process of complexity and change had already effected a transformation of social structure and life style, a number of powerful intellectual movements led by great personalities arose. In China the semi-mythical figure of Lao Tzu, *ca.* 650-600 B.C., followed by the scholar-sage Confucius, 550 B.C., put an entirely new qualitative aesthetic and intellectual stamp upon the already ancient and traditional Chinese civilization.

In India the development of the Brahamanids, *ca.* 700 B.C. (ritual conduct and a philosophy of worship), followed soon after by the Upanishads, 700–600 B.C. (early metaphysical speculation), denotes the existence of a vigorous and thriving philosophical movement within the ruling Indo-European tribal society that had entered and taken over the subcontinent centuries earlier. Shortly after, the appearance of the Buddha, *ca.* 550 B.C., his powerful personal calling and his ethical idealism, had its enormous impact first on India, then throughout the civilized areas of east Asia.

In the West, from about 750 B.C. to 600 B.C., the Hebrew prophets Amos, Hosea, Isaiah, and Jeremiah represent a series of thinkers who attempted to protect an ancient and conservative ethnic and religious tradition from regression and dilution. They developed and advanced this religious tradition into a wholly new and self-conscious intellectual, moral, and social plane. To the north and west across the Mediterranean, the Greeks had been slowly evolving from their Achaean tribal traditions into small urban trading centers.

About 600 B.C., two men on opposite shores of the Aegean Sea propounded and acted on a number of intellectual suppositions about the underlying metaphysical nature of things, in effect precipitating the development of a wholly new category of thought— philosophy. In Athens a poet-teacher and businessman, Solon, rose to political prominence as a result of a combination of political necessity and personal and social vision; and in Miletus, Ionia (the Greek settlements on the western coast of what is now Asiatic Turkey), Thales, another entrepreneur and intellectual.

What begins to occur historically is different from the usual random flow of events that determines informal educational patterns. Rather, it is the conscious and deliberate choice of values and ideas by which people decide to live and educate their young that determines the condition of social life. For the first time, people accept responsibility for actions determined by decisions consciously aimed at. No longer can the gods be blamed for inflicting pain or be praised for good fortune.

Why were these religions and philosophies created? What cultural or historical purpose did they serve? Note that we here already assume a nontheistic explanation. Religions and philosophies are cultural phenomena. And like other cultural phenomena, they are generated from the contexts and needs of the existing state of society. Thus, even as abstract a level of thought as "philosophical awareness," when it is produced and nourished in such widely separated civilizational climes, must represent a cultural need.

The educational function of philosophical awareness and its tangible expression derives from the nature of civilizational life, from its complexity and the rapidity of social change. Philosophy serves as a cognitive guide to that society's assertion of both whither and why. The philosophical attitude allows people to face the innumerable possible cultural permutations of a rapidly evolving society and subject these dynamics to a preemptive criticism. Only one set of many possibilities is chosen. These choices constitute value systems whereby the character of one's society is formed socially, culturally, and politically.

Every important philosophy teaches not in terms of the now that exists, but of the tomorrow that is to come. And in pointing the way to the future, in demanding decisions from us, it hopes to bring about the predicted and not the untoward. In this way the philosophical calls forth a wholly new conception of education: as a critical tool for effecting the various social goals of humanity.

We do not wish to leave the impression that because the philosophical mode of thought and formal education are natural outcomes of a historical evolution of society they develop and take hold with little pain or travail. Quite the contrary. The informal mode of slow and mostly imperceptible changes—even of stagnation—is just as natural and sometimes far easier for people to live with. It is, after all, the basic adaptive level of humanity. In many ways, however, it wars against the creative drive. Innumerable thinkers have explored this duality between habit and innovation. Inevitably, those innovators who warn society of the perilous consequence of one course of action rather than another, and the necessity for instituting a shift in purpose for the society—a revision in education—suffer the wrath of a society. Such intellectual and religious martyrs litter the landscape of written history. Darlington, the evolutionary biologist, notes the role of the prophets in Jewish history. The prophets came from all walks of life—they were farmers, villagers, shepherds, scholars—and they attempted to lead their people into a way of life more in tune with their committed destiny than the easy, corrupt, or enslaved state into which they had fallen:

> What the prophets of the old kingdom had been asserting with their splendid phrases was the dramatic polarity and opposition between the transient interests of the political state and the durable interests of individual belief and integrity. What the prophets of the Exile were asserting no less splendidly was that their religion, their rituals, laws and chronicles would preserve

the Jewish people more effectively than the power of Babylon could preserve the greatness of its Empire. This was a practical policy as well as a spiritual doctrine. And it succeeded. It proved to be true. For in fact Babylon fell and the Jews survived. The prophets preserved the Jewish people. And the Jewish people were thus able to preserve the prophets.[4]

This is a clear statement of the educational role of a great philosophical religion and the teachers who passed on their message to all members in that culture, young as well as old. It is in terms of preserving such fundamental values that a society organizes a formal educational structure to ensure that that most important dimension of the society (and yet its most ephemeral possession)—the system of ideas and values by which it helps to define and re-create itself—is preserved for the future.

SUMMARY

Formal education is a product of a new qualitative level of human life. Complexity and social change, products of human activity in culture, eventually create civilizations. Civilizations are born in self-consciousness. They give rise to philosophies that represent humanity's basic need to know, to find explicit meaning and coherence to the structure and dynamics of society.

Formal education, with all its institutional apparatus of schools, certification, and teachers, is thus an intellectual bridge between one generation and the next. Its purpose is to guide the young as they mature to control their destinies by giving them an ideational map to the future. Thus, the young can preserve the stability, coherence, and meaning of their culture even while it rapidly evolves.

If the philosophy is in conflict with experience or does not illuminate problems as they arise, or even does not mesh with the informal cultural ground of life, there will be trauma. The educational system will be the first to falter. Then a reconstructed set of philosophical ideals will become necessary to refurbish the fabric of meaning and gain control over the social structure.

Thus, as Bernard Bailyn has pointed out, as the first flush of religious unity faded in the American colonies of the late seventeenth century—due in part to their successful adaptation and multiplication as well as to their push toward the western frontier—a

4. Cyril O. Darlington, *The Evolution of Man and Society* (London: Allen & Unwin, 1969), p. 190.

process of social and religious disintegration and educational lassitude set in. Intellectual and social changes were arriving from across the seas. This trend continued into the eighteenth century, then began to spread alarmingly. The response of the various authorities was educational. During the 1740s and '50s, along with a great religious revival, an extraordinary interdenominational educational effort was begun along the length and breadth of colonial America. The various sectarian groups attempted to stabilize the structure of their beliefs and therefore the shape of their society for now and for all future generations. Not only primary schools for the young, but colleges to train the new leaders would be necessary in the creation of this formal educational system.

> Their aims in education [sectarian groups] were not served by a neutral pedagogy that might develop according to its own inner impulses and the drift of intellectual currents. The education they desired and created was an instrument of deliberate group action. It bore the burden of defining the group, of justifying its existence by promoting the view that its peculiar interpretations and practices conformed more closely "to those of the early Church as pictured in the New Testament than the views and policies of its rivals." And it was by carefully controlled education above all else that denominational leaders hoped to perpetuate the group into future generations. . . . Education, so central to their purposes, was deliberate, self-conscious, and explicit. The once automatic process of transfer would continue to operate only by dint of sustained effort. Education was an act of will.[5]

The stringent test of any educational system is not its truth but its workability. Some systems are so loosely built that they comfortably undergo periodic restructuring. Others are so rigidly ordered as to resist the shifts and changes necessitated by an interim reshuffling. In the end, the latter system will explode and disintegrate. Thus, we should judge current educational establishments less by their present turmoil or peace than by their long-term effectiveness in bringing the young into useful maturity.

The only way that a society might avoid the constant intellectual examination demanded by the formal mode of education would be to experience a slowing up of change and innovation—by simplifying

5. Bernard Bailyn, *Education in the Forming of American Society* (New York: W. W. Norton, 1972), pp. 40–41.

life styles and social roles and steadying the social structure from generation to generation. Then the traditional dynamics in informal education would regain their importance in determining "good normal behavior" much as they did in the richly textured yet stagnant Oriental civilizations before their contact with the West.

Part

2

**Historical
Perspectives**

4 The Early Educational Traditions

Colonists arrived in the New World in the early years of the seventeenth century. They came to secure a set of philosophical and religious values whose possibility for transmission through formal education had become threatened. The Puritans were attempting to retain a conservative tradition that had been attacked by a completely new set of informal social patterns. These conditions were undermining the rigorous intellectual and social foundations of Calvinist tradition.

Once in the New World, with the necessity for strenuous efforts for survival, the hard, bleak religious tradition was buffered by the isolative qualities of the Massachusetts Bay Colony. The meager resources of an undeveloped environment, without the temptations offered by the perfumed and silken society left behind, provided its own natural discipline.

It has been argued, and with validity, that while the Protestant Reformation was a reactionary religious and intellectual movement envisioning the ancient Augustinian ideal—which had long disappeared from the sophisticated "establishment" Catholicism of the Sorbonne in Paris and St. Peter's in Rome—it would still set loose a number of intellectual and social ideas, e.g., universal literacy and the separation of church and state, that later were to transform Protestantism into a vanguard movement for modernization. Nevertheless, at first it attempted to separate itself from the secular embellishments of the Renaissance papacy and the sterile scholasticism of the professors in Paris, one of whose members had been the disenchanted John Calvin of Geneva (1509–64), who had given the movement intellectual force that had to have important educational consequences.

ONE

The Puritans first landed in Massachusetts in 1630. By 1635 a Latin grammar school had been established. A year later, Harvard College was established for the education of literate and scholarly ministers. In the 1640s a series of institutional arrangements were made for the education of the bulk of the young of the colony, either in Dame schools, grammar, or secondary schools. The "old deluder Satan" laws of 1642 and 1647 mark the transition from persuasive attempts by the colonist leaders to stimulate education to perpetuate their system of values, thence to use legal injunctions to induce the various communities of the colony to establish schools, levy taxes to support them, hire teachers, and so forth.

It is no accident that New Town, the original name of the town where Harvard was established, became Cambridge, commemorating the institution in England from which many of the colony's founders had graduated. These men saw in a formal system of education the way to protect and propagate their system of values down through the generations, protect their commonwealth from random change, give meaning and identity to the various facets of their life style, and provide a symbolic code by which the exigencies of life here on earth could be met with intelligence and reason, preparatory to their ascent to the eternal commonwealth that lay beyond the material and sensory.

For almost three-quarters of a century the pace of change was so slow that the calm sense of continuity was almost untouched, which aided the gradual process of institutionalization. Adding to this was the maintenance of a relatively simple political, social, and economic structure.

What was gained in the relentless struggle against the natural forces was a better living in quantitative terms. The fishing industry increased and became a rich resource; farming and lumbering provided country as well as town folk a secure livelihood and market. During this period there was a steady but assimilable population increase. The rule of Cromwell and the Puritans in England had closed off the urgent causes of emigration from England, and for a few decades the colonial Puritan tradition was insulated and stabilized. It also made them increasingly independent.

The gradual increase in population pushed the frontiers beyond the coastline and the established settlements. In an attempt to secure the same educational results along the frontier as in the coastal villages, the colonial authorities instituted "moving schools" in the 1660s. Life on the frontier was harder; amid renewed struggle one generation removed from the original religious and intellectual influence that had provided the impetus for the establishment of the commonwealth in the first place, education was less effective. In addition, dissident religious groups had left Massachusetts for Providence and Hartford. While formal education was uppermost in their minds, too, at the very least to secure the intellectual and moral grounds for their own independence, it did detract from the imperious control of the philosophical raison d'être by the Puritan elite of their New England homeland.

These were small motes in the clear-eyed vision that constituted the unity of informal and formal education in seventeenth-century Massachusetts. The greater disturber of this equilibrium occurred toward the end of the century. It was brought about by worldwide commercial and scientific changes. Inevitably, these would reach the colonies.

Wealth and security were certainly part of the Protestant tradition. The Puritans thus could not block those secular means for acquiring them and ultimately the scientific thinking that produced them. The technology that built fine ships, utilized compasses and astrolobes, produced efficient farming and milling equipment, and developed guns and powder to protect these acquisitions had to be somehow absorbed into the Puritan intellectual world. In fact, the Protestant ethical tradition bestowed a moral blessing on wealth and achievement. They were a sign of God's acquiescence, the only sign people could rely on that might give a hint of personal destiny when mortal life departed.

The raw materials that issued from the natural resources of the colonies—for the most part through Boston's natural harbor—were exchanged for the manufactured goods of England as well as goods from more exotic lands across the seas. There was wealth to be had from these colonies, perhaps in quantities far larger than in the limited, controlled materialistic imaginations of the Puritan fathers. The "glorious revolution" of 1688 in England brought this situation to a head.

TWO

The accession of William and Mary represented a final victory of Parliament and the new middle-class mercantile elite over the landed aristocracy. Now, through colonial conquest via seapower and the international trade that necessarily ensued, England, a full century after her defeat of the Spanish Armada, was ready to inherit the Spanish mantle as the dominant maritime power in the world.

In 1691 the impact of these events on the Massachusetts Bay Colony was recorded, as rule over the colony reverted to a governor appointed by the crown. The colonists would no longer control the destiny of this commonwealth. The small group of religious deviants—Methodists, Quakers, Presbyterians, and the like—that heretofore were tolerated in Boston only for practical reasons began to swell through immigration from England and abroad. New churches were founded, but only after a protracted struggle. The larger secular rights of the populace were gradually established and emancipated from theological control.

There were too many things that people could now afford and too few reasons to deny themselves these formerly forbidden luxuries. The town of Boston became a small city during the last decade of the seventeenth century. Even the relative anonymity associated with city life now became possible.[1] The only response to attempts to protect the well-integrated religious status quo, beyond a holding action, was an indirect, psychological one.

The famous witchcraft trials (1690-92) occurred in Salem, a community on the periphery of this new urban environment. Perhaps one ought to take into consideration the fact that this set of events took place under indigenous moral and social conditions, not regard them as symptoms of a more pervasive change in the intellectual and cultural climate. Yet one wonders whether such bizarre events as those that occurred in Salem could have happened under the tough-minded Puritan hegemony of John Winthrop, John Cotton, or Increase Mather.

Certainly by 1690 there was a sense of dissolution of the old fiber. The hysteria of this community in Salem and the barbaric resolution of its affliction are indications of the fearfulness that comes when the traditional value system is given a shaking. Perhaps it was symptomatic of a last-ditch subliminal attempt to secure the bastions of a culture and to protect its educational patterns and the meanings that needed to be succored in order to maintain the tradition.

The process of change was slow but relentless. Those who refused to bend to new ways would find no permanent contentment.

1. An unpleasant Englishman, noting the marked turn from orthodoxy by the year 1699, declared, "Money their God, and Large Possessions the only Heaven Covet."

Cotton Mather, whimpering successor to stern and solemn Increase Mather, epitomizes the erosion of the old truths. While the content of the doctrine does not change appreciably, the tenor of Cotton Mather's missionary teachings to his congregation do. Mather's enunciations to his flock betray a loss of confidence. Rather than a demand for obeisance to God's will, there is a plea—solicitous, almost deferring—for their obedience.[2]

Increasingly, the world of Boston—the craftsmen, merchants, entrepreneurs—merged with worlds of similar interest in New York, Philadelphia, Baltimore, Richmond, and Savannah. And the more traditional Christian élan withdrew to New Haven, Connecticut (Elihu Yale), Northampton, Massachusetts (Jonathan Edwards), and other momentary byways that were not yet on the mainline of the contemporary cultural dynamics. On the one hand we see in the writings of Jonathan Edwards an imperious religio-intellectual educational tradition with no rivals when it came to integrating the greater part of an individual's informal familial, communitarian, moral, social, and aesthetic existence. On the other hand was the steady, insistent knock of the practical economic demands evoked by the same forces against which both Luther and Calvin had fought and which the colonists had tried to avoid by coming to the New World.

Now the enemy was within. Who could deny the religious neutrality of warm woolen goods, fine mahogany furniture, carriages, and the like? These objects were indeed moral symbols. Those individuals who purveyed and purchased these goods were members of "our own" community. It thus followed that with the winds of economic and technological change came subtle social and educational alterations.

THREE

When a seventeenth- or eighteenth-century merchant used the expression "when my ship comes in," it was by no means an empty hope. Gone were the days when mythical serpents or monsters were feared. Now the merchant could rely on the skill of the crew to keep the boat seaworthy and maintain health (prevent scurvy); the skill of the captain to use the most precise sailing techniques; and the

2. At one point Cotton Mather directed an inquiry to England to ascertain some facts as to one of the new discoveries of which he had recently heard. Does the telescope indeed give new evidence as to God's grandeur and achievements? See Vernon Parrington, *Main Currents in American Thought* (New York: Harcourt, Brace, 1967), 1:116.

skill of the navigator to handle the compass, sextant, and astrolabe.

Scientific attitudes, whether applied to seamanship, agriculture, manufacture, banking and accounts, would inevitably triumph in terms of enhancing one's competency in dealing with an evolving society. The self-abnegation, even the Puritan rationalizations of one's moralistic work habits and the harsh set of community restrictions established by the theocracy, now seemed out of tune with the exhilarating sense of social possibility that was revealed to people by their expanding intelligence. Even the sense of sin evaporated as individuals projected their energies into the social and physical world rather than into the succoring of their own souls.

Some of these children of the new enlightenment accepted the powerful intellectual tools of this science so unreservedly that they sought to overthrow completely the old intellectual and moral order—Christianity. They saw the inevitable triumph of this new educational revolution; according to their logic, the management of this new commercial middle-class world that had descended upon the West was to be the responsibility of science.

One might articulate the situation as follows: The "philosophers" of the Enlightenment felt that a new formal system of education necessitated the replacing of the older integration in which religion had encompassed a complete culture—both informal life style and formal institutions and beliefs. Free souls that they were, they expected that, given time, reason could also reconstruct the informal world of cultural symbols. Yet, because of their inchoate sense of appropriateness, even conservatism, most citizens did not see the new science as a replacement of Christian culture. Rather they saw that with a natural shift in its structure, Christian thought might accommodate science. Thus, Deism and Unitarianism represent Protestant adjustments to the change; they eliminated the more dogmatic theological characteristics of the old Calvinist creed. The inner flexibility of Protestant thought—its fundamentally individualistic anticredal bias—coupled with its highly fragmented organizational structure—allowed a continual series of intellectual adjustments that accommodated it to the widening horizons of this new era.

Thus, Locke and Newton, Jefferson, Washington, and the Adamses were enlightened Christians. The world was still moving slowly enough from generation to generation in terms of changes in the formal intellectual scene as well as in the socioeconomic structure of life to allow the informal cultural fabric and its intimate educative symbolism to remain whole.

Kings College (Columbia), 1754, in New York and the College of Philadelphia (University of Pennsylvania), 1749, were essentially bourgeois educational institutions to train men to function competently in this new society in law, medicine, and the arts. Yet ministers, too, were prepared, and the institution was inevitably governed by the religious elect of the community. The commitment of the Protestant elders to their community, family, their sense of responsibility, the continuity of a host of moral and institutional relationships were neatly sustained in spite of this essentially radical shift of the intellectual and educational sightlines.

The men who participated in the Continental Congress of 1776 were vastly different kinds of people than those who oversaw the Massachusetts Bay Colony 125 years earlier. They could proclaim themselves rational Christians; they were committed to the maintenance of a fabric of meaning in society, from the highest metaphysical views of the universe down to day-to-day political, social, and moral commitments and actions.

One cannot argue from this set of events that what occurred in the colonies, then in the new nation as a whole, was both a triumph of a new truth and an advance toward ultimate rationality. Those intellectual and philosophical dogmatists who would have argued for the complete overthrow of the old order, perhaps even through state control of all formal educational agencies, could not have been aware of the critical importance of the informal patterns of belief and behavior for the average citizens. The Christian tradition had made too deep a mark on their souls and therefore on their most intimate living arrangements to be dissolved so easily by logic alone.

What happened, then, even as mid-eighteenth-century men went out into the city streets (private tutors, academies) to obtain the kind of education in navigation, bookkeeping, modern foreign languages, natural philosophy, botany, etc., and in a sense abandoned the theocratically controlled public school, was that the Christian value system was absorbed into their way of life. They accepted it increasingly as an informal element in their belief system—for the communal, familial, moral, cultural, and ritualistic purposes. They accepted an attenuated theism, e.g., the view of God as the creator and adjuster of the great mechanical clock that was the world, even if the price was a jerrybuilt set of philosophical accommodations necessary to preserve the existing fabric of meaning of this slowly evolving semifrontier culture.

FOUR

We now have a culture that by the first decades of the nineteenth century was undergoing the beginnings of an accelerating process of social change. By and large, the informal culture—an agrarian Christianity—bereft of the traditional fixed class and feudal relationships of Europe, had freed itself of the more coercive theocratic elements of the Puritan tradition. For one, the Anglican culture of the Middle Atlantic states blended a more benign religiomoral structure with an easier climatic environment. In addition, the great move—with its attendant primitive conditions—that had just begun rendered religious control difficult. Indeed, it was rare during this period to find a person on the Appalachian frontier who had seen, much less could read, the Bible.

Here and there in New England, in towns that had remained static and insulated, a strong theocratic tradition survived, even while shorn of its official prerogatives. Horace Mann, born in Franklin, Massachusetts, in 1796, could look back upon this tradition when he recalled this village of his childhood:

> More than by toil, or by the privation of any natural taste, was the inward joy of my youth blighted by theological inculcations. The pastor of the church in Franklin was the somewhat celebrated Dr. Emmons, who not only preached to his people, but ruled them, for more than fifty years. He was an extra or hyper-Calvinist,—a man of pure intellect, whose logic was never softened in its severity by the infusion of any kindliness of sentiment. He expounded all the doctrines of total depravity, election, and reprobation, and not only the eternity, but the extremity, of hell-torments, unflinchingly and in their most terrible significance; while he rarely if ever descanted upon the joys of heaven, and never, to my recollection, upon the essential and necessary happiness of a virtuous life. . . .
>
> The consequences upon my mind and happiness were disastrous in the extreme. Often, on going to bed at night, did the objects of the day and the faces of friends give place to a vision of the awful throne, the inexorable Judge, and the hapless myriads, among whom I often seemed to see those whom I loved best; and there I wept and sobbed until Nature found that counterfeit repose in exhaustion whose genuine reality she should have found in freedom from care and the spontaneous happiness of childhood. What seems most deplorable in the retrospect, all these fears and sufferings, springing from a belief in the immutability of the decrees that had been made, never

prompted me to a single good action, or had the slightest efficacy in deterring me from a bad one.[3]

The late eighteenth and early nineteenth centuries were an era of general educational flaccidity in terms of school organization or governmental support of education. Note the rejection by the House of Burgesses in 1779 of Jefferson's plea for a general reorganization and systemization of education. Such a system potentially would have reached into every corner of Virginia to yield a steady supply of talent for entry into this new culture of reason, science, the arts, and political democracy. What the revolutionary elite—the Franklins, Washingtons, Jeffersons—had achieved, they had achieved through the force of their personal wills. The energies of Franklin are noteworthy. His many inventions, his excitement and openness to innovations from abroad, save in one rejected area—religious disputation—exemplify the aggressive scientific mentality of this era, as expressed in almost every area of social intercourse.

In a visit to Jefferson's Monticello, one cannot but be impressed by this brilliant and inventive generalist. In every area of his life— the modern architectural design of the house and the layout of the gardens; the experimentation with new agricultural techniques; the furniture designed for special functionality; the broad-ranging attempt to see the new, the possible in every aspect of traditional life—we see represented a reverence for the power of the mind to break loose from the foundations of habit. With every innovative breakthrough, man expected to slough off another of the material bonds of want and privation.

Yet this American elite was not interested merely in freeing itself from the restrictions of necessity. It was more interested in cultivating those cultural opportunities that were now available—in music, the arts, literature, science, politics, architecture, agriculture. The deist culture was both a bond to traditional personal and social obligation (through their Christian religious as well as Anglo-European heritage) and also the rich soil of the informal educational tradition, fertile and flexible enough to provide for growing roots to sprout luxuriant foliage.

The work of elitist groups such as the Royal and Lunar societies in England and Benjamin Franklin's Philosophical Society in the New World would convey only long-term intellectual consequences to the people. These groups both reflected and stimulated the

3. Mary Mann, *Life of Horace Mann* (Boston: Walker, Fuller, 1865), pp. 13, 15.

growing transformations that owed much to the gradual insinuation of the scientific and secular approach to life and reality. Thus, while the new revolutionary tradition in France and the United States had symbolized a release from the old social and philosophical controls, the impact on the thinking of the masses as contrasted with the elite was small. What did happen was a general if gradual acceleration of change that eventually did affect the lives of the common people.

Between 1720 and 1801 England increased in population from 6 million to 9 million.[4] By 1850, there would be over 20 million Englishmen. Prussia grew from 2.3 million to 5.8 million between 1740 and 1783, Saxony from 1.6 million to 2 million between 1722 and 1802. France between 1700 and 1789 rose in population from 18 million to 24 million. In the eighteenth century, the cities made one of their quickest growth spurts. London increased from 675,000 to 865,000, Paris from 500,000 to 670,000, Berlin from 29,000 to 141,000.

America, which had almost 4 million people in 1790, by 1815 had grown to 13 million, with scarcely a half million of the increase accounted for by immigration. In the new nation, as in the Old World, this increase was largely among the poorer part of the population. And indeed, because of the expanding frontier, the relatively undeveloped state of things in the United States, and the slowness with which worldwide trends would be reflected here, the two cultural eras for a time overlapped.

Horace Mann could be born in Calvinism, be educated at Brown University, a Baptist institution, maintain his Unitarianism, and commit himself for a career in educational reform under the nestling sponsorship of New England Transcendentalism. At the same time that the Jacksonian masses were dissolving the barriers of political exclusiveness that were established through property qualifications, that paradigmatic intellectual aristocrat-cum-democrat, Thomas Jefferson, in 1825 was finally seeing his dream of a state university—staffed by the best professional talent that could be enticed from Europe—established in his western Virginia homeland at Charlottesville.

The cultural wave that overtook both Europe and America is epitomized in a new and unexpectedly improved status and role for religion. One can only hypothesize an explanation for this phenomenon, that the Enlightenment culture was too distant and abstract in both role and function to touch the lives and feelings of the masses. Certainly the old fundamentalist religion was in the

4. William O. Henderson, *The Industrial Revolution in Europe* (Chicago: Quadrangle Books, 1961), p. 7.

main only a historical memory. New influences were undercutting the pervasive impact of Newton and the physical sciences. A renewed awareness and cultivation of history was observable; the arts were now exemplified by their concentration not so much on form and structure but on personality and emotion; interest in biology and nature was renewed now that its fearsome theoretical immensity had been brought under intellectual and technological control in a more scientific agriculture. A feeling of oneness with nature was experienced, and once more deity was invoked to explain this phenomenon. The philosophies of the German romantics Fichte, Schelling, and Hegel replaced Leibniz and Kant. In England Coleridge succeeded Hume, in France Rousseau replaced Voltaire.

This was also true for the United States. New Englanders Thoreau, Emerson, Hawthorne, and Mann explored a new religious, social, and educational message. The heart must meet its own needs, even as it joins with reason. "Transcendentalism" was exhibited in a new spirit of communalism. An attempt was made to fuse informal culture and education with the religious rationalizations for the work ethic. Even then, early in the nineteenth century, a feeling of revulsion was building toward that hidden cancer, slavery, that absorbs so large a part of the American experience.

Science had not disappeared from the scene. It was still a powerful guide and disciplinarian in deciding which direction this new "romantic, religious" culture could go. First, the destruction of the unique integration within eighteenth-century rationalism of science, philosophy, religion, and politics had resulted in the establishment of separate bastions of academic science within the walls of specialized institutions epitomized by the Ecole Polytechnic in Paris. Here, the enormous theoretical possibilities of the physical sciences and mathematics were being revealed. The second impact of science was in the industrial establishment now sweeping over Europe wherein these theoretical discoveries were being rapidly put to practical use.

FIVE

At any one period of time in a complex culture, as long as the process of social change is not violently rapid, there exists an interesting mix of old and new trends, none ever fully realized; only a tenuous integration occurs. But amid this unity, and even within the various elements of culture moving at different speeds in their evolution and in possibly different paths, the total impact is such as to make life slightly ambiguous in meaning and direction, at the same time interesting and full of portent. The very nature of modern culture, given its inner dynamics, makes it impossible for a citizenry to accept a static environment. So the essential impetus of life is transformed mentally into an acceptance of whatever constitutes orthodoxy and normality. This sense of the ordinary can be accepted as long as the pace of innovation can be absorbed both in the informal education environment as well as intellectually through formal educational means. This rapidly evolving situation existed in that fascinating half century after 1800.

As early as 1815, an estimated 100,000 people, mostly women and children, were employed in the textile mills of New England. This constituted the first phase of the industrial revolution in America and the beginning of the creation of an urban proletariat in the United States. Squalor was rampant on the streets of the new cities during this period—in Boston, Baltimore, New York, and Philadelphia. It was at this time that the Lancastrian monitorial system of education was introduced, wherein large numbers of children could be taught basic reading and writing skills by semi-educated adolescents guided by a poorly paid master often of checkered background.

Even so, a steady surge of optimism and altruism prevailed. The common man came into his own; this ushered in an era of the "common school." The purpose of the common school was to unite a disparate and widely dispersed population in a rapidly evolving era of agricultural wealth, commerce, and growing industry. This educational movement had several aims: to bring about a national consciousness and sense of the inherent equality and possibility in man, and to accommodate him to a future with as few practical limitations as possible, and those subject to amelioration. The old Enlightenment intellectual vision of limitless horizons was in America being fused into a practical vision, and this in spite of the existence of diverse and perhaps incommensurate intellectual traditions.

The mentality that created the steamship, the railroad, and sent clipper ships halfway around the world coexisted with a Thoreau, for whom these trends and the style of life they produced were anathema. Schools were created with public tax monies. A non-denominational Protestantism was established to foreclose the possibility of internecine religious agitation while America tried to absorb a new flow of Catholic immigrants. Elsewhere, frontier farmers under the most primitive conditions were still struggling to eke a bare existence from the soil. At the same time, the Brook Farm community in Massachusetts was established—a bucolic cooperative haven from the pleasures, temptations, and vices of urban life.

Those same instigators of public education who sought to preserve public morality and good citizenship were for the most part the new religious reformers, romantics, and idealists who even then found urban blight intolerable, though it was still only an incipient menace as compared to the real thing in England and France. The kinds of cognitive skills that increasingly were taught in these schools to more and more children necessarily had to further the advancing scientific and industrial culture.

One might summarize this first half of the nineteenth century as marking the beginning of the separation of the two cultures. The scientific and industrial culture, increasingly specialized and technically oriented, burgeoned through people's powerful strivings to throw off their dependence on the accidents of nature, to conquer time and space and acquire the amenities of life. These amenities were now being produced by the economic system in increasing quantities, inevitably adding new dimensions to experience. Implicit in this developing structure of knowledge was a view that science had begun to unravel the mysteries of nature and would soon penetrate the ultimate realities of the universe. With every industrial advance, these assumptions were supported, also enhanced, in terms of rising human expectations. For the moment, this manifestation did not extend beyond the material and economic side of things. The communitarian bases of life, whether farm, village, or city, remained secure. As individuals moved from their parochial villages or farms onto the comfortable plateau of urban middle-class living, they took upon themselves the somewhat more progressive value systems and cultural attitudes therein purveyed. But they still cherished and protected their past.

The religious and humanistic culture within which most of the populace lived and which nurtured the drive for formal education (there was in the beginning an ambivalence among the industrialists as to the usefulness of schools) drove its roots deep into the informal value system. It should not be thought that the only sources of strength of the nondenominational Protestant agrarian village culture lay in the slow-moving pace of evolving traditional values.

A rich new philosophical movement flowed out of Europe in the early nineteenth century into our own world. Dominated by the absolute idealism of Georg W. F. Hegel and translated into various liberal American philosophies—Transcendentalism for one—it gave philosophical sanction to the assumed belief in an all-encompassing divine force that had been manifested upon this earth in the form of an egalitarian social ideal. The literature, music, and community life of our nation was constructed out of these ideas and was centered on the Protestant church, the fundamental institution in America that could claim that necessary historical connection with the past.

Essentially the two worlds of small town and industrial center remained apart. Only a few intellectuals would pursue the implications of the two inevitably disparate philosophical traditions they represented. That they logically conflicted and would in the end have to confront each other could not be foreseen. The many colleges created by private religious groups as well as the several state universities trained their ministers, lawyers, doctors, and gentlemen, as before. Each area of life and thought fulfilled different current needs. As yet, there appeared to be enough intellectual room for diversity.

As late as 1882 at Johns Hopkins University, two areas of graduate studies could still coexist in a measure of equality. Even there, one could recognize the inherent conflict of social dynamics, ethical value systems, and basic metaphysical claims between the distinct positions. Daniel Coit Gilman, president of Johns Hopkins, is said to have confronted the young John Dewey in a hallway of that institution. Well aware that Dewey was not only bright but inordinately ambitious, Gilman decried his involvement with the Hopkins philosophical wing, especially as represented by Dewey's teacher, the Hegelian idealist G. S. Morris. With such faculty as G. Stanley Hall and Charles S. Peirce representing the scientific mentality of the time, it seemed obvious to Gilman that here lay the future. Dewey was warned that he might be wasting his energies on a discipline that was destined for oblivion. Dewey did not listen; he remained faithful to Morris and followed him to the University of Michigan upon receiving his doctoral degree. But not too long after, he too succumbed to the explanatory power of the new science and embarked upon a new philosophical road that constituted a vindication for the prescient Gilman.

5 | The Transitional Generations

In 1859 Alfred Krupp, son of an unsuccessful and impoverished iron smelterer, gained his first large contract. The Imperial government of Russia put in an order for 120 steel cannons of large bore. In that same year, across the seas in the United States in Pennsylvania, E. L. Drake drilled the first oil well. Further west, again in 1859, Horace Mann died. The dynamic inspirer of the Common School, born in the final decade of the previous century in a New England town in which the old colonial tradition had still survived, succumbed at his unique coeducational college, Antioch, in Ohio. He had spanned two eras. Back east, in Burlington, Vermont, in the heart of New England, in this same year, John Dewey was born. A new world was being created.

Shortly, the American Civil War would teach Europe the full meaning of the new industrial age and the possibilities inherent in the marriage of industry with the military. Germany, under the tutelage of such men as Alfred Krupp, would take this marriage one step further, as is clearly shown in her efficient smashing of France in 1871. The union between scientific scholarship, formal education, industrial technology, and military and political power was to be sanctified by history. Thus the inevitable cultural breakthrough began; it is with us still.

The year 1859 saw other events that were important turning points in this revolutionary era. In *Darwin, Marx, Wagner*,[1] Jacques Barzun has written of the impact produced by these men in shaping the generations yet to come.[2] Darwin's *Origin of Species* brought to full fruition the search for a naturalistic, indeed objective, theory of biological evolution. Darwin produced a conceptual mechanism

1. Jacques Barzun, *Darwin, Marx, Wagner* (Garden City, N.Y.: Doubleday Anchor, 1958).
2. Sigmund Freud was born in 1856.

(mutation, adaptation, natural selection) for understanding the evidenced changes. His theory became a magnificent heuristic device for examining a host of other phenomena and areas, from psychology to anthropology; it literally changed our view of ourselves and the biological world.

Karl Marx's *Critique of Political Economy* represented only the first phase of *Das Kapital*. The scientific spirit had bred into Marx an awareness of the epochal confrontation of industry with the historical processes of society. The *Critique* represented an attempt to reformulate these processes in the light of Marx's special philosophical insights. It gave careful attention to the process by which power, class, and economic advantage had interacted not only in history but also in his own era to produce the particular social configurations of the time. It also held out hope to masses of downtrodden that they held their fate in their own hands.

In *Tristan und Isolde*, Richard Wagner had introduced wholly new harmonic, orchestral, and dramatic effects into the symphonic as well as operatic traditions. And while the revolution that Wagner promised was completed by successor composers, his genius served to place before the cultured classes yet another example of the unheralded cultural fertility that had been produced since the days when the first modern trends had startled Renaissance Europe.

ONE

For almost three hundred years, from the early seventeenth century to the threshold of the twentieth, the formal revolution in intellectual ideals had gradually but inexorably displaced to the sidelines the major religious forms from their dominant position in the minds of the educated classes. More and more, the religious role centered itself in the informal culture; it became the traditional glue of ritual, commitment, and a sense of history needed by family and community in order to function.

The entire process of displacement had been gradual enough so that the aristocratic élan of society—the sense of legitimacy, authority, and continuity—had been maintained; it had moved smoothly from one historic point to the next. By the middle of the nineteenth century, a new factor was completing its incubation. It took the prescient genius of Karl Marx to enunciate it in its modern embodiment and characterize its revolutionary portent. To come was a proletarian surge that would complete the revolutionary process.

These thoughts had not begun with Marx. Rousseau and Vico

had predicted its coming in the eighteenth century. From the days of Jefferson and Jackson, our own proletariat—the frontier farmer and the city worker—shaped the peculiar indigenous American character. Yet Tocqueville could recognize, note, and report it to the world.[3]

The impact of the intellectual and cultural revolution on the character of informal culture began almost surreptitiously with the demographic advance of the eighteenth century. But it grew with tangible impact in the cities of the nineteenth. The world of common-sense social experience was undergoing a sharp revocation. It would become necessary to translate the formal educational culture to the masses, for now they figured importantly in the industrial transformation of their societies. A new formal educational structure would have to be established to bring order to the chaotic advances taking place and to integrate people's lives in both the formal and informal domains. Otherwise, could they discipline themselves to function under such radically new cultural circumstances?

In all parts of the civilized world, the search went on to find the most efficient form of national education. The shape and particular character of the education in each society were determined by indigenous influences—Pestalozzi, Froebel, Victor Cousin, Horace Mann. But there can be no doubt that the entrance in all these societies of the proletarian class of urban-dwelling factory workers into a pivotal position on the blade edge of the plow of social change made an educational switch necessary to rescue the workers from their perennial agricultural oblivion.

Even in the predominantly rural nineteenth-century society, in the stability of that middle America of Sherwood Anderson's *Winesburg, Ohio,* which we recall with such nostalgia, embarrassment, and dread, the old sense of place, the slow rhythms of familiarity and ennui, was to be permanently eroded by the end of the second half of the nineteenth century. The American public school would help us to shift our acceptances of reality onto a new plane of activity and thought.

TWO

In the 1840s and '50s, the tax-supported Common School was gradually established throughout the East and Midwest. At the same time that it introduced a modicum of literacy into the popu-

3. Alexis de Tocqueville, *Democracy in America* (New York: Knopf, 1945; first published, 1830).

lation, it also began to superimpose new social goals. Normal schools were established in various states of the East—Massachusetts, New York, Connecticut—to train teachers beyond the elementary level of literacy with which many of them were previously equipped. The few existing public high schools, if not on a level with the better private secondary academies that channeled their few graduates into the exclusive liberal arts colleges such as Princeton, Harvard, and Yale, at least gave off an aura of expectation of improvement. Throughout the land, there was an appreciation of the meaning of educational standards as established by the various states for the common educational good.

Compulsory education laws began to be enacted; the first was in Massachusetts in 1852. By 1890, a large number of states were enacting and enforcing these laws. Literacy was no longer to be considered a luxury but a necessity in the increased complexity of a life whose pace was so rapid. In 1862, in the midst of a brutal, internecine, civil war, the Morrill Act was passed. Through funds that came from the sale of federal lands, it allocated moneys for the support of mechanical and agricultural training in state colleges. Thus began a sharp rise in the activities of the public universities. Most of the activity occurred in the relatively undeveloped states of the Midwest.

The spread of universal elementary education in the latter part of the nineteenth century began to produce a small but active cadre of professional educators. In 1857, inspired to self-consciousness perhaps by (1) the religio-philosophical ideal of universal enlightenment and (2) by the growing discrepancy between knowledge and sophistication in the intellectual elite and simplicity and backwardness of the masses, a small group of male schoolmasters established the National Education Association. At first, it was the self-consciousness of self-protection, social and economic improvement that characterized their activities. Eventually, a nationwide organization would develop to foster research into the problem of modernization and the facilitation of this educational enterprise.

In 1858, at a small training school in Oswego, New York, the principal, Edward Sheldon, introduced Pestalozzian "object lesson" materials. These were expected to supplant the more traditional book-oriented learnings of the past. A wave of receptivity greeted this new "panacea," perhaps reflecting even at this early stage of public education the intense search for the new, the better, the more scientific or true educational method.

In Saint Louis, Missouri, German immigrants, a large percentage of whom were displaced intellectuals from revolutionary turbulence and intensely interested in education, established in the 1860s and '70s, under the leadership of Carl Schurtz and William Torrey Harris, a first-class public system of education that began with a public kindergarten (1873). It was modeled on the idealistic philosophy of Friedrich Froebel.

Secondary schools supported by tax moneys had existed since the 1820s in the larger cities (Boston, New York). But until 1872, the principle was purely a local option. Therefore, a huge gap intervened between the general populace getting an education in a one-room schoolhouse and that small group of elite in the liberal arts college and the few enterprising sons of the rising middle class who attended state colleges and universities. Until after the Civil War, the secondary school was most likely a private academy—Deerfield, Phillips Exeter, Mount Holyoke, or Elmira.[4] In 1874 the Michigan State Supreme Court upheld taxation by the city of Kalamazoo for the support of its high school. This swept away a tacit barrier of this form of education, and soon the public high school was the dominant institution for the education of young adolescents.

Even the structure of higher education was to undergo rapid transformation during the late nineteenth century. The impact of the ingenious German system of education, encompassing the child from the cradle to the university, was influential as a symbolic example, especially after the Franco-German War of 1871. The Prussian system, wedded both to a heavy emphasis on scholarly research and to the practical needs of a burgeoning industrial machine, stimulated grave questions about America's English-modeled undergraduate college. Jefferson's University of Virginia, established with some of the finest European teachers, was now essentially no more than a finishing school for gentlemen. The state colleges were as yet institutions giving practical if necessary instruction for the development of the farm economy and at the same time raising the educational tone of their respective states.

Yale gave the first Ph.D. in 1861. But it was Daniel Coit Gilman who, in establishing Johns Hopkins University in Baltimore in 1876, enunciated a new theme—postgraduate education modeled on the German university, intended to stimulate the sciences while not ignoring the humanities.[5] Rather than continuing to create the cultivated gentleman or skilled farmer, Gilman sought to develop a

4. By the end of the century, the upper classes had withdrawn to even more exclusive boarding high schools: Groton, Choate, Hotchkiss. See E. Digby Baltzell, *The Protestant Establishment* (New York: Vintage, 1966), pp. 121–35.
5. Railroad wealth (Baltimore and Ohio) was instrumental in establishing Johns Hopkins.

researcher in the vanguard of knowledge. He explicitly committed his university to research and the advancement of knowledge. The goal was no longer the semitutorial shaping of a young gentleman —in loco parentis. The students' freedom to learn would be balanced by the research and teaching freedom of the professor.

THREE

Burlington, Vermont, though one of the larger towns of this rural state and destined soon to be the home of its state university, was only a microcosm of New England society at mid-century. It was an easy amalgam of town and country life. Work was hard, the fruits meager yet steady enough to sustain a sense of security, intimacy of relationship, and the typical democratic ideals of participation by most elements in the community.

John Dewey, of lower-middle-class background (his father was a grocer), attended the local university. In the mid-1870s, the University of Vermont had eight professors and two hundred students. It is said that the germ of meaning to Dewey's own education did not take hold in this middling student until his last year of college when he read T. H. Huxley's *Principles of Biology*. While the experience did not stimulate him to become a scientist, it started him down the road of intellectual development which a few years later led him to undertake graduate study at Johns Hopkins.

At Johns Hopkins, Dewey, by then a novice philosopher, encountered two distinct faculties: the aggressive, energetic scientific departments, then represented as we have noted earlier by scholars such as Charles Sanders Peirce and G. Stanley Hall; and the humanities departments, represented by his own mentor philosopher, G. S. Morris. In 1884 Dewey received his doctorate and, following Morris, moved to the University of Michigan, then a burgeoning, dynamic state institution.

It was not until 1890, when he was stimulated by a close reading of William James' *Principles of Psychology* (a Darwinian and functional approach to thinking and behavior) that Dewey was persuaded to abandon his Christian idealism and finally throw in his lot with the scientific wing, the wave of the future. It is not unfair to claim that by the year 1890 the general shape of American formal education, as it was beginning to respond to the new industrial era and the coming twentieth century, had been institutionally defined.

The 1890s saw a flurry of concern and study that concentrated on the structure of American education. Graduate education had by now won its place on the American scene. Dewey would join a distinguished faculty at John D. Rockefeller's new University of Chicago in 1894, as chairman of a combined Department of Philosophy, Psychology, and Pedagogy, eventually to become a School of Education. In New York, the Institute for Industrial Education had become Teachers College, Columbia University, predominantly a graduate school of education for training teachers and engaging in educational research. Indeed, the profession of education had begun to coalesce during this decade, and the training of large cadres of teachers and administrators became a matter of national importance. The number of high school students had increased radically because of the impact of the Kalamazoo Decision (1874). The rate of increase, from 110,000 to 202,963 in 1890, practically a doubling in every decade, was to continue until the 1940s when a leveling off began.

A by-product of this expansive trend was the work of two commissions. The first was the Committee of Ten (1893), headed by Charles Eliot, which recommended a series of liberal arts academic disciplines by establishing the high school as a terminal educational experience for the masses. Yet these requirements were little different from those taken as prerequisites for college entrance by the pupils who intended to continue their education for another four years. Second was the Committee on College Requirements of 1899, which in general supported the first group.

Another group, also meeting under NEA auspices, but several years later, suggested shortening the eight-year grammar school to six and lengthening the high school years to six, giving due regard to developmental differences in the young. In this latter suggestion we see the first manifestations of the ultimate emergence of the American educational system from long-standing acculturation demands of the agricultural life style. The young were mastering skills much more rapidly due primarily to their greater exposure to modern currents of life. It was several decades before the above important structural suggestion was worked out; it finally issued in the junior-senior high school movement.

One cannot understand the developments in institutional education without appreciating the explosive advances in science and industry.[6] The proliferation of new inventions, industrial methods, and technological know-how was epitomized in those socially devastating inventions, the automobile and the airplane, which were

6. Daniel J. Boorstin, *The Americans: The Democratic Experience* (New York: Random House, 1973).

developed almost within a decade of each other. The gradual dominance of the United States industrially and technologically was hinted at in the Spanish-American War and fully realized in World War I. The systematic contribution of the schools to our economic life had heretofore been rather minor. Up to now, the freedom and openness of our culture and the ingenuity of the entrepreneur had more than made up for the lack of system in our approach. Yet when one could appraise what the Germans had done with fewer resources and what the Japanese even then had been able to achieve in so few years, capped by their destruction of the Russian czar's forces in 1905—by a sustained, organized pooling of all resources by various segments of the culture—our domestic need for greater governmental involvement became urgent.

State laws concerning compulsory education were tightened. Expansion of support of public schools by state revenues in addition to local taxation became the prelude to greater statewide involvement, such as the establishment of the Board of Regents in New York State to determine standards of graduation from high school, curricular synchronization, and other programs that would fit an increasingly mobile society. In addition, the upgrading of teacher training from normal school education to at least the basic college skills in newly expanded "state teachers colleges" became necessary. The federal government, heretofore aloof from educational participation by constitutional injunction (residual powers left to the state, Tenth Amendment), even felt the need to support vocational training. The Smith-Lever (1914) and Smith-Hughes (1917) programs that were established in specialized high schools (primarily in New York City and the East) or as part of a more comprehensive high school program (the basic pattern throughout the midwestern part of the United States) constituted the first permanent federal involvement in public education. The result of this buttressing of the various middle-level skills, sorely needed in an industrial world, resulted in a greater dollar support of each vocational student than his academic high school confrere.

FOUR

It was also in the decade beginning in 1890 that those philosophical tendencies that first surfaced shortly after mid-century (1859) began to coalesce into one unified intellectual movement that moved into the schools. The disparate disciplines in the physical, biological, and social sciences had united themselves into a new and progressive consideration of the major social and educational issues of the period. Note this list of American scholars: Oliver Wendell Holmes (law), Thorstein Veblen (economics), Charles Beard (history), William James (psychology and philosophy), John Dewey (psychology, philosophy, and education), Charles S. Peirce (scientific philosophy), George Herbert Mead (social psychology), Albion Small (sociology), William MacDougall (social psychology), W. H. Kilpatrick (educational philosophy), Lewis Henry Morgan (anthropology), E. L. Thorndike (education and psychology), Franz Boas (anthropology). They literally rocketed a new scientific ideology into the American scene. The results for the common people were that, in one generation, they swept permanently into the past the intellectual underpinnings for the dominant religious and idealistic metaphysics of the early and mid-nineteenth century.

Philosophy is surely the queen of sciences. And the reigning philosopher of the time, John Dewey, was the logical choice to set forth the ideological ground for the movement and point the way to its broad applicatory significance. In the beginning, Dewey traversed the domains of psychology, education, and philosophy, thence to extend his philosophy into a general method of thought and analysis. His philosophy would also be used to indicate the relationship of the various disciplines of knowledge to individual and social experience. Dewey was creating, as Galileo and Locke did before him, the ground for a new rationalism. This rationalism had to come to terms with the scientific-industrial complex that had been thrust upon the world and also to determine the role of society and its formal educational system in controlling and guiding this unruly young giant. Philosophy and education would be utilized to keep technology to its commitment to the American egalitarian and democratic dream.

The Deweyan metaphysic encompassed several aspects: the traditional scientific respect for experience and experimentation, the withholding of judgment until publicly ascertainable evidence was commanded, a freedom from fixed belief, and a commitment to those propositions that could be tested through ordinary sensory means. In the pragmatic theory of meaning (C. S. Peirce)—which anticipates the tenets of that reforming European philosophical movement, the Vienna Circle (logical positivism)—it was asserted that only those questions that are capable of public and scientific resolution are worthy of intellectual and educational concern. The inquiry into the various mythological belief systems of religion and philosophy was seen by Dewey and the other pragmatists as a spurious effort, a luxury affordable only in the relatively quiescent atmosphere of preindustrial times.

Dewey was an evolutionist, deeply committed to the Darwinian views on change. *Homo sapiens* is a biosocial animal organically endowed with a need for societal stimuli. Even at the height of the psychological Darwinism of his own colleagues Edward Thorndike, John Watson, etc., Dewey saw that the social-conventional matrix of human existence reflected characteristics too complex to be treated or evaluated as one might more simply directed living creatures who merely *learn* and are not *educated.* Yet humans face the same constantly evolving challenges as all creatures. And if they are endowed with few inborn responses to deal with the environmental challenge, their future will be decided by the manner in which they formulate their more generic social responses.

In an ever changing world, it is how skillfully human beings respond to the inevitable social and personal dislocations that arise out of complex and interlocking institutions that is vital. Only by applying a rational methodology of inquiry into cause and consequence can people avoid the disasters that have occurred in the past. Thus the problem-solving method was introduced by Dewey into formal education, the key institution for accommodating the young to a controlled process of social change. The ramifications of this method as applied to education were first revealed in Dewey's early lectures at the laboratory school of the University of Chicago, "The Child and the Curriculum" and "School and Society," 1898–1902. He went to Columbia University in 1904. Thence in 1916 came his most comprehensive statement, *Democracy and Education.*[7] Herein is set forth an approach to education that is not rooted in fixed quantities of traditional knowledge to be absorbed uncritically; rather it is a dynamic and interactive approach to experience that sees the significance of knowledge in terms of its consequences for human behavior.

Here was also demonstrated the Deweyan concern for the democratic process. For if we dissolve a structure of human sociality founded on tradition and fixed belief, then we must substitute something just as sure, a gyroscope for an always evolving world. The solution, to Dewey, was the only one which his own experience and the corporate American tradition would allow, the democratic process. The democratic process meant more to Dewey than merely the performance of certain activities—meeting, debating, and vot-

---

7. John Dewey, *Democracy and Education* (New York: Macmillan, 1916).

ing—or the establishment of institutional structures—the various divisions of government, checks and balances, a written constitution, and a bill of rights. Though of course these were essential.

But even more important was the substantial fabric of democratic life, where the canons of logic and action give direction and flesh to the externals of democratic life. This can be realized by a willingness to face the issues of experience with a secular attitude toward reason—the problem-solving frame of mind. Dewey and his antiformalistic confreres in the various fields of study would have evicted all the time-honored shibboleths of traditional society and searched for standards and values more in keeping with this new era.

Democracy and education would be joined together in a quest for public rationality, using universally observable criteria of meaning and truth. The schools must educate the young to participate in this process; they would learn by doing. Dewey did not expect that any great social questions would be decided overnight by an immediate plebiscite. But by promoting a general, open debate by the various publics in our nation, he did expect that eventually the most workable and scientifically warrantable solution would emerge. For every new problem, we would attempt to bring about a temporary equilibrium in terms of evoking majority acquiescence. The goal of the public schools would be to absorb the great mass of young into a nationwide system of education. By exposing them to the challenges of choice at every point in their development and growth, the schools would prepare the young for public responsibility.

FIVE

The impact of Dewey and his Progressive cohorts varied, both in education and in the larger intellectual community. Certainly the schools and teachers, especially on the elementary level, began to reverse their traditional formal styles. New child-centered curricula were developed. There was a new sense of participation by this growing profession in the intellectual dialectic of the times. One might doubt that this pragmatic philosophy penetrated deeply into the body politic at first. The process in education, in the political and social arena, was gradual. The American social scene was growing in complexity at such a rapid pace that no one set of ideological influences was likely to affect more than a small sector of the public consciousness. It was only in the 1930s, in a time of social crisis (under the aegis of the New Deal) that the Progressive social philosophy came into application.

In the first two decades of the twentieth century, under the cumulative impact of a flood of immigration and a vast expansion of industry, the great dynamo of our society was in the economic domain. Intellectuals, in attempting to guide and shape the direction of this evolving society, were indeed riding a tiger. Population growth was a significant aspect of this change in direction. The population had expanded from about 40 million in 1870 to 105 million in 1920, and millions of these were immigrants who had poured into the United States during this time, largely from non-Anglo-Saxon lands. For example, of 8 million immigrants who came to the United States between 1900 and 1910, half were from Eastern and Southern Europe. From the beginning of large-scale immigration after the War of 1812 until the mid-1960s, fully 43 million had come to the United States. And they still come. In 1900, at the height of the influx, one-third of the United States population was foreign born.

If one could point to an important set of educational ideals for which the progressivists in education—Dewey, W. H. Kilpatrick, Boyd Bode, James Russell (all except Bode based at then dominant Teachers College, Columbia University)—prepared the ground, it was that of absorbing the great numbers of young, acculturating them to American democratic ideals and sending them out to participate in this new technological society. The goals of the system were clear.

The economic and technological systems were insatiable in their demands for skilled hands. In many cases, specialized demands existed that could have been fulfilled by the schools, from the business bureaucracy, the factory, or the mill. Yet with few exceptions, the goal of the American high school, still the major terminal institution (college enrollments were rising more slowly—as late as 1940 only 4.6 percent of the adult population had graduated from college) was that represented in the vision of the 1892 Committee of Ten: a generalized academic program broadly adapting to new knowledge and experience in the sciences, yet one that retained a sense of the cultural tradition in the arts and humanities. Such a curriculum was thought to be the most likely road for producing a person who could meet the changing requirements of the outside world.

Throughout the first half of the twentieth century a drumming insistence on the redemptive role of the public school emanated from liberal thought. The Progressive movement, which had assumed philosophical leadership at this time, argued for the secular scientific vision as an outcome of education. And in addition, it offered the classic all-encompassing slogan: every child should receive an equal education. The philosophical and qualitative orientation was gradually superseded by the simpler and more emotionally redemptive commitment (Bernard Bailyn called them educational missionaries) to seeing the net of public education thrown wider and wider.

Equality of opportunity in this land of almost limitless economic and social hope could be achieved only through the public schools. In this era of constantly expanding knowledge and new technologies, both high school and college education became the preoccupation of this crusade against the darkness of ignorance. The missionary element was noticeably intensified in the writings and teachings of the so-called social-reconstructionist wing of the Progressive movement in education. Such individuals as William H. Kilpatrick, George Counts, and Harold Rugg, all at Teachers College and all influenced by Dewey, saw the schools not only as an individually liberating institution, but also one which, in Rugg's phrase, would become a conscious agent in the Progressive improvement of the social order.[8]

For those who lived through this era of great hopes, albeit amid pessimism, into which wars and depressions temporarily intruded, the powerful formal educational ideal seemed at least not to undermine the basic value commitments in the informal culture. Substituting the car for the horse and buggy, listening to music on a phonograph or radio, watching a film instead of a vaudeville show added richness and variety to the world.

One might be able to travel farther by railroad or live in a more complicated city. Yet relatively few could afford cars for mere joyriding; cities were still carved up into neighborhoods where people still shared the problem of earning a living, facing the unknown, and raising families. There was hope, but rarely great expectations.

Religious life, made more complicated by the addition of millions of people of different ethnic backgrounds, was richer by virtue of its binding role with the European past. For indigenous American communities in city and country, the sense of tradition and origin, and the necessities of life, still helped to keep the commitment to a community, if not the orthodoxies of literal belief.

Part of the educational task of uplift that the schools provided was a first-time exposure to the great cultural tradition of the West.

8. Harold Rugg, *Culture and Education in America* (New York: Harcourt, Brace, 1931).

The knowledge of the literature, the fine arts, and the music, coming as it did out of that same source as did those vistas in the sciences and social sciences, served to open a realm of cultural aspirations as part of this formal educational tradition that seemed not at all to conflict with what was sensed as good and permanent in family and communal life.

Thus, the elementary school, high school, and college acted to build out into this larger world of knowledge, refinement, and social opportunity that seemed to be joined with the perennial values of the informal culture. True, the flapper age of the 1920s extended the chances that one took in terms of moral and behavioral freedoms. But few seriously considered that the kind of life portrayed in the novels of F. Scott Fitzgerald represented more than examples of the doomed decadence of a small and spoiled class.

Up until the end of World War II, American education served a wide variety of social, cultural, and intellectual ends without evident inconsistency. Strands of the historic past existed between the generations, the raw necessities of economic and political survival kept the American people relatively uncommitted in their values. They could, for example, vote heavily for Franklin Roosevelt, be religiously and socially conservative, indulge their leisure hours in popular culture—jazz, slick magazines, the cinema—yet respect high culture, learning, and work.

As fast as the world was changing up to mid-century, led by the institutions and ideals of formal education, there was an implicit belief that the realm of intimate values—the family, the community, morality, the aspirations for a life balanced between the externals of career and the intrinsic satisfactions of the private world—would be maintained. This informal culture was thought to be infinitely fertile in renewing itself to fit the changed conditions of external life. In renewing itself in the inner lives of individuals and communities, it was presumed that this creative potential could be passed on into the larger contexts and institutions of cultural existence.

We would have a world of technology and social change. But we would indefinitely renew our communities, develop new poets and writers, composers and architects. Our religious orientation might change, but new philosophical adventurers together with scientists and humanists would work toward an ever renewable flowering of the creative vision of our people.

6

The Great System

ONE

In the decades before World War II, the United States of the average American was in the main a poor country. Certainly its masses were better off than in any other society in the West. By and large, the vast majority of workers in factory, field, or office had to struggle to maintain a base minimum existence. But the minimum was being redefined in an era of great changes and rising expectations.

From the industrial centers of twentieth-century America a nourishing stream of goods and amenities had begun to flow. Many middle-class Americans had cars. Almost all had electricity, and indoor plumbing was the rule. Refrigerators, phonographs, cameras, and radios were increasingly ordinary purchases. Apartments and offices had central heating and elevators. Movie theaters were everywhere and with them came a visual taste of the outside world. With the car, the bus, the railroad, and soon even the airplane, people were able to determine their own life style in a way that had never been known before.

The first trickle of migrants moving west to California and the Pacific Coast was followed by a wave of poor during the Great Depression. This event, while it sharply curtailed America's sense of rising expectations, merely whetted appetites for what was possible. This sense of possibility, stimulated by the great technological changes, was as much a historical cultural transmutation as it was the mere expectation of greater quantities of material things.

People saw themselves being liberated from the domination of the past. The very word *tradition* meant the moral proscriptions of the past—small towns, social condition of birth, church, family, neighbors. The old beliefs seemed like implacable barriers to a startlingly new vision of the future that was being purveyed in the movies, slicks, even in the school.

Before, during, and after the Tennessee Scopes Trial (1925), the public school was increasingly reflecting the values, substance, and organizational orientation of the modern scientific technological community. The curriculum and the structure were no longer geared to family, community, and tradition, but to new professional, academic, or industrial careers that reflected the upward and outward mentality of each subsequent generation. One could hypothesize that the skills accumulated for almost four decades were pent up and only incompletely released and applied by the American social system. This resource had to wait for release until and after the conclusion of the Second World War in 1945.

The twenty to twenty-five years after the end of World War II mark a unique period in the history of the world. For the United States it represents both a break with the cultural traditions of the past and the fulfillment of a social vision that our people had no right to expect.

Our success was such as to stimulate attempts at imitation by the rest of the world. The affluence and expansiveness in the demographic, economic, and technological fields were prepared for by our special position at the conclusion of the Second World War. When, in 1941, Franklin Roosevelt proclaimed to an admittedly skeptical people that we would produce 60,000 airplanes a year, the impact of depression psychology was still upon us.

By the end of the war, we had proved our resilience, our educational capabilities in utilizing modern science, military and social organization to overwhelm the enemy; we were triumphant, unscathed, and brimming with energy and ambition. Historically, the only other country that has held a correspondingly central position in defining the character and destiny of an era such as the United States did in this period was Rome in the year 27 B.C.

Rome in 27 B.C. (which commences the era of Augustus) was by and large freed of external opposition and internal factionalism. She had begun to consolidate and integrate her conquests and to create an international social and political order. Led by administrators, architects, engineers, and military officers, this society elicited vast energies from indigenous populations throughout the world. It was the most efficient social machine yet known. Concerned primarily with economic and technological development and determined to keep the peace at the borders and law within, it first served the interests of a ruling oligarchy in the home city of

Rome and indirectly the sense of legitimacy and continuity of the people without for several centuries.

The massive American productivity of war materiel and the advanced technologies and corporate organizational experience served the United States well in this respect in the post–World War II period. The evidence of this expansion of productivity in consumer goods and the altered structure of our society is before our eyes. This was an unprecedented era of full employment, in spite of a massive increase in population (from about 130 million in 1940 to over 210 million in 1973). It was predicated on the abilities of a highly educated society, an advancing technology—especially in the consumer areas—almost unlimited cheap natural resources, and a large continental society to be used as a social and economic palette for this experiment in cultural engineering.

Millions of cars rolled off the assembly lines each year; highways were in a constant state of expansion, as were bridges and the extensive petrochemical industry that fed the insatiable transportation industry. Soon a suburban culture was born, along with a dynamic and transient society where the automobile represented merely one phase of a culture that now defined itself in terms of the acquisition of an always ascending level and variety of consumer products—refrigerators, TVs, hi-fis, washers, dryers, dishwashers, stoves, deep freezes, cameras, etc., etc., some in multiple quantities, his and hers.

The enormous abundance and cheapness of resources resulted from the heightened efficiency of technology in extracting them easily and the relative weakness and economic needs of those nations from whom the resources were imported. In our own society the development of pesticides, fertilizers, and irrigation techniques unleashed a bounty of agricultural products. Food was cheap and never wanting. But there was one unpleasant side effect. Technology began to displace the small resident farmer and his family with those who could expand into semiindustrial operations. The urban population expanded accordingly, feeding the building boom in cities and suburbs in a frenzy of expansion.

When Michael Harrington in 1963 wrote *The Other America: Poverty in the United States,* he estimated that between 20 and 25 percent of Americans—some claimed only 15 percent—lived in poverty at a time when the nation was unbelievably wealthy.[1] But to grant that between 75 and 85 percent of the population lived in a

1. Michael Harrington, *The Other America: Poverty in the United States* (New York: Macmillan, 1963).

state of relative middle-class affluence is to describe social conditions that are historically unprecedented.

This condition of relative and widespread abundance can be seen in terms of gross national product, the total value of all the goods produced and services rendered in any one year in our nation. In 1944, at a time when the American war machine was in total activation, the GNP was about $353 billion. Thirteen years later (1957), it had grown by another $100 billion. In less than thirteen more years (1969), it had added almost $300 billion more to a grand total of $728 billion gross national product (all figures adjusted for inflation).[2]

Another way of seeing this yearly and cumulative expansion of production is to note that the total growth of American economy from 1950 to 1969 (19 years) equals the growth from 1620 to 1950 (330 years).[3] One does not see merely dollars and cents in these figures, or bricks and mortar, refrigerators and cars. One perceives a tremendous overhauling of a way of life, patterns of interacting with other people, relating to jobs, communities, even one's own family ties.

This wealth goes into personal ornamentation, into new awarenesses, travel, spending or saving, into institutions that accumulate wealth and power. These must be organized to draw in individuals and shape their lives in terms of their basic rationale for existing. But it is not merely as accidental as that. For, once the methods are perfected for extracting, transporting, fabricating, and distributing and consuming this wealth, techniques must be devised for maintaining the pattern of organization and indeed the rationale for accepting the utopian ideal of affluence as a reality as well as an expectation.

Thus the great system was expanded to the communications medium, where a unique educational and cultural enterprise was born. This enterprise was to utilize the traditions, values, fears, and loves of the masses as a means of involving them in the cycle of consumption and luring them into accepting social conditions that would necessitate their inextricable immersion in it. This would ultimately keep the people happy and productive. The system depended on the maintenance of a high degree of affluence and of an educated population; thus, it needed efficiency and education. The internal national competition for this wealth that shaped the new

2. Edwin L. Dale, "The Economics of Pollution," *American Air Lines Magazine*, March 1971; reprinted from the *New York Times*, 19 April 1970.
3. Ibid.

values of Americans was soon followed by the challenging resurgence of the Western nations. No person or society would get a free ride without skills. And the more skills one could accumulate, the higher on the economic and institutional ladder one might climb.

TWO

The United States, in gratitude for the sacrifices of millions of young men during World War II, set in motion the GI Bill, one aspect of which granted educational opportunities—subsidized by the federal government—in any accredited educational program the veteran might choose. For most veterans, this presented an opportunity to obtain a college education that ordinarily they would not have been able to afford. It made so many millions of Americans aware that there was an aspect of education not alone reserved for the very advantaged that the stimulus for higher education was significant. A college education became not merely a luxury but a necessity in the minds of the American people.

The impact of skilled graduates on an economy beginning to take off technologically could not have been envisioned beforehand. This, together with a sprinting post-World War II birthrate, had epochal results within education, both formal and informal.

At first, the deep egalitarian aspiration for opportunity for the enhancement of cultural life for all citizens played an important part both in the GI Bill and the expenditures on the state and local level for the building of schools and the expansion of college facilities. Education was a good thing. It allowed for a variety of talents to emerge from all classes of society.[4] Individuals and their communities would be better able to appreciate the great intellectual and cultural landmarks of the Western tradition and to become part of this heritage for our mutual enhancement.

The statistical record reflects a growth that gradually transformed our ideals, however, from the philosophical and cultural to a new level of perception. In 1940, during a depression, there were 1.4 million students attending college. The total expenditure for that year for public and private colleges was $675 million. The immense increase in expenditures that took place after 1945 had soared to $10 billion by 1966 and $20 billion in 1972. At that time it was estimated that over 9 million students were attending college-level institutions.

Public school expenditure, which in 1940 was estimated at $2.3

4. It was this egalitarian impetus that was behind the agitation that finally led to the *Brown* (desegregation) decision of 1954.

billion (for 30 million students) had increased by 1968 to $35.5 billion and finally to $45 billion in 1972. The total number of students in all noncollegiate institutions having reached a peak of about 61 million students in 1970 had by 1974 fallen to 58.6 million. Yet, because of inflation, the cost had risen from about $70 billion (1970) to almost $110 billion in 1974.[5]

A. H. Raskin of the *New York Times* estimates that in the ten years 1963–73 the total annual expenditure for education at all levels, public and private, had increased from $29.3 billion to $83.5 billion (none of the above comparative figures adjusted for inflation).[6] Even allowing for inflation, it must be realized that this kind of economic investment in an endeavor—education is but a set of beliefs, awarenesses, intellectual competencies and in such a large measure is an intangible—must in some way have been altered in its very basic character.

Thinking beyond the building efforts, we progress to the enormous need to recruit teachers, to regulate and standardize curricula. The need merely to manage an operation such as this must be such as literally to exhaust the attention and concerns of those involved. The outcome of the expansion of schooling was to absorb it fully as an institution into our corporate structure. As Kimball and McClellan put it, the size, complexity, and interdependence of our corporate structures make it impossible to avoid being drawn in. Educators as well as all participating citizens must accept this altered character of social life.

> In short, the price of being an American is "being" an organization man. Autonomy is not . . . a viable alternative. On the contrary, the very attempt to discover an alternative is a form of mental and social illness, a denial of reality. The important question is not whether, but what kind of organization man.[7]

The question of how to define this new reality and give it a sense of direction beyond those admittedly decentralized and relatively independent programs of the state systems of public education and the diverse college schemes that had developed over the years was finally answered in the late 1950s. In 1957 the Soviet Union orbited the first Sputnik, beating the Americans to an important first in a critical technological and scientific area. We sought for reasons.

5. U.S. Office of Education, cited in *Newsweek*, 16 September 1974.
6. *New York Times*, 9 September 1973. This is a conservative figure.
7. Solon Kimball and James McClellan, *Education and the New America* (New York: Random House, 1962), p. 315.

What with our stunned pride, the latent fear of the communist bloc that came on the heels of the Korean war, the Hungarian revolution, and the generally threatening visage of an expansionist Soviet society, we concluded, rightly or wrongly, that our indigenous educational system might be at fault.

The older idealism, philanthropy, and child-centeredness of the Progressive educational system were already well out of tune with current postwar perceptions. The conservative critics of this tradition, who criticized the old leadership as much for their left-of-center social and political orientation as for their progressive educational views, gained a new ally—national defense. Admiral Hyman Rickover, head of the atomic submarine program, wrote and lectured widely in an attempt to upgrade standards in education, in favor of the more efficient production of scientists and technicians and against any soft-hearted educational efforts that indulged the private needs of the individual.[8]

The National Defense Education Act of 1958 was a direct response to the Soviet educational challenge. At first, it put federal moneys into the training of foreign-language teachers and guidance counselors, the latter the better to funnel talented young people into the most efficient educational pathways. Soon, moneys for the training of science and math teachers were added, increasing at the same time the already extensive federal involvement in education.

In 1953 the United States Office of Education was made part of a new cabinet level department, Health, Education, and Welfare. And while at first the federal outlays were negligible, by 1955 they had risen to $377 million. Five years later, in 1960, the total was $866 million; in another five years it had almost doubled, to $1.5 billion. When one considers that the federal budget for 1973 included a total of $110 billion for all forms of social welfare, much of it administered by HEW and designated for education, the extent of this federal organizational involvement can be appreciated.

As the American educational and technological machine began to synchronize its efforts, the threat of Soviet and Chinese communism receded as factors in determining the direction of education. A more ecumenical figure, James Conant, former president of Harvard and a distinguished scientist in his own right, was requested by the Carnegie Corporation to undertake a study of the American high school with a view toward the improvement of its organization; this was as prelude to the upgrading of the program.[9] The impact of

8. Hyman Rickover, *Education and Freedom* (New York: E. P. Dutton, 1959); also, *Swiss Schools and Ours: Why Theirs Are Better* (Boston: Little, Brown, 1962).
9. James B. Conant, *The American High School Today* (New York: McGraw-Hill, 1959); also, *Slums and Suburbs* (New York: McGraw-Hill, 1961).

Conant's studies was to defuse the politically contentious battles over philosophy and control of the schools and edge toward a consensus. No longer would progressivist or conservative do battle over programs, teacher training, or even long-range goals. The entire society would pull together toward a middle-of-the-road effort. The increase in efficiency, competence, and knowledge could be seen to have beneficent outcomes for the society as a whole, for both localities and individuals. In a world of such rapid social change, the inertial force of advance seemed to unite all those previously diverse educational strands.

Clark Kerr, who, as president of a farflung yet completely integrated university system in California, developed the paradigm of the modern educational system, put the situation this way:

> Knowledge has certainly never in history been so central to the conduct of an entire society. What the railroads did for the second half of the nineteenth century and the automobile for the first half of this century, the knowledge industry may do for the second half of this century: that is, to serve as the focal point for national growth. And the university is at the center of the knowledge process.[10]

Kerr's technocratic visions were temporarily blurred when he was swept out of his post at the University of California by the student rebellions of the late 1960s. However, he was soon at work for the Carnegie Commission in Higher Education, calling for more moneys to be poured into higher education.

The role of the tax-exempt foundations, some 22,000 operating in the early 1970s, is worthy of mention in this respect. These organizations, ostensibly nonpolitical and tax exempt because they dispensed funds to the public, were estimated to have $20 billion in liquid funds available to them.[11] John Gardner, former head of the Carnegie Commission, once stated that in any one year about $12 billion was given by foundations to a variety of charitable, religious, and educational organizations. The Ford Foundation alone is said to have given away $2 billion, much of it to education.

Throughout the 1950s and '60s, these foundation grants, tied in as they were with specific programs, institutional or educational, did much to shape American education toward creating a unified

10. Clark Kerr, *The Uses of the University* (Cambridge, Mass.: Harvard University Press, 1963).
11. Chris A. De Young and Richard Wynn, *American Education* (New York: McGraw-Hill, 1972), p. 443.

technological- and consumer-oriented society. As each school or college expanded or modernized, it became caught up in a cycle of needs that could not be ignored if it wanted to survive. Between the state legislatures, the federal government, and the foundations, the twig was shaped.

Local school districts, under pressure by suburban parents oriented toward and committed to this new and exciting way of life, acquiesced to increased school taxes, which in some areas amounted to what would a decade earlier have been considered confiscatory taxation. Private secondary schools and private colleges, likewise dependent on donations from the well-off, fell into line to develop curricula and standards that meshed with the achievement goals established in Princeton, New Jersey, by the Educational Testing Service.

As the inheritor of the responsibility for assessing individual academic competence, and thus assisting secondary and college institutions in matching individual talents against a common denominator, this Carnegie Corporation offspring became a cultural and educational arbiter of extraordinary power. In establishing standards of intellectual ability and opening or closing the door of opportunity to the young, it markedly assisted in focusing national standards and developing objective criteria for our achievement-oriented society.

The tentacles of this organizational and credentialist octopus moved far and wide into areas only tenuously related to education. Thinking about education came to mean being absorbed with organizational matters. Schooling had become a commodity to be purveyed rather than an intangible exploration concerned with intellectual and cultural ends and the deepening of values. As wealth and power began to pyramid, teachers began to organize. Soon after, as the National Educational Association or the American Federation of Teachers closed down school systems such as that in New York City, we were reminded that power breeds counterpower.

The size of institutions also reflected this economic and institutional view of what formal education had become—something to be sold in the most efficient manner. Institutions such as the state university were expanded so that, at one point, several approached enrollments of 50,000 students. As the pressure for educational integration increased in the 1960s, the early expectations from the *Brown* decision (1954) not having been met, a new organizational and social panacea was proposed—educational parks. This product of the efficiency experts' brightest dreams would encompass a series of schools, elementary through college, where thousands of children could be brought from various outlying locations. Here they could be cheaply processed, using shared cafeteria, recreational, library, heating, and custodial facilities. An additional virtue would lie in the possibility of using educational parks for "desegregation and integration in bringing all the children of a large section of a city into one centrally located set of institutions." [12]

THREE

It was clear that the megalomania for growth, prosperity, and power that had fixated our society's formal ideals had also permeated every element of the educational structure. Seemingly only one aim in education had any meaning for those who had inherited the power to dispense the wealth that moved the system: to absorb education at all levels into one single national system committed, if not to a genuine egalitarianism, at least to forming a uniform economic and social vision of what constituted the good life.

Even as it lurched outward and upward in dimension and momentum, as it seemed to be reaching the pinnacle of its aims, the structure began to show fissures. A new generation was entering college in the mid- to late 1960s. These students had never known anything but the affluence of the postwar period. They were not grateful for any opportunity that might have otherwise been denied them. They did not consider themselves fortunate. Higher education, as education in general, was an assumed right. These students were products of the system, yet they found the system wanting.

These were young people who had been raised on travel, transiency, and the self-indulging fulfillment of every material or physical desire. The development of the birth-control pill in 1960 had created as a reality what before was only a tantalizing dream—unlimited sexual adventures without moral, psychic, or religious obligations. What our commercial mass media had only hinted at, as a lure for symbolic gratification, was now a perplexing reality.

The explosive rebellion against the concept of in loco parentis in the colleges, the politicization of the young in the struggle against the Vietnam war, and the riots of the minority poor in the ghettoes reflected an unexpected countertheme to the prevailing cultural ethos. It was not merely the millions of youth that surged into the age brackets 15–24 during the 1960s (12 million more than in the '50s) that emphasized the extent of this rebellion. It was also

12. *Educational Parks* (New York: Center for Urban Education, n.d.), pp. 1–4.

the trend toward a counterculture of values—drugs, sexual confusion, communes, nonresponsibility.[13]

Finally, while the turmoil of the late 1960s and early 1970s was largely nonviolent, it was a revolt without gusto, enthusiasm, or intellectual direction. Somehow our society had come apart at the seams (as did the other Western societies) at its peak moment of euphoria. The ecological and natural-resource crisis that followed on the heels of these troubles was an anticlimax. Americans already knew that something had gone wrong in our formal system. And if an end to the heady affluence of the postwar generation was going to be forced upon us, perhaps it was just as well that the pressures were externally applied.

FOUR

We need to understand why the great system flourished so mightily in society and in education and why it just as mightily cracked and almost splintered apart. Today, dire necessity and the inertial impetus of staying with what is until something better is offered are barely holding it together. Our social and educational scene is one of such widespread disaffection that it does little good at this point to reiterate its defects and the details of its exhausted features. We must look elsewhere.

To answer the question of why, both generally and tentatively, we must first examine the changes that occurred in the formal structure of education. At one stroke we transformed an idealistic system of culture building that connected reason and knowledge, competency and commitment with a value system that united our intimate personal world with the public world. Education, the pursuit of knowledge, science and technology were tapped in our attempts to remedy a defect in our material lives, and to enhance our cultural existence, to improve and deepen it. The means, ends, and limits of formal education were clearly understood.

As success overtook us, this clear connection between the formal and informal was effaced. The ideal of social and economic equality, aspired to in the context of a broad philosophy of the democratic life, was supplanted by the "wisdom" of economic growth and powerful institutions. What values could withstand the asphalt highways, glass-walled office buildings, or the government science and research grants? Because growth seemed to make life easier, it

---

13. The theme of extended nonresponsibility or juvenalization has become central to James Coleman's analysis of youth and educational instability.

had to be good. Formal education was forced into this system of valueless consumption, careerism, and consensus.

The steady escalation of material demands, the accelerating pace of social change, and the nomadic character of family life have had their impact. The strength and stability of our perception of life, our willingness to strike out on more personal or individual pathways of belief or action are inevitably undercut. Alvin Toffler claims that between March 1967 and March 1968, 36.6 million Americans (not counting children under one year) moved their residence. In seventy major American cities, including New York, the average residence in one place was four years.[14]

The primary cause of this is the dissolution of the structure of community life effected by the institutions of the great system. The mobility that these institutions have fostered has torn up not only economic roots but also the entire nexus of authority in our social and cultural tradition. Kimball and McClellan put it this way:

> The concomitants of family lineage, hereditary occupation and wealth, and participation in community ceremonialism no longer have significant cultural meaning; and the institutional linkages which once tied class to class have no spatial base upon which to operate. The differences within metropolis are not the sum of spatially discrete residential localities but the projection of the remote superstructures.[15]

For an educational system to falter, the philosophical system, the set of values and assumptions about human beings, society, and reality had to be questioned. As in human life, education is founded upon a small set of conventions, upon agreements between people about things and attitudes. It is a fragile creation, no more than a breath of air.

In the last few years there has been a deep and as yet inchoate questioning of those assumptions that swept the present educational system into ascendancy over the past century and a half. The intensely rapid, indeed dizzying rate of social change has perhaps had its reaction in an almost equally rapid disaffection. In order for the present system to have flourished, it had to build upon agreements made which, while they inaugurated the new, aided in throwing out the old.

The advance of Western technology, the attack upon the problem of economic survival, the vision no longer of barely enough but of a bountiful repast, necessitated many readjustments in our infor-

---

14. Alvin Toffler, *Future Shock* (New York: Random House, 1970), pp. 72–74.
15. Kimball and McClellan, *Education and the New America*, pp. 132–33.

mal culture as well as in our overt beliefs and institutions. This trend occurred worldwide. The fruits elsewhere in the world have been bitter; in the industrializing totalitarian nations, traumatic. For fortunate America, it has been easier. A vast, undeveloped, and open society needed to throw out hardly anything to start out anew. America, even in 1859, was still an infant, still a year away from its first maturational experience in blood, the Civil War.

During the interval between then and the present time, the American educational system was the spearhead for the new world. Americans rejoiced in its coming. It was hardly a conspiracy of the powerful. But like all other innovative trends, especially those with such unique dynamic force, the values they introduce and propel into reality are not imposed upon a vacuum. Inevitably they will displace other values. Indeed, they must fight their battles for the minds of people to induce their consent and their goodwill.

The formal ideals of the nineteenth century were at first displaced by rationalistic scientific and morally egalitarian values, and then by the realistic preoccupation with power of the affluent society. The deeper informal culture, the traditions and authority of the past, have unfortunately been torn up, and nothing as firmly rooted has since taken hold. The rapidly evolving institutional face of American society and the surge for the good life have themselves become an informal culture; they have become a repository for what passes as values.

But these are tinsel conjured up by advertising agencies and the mass media to mesh with the interests of the great corporate structures. In fact, we are enjoined not to believe in stable truths, right and wrong, or established canons of the beautiful or good. Our informal culture is permeated by a relativism in values and beliefs that allows us to be manipulated by the functionaries of the great system.

The public schools and colleges, by becoming mirror images of the corporate world, have consciously and deliberately eliminated strong value commitments, standards, beliefs, and a sense of uniqueness and identity. Nothing in education as it has evolved in the last generation can be allowed to interfere with the perceptions of our citizens as members of a homogeneous consuming society.

Though recent events have sapped the authority of the corporate structure, punctured the myth of its purported efficiency in planning for our material wealth, and rejected its blatant tampering with certain rhetorical trappings of morality and honesty, the young have inherited only a lacuna, an emptiness. Some ask, as the great system crumbles, Are we now to become pawns to the winds of history?

Part

3

Institutions
and
Issues

7 | The High Wall of Separation in Religion and Education

In the first third of the nineteenth century there were still ministers in smaller New England communities who would with methodological regularity inspect the local schoolhouse to ensure the continued moral and spiritual health of the young. These ministrations were directed at teacher and textbook as well as the attitudes and behavior of the susceptible pupil. In a time of changing values, it was a reaffirmation of the primacy of soul over body. By the 1830s, however, such supervision and control were gradually diminishing.

This is not to say that religion was on the wane during this period, though the theocratic hegemony over the colonial society had been dissipated by the winds of the Enlightenment. The First Amendment, which read, "Congress shall make no law respecting an establishment of religion, or prohibiting the free exercise thereof," eventually made its impact on New England. The multiplicity of sects, the division of the old Calvinist church into Congregationalist and Presbyterian groups, as well as the rise of Unitarianism—increasingly subscribed to by a substantial proportion of the elite in the larger towns and cities—made the relationship between church, state, and school increasingly sensitive, fraught with too many unsuspected schisms to risk cementing, except by the rigidly zealous.

By 1827, Massachusetts had passed a law prohibiting the purchase of sectarian books by any publicly supported school. Earlier, in 1823, the Woodstock edition of the New England primer had substituted the frailties of an ape for "In Adam's sin we sinned all." Older books, such as Cotton Mather's *Spiritual Milk for American Babies,* and even certain eighteenth-century stalwarts by Thomas Dilworth, George Fox, and William Penn, which combined spelling and grammar, fables and religious homilies, were being discarded in favor of more functional texts which had less controversial material and would thus appeal to a wider audience.[1] The commercial element, whose entrance in the 1830s coincided with the widening acceptance of common school education, no doubt had a certain influence in cleansing sectarianism from the schools.

The theme that held the greatest prospect for stability for the schools was the hope for the creation of a vitiated nondenominational Protestantism, one that could be agreed upon by all sections of the community. A significant shift had occurred in the sources of religious belief. The stringent Calvinist fundamentalism, which had conflicted in so many areas of public belief and behavior with the Enlightenment, had temporarily retreated. The sources now came from philosophical idealism, which was sweeping the Continent, and from domestic Transcendentalism, which had found its own peculiarly American shape.

Eventually it was the original views of Martin Luther that helped to harmonize the new nondenominational Protestantism. Here, the individual's right to find his own sources of religious illumination as derived directly from the Bible contrasted with the more rigid American forms of Calvinism. By the mid-eighteenth century the enforced codes of theological orthodoxy and the political and social rigidities that Congregationalism had seemed to sponsor had lost their relevancy and persuasiveness.

Certainly the moral history of the Old Testament and the enigmatic mysteries in the New Testament were still held to in the sacramental and devotional contexts of churchly life. And the contemporary nineteenth-century philosophical abstraction concerning the relation of God to an overarching system of Mind and Thought saw all of life united in terms of its Being and destiny and was well within the limits of belief as set in the holy texts. It held up as well in the evolving structure of scientific and philosophical thought.

To the Christian citizen in America, the issue was no longer either a secular or a fundamentalist view of reality, but rather how this broader Christian idealism could be maintained in the American scheme of things without being devastated by fruitless sectarian controversy. The firmness of Jefferson and Madison in their fight against the establishment is voiced in Jefferson's letter to the Danbury Baptists in January 1802: "The First Amendment has erected a wall of separation between Church and State. That wall must be kept high and impregnable. We could not approve the slightest breach."

1. Newton Edwards and Herman G. Richey, *The School in the American Social Order* (Boston: Houghton Mifflin, 1963).

The arrival in the 1830s and 1840s of large groups of impoverished Irish Catholics within a relatively homogeneous religious America added an element that quickly drove out the last doubts as to the future secularization of the schools. The small resident Catholic minority, now buttressed by numbers as well as the egalitarian Jacksonian political climate, soon made their weight felt through the religious hierarchy. The use of the King James version of the Bible in schools was unacceptable to them, and for their children to be educated with the Protestant majority in the secularized public school was anathema to the hierarchy of the church. An insistent demand for support for their own schools began. Barring this, they asked for separate but equal treatment in the public school, i.e., reading from their own sacred texts. Pressures from Protestant churches and lay groups were such as to convince the political leaders in New York State and Pennsylvania to remove the schools permanently from such controversy.

Governor William Seward and the head of the New York State Common Schools, John C. Spencer, pushed through the Maclay Bill in 1842, which permanently enjoined any board of education from giving public funds to sectarian schools. Bishop John Hughes of the Catholic diocese in New York only partially achieved his goal when the Public School Society of New York, which had been the distribution point for any philanthropic, state, and municipal funds that were contributed to a variety of nonchurch schools (pauper schools run in the Lancastrian monitorial tradition), was dissolved and a truly public but secular system established. There could no longer be covert public support of Protestant-oriented schools.

In Philadelphia, in 1842, a similar request from Bishop Patrick Kenrick for reading from the Douay Bible induced much debate, resulting in riotous controversy two years later. The schools eventually were freed from the varied religious demands for Bible reading and the rebuffed Catholics gradually commenced building a parallel parochial school system. There were no diversions of school funds after 1840. A number of states amended their constitutions to prevent public support of religious schools, including Massachusetts in 1855. Others wrote such provisions into their constitutions on entering the Union.

It must be remembered that the political leaders, in shunting aside involvement with religious factionalism in the schools, were not abandoning their strong religious association; American education would not suddenly become secular or godless. The common schools during this period had won a place in the pocketbooks of the

American taxpayers, thereby avoiding greater evils. These included denying masses of children of the poor any institutions of socialization. This was especially critical for the new immigrants; a great need existed for integrating them into American society.

For the most part the funds were meager, education still being in the main private and sectarian, and most religious groups content as yet to run their own secondary schools and colleges. Compulsory education was a thing of the future. For those who wanted and needed some basic schooling, the common school, a peaceful as well as passive creation, answered the contemporary demand.

American schools were not completely free of religious involvements. But at the very least, legal precedents were set that cleared the way for future political decision making. Americans were thus able to follow a comfortable path of educational development within an established and agreed-upon pattern of value choices. The schools would reflect the modality of attitudes in the general community and at the same time cultivate those intellectual skills and attributes that were the fruits of the Western and Anglo-Saxon tradition. They would nurture science without simultaneously fostering atheistic trends that would conflict with that portion of the public being taxed for their support.

The question arises as to why, especially after the Civil War, as industry and science began to reflect new social trends and intellectual styles, the problem of the relation of religion and education remained relatively quiescent. Not until the 1920s was legislation considered that reflected the development of a new challenge divided between religion, ethnicity, and the state. In the meantime, during approximately seventy-five years of rapidly shifting social horizons, religion maintained its peace with the educational and political structure.

RELIGION AND INFORMAL EDUCATION

The substantial number of citizens who are committed to faith in religious institutions and support them with their time and dollars certainly reflect a much deeper allegiance than the purely theological tenets, which purportedly function as the foundations for the faith, could be expected to earn. Today, given the general metaphysical commitments of our people, the existing edifice of formal religion is an even more impressive testament. When one examines the various writings concerning the relation of the American religious institutions to both the political and the educational structure, there can be little doubt that even the most fiery proponents of complete separation were sympathetic to religion and saw in this separation a guarantee of its continued cultivation.[2] Here, it was implied, existed the deepest and most personal elements of freedom, choice, and commitment that could be ascribed to man's experience.

The problem of the religious dimension of man has been treated by innumerable scholars. Certainly, at this stage in a long evolution of discussion and debate, one could with reason, as did Benjamin Franklin, turn away from endless and fruitless debate and go on to other more solvable issues. But the question of the religious would again return to haunt us, as it has in the Soviet Union and Communist China, where religion has been overthrown from official favor yet exists on the fringes of the polity; it is an escape valve for the aging faithful. Then through the front door a new faith comes marching in, replete with the familiar institutional panoply: sainted founders and martyrs, a literature accepted as holy writ; solemn ritual and festivals; religious shrines and tombs; and the inevitable awful secular punishments visited upon the unfaithful, heretics, schismatics, and nonbelievers in the state religion.

The need for religion is undoubtedly deep. Human beings are born bereft of instincts that would fix their course in life. Their existence is a series of choices that are made available to them by personal vision, an awareness of personal and transcendental experience that breaks through the given of cultural life. Understanding itself seems to span realms beyond common sense. These exist in the micro- and macro-world of science, in the future, where things can be imagined but not seen, and back again in time to a period that borders on the ultimate beginning. Human beings are born into one epoch but know many others. They live in one society, the motherland, but may choose to fulfill themselves in another. And finally, death must come. One's entire life is colored by its imminence; a premonition of dust and nothingness is a constant companion.

And so people hang on dearly and tenaciously to what is: loved ones, symbols of community and nation, a structure of belief that will act as a guide in ordering life, in mastering the inchoate passions that drive people on to conjure up new symbols of meaning.

The nineteenth-century Christian lived in two religious worlds: the world of formal thought wherein the doctrines, theological and

2. J. Freeman Butts, *The American Tradition in Religion and Education* (Boston: Beacon Press, 1950).

institutional, were subject to analysis, criticism, and emendation; and the informal realm, in which the most intimate life style and personal behavior were wrapped up in a nexus of relations—familial, community, historical, psychological. The richness of the Christian tradition, whether Catholic or Protestant, had sunk such deep roots in the fabric of American society that the various philosophical debates touched only a few. These lived on the intellectual and social frontiers. They were emancipated, as the common person was not, from prosaic community restrictions. They were emancipated as well from a world in which one's discursive beliefs, scientific or academic, had a direct impact on one's actions and style of living.

For the most part, Christian Americans lived their Christianity in terms of a church, a minister or priest, who was directly involved in their lives at birth, communion, marriage, illness, and death. Neighbors and communicants who shared their conjoint historic experiences intermarried, had children, and identified the destiny of the young and old with a tradition that was deeper, more intimate and mysterious than the external political world. This tradition also gave forceful significance to the inchoate awareness of the societal and communitarian demands for moral restraints and behavior. Finally, it was the foundation for a life in which the easy, decision-less, instinctual specificity of animal existence was not possible.

The world of religion, far more than merely explaining the abstract structure of external experience, explained the world of internal experience. In marking out the limits of the sacred and profane, the "shalls" as well as the "shall nots," it served a perennial function of establishing the deepest roots of the social and moral law. Schools and legislatures could attend to the matters of writing, counting, and reading and the external aspects of man's material arrangements. The church in America was still united with its constituency in maintaining the internal fabric of meaning.

CATHOLIC CONCERNS

In the latter part of the nineteenth century, compulsory education laws were being passed with greater rapidity, thereby shaking the contentedness of the Catholic church with the educational status quo. Too many children were attending free state schools, including many Catholic poor. Catholic educators for the most part began actively to agitate within their congregations to build and support a refuge from the Protestant secularism that seemed to be engulfing public education. Certainly in homogeneous Protestant communities the legal restraints against the use of the King James Bible were more ignored than obeyed. Even in New York City as late as the 1930s, in schools where a Protestant majority existed only among the faculty, this tradition endured at school assemblies.

In the late 1880s there was some resistance on the part of lay and clerical Catholics against the new compulsory education laws. Catholic schools were not yet able to compete with the publicly funded schools. Liberal Catholic Archbishop John Ireland, in an address entitled "Schools" in 1890, supported compulsory attendance in the state schools as an integral part of the American tradition. He was vigorously attacked (especially by the German-American wing of the Catholic hierarchy) for downgrading parish schools, advocating state over parental authority, and supporting Protestant interests in the public schools. Letters urging his excommunication were purportedly sent to Rome.

In a famous letter of explanation, also 1890, sent to the leading American prelate, Cardinal Gibbons, Ireland argued in his own defense that the American people had by now made a deep and unchallengeable commitment to public education. In supporting this institution he was not attempting to undermine the rights of parents for free choice of schools. Nevertheless, the state did have a right to prevent the extreme abuse of the child, which total ignorance might entail. In fact, schools having some sectarian Christian character, whether Protestant or Catholic, were certainly better than completely materialistic schools, a growing tendency in the society even then.

Ireland did suggest the merit of the Poughkeepsie plan, by which Catholic priests and nuns or laymen teach in public schools in predominantly Catholic districts, even if their crucifix was removed during school hours and even if the subjects taught were secular. However, "pupils are Catholic, teachers are Catholic, the atmosphere is Catholic; all secular teaching is from Catholic minds and Catholic hearts."

In a suggestion that was a premonition of a later era, Ireland argued for state support of all schools, private and parochial as well as public. He felt that this, rather than building up the parish school, ought to be the main thrust of Catholic educational enterprise:

> My appeal for State Schools fit for Catholic children has been censured under the plea that a Protestant state should touch nothing Catholic. But America is not a "Protestant State," and if Catholics pay school taxes they should receive benefits from

them. The burden upon our Catholics to maintain parish schools up to the required standard for all the children of the Church is almost unbearable. . . .

It is well, too, to remark that our public schools, in many places at least, are not *positively* bad. They are not "hot beds" of vice; neither do they teach unbelief or Protestantism. Teachers are often good Catholics; or at least they are gentlemen or ladies, decorous in conduct, and generous toward our faith. I know well the immense advantage to children of positive dogmatic teaching in school; yet, where the school is as nearly neutral as can be—the family and the Sunday School can do much. . . .[3]

Ireland was well aware that the pace of change was swift and that a tradition of common schooling developed to provide a semblance of literacy for the masses had been transformed into a vast social undertaking by which the masses were to be lifted up to a new level and style of life befitting an industrial America. Catholics, committed to no particular style of society or economics, and content to minister to the souls of the membership through church structure, were left increasingly in the wake of an industrializing, semisecular Protestant world. In some way, Ireland thought, the vast moneys available to Protestant philanthropy and the tax-supported state schools had to be shared with the Catholic schools. Perhaps the conservative majority saw the futility of attempting to gain government support for parochial education since the sectarian Protestant groups had apparently reconciled themselves to its loss and had adjusted accordingly. Yet Ireland stands as a lone and insightful visionary perceiving a future when his ideal plan would become an utter necessity for the basic survival of the Catholic educational system.

ACCOMMODATION AND CONFLICT

A tremendous drive for social, intellectual, and economic accomplishment pervaded nineteenth-century Protestant America. It is found in Horace Mann's vision of the common schools as well as the entrepreneur efforts of the Goulds, the Hills, and the Harrimans. Not accidentally, much of that wealth returned to the public good. Andrew Carnegie made a religion of philanthropic work, arguing against the egalitarian, socialist redistribution of wealth that would

3. Herbert M. Kliebard, ed., *Religion and Education in America: A Documentary History* (Scranton, Pa.: Intext, 1969), p. 99.

attempt to raise only the bottom. How else could Samuel Tilden endow the New York Public Library with so many millions, or the Cooper family contribute hundreds of thousands for a free institute (Cooper Union) for the arts and sciences?

There are many other examples. The structure of much of our great educational, scientific, and cultural institutions derives from that aggressive Protestant spirit that saw in such quasi-secular enterprises a redemptive dimension of individual acquisitiveness. It is seen in John Dewey's driving ambition to be a philosopher so that he could further his teacher's (Morris) view that Hegel had scientifically proved the existence of God. For many years, until his pragmatic and scientific conversion in 1890 after reading William James, he had been a devout evangelical Christian, faculty adviser to the Christian Association at Michigan University, always searching for a new and more progressive bottle for the traditional Christian wine. Perhaps the transformation of our society itself manifests a combination of the search for a new environment of the ultimate truth by the infinitely flexible Protestant mind with the scientific demands of logic for a universe subject to one homogeneous system of laws, a universe unmarred by qualitative variability.

Thus we answer, at least tentatively, the question as to why there existed that curious relationship of religion with the enormous, galloping educational and industrial machine that had enveloped America for almost three-quarters of a century. Religion, in its Protestant transformation, did not abandon the schools. Protestantism transmuted itself so that it could live in the world of science and technology, but also in the communal lowlands of belief—the fertile sources for the essential Protestant communitarian morality. Here was a unified public nondenominational system of education that fed the redemptive social ideals of American Protestantism by slightly easing the existing inequalities. This left the industrial system uninhibited in creating its own definitions of America.

Not until after World War I did several controversial issues involving religion and government in education manifest themselves. By then, a different power situation was reflected in the relationship of religion and education, and ultimately a critical change in the informal culture of mainly Protestant America.

By the end of the war, it was clear which way technology was leading the country. The United States was still for the most part poor and working class. But it had an exuberant sense of expectation and power. It was now the greatest force in the international scene. More and more, the school, through the state boards of education, curriculum control by large publishers, state-financed support, and national teachers associations, looked away from the community to the economic and political scene. The power of education to influence one's economic future was well advertised during these decades (1920–40). Usually the education attained in one's community became the means for departing for the big city. Small towns and cities were sapped of their most aggressive and able young; and large cities were enriched by masses of unattached, ambitious, and institutionally oriented people.

The state had been attempting to cut down the power of local boards since the last third of the nineteenth century, if not before. In 1919, Nebraska passed a bill, no doubt as a consequence of the war hysteria, against the right of any public, private, or denominational school to teach a language other than English below the eighth grade. This law did not care to stipulate the pedagogical role of English in the school, merely that *another* language was not to be taught before a certain age, implying its opposition to bilingualism. (Latin, Greek, and Hebrew, all dead languages, were not proscribed.) The U.S. Supreme Court decided in 1923 that this was a gross infringement of the rights of the individual.[4] No special emergency warranted such drastic action.

The Supreme Court certainly did not intend to restrict the rights of local boards to decide whether or not to teach foreign languages. But it ruled that such a statewide proscription on *all* schools was unconstitutional unless there were a state or national emergency. Justice Holmes demurred. He saw the value of a universal acquaintance with English.

> Youth is the time when familiarity with a language is established and if there are sections in the State where a child would hear only Polish or French or German spoken at home I am not prepared to say that it is unreasonable to provide that in his early years he shall hear and speak only English at school.[5]

In Oregon a law passed in 1922, to be implemented in 1926, that further exemplifies this new and powerful stance of the state with regard to the now essentially public and secular nature of the educational enterprise. In this case almost all children between the ages of eight and sixteen were mandated by the state to be sent by their parents or guardians to a public school. (There were some excep-

4. Ibid., pp. 115–20. See also discussion on p. 285 of present volume.
5. Ibid., pp. 120–21.

tions.) No doubt the impact of science and industrialism had forged a new dimension to the formal system. The universality of science and technology and the intimate relation of political and educational power to their smooth and integrative functioning virtually necessitated the establishment of a unified fabric of education. And in Oregon liberal political and educational leaders thought a significant break with the diverse patterns of the past might be enacted.

Butts and Cremin phrase it as follows:

> Those who favored the law hearkened back to the arguments used in building the common school ideal of the early nineteenth century. They claimed that the demands of citizenship required the state to see to it that all potential citizens be given appropriate training for their responsibilities; that the increase in juvenile delinquency followed upon an increase of numbers attending nonpublic schools; that attendance at a common school would prevent religious hostility and prejudice; and that instruction in American government and institutions for immigrant children could best be done when children of all classes and creeds attended school together.[6]

Justice McReynolds, who also delivered the majority view in the Nebraska decision, agreed with the pleas of the Oregon appellants insofar as their individual rights to engage in such enterprise to teach in or run a private school constituted an expropriation of property and interfered with the liberty of parents to educate and bring up their children, and the law was struck down by the Court.[7]

The most famous legal battle involving religion was the Scopes trial that took place in Dayton, Tennessee, in 1925. A young biology teacher, John Scopes, had challenged a state law that prohibited the teaching of evolutionary theory in the public schools. William Jennings Bryan acted as a friend of the state; he was opposed by Clarence Darrow, who represented Scopes. The result was an affirmation of the state and the dismissal of young Scopes. In the meantime, much nationwide publicity had undermined the essentially conservative and antiscientific attitudes of the rural folk and their supporters who had rallied behind the unfortunate Bryan. Not until 1966 did the Court rule that this state law was unconstitutional.

While each of these earlier decisions might appear on the surface

6. R. Freeman Butts and Lawrence Cremin, *A History of Education in American Culture* (New York: Henry Holt, 1953), p. 526.
7. Kliebard, *Religion and Education in America,* pp. 121–26. See also chap. 14 in this volume, pp. 285–86.

to support traditional values, private schools, conservative curricula, and ethnic rights (in the Nebraska case), the very existence of a private and sectarian school system (in the Oregon case), and the values of traditional religious beliefs about the nature of man (in the Tennessee cause célèbre), they all reflect the growing impact of a new culture. Its dual tendrils—formal and informal education—were attempting to establish themselves both in the legal framework of the public society as well as in the ethos, feelings, and perceptions of the masses.

The public school establishment, reflecting as it did the new organizational frame of the technological society, was instrumental in attempting the dissolution of the last remaining islands of privateness. In the Tennessee example, we have a regressive, rural-oriented state policy ridiculed and ultimately rendered ineffective by the power of the "intellectual establishment." These events serve to emphasize the enormously effective claims for truth and social relevance of the trend toward modernization. What had not yet been in fact achieved in terms of these legal decisions (the dominance of the public over the private sector) would inevitably have to occur elsewhere in society, given the long-term evolution of these trends. Educators and politicians saw them occurring in our society. They were now both marching to the same tune.

SECULAR DOMINANCE

A new culture in America was born in the 1920s. It was a social and moral revolution constituted by the automobile, Prohibition, radio, movies, and a new awareness of the secular dimension of personal and social life. To Marx and Darwin we now added Einstein and Freud. The lid was off the old social restraints. A new vision of reality was being created in America, synthesized from the literary perceptions of such as Sinclair Lewis, John Dos Passos, Scott Fitzgerald, Ernest Hemingway, as well as Cecil B. DeMille, Charles Chaplin, and Jean Harlow.

The Great Depression and World War II were a hiatus in the inevitable confrontations that had been posed in the 1920s. The ending of the war and the era of prosperity that followed loosed a tremendous flood of educational reconstruction in both the lower schools and the colleges. And while public and private sectors responded with vigor, it was obvious that because of inflation, the absorption of the private dollar of the middle class in matters of economics and material necessities, the parochial school would suffer. The workingman at last saw a middle-class vision as a distinct possibility—a house, a car, work-saving appliances, a television set. The private sector of education would have to provide an even better argument for its existence than diversity and private values. In this new atmosphere of material possibilities and affluence, and after the public travail of a depression and a war, private values and private schools were hardly a general ideal.

The Protestant and Jewish leadership, which had committed itself to the public interests of the state school, set about their own religious construction confident, yet ultimately progressively more impotent, in terms of their influence on changing and dwindling congregations. The Catholics, on the other hand, still staunchly hierarchical and well organized, now with an enlarged and vocal constituency, began a drawn-out and contentious agitation for the kind of support that John Ireland had seen as critical for the survival of their schools.

Hindsight allows us to perceive this movement not as the arrogant empire building of a powerful and conservative constituency, but as the "last hurrah" of a religious denomination that had survived early vicissitudes merely by enduring. Under the aegis of a number of able and aggressive bishops—Stritch, Spellman, Cushing, MacIntyre, and the popular polemicist Fulton J. Sheen—the Catholic image became acceptable. It connoted tradition, stability, ritual pomp and panoply in a world that seemed to be swirling away in change and instability. There were even large scaled conversions of conservative Protestants to the faith; Clare Booth Luce is but one well-known example. In 1900 the parochial schools had 554,525 students. This constituted about 5.2 percent of all children attending school. By 1957, with a Catholic school population of 4.4 million, they counted 11.9 percent of the total school population. It continued to grow, to about 6.5 million in 1965, before beginning to level off.

The Catholics wanted a share of the public tax moneys being increasingly expended on public education. The *Everson* case (1947) was probably the most significant victory for the Catholics, for it created a wedge by which a variety of kinds of support for parochial and private school pupils might be initiated. The specific issue here —the provision of bus transportation by local districts for children in all schools, public and private—was upheld by the Court. It argued that such aid constituted a public-welfare grant to the child and not the school. In support of this view it cited an earlier case in

Louisiana, the *Cochrane* case (1930), in which secular school books were loaned to children in all private and public schools. Now, if the state or district wished to provide health services, lunch programs, etc., to the child directly (either in or about the school), this could be done.

The issue of having clerics enter a school to teach religion to children of their own faith was decided in the *McCollum* case (Illinois, 1948). The Supreme Court decided in favor of the secularist complainant. In an ancillary decision, the *Zorach* case (New York, 1952), a state law providing released time for children who wish to leave school early to attend religious classes in their own churches or synagogues was supported by the Supreme Court. In a later case, *Engel* v. *Vitale* (New York, 1962), the Court declared unconstitutional a nondenominational Regents' prayer to be used in all public schools: "Almighty God, we acknowledge our dependence upon Thee, and we beg Thy blessings upon us, our parents, our teachers, and our country. Amen." [8]

It is clear that with the exception of the *Everson* decision (1947) and the concurring views of the Court in *Central School District* v. *Allen* (New York, 1968), in which it was decided that secular books could be loaned to pupils in private and parochial schools, the drift of judicial opinion was not favorable to religious education.[9] And while it was true that each decision that ran against religious involvement in education or governmental support for religious schooling was met with dismay by a significant proportion of the public, the outcry was not enough to stimulate a constitutional amendment that would dismantle the "high wall of separation." The public had committed itself to a secular stance in its social life, and those of strong sectarian preferences would have to foot the bill. Religion would be increasingly enclosed within its sanctuary of privacy.

The period after World War II can be summarized as having begun in a burst of renewed interest in religious matters. Religious institutions and values were strengthened; church membership increased, especially Catholic; and attempts were made to renew historic and traditional ties where they had been disturbed by war. It was accompanied by parallel campaigns in both the intellectual and polemical spheres. In addition, numerous groups, both lay and legislative, attempted to support religion either in terms of tax sup-

8. Sidney N. Tiedt, *The Role of the Federal Government in Education* (New York: Oxford University Press, 1966), p. 121.
9. See Kliebard, *Religion and Education in America*, pp. 232–47.

port for school services or for Bible reading, prayers, released time, and so on. By and large the trend was not aimed at the full realization of these goals in social and educational policy. John F. Kennedy, as a Catholic President of the United States, exemplified a truth long existent in Catholic doctrine, in which a Catholic's commitment to his faith qua faith is distinguished from his political, social, and educational views. Occurring as it did in the sharply modernizing atmosphere created by Pope John XXIII, it dissipated the Protestant fear of the Vatican and brought Catholics more fully into the secular mainstream. It also softened the more extreme interpretations of the 1931 encyclical injunction of Pope Pius XI, in which the theme had been "a Catholic school for every Catholic child." [10]

The liberalization of the image of Catholicism was reflected in a diminishing of the urgent agitation for public tax moneys for the support of Catholic schools. The increasing economic burden that the public schools thereby incurred was only part of the problem. There was in general an acquiescence to the truth that the schools ought not be subject to sectarian agitation of any kind. The fear of polarizing the public over this issue or others, such as nonsectarian winter holiday festivals (Christmas-Chanukah) or school prayers, indicated a real consensus that no one wanted to disrupt.

Other factors intervened to turn the public's concern elsewhere in education. Specifically, school busing and forced integration became critical educational motifs. (Unfortunately, a good proportion of the population was willing to turn these into political issues.)

But in religion itself there was a trend that would give rise to a concern as to the direction of this important dimension of our lives, no less its role in education and schooling. It was evident in the radically altered image of the clergy, explicitly presented by religious leaders themselves, to meet the changing circumstances of our society. We do not know what the ultimate result will be of the thrust for modernity and relevance. One can only describe it and suggest some of the questions that are implied for the institutional church and synagogue and for the role of religion in the lives of the community, school, and individual.

Will Herberg predicted this change in his *Protestant, Catholic, Jew.*[11] He noted that the distinctions, which had heretofore set off the special nature of these great faiths and transmitted their historical message to their respective constituencies, had begun to dis-

10. Pius XI Encyclical, *Christian Education of Youth* (1931).
11. Will Herberg, *Protestant, Catholic, Jew* (New York: Doubleday, 1955).

solve. The process of ecumenicism, given great impetus by Pope John XXIII, continued to expand. Not only the diminishing sectarian values in the schools, but also joint festive observances had, as noted, brought a measure of harmony to the schools. The modernization of Jewish traditions—holiday and food restrictions, clothing and the appearance of the new rabbinate, even a politically active rabbi (Meir Kahane)—was also significant.

The Catholic church had responded with modernizations of its ritual, the use of vernacular in the Mass, elimination of certain food restrictions, admission of women and married men to certain ministerial roles, modernization of dress for nuns, and finally a great change in the character of Catholic higher education. Lay control was established in most colleges and universities, thus making them eligible for a variety of federal and state grants. Admission procedures were also liberalized; non-Catholics would now be allowed to attend nontheological areas of the curriculum.

Of course, as the distinctions of these minority religions were effaced, the likelihood increased that they would begin to resemble the majority Protestant religions. To Herberg, this was regrettable because a bland, undifferentiated religious uniformity could lead only to a religion without distinctive philosophical claims. In the end, as their claims to a unique vision vanished, they would exert less and weaker moral influence over their constituencies.

The clergy's response has been interesting. The message of a few forceful clergymen—Billy Graham is one—has been primarily evangelical. However, by and large, the clergy that have reached the headlines and dramatized their new involvement have been the political clergy. From the time of Martin Luther King and the Montgomery, Alabama, bus boycott, a new religiously ecumenical group of socially involved figures—William Sloan Coffin, Robert Drinan, James Pike, Fathers Berrigan and Groppi, and the aforementioned Rabbi Kahane—has forced the public to view them in their new role. These religious leaders have used their moral authority to further secular causes. Note the changing role of such Catholics as Father Theodore Hesburgh, president of Notre Dame University, who for several years was chairman of the Civil Rights Commission in Washington, or Sister Jacqueline Grennan, who abandoned her habit and the presidency of Webster College in Missouri (a Catholic women's college) to marry and become president of Hunter College, CUNY. (Interestingly, this college had a long tradition of lay Catholic presidents.) The large Catholic minority in New York City was either silent or applauded this historically unusual transformation.

CONCLUSION

The first blow to have important educational consequences for the American religious tradition was that brought about by the scientific revolution of the seventeenth century, though its political and economic consequences were not felt until the following century. While science raised an aura of skepticism concerning much of the philosophical and theological underpinning of this religious structure of belief, e.g., the ontological reality of God and the more literal social and moral extrapolation that derived from such beliefs, the structure of social and moral life that exuded from the churchly tradition remained secure.

There are many ways of believing in Divinity, some as profound and relevant today as they were hundreds of years ago. For after all, the scientific understanding of man and the physical universe cannot alone explain the miracle of human consciousness, the awareness of moral law, and the mystery of birth and death.

It was when the industrial and social revolutions of the twentieth century began to tear out those communitarian roots that tied minister and congregation together that the last semblance of the authority of organized religion was broken. When birth-control pills, pornography, drugs, sexual permissiveness—all of them social aspects related to our religious life and all previously forbidden by the church—were catapulted into our laps, the breakdown of authority became especially apparent among the young. The present frenzy of political and sociological activities engaged in by churches and synagogues in order to reclaim some moral authority is interesting and perhaps even exciting in the short run. Will their quest for social redemption, whether through racial equality or antiwar causes or in the psychological areas of personality adjustment and counseling, lose for them their unique role and historic position of authority even as it gains "relevance?" Or is relevance today only a synonym for a contemporaneity that lacks historical perspicacity and vision?

It is ironic that as the substance of religious authority dissolves as an educational force, the surface institutional façade grows. We still pour our wealth into half-empty churches and synagogues and schools of theology. And there is still a resurgence of involvement in religious *experience,* e.g., the recent interest in the occult by the young, as well as the academic study of religion. The quest for meaning among young people is perennial. It is part of their birthright and eventually their responsibility to continue that tenuous cultural fabric of civilizational life where thought is prelude to action.

Is religion as relevant now for an American educational experience as it has been in the past? If we ask this question in terms of our definition of formal education (chapter 3), the answer must be in the affirmative. For we define religion, not in opposition to philosophy, but as one of its dimensions. Those aspects of philosophical thought that have been absorbed by the sciences can never alone answer our concerns; describing in objective terms what we also feel as private beings. We can know about birth and death and love as objective realities. But how do we handle them as individuals or, conjointly, as cultural beings?

Andrew Greeley has expressed this need for meaning and an ultimate interpretive scheme,

> . . . [which need not] be based on a traditional religious scheme or institutionalized in a traditional church.[12]

More positively, he states:

> Life has no direction at all unless it has some ultimate direction. Approximate direction in the midst of an ultimate existential drift produces an overwhelming sense of a "bafflement," which some men may be able to tolerate but which most men reject. Man will no longer need a "faith" only when he has evolved beyond the experience of bafflement.[13]

This realm of personal or private experience touches on many traditional religious areas. They are all part of the human search for meaning, a search which is prelude to thoughtful action. As such they must be included as part of what we teach to the young. These religious problems may exist primarily as private or interpersonal issues of belief and behavior. But they aid us in creating a bridge of ideas and understandings to the totality of experience. The need for continuity, the passing of the baton from generation to generation, can in this way be maintained in terms of the retention of traditional values as well as progress and improvement and adaptation to what will come. One has the awful presentiment that incipient dissolution will be the price of adaptation to the new by the religious institutions and their ancillary educational activities. But this need not be the inevitable outcome of even rapid historical change.

12. Andrew M. Greeley, *Unsecular Man* (New York: Shocken Books, 1972), p. 83.
13. Ibid.,

Before the shape of future religious activity can be seen, we will have to wait until our society has reintegrated itself and has begun to spin a philosophy that will stabilize our movement and give it some direction. That formal education needs some form of religious depth to achieve its new philosophic mission is an incontrovertible historic reality. That the present form of religion is incompatible with the current trend of social development is likewise a social fact.[14] Thus, we must look to the future, where religious interest will be once more resurgent not as social salvation or psychological therapy but as a means of confronting those perennial personal and communitarian questions that we must inevitably face.

14. The writings of Robert Bellah on the American civil religion is a reflection of this trend. See William G. McLoughlin and Robert N. Bellah, eds., *Religion in America* (Boston: Houghton Mifflin, 1968).

8 The Teaching Profession

THE CALL TO TEACHING

On a hot August day in Philadelphia in the year 1857, forty-three delegates representing ten state associations of public school teachers met to sign a constitution that would affiliate their respective organizations in a National Teachers' Association. The purpose of this new association was "to elevate the character and advance the interests of the profession of teaching and to promote the cause of popular education in the United States." [1]

It was a small and inauspicious beginning to what was soon to become a unique institutional phenomenon in the history of education. This organization was the product of a quarter of a century of constant agitation by a variety of political and social reformers for tax-supported free schools for citizens of all classes, at least through the grammar school grades. The success of this drive to establish the Common School, an institution that would have the efficiency and pervasive spread of the newly developing German public schools, the intellectual élan exemplified in the centrally controlled French schools, yet with the still incipient localism of the British schools, was the reflection of their achievement at this charter meeting.

These gentlemen had thus enunciated their independence from their social-reformer sponsors—the Horace Manns, Henry Barnards, and Thaddeus Stevenses. They were of course indebted to the great intellectual and political skills of these and others, including college presidents such as Francis Wayland of Brown, and normal school leaders such as David Page and Edward Sheldon.[2] But they also felt

1. Elwood Cubberley, *Public Education in the United States* (Boston: Houghton Mifflin, 1947), p. 709.
2. David Page, *Theory and Practice of Teaching* (1847); Edward Sheldon headed the Oswego State Normal School in New York, around 1853. Also see Cubberley, *Public Education in the United States,* pp. 385–86.

that their role as practitioner, their growing numbers, and the fact that the common school in this second half of the century was an indisputably permanent institution on the American scene warranted this new venture in corporate concern. At first it was limited to "gentlemen." But with the insistent persuasion of an increasing percentage of female teachers, its constituency was broadened in 1866. In 1870, it reorganized radically as the National Education Association. It now had four departments, the result of an amalgamation with parallel groups that had developed during these years. The four departments were school superintendence, normal schools, elementary schools, and higher education. In this general form the organization retained its dominant position as professional spokesman for over a hundred years.

As Tocqueville had noted earlier in the century, Americans have an almost unquenchable passion for organized activity. And with the swirl of political parties, labor unions, and citizens' groups of almost every kind came organizations not only for the establishment and running of the schools but also more generic groups for proseletizing and propagandizing the cause of public education. Josiah Holbrook's American Lyceum (1826), the Western Academic Institute (1829, Cincinnati), and many others sponsored lectures for the diffusion of the new knowledge that was sweeping the world, and to argue for institutions to bring this knowledge to the young. While America was yet a society of the "poor," still it was a society of people who held their heads high, who could and did aspire for a better and richer life and had confidence in the future. In addition, many philanthropic groups sponsored schools for the poor, and remnants still existed of the eighteenth-century town school. Together they provided the steady push for the legal establishment of a tax base to support this new institution.

Then the need arose for teachers. Candidates came from many sources, including young ministers awaiting their first parish. In the main, however, those entering the teaching profession did not come with the highest social credentials. The old image of the indentured servant working off his passage by teaching still lingered. Also, it is no accident that so many interesting innovators in education came to the field after experiencing failure in one or more of the manly professions or vocations, e.g., Rousseau, Pestalozzi, Edward Sheldon, Friedrich Froebel.

The most important development for the creation of this unique profession was the normal school. The normal school was specifically designed to train teachers. Its earliest antecedents were the

Lancastrian Model Schools (1818) established to train their own teachers, and the private tuition school opened in 1823 by the Reverend Samuel R. Hall in Concord, Vermont. Hall was concerned both to provide for the basic education of the teacher and to impart his knowledge of the "Art of Teaching." He later wrote the first American pedagogical book: *Lectures on Schoolkeeping* (1829). In addition, James G. Carter, a Massachusetts political leader, established his own private training school; significantly, he attempted to obtain state aid for it. This was in 1827, in Lancaster, Massachusetts.

There was progress. In New York, teacher training began about 1818, through the prodding of Governor DeWitt Clinton. Clinton advocated various forms of teacher training for the common school teacher as well as for teachers in the monitorial (Lancastrian) system. Especially interesting was his suggestion that the many existing private academies be used for the training of teachers. At that time, the academy, ostensibly a secondary school, served the same basic age clientele as the liberal arts colleges. Yet because it was organized for more general academic training and was less rigorous or classical, it seemed perfectly suited to train future schoolmasters.[3] The state would aid those academies; indeed, by 1835, five academies were offering this training. Philips Andover in Massachusetts was among those which instituted such courses.

Throughout the 1830s, especially in Massachusetts, an incessant campaign was underway to establish these publicly supported schools with attached model elementary schools. Men such as Carter, Mann, the Reverend Charles Brooks, and David Page utilized the various reports of Victor Cousin (France) and Calvin Stowe (United States) on Prussian training methods to persuade their respective recalcitrant state legislatures.[4] The first state normal school was finally opened in 1839. The idea spread rapidly; by 1860, twelve state normal schools (four in Massachusetts), one city normal school (established in Saint Louis by Carl Schurz), and six private schools existed. While a majority of the students were women, no small number were men.

The need for teachers was extensive enough that both for the lower-grade common schools and for the few public high schools that existed men from many walks of life were attracted to teaching. But as the normal school idea spread and as the commercial and

---

3. See Yale College report of 1828.
4. Page became first principal of the State Normal School at Albany in 1844 at the recommendation of Mann and Barnard. He wrote a very popular book, *Theory and Practice of Teaching* (1847).

industrial base expanded–thus giving men more opportunities than farming–the number of women who entered teaching grew accordingly. After 1880, male hegemony in the classroom, except for the high school, had disappeared. The common school and its normal school training adjunct dominated the educational scene.

Henry Barnard is credited with establishing in Connecticut special institutes that were offered to teachers either before or after their school terms. These consisted of intensive courses in the methods of teaching, or "common branches." Prominent educators gave guest lectures that would complement the formal course. This idea spread rapidly throughout the East and Midwest after 1840. In some states it was the only teacher preparation offered. In others it was a supplemental or refresher course similar to today's summer session.

In 1859 the Oswego Normal School (New York) instituted the Pestalozzian "object method" in its teacher-training program. Edward Sheldon was the guiding force behind this move. The education-hungry American public began a long-enduring debate over methodology that not only made Oswego a leading teacher-training institution but radiated its influence throughout the United States through its graduates. Colleges and universities also became interested in the "problem" of education.

Lectures on the "art of teaching" had been given since 1831 at Washington College, Pennsylvania, between 1850 and 1855 at Brown University, and at Michigan since 1860.[5] Thomas Gallaudet announced a series of lectures on teaching at Washington Square College (New York University) for 1832–33, but they were never given. In 1873 a professorship of Mental and Moral Sciences and Didactics was established at the University of Iowa (teacher training had existed there since 1855). This was expanded to a College of Normal Instruction in 1878, which eventually became a School of Education. In 1879 at the University of Michigan, in 1881 at the University of Wisconsin, in 1884 at North Carolina, Missouri, and Johns Hopkins, and in 1886 at Indiana schools of education opened. In 1887 Teachers College, Columbia University, was established. Both the University of Chicago and Stanford established classes in pedagogy at their founding in 1891.[6]

Thus we can establish a steady interaction between the development of the profession and the growth of the public schools. The

5. R. Freeman Butts and Lawrence Cremin, *A History of Education in American Culture* (New York: Henry Holt, 1953).
6. Cubberley, *Public Education in the United States*, pp. 690–91.

quantitative factor was critical. Also important were the intellectual and social élan of educational discussion and the quality of concrete programs designed to improve teacher training and to study the nature and practice of formal education. Between 1880 and 1910, with such intellectuals as G. Stanley Hall, Edward Thorndike, William James, John Dewey, George Herbert Mead, Charles W. Eliot, and William T. Harris dominating educational discussion, much of it at the annual conclaves of the NEA, the NEA was being established as a unique voluntary association mediating between the general public and governmental bodies regulating education. In 1894 the Committee of Ten, whose leading figure was Charles W. Eliot, while its membership was dominated by college presidents, was still under the auspices of the NEA.

THE SHAPING OF THE PROFESSION

During this period the small elite membership of the association had the effect of transforming it into a group of immense power and influence. Thus, whatever diverse innovations were tried throughout the country under its auspices, there was a tendency to canonize them as "good educational progress." Not until 1916 was a research division established in Washington. This provided a new role for the organization. It was now an actual bureaucratic institution designed to formulate its own standard of good practice and to purvey it as official dogma.

Another factor in the rise to official guidance, if not domination, of the educational profession by the NEA was the gradual elimination of the local district and the popularly elected district superintendent. In 1874 the Michigan State Supreme Court confirmed the right of the city of Kalamazoo to support a local public high school. The argument was that the state was allowed to tax for the university and the locality for the common school, but a public high school was not permitted. By now, public high schools were fairly common in the East and thus such an enterprise would not be contrary to public expectation.[7] Wisconsin and Minnesota courts shortly confirmed the Michigan ruling, and the high school rapidly became the most dynamic educational institution of the late nineteenth century. It almost completely displaced the private academy, though the academy was even then in gradual decline.

7. John D. Rockefeller's mother is said to have moved from western New York State to Cleveland, Ohio, about 1855 so that her son could get a good secondary education at that city's Central High School.

The remaining years of the century saw a gradual normalization of the structure of public education. The work of the 1894 committee was essential in this respect. The schools were gradually removed from the battleground of public cause and social ideal. Even small and isolated districts coordinated their systems, from kindergarten to high school. Over twenty-two states had established such consolidation plans by 1905. Also at about this time, compulsory education laws had begun to spread out from the North and Midwest into the South.[8]

There were other noteworthy changes. The superintendent and the principal were now shifted from their roles as quasi-political and philosophical leaders to their constituencies. With each year, the professors of education, especially those in the national leadership of the NEA, were assuming the role of educational leader. Scholar educators such as Francis Parker and William T. Harris were ever fewer in kind and number. Colleges and universities responded to this shift by establishing courses in administrative technique. No doubt many ambitious teachers saw in educational administration as it functioned at this point an attractive prospect. For no longer was there the responsibility of facing down an alert constituency with regard to the broader issues of educational policy, as had been true in former days. Besides, the enormous constructive work of building schools, finding qualified teachers, overseeing school management, purchasing supplies, and coordinating the diverse programs of the schools was enough to engross any group of professionals.

Indeed, the schools were increasingly seen as the educational correlates of our rapidly expanding industrial system. The comprehensive high school, which became the American solution to the track system of the European schools, absorbed within itself a diversity of functions—academic, vocational, commercial, and even a minimal "general" diploma program, now that compulsory education laws were making attendance mandatory well into the high school years. In this massive operation (doubling every ten years between 1880 and 1940), the cult of the efficiency expert and the dynamic school manager gradually eclipsed the scholar as the paradigm of an educational leader.

8. James W. Guthrie reports that in 1900 there were 100,000 operating school districts, which had been reduced to about 16,000 in 1974. A school board member in 1900 represented 200 people, in 1974 about 3,000. See "Public Control of Public Schools: Can We Get It Back," *Public Affairs Report of Institute of Governmental Studies* 15, no. 3 (June 1974).

> The tragedy was that educators were forced to assume too soon the role of experts and that in so doing they either turned their attention to cost accounting ... or to simple mechanical problems. .... This pattern was followed by other administrators who, in their conception and application of scientific management, changed its original meaning. These men were not scientists who were interested in inquiring into the nature of the educational process. They were undoubtedly dedicated to and genuinely concerned about improving public education but they were under continuous pressure to economize and to operate the schools in a businesslike way and this fact, added to their inability to carry out scientific research on more profound problems, led them to devote their attention to applying the scientific method to the financial and mechanical aspects of education.[9]

Within the NEA, the administrative division gradually became the dominant force. It was not merely a matter of numbers of children that was increasing the population of schools; at the same time, the numbers of teachers were increasing also. Rather, a great, overtly silent and internal debate about the nature of discipline and the preparation of teachers and therefore the constituency of the schools took place, which inevitably caused the association to evolve in the manner it did.

The excitement about educational advance and innovation brought many highly competent intellectuals into the field. A sense of limitless possibilities for public good arose. The importance of studying education was seen from the standpoint of philosophy, scientific psychology, history, and sociology as well as pedagogical theory.

Thousands of students poured into the normal schools and the state teachers colleges. (By 1920 there were forty-six such institutions.) Many of these students had only a rudimentary secondary school education, coming as they did from rural and small town environments, so a great change took place. These recruits looked upon teaching as a steppingstone onto the middle-class ladder. They reflected little of the intellectual or cultural sophistication of the new leadership in the universities. The general tenor of their education was thus diverted from the intellectual orientation developed by these leaders. More and more, they were offered methodological "how to" courses of a basic vocational orientation.

9. Raymond E. Callahan, *Education and the Cult of Efficiency* (Chicago: University of Chicago Press, 1962), p. 93.

Abraham Flexner, fresh from his critical analysis of the short-comings of medical education in the United States, examined this problem in his *Universities: German, English and American.*[10] He did not concern himself with the nineteenth-century pattern of German teacher education, wherein on the lowest rung of the educational ladder, Prussian schoolmasters were but one step above their students in training and status. Flexner focused on the observable trend in the United States toward a watering down of the curriculum. He argued in favor of a teacher-training institution modeled on the highest attainments of the German university's search for knowledge. He would have the United States reject the model that was rapidly taking over and being facilitated by the newly introduced system of state certification requirements for teaching. Instead, university training in education ought to be concerned with philosophy, psychology, and history as they relate in their various ways to the educational process. The other alternative was indeed to accommodate to the mass pressures for some kind of higher education for teachers. Inevitably, it would be an inferior version and would thus detract from the progress of the profession.

Although one must respect the spirit and intent of men such as Flexner and Nicholas Murray Butler, who, before he left the presidency of Teachers College for Columbia University, attempted to retain its intellectualistic orientation, the times were against their proposals. The nation was moving onto a new plateau of life, and it was the task of the profession to lead the way. Public education in these decades, 1880–1920, was the primary institution utilized to help establish a new social order that would harmonize with concurrent material changes. To exist in, if not to master, this new world, not only literacy but also a wide variety of formal skills never before considered essential, except for a very small portion of the population, became necessities.

The moral fervor that surrounded this mounting tide of educational change was promoted and directed primarily by the members of this new profession. The vision was of the all-sacrificing schoolmarm giving up both marriage and the small social pleasures of the outside world for her endless devotion to the young; the paeans of such immigrants as Mary Antin, who remembered the small kindnesses and encouragement she received as a small child newly arrived in this country (1894).

10. Abraham Flexner, *Universities: German, English and American* (New York: Oxford University Press, 1930).

> Whenever the teachers had anything special to help me over
> my private difficulties, my gratitude went out to them, silently.
> It meant so much to me that they halted the lesson to give me a
> lift, that I needs must love them for it. Dear Miss Carrol of the
> second grade would be amazed to hear what small things I
> remember, all because I was so impressed at the time with her
> readiness and sweetness in taking notice of my difficulties.[11]

Thousands of teachers, for very small remuneration, many who
were graduates of newly established semicollegiate institutions and
who might never have obtained degrees were it not for this pervasive
democratization process, committed themselves in turn to lending a
helping hand to those who followed them. One cannot deny that the
teaching profession had an integral part in training the young for
participation and functioning in our industrial society.

The rhythms of the farm and the small town were far from the
rhythms of formal education and the modernizing society it purported to serve. Perhaps that is why farmers so often opposed the
public school until after the mid-nineteenth century. For, in taking
so many of the young off the farms and out of the towns into the
cities, the public school had fostered alien social and philosophical
allegiances. On the other hand, in the process of modernization the
poor, oppressed, and ignorant, whether native born or immigrant,
were given a new lease on life. This became the teachers' sacred if
secular mission.

On examination, it is unusual for a society to hand over so freely
and with such minimal controls to an organized group of teachers
the prime responsibility for facilitating the shift of entire generations
from one level of life and its concomitant values to another. The
informal alliance of "educationists" in departments and schools of
education, professional organizations—also confederated loosely as
state organizations within the larger hegemony of the NEA—school
boards, and state departments of education had securely established
themselves as a secular scientifically and technologically committed
group of institutions with the goal of bringing together the disparate
populations of the United States into one politically and ecumeni-
cally united society. Yet it still purported to cherish individual
initiative and a measure of independence from federal and state
domination. Almost unlimitedly optimistic expectations of good
arose from the advance of public education in terms of knowledge
and mastery of the environment.

11. Mary Antin, *The Promised Land* (Boston: Houghton Mifflin, 1912).

SERVING A NATION

In 1918 there were only about 10,000 members in the NEA. America had just won a world war. She had been catapulted into a position as the most powerful nation in the world and as the defender of democracy and freedom from the tyranny of traditional autocratic oppressors. By 1930 the NEA had expanded to 220,000 members. Now loosely organized through the various state organizations and under the aggressive leadership of superintendents and administrators, it developed a self-consciousness that was epitomized in that much-maligned word *professional.*

Perhaps this self-consciousness was stimulated by the organization in Chicago of the rival American Federation of Teachers (1916). The AFT was sponsored by the American Federation of Labor (AFL). John Dewey, who had also helped to found the American Association of University Professors, was its first member. There is no doubt that the NEA at this time was securely controlled by the various administrator organizations, National Association of Secondary School Principals, the Association for Supervision and Curriculum Development, etc. These groups did not at first conceive of their role as essentially that of contributors to an atmosphere of social quietism. Further, the classroom teachers seemed not to protest this structure of professional domination.

There was a pervasive atmosphere of evangelicism, of "doing good." Teachers trooped in by the thousands to hear the various sages and savants of the profession advise them of the best method of "teaching the child and not the subject matter"; how to gear curricula to the emotional and intellectual readiness of the child; how to develop reading plans from a set of basal readers; how to restructure the classroom for individualized teaching and learning; etc.

At Teachers College, Columbia University, a philosopher and associate of John Dewey, William Heard Kilpatrick, lectured to hundreds of students each semester on the project method and other progressive approaches to curriculum and society. His lectures on the enhancement of the individual through concrete experiential learning and the consequent betterment of our democracy by all of these participating members dazzled thousands of prospective teachers. To this day, the Horace Mann Auditorium at Columbia Teachers College is exalted in the memories of several generations of American educators who enthusiastically crowded the aisles to hear that unique galaxy that existed at Morningside Heights in the 1920s and '30s.

One of the most interesting facets of the secular proseletizing for the public schools was the development of the vision of "professionalization." Usually thought of as limited to doctors, clergy, judges, lawyers, perhaps even the military, professionalization as a goal became an internal obsession that explains a part of the history of the NEA and the teachers themselves from 1920 to about the mid-1950s. The social origins of the majority of teachers offer a partial explanation—working class, farmers, petit bourgeois. They were searching for the relative security of the civil service, yet striving for the quasi independence and status that recognition as a professional would signify. (By 1950 there were 450,000 members in the NEA.)

One can look to this period as epitomizing one of the high points in American institutional life. With advances in knowledge, in social democracy, and in internal cohesiveness came an increasing preoccupation with public education as the means by which old values would be given new life in the world of the ever new.

The vision of professionalization that began to affect public education came about at the same time as the self-conscious awareness of the social upheaval began to imprint itself on the public mind. Just as the medical profession was beginning to benefit from advances in the health sciences, teachers too began to see themselves as serving a far higher cause than ordinary school-keeping tasks would have connoted.

But it was not merely to serve their own advantage or to rectify an economic and social slight that moved them in the direction of professionalization. A renewed aspect of that zealous secular Calvinism exhibited itself to be an ineradicable factor in the American consciousness.

The first theme in the motif of professionalization was social service. Here, unlike other and more crass vocations, the purity of the professional commitment was tested. And it was here the teacher argued that in terms of advancing the American social good, the values of democracy, respect for reason and knowledge, care for the personal and educational welfare of the child, the teaching profession could not be beaten. And what was their key claim? It was achieved within a public tax-supported school system wherein no ulterior economic motive of personal gain could be involved. And of course, in turn, the laws for compulsory education and the pervasive establishment of public schools signified on the part of the consti-

THE TEACHING PROFESSION   117

tuted authorities that education was an obligation of society for which teachers were a critically important element.

A second aspect of the search for professionalization was the existence of a body of knowledge and specialized training. Many people do public good and perform critical tasks—sanitation workers, plumbers, firemen, bus drivers. A social service without a body of knowledge—usually a body of theory—to be absorbed through special training cannot claim to be a profession. The analogy with law and medicine or the ministry is clear here. The lawyer needs to know the existing legal statutes and the critical court cases (jurisprudence), and he is also trained in legal and political theory as well as moral philosophy. The doctor must know physiology and chemistry, among other disciplines. A general theory of the sciences also could be considered essential even before the apprentice M.D. gets down to the more detailed training of his own specialty. So too with education.

The arguments of Abraham Flexner concerning the relationship of philosophy, psychology, history, and sociology to teacher training are here germane.[12] Specialized training should ideally be presented with regard to the relation of theory to practice, for a professional should never be told exactly how to do something. No particular rule will hold for all or even a majority of the cases. Here a rich theoretical understanding is crucial to intelligent independent action.

The progressive philosophies of Dewey, Kilpatrick, and Boyd Bode (of Ohio State), the work in psychology of Edward Thorndike and L. M. Terman, and that of Harold Rugg in statistics and social studies education, as they penetrated into professional education, provided a contemporary educational literature to supplement the historical tradition. Unfortunately, much of the professional training of teachers was nonintellectual—how to use teachers' manuals in drawing up lesson plans, how to check attendance registers. As noted, we must attribute this watering down of teacher training to the immaturity of most of those who taught in these small state and private teacher-training institutions. It was difficult to recruit sophisticated faculty, especially in professional education, itself a fledgling discipline.

Thus one could argue in theory that an important body of literature existed or could exist unique to the teaching profession. (This was a crucial issue, for an ordinary liberal arts education could never suffice as a standard of professional competence.) Unfortunately, the

12. Flexner, *Universities: German, English and American.*

exigencies of turning out thousands of teachers in a short period of time made standards questionable, both in course content and faculty quality, thus opening the profession to considerable criticism and ridicule throughout this period.

With each ounce of altruism and aspiration, a balance of self-interest was in order. Though the leaders of the profession well knew that the education profession would be respected and admired in a quaint way, only organizational strength and economic power would be taken seriously as a reflection of professional influence on social policy. At this point the teaching profession failed to meet the test and the standard set by the medical profession. Here, in the control of state licensing procedures and entry into the profession, this weakness would have long-term if surprising organizational consequences. State boards of education had been set up to oversee fulfillment of criteria for licensing and certification. This constituted an important part of the growing role of the profession. These certification requirements consisted mainly of a college degree and course standards in professional education, but not a standard of practice except in terms of the successful fulfilling of student-teaching requirements.

Control of entry was in the hands of state boards. The NEA, often working in concert with school board associations and PTA groups, supported lay control because it maintained close communication with the citizenry. (In New York the Board of Regents consisted mostly of laymen, not teachers.) On the other hand, the control of admissions, as for example by the medical profession—in this case the AMA—was clearly a critical factor in their achieving economic affluence. By regulating the licensing of hospitals and schools of medicine, the profession could control the numbers that entered and thus exert a quiet but effective economic sanction over the cost of medical care.

The ambivalence, partly justified, of the NEA to control the teaching profession in terms of licensing or entry made it susceptible later on to attack by the growing and belligerent AFT. As school populations burgeoned, resulting in increased demands for teachers, admissions criteria would be often suspended, and a new influx of teachers appeared, ready to be licensed. This further debased what little economic leverage the teachers could exercise. Taking place over many decades, this attitude wreaked havoc on their evolving sense of professional dignity and autonomy.

Professional autonomy was a key element, if a weak link, in the development of a proud and independent education profession. It constituted the individual's awareness that though one has absorbed a common body of theory and practical knowledge, has similar problems of work with other teachers, one will be free to excel or to fail, to be rewarded or not in accordance with the level of fulfillment of the general standards of the profession. In teaching, the development of tenure regulations protected most teachers from unreasonable and peremptory dismissal or harassment without serious cause once a probationary period had been successfully served. But in reality there was little opportunity for highly skilled teachers to show significant innovations—a fixed salary schedule precluded this—and merit pay frightened off more teachers than it attracted. Nevertheless, higher pay for more education or advanced degrees eventually became common practice.

Certainly the limited autonomy given to teachers presumably because they worked with large numbers of students in a "state" setting precluded the independence of initiative and judgment that the doctor or lawyer enjoyed. The constant supervision by principals, the standardization of texts and methodology, the scrutiny over a teacher's personal life (a holdover from the nineteenth century) limited the range of personal action that this principle entails.

Most crucially perhaps, at least in terms of more recent values, teachers were unable to decide who they would or would not teach, whether or not they could teach successfully under existing conditions and still maintain their professional standards, whether or not they could fix their working conditions in accordance with the ascertained educational need, and of course, in the final instance, they were unable to exercise any control over their remuneration. In this general area much had to be achieved before parity with the other professions could be attained. The NEA, beholden as it was to the administrative quietism of its leadership, did little in the years of its unchallenged hegemony (1920–60) to effect real progress.

In general, the NEA attempted to encompass the largest and least controversial consensus. Thus can be explained the rapid expansion after 1910 of the organization, its poor showing in civil liberty and tenure cases involving the rights and jobs of teachers. And while the AFT was much more militant in fighting for the civil and professional rights of teachers, it represented a pitifully small number of teachers and a partisan position in public education that most American teachers rejected.

This was the case with Progressive education. As Lawrence Cremin has pointed out, while the NEA, at its various conventions, in its research reports, and through its journal, purveyed the values of

Progressive education, including those advocated by the more ideological Progressive Education Association, it never went further into the philosophical domain than to mildly advocate the new pedagogical methods as progressive and modern.[13]

The mainline attitudes of the leadership of the NEA did not pursue to the ultimate conclusion the vision of professional control and independence. Along with the awareness that American education was riding a universalistic crest of social consensus and economic advance was a grudging openness to other institutions of society, business, government, even religious and community organizations (PTAs). In this sense the NEA, and to a lesser extent the AFT, saved itself from the ideological debacle that overtook the Progressive Education Association in the 1940s and '50s, which led to the later radical shift to a political and organizational structure directed to economic and institutional survival.

In the main the NEA remained a heavily decentralized organization whose central function, and one which cannot be denigrated, was involved with various kinds of educational research. The research division, founded in 1916, sponsored innumerable journals as well as special reports. It added importantly in lifting the educational profession's vision beyond the practical mechanical efforts of administrators' or classroom teachers' daily routines.

And one could argue that a good beginning had been made toward the ideal of parity alongside the more distinguished professions, medicine and law. As such it was the continuation of a tradition of educational writing that can be traced back to 1818. By 1852, eleven journals were in operation, some in existence for only a few years. In 1855 Henry Barnard's *American Journal of Education* appeared. Though he had been associated with an earlier periodical on education, his sponsorship led to its continuance until 1881. In addition, a number of state teachers' association journals carried on an exchange of educational information throughout this late-nineteenth-century era.

Always the vision of social science, the vague hope for an enlightened and unified democracy, illuminated the aspirations of most of the membership in the various educational associations. Codes of ethics were drawn up and passed that exhorted the teachers to behavior that could only rival that of the saints, but couched in vague language that rarely led to expulsion from the group for violations of the code. While the ultimate shape of American society

13. Lawrence A. Cremin, *The Transformation of the School* (New York: Knopf, 1961), pp. 275–76.

and education was still in flux, it was understandable that this inchoate coalition of teachers, administrators, professors, and counselors could coexist. The unification in terms of social ideal and intellectual growth, the general state of economic deprivation of the majority of the people, and the possibilities for the common good in education made public education, along with the teaching profession, one of the most powerful symbols of nationhood that brought us together as a people.

THE QUEST FOR POWER

A radical redirection in the character of the teaching profession can be traced to the post-1945 boom. Economic growth of an unprecedented sort and a major expansion of the population took place that reshaped the structure of education. Great populations picked themselves up out of the cities and moved to the suburbs, often commuting back to the cities and their jobs. The residential areas of the cities were increasingly remaindered to the new black and Latin poor.

The large new core of teachers that was recruited to suburban schools was a young and aggressive group. These teachers were determined to benefit from a sellers' market, by a residue of goodwill for education, the ideals of professionalism among teachers, and their own ambitions for the young. The situation was unique because large portions of the United States—the agricultural hinterlands and the cities—were left behind in the economic race. In the 1950s estimated average earnings of public school teachers ranked fourteenth in a list of eighteen professions. Below them were social-welfare workers, librarians, clergymen, and dieticians.

In a nation that purportedly doted on education and gave so much lip service to the ideals of the public schools, this was particularly galling to the urban teachers increasingly depressed by a unique set of potentially explosive circumstances. The new minorities in the urban school were unlike the old. They suffered a deprivation that made teaching in these schools difficult and often frustrating. In New York City the situation was exacerbated by the fact that all educational directives were handed down from one central place—110 Livingstone Street in Brooklyn—too far from the needs and problems of the teachers. Yet a rigid set of institutional controls made any kind of autonomous innovation difficult and made flexibility in curriculum planning to meet unique situations in the various schools almost impossible.

The first explosion occurred in New York City in 1960. It would bring about a new face to the teaching profession. The NEA was still a loose confederation of organizations with about 800,000 members. Incredibly fragmented in New York City, its organizations represented virtually every discipline, administrative category, and ethnic group. These groups corporately had done next to nothing to alleviate the rigid circumstances under which the teachers had to function or to improve the economic situation of the teachers in relation to the residential suburbs.

The AFT led the way out of this jungle of frustrations. Founded in 1916 by a combination of labor leaders and educators, including John Dewey, it had not had much success in attracting teachers. Its union affiliation and working-class image deterred teachers from joining, except for a small core in the Midwest. Its total national membership in 1960 was between 30,000 and 40,000.

A campaign waged by the union, especially among the junior high school teachers, led to a strike by its membership and allies for the right to a collective bargaining election. The New York City Board of Education finally acceded to this demand, and a vigorous election was waged. The NEA affiliates attempted to band together to contest the election, but they were too disorganized, aside from being tainted with their prior ineffectiveness, to persuade an aroused group of teachers. The final vote was 20,045 to 9,770 in favor of the AFT affiliate, the United Federation of Teachers.

This was the beginning of an avalanche. In city after city the AFT won converts and collective bargaining elections. Myron Lieberman could predict in his *Future of Public Education* in 1962 that the AFT would have a membership of 250,000 by 1970 (actually it came to 180,000).[14] Almost immediately, the NEA came to life; it saw that a wholly new situation was in the professional winds. Led by the Utah delegation of teachers, which had likewise suffered at the hands of that state, the NEA classroom teachers asserted their dominance; by 1964, the NEA was calling for "professional negotiation" elections in areas where they were strong so as to assert their exclusive contracted "bargaining" rights with school boards.

This revolution had naturally frightened school boards and they countered with this statement:

> The authority of the board of education is established by law
> and this authority may not be delegated to others. Strikes,

14. Myron Lieberman, *Future of Public Education* (Chicago: University of Chicago Press, 1962).

sanctions, boycotts, mandated arbitration or mediation are improper procedures to be used by public employees who are dissatisfied with their conditions of employment.[15]

But this objection was to no avail. A new mood had overtaken the education profession. In many ways the arguments of Myron Lieberman were critical in defining the new attitude of teachers and what they stood for in affluent postwar America. The argument centered on the fact that teachers were important purveyors of an essential service to our technological society, i.e., the knowledge and pedagogical skills essential to maintain our standard of living.

Teachers over the years had been ill served by society in general as well as by the specific organizations that purported to represent them. These latter had been content with an honorific status for the profession rather than tangible benefits. All other groups organized for their own advancement had mobilized effectively for the enhancement of their status, especially the medical profession, which perpetually engaged in the strike, i.e., withholding services from those who could not pay. And yet no one denigrated doctors for their unprofessionalism, even when they dried up possible entry into the profession (shortage of places in medical schools) by creating artificial shortages. By this single act they had in addition put a greater economic premium on their services.

No, the rule in today's society, so argued Lieberman, is power. Those who can muster power will be able to deal effectively with the larger society. To do this, one principle remains preeminent—strength in organization. Even if illegal, the strike was the only way to make officialdom take notice. Without teachers, especially on opening day in September, society would be in a bad way. And who would replace them? Henceforth, the teachers must take their place alongside the other institutional organizations in the corporate society, whether professionals, workers, corporations, or the great variety of vested interest groups in our nation. Society will take cognizance of their demands in direct correlation to their strength and ability to make felt their important needs.

But just as the power of school boards was met by the power of teachers' organizations (the NEA, soon almost a million strong, had their share of strikes), so too the power of the teachers would be confronted. This occurred, again in New York City, during a horrifying series of strikes by the teachers' union in 1968. The complex set

15. National School Board Association, in *Saturday Review* 46, no. 42 (October 1963).

of events centered around an experiment in local control in Ocean Hill, the Brownsville section of Brooklyn, a predominantly black area. Some citizens made demands on the union in terms of placing and discharging teachers, which the union felt would be the first step toward the dissolution of civil service protection as well as their hard-won collective bargaining contract.

The people's right to local control was countered by the traditional professional rights of the teachers' organizations. The resulting face-off was bitter and not without traces of racial and religious conflict. As Martin Mayer described it, the argument of the community was remarkably similar to the original demands of teachers against the administrative bureaucracy:

> The argument which sustained the drive to decentralize the New York schools was an insistence on the need for "accountability." In the centralized structure there were, simply, too many distant authority figures who could be blamed for unpopular decisions, for failures to respond to requests by the parents whose children were, presumably, the beneficiaries of the enterprise. Too many people could say no to any change in existing procedure—especially any change involving the reallocation of money or personnel.... Decentralization would knock away the crutches, would require the local hierarchs to be leaders rather than bureaucrats, would promote responsibility through increasing authority.[16]

In the end the war between two principles, (1) local control by lay authorities over personnel, use of budget moneys, and curriculum; and (2) the rights of teachers to negotiate with larger authorities for the maintenance of professional control over those same areas that the locals now vied for. The strike resulted in a social disaster that predictably had long-range implications for the profession. As Mayer stated, "The New York teachers' strike of 1968 seems to me the worst disaster my native city has experienced in my lifetime." [17]

In 1970 prolonged and bitter teacher strikes by the AFT in East Saint Louis, Illinois, Newark, New Jersey, as well as New York City were broken by a combination of tenacious and resistant school boards, state antistrike laws, and an apathetic, even hostile public. Power achieved, the public was not sympathetic to any further

16. Martin Mayer, *The Teachers Strike: New York 1968* (New York: Harper & Row, 1969), p. 111.
17. Ibid., p. 15.

encroachment by the professional teacher organizations. In addition, the cities themselves were inhabited by poor minority groups that looked upon the teachers as colonial exploiters whose income seemed astronomical by local contrast. Finally, the crest of the birthrate had long been passed; each year brought diminishing pressures on school boards for more teachers. The teachers' organizations had been unable at this critical moment to halt the production of more teachers. Their bargaining position was thereby even more significantly eroded.

What had happened to the teaching profession in the 1960s is that it had finally found the key—organizational power politics—to gain for its members the wealth that had become available to other politically more sophisticated groups. By calling upon a reservoir of goodwill accumulated over the years, and with the addition of the strike, it had gained a breakthrough to economic parity.

Used successfully over and over again, the strike revealed two factors to the American people: (1) teachers as professionals, like members of any other group, were out to get what they could for their profession in any way possible; and (2) it punctured one of the last remaining myths of the old corporate dream for America, that of various publics pulling together to achieve a social and philosophical consensus built out of mutual self-sacrifice.

The teachers were no different from anyone else. The buffering dimension of community responsibility was gone; everyone was out for himself in this dynamic, hurtling superorganization called America; the teachers were now merely one of the bunch. They would get what they could, but only in the flailing competition of countervailing power.

Our sense of community and school had long been dissolved. The national idealism that brought us such an exhilarating victory in World War II was muddied in corporate affluence and Vietnam. There was little that the education profession could evoke to revivify the symbolic allure of public education. Albert Shanker reflected this well in his 1974 campaign for the presidency of the now 400,000-plus-member AFT. "When we united, we decided that we wanted to stop being losers. You don't keep power by running an organization with amateurs." An aide added, "We are running a large corporation and it has to be administered." [18]

18. *New York Times*, 24 March 1974.

Postscript

With the collapse of New York City's finances in the fall of 1975, the city had to turn to Albert Shanker and the local teachers' union to use their pension funds to purchase Municipal Assistance Corporation bonds to help the city stave off bankruptcy. The dawning realization that the two power structures were now inextricably linked, had a dampening impact on the union membership.

The United Federation of Teachers had made its original power play when Mayor Wagner turned them down for salary increases in 1960. He did find monies to deal with a snow storm and a hurricane which struck soon after. The mayor's explanation to the union leaders was that the money was reserved for disaster relief. The union thereupon transformed itself into a disaster for the city. The subsequent strikes were the product of this strategy.

By late October 1975, the worm had turned. The city now had become a disaster for the union. As *The New Yorker* reported it, "On Friday, this self-appointed disaster [Shanker] the equal of snowstorms and hurricanes had met in default [N.Y.C.] a disaster that was his match"[19]

19. *The New Yorker,* 27 October 1975, p. 33.

9 | Minorities

THE HISTORICAL CONTEXT

America has always had minorities. But until the middle of the nineteenth century it had no real minority problem. In the first two centuries the minorities had either blended together slowly through mutual intercourse or, as in the case of the blacks, had remained a submerged and ignored caste. The Dutch, English, French Huguenot, Swede, German, Anglican, Puritan, and Catholic evolved along with one another. These groups all represented North European cultures of roughly similar civilizational styles and moral patterns. Over a long span of generations, natural proximity allowed for their gradual assimilation under the English and then the revolutionary Anglo-Protestant political hegemony.

In this early phase of American life the crucial surface issues of political and economic development took precedence over the cultural and religious factors. Then, in the 1840s, there was a new influx of immigrants. At this point, the issue of majority-minority relationships was raised. Here, the informal cultural worlds of ethnicity and national origins were being intruded into a heretofore neutral political scene. Now the public educational system became involved because its function was to educate the children of the poor and ignorant. It must always be ready to face any new cultural or religious changes that might have unknown potential in the political and social scene.

These new immigrants constituted a halfway house between English orthodoxy and the comfortable open-door policy to all comers that later attracted the masses from the east and south of Europe and Asia. The Irish and German immigrants headed mainly for the cities and towns of the East and Midwest. In religion and language they were different from the majority, but in appearances (except for economic and class differences) they fitted in with the Anglo-Saxon "racial" context. They became gradually absorbed into a structure of political and economic life where differences— Celt vs. Saxon vs. Teuton—became increasingly irrelevant to the new industrialized and urban patterns of life.

The Irish Catholics, dominating as they did the hierarchy of the church in America, soon established their own school system. And they soon found their way into a number of areas of American life, e.g., politics and police. Coming in the 1840s (during the time of the Irish famine), they were over 25 percent of the population of New York City in 1850 and at least one-third of its population in 1890.

By mid-century, cities such as Cincinnati and Saint Louis in the Midwest had become heavily German. Though they were predominantly Catholic (many were from the Rhine areas of Germany), they did not press the issue of parochial schooling. Perhaps this was because the German system of state schooling was largely regional in structure, i.e., Catholics controlled education in the geographical areas where they were predominant. Many of these Germans were liberals who had been forced to leave an increasingly reactionary Prussian society. They thus brought to their involvement with education a keen interest in the social ideals of the public schools and an intense academic and intellectualistic bent. Also they were receptive to the educational innovations that were now issuing from Germany. Thus the educational theories of Pestalozzi, Froebel, and Herbart always received a sympathetic hearing in the German strongholds of the Midwest. While it was W. T. Harris who introduced Froebel's vision of the kindergarten into the Saint Louis school system, German leaders such as Dr. Carl Schurtz prepared the ground for these innovations. Germans were also intrumental in starting a number of sectarian colleges in the Midwest, such as Wittenberg, Otterbein, and Heidelberg.

At least until the 1870s, a healthy tension or balance existed between the private community life of the minorities and their gradual entrance into the public world. What about the anti-Catholic rioting in the cities during the mid-century? Certainly there was a strong element of anti-Catholicism in such rioting. But economic issues were also crucial factors. In this first wave of non-Protestant Anglo-Saxons were immigrants of incredible poverty; they were perhaps even primitive by comparison with the native American population. This would constitute a pseudo-cultural difference that economic progress could render inoperative, Simultaneously, parochial schools were being founded and patronized. Combined, these factors exemplify the causes for the tensions that resulted in such rioting.

The workaday daytime world could be temporarily neutralized in the private cultural world of family, friends, and community by night. The private culture helped to bridge the gap between old and new.[1] It was the best of all possible worlds. People could retain their deeply rooted ethnic familiarities and values and still obtain a small share of the enormous material opportunities available to all citizens.

America was vast enough, open enough, and was going through such rapid social and intellectual changes that the variety of ethnic and cultural values that existed hardly seemed relevant. Those who held onto their European identities did not personally feel the full impact of the Americanization process. They thought their own value system was secure, though they sensed it was changing. It was vital that the basic structural feature of these minority groups last over a long enough period of time to allow the generations to communicate, to buffer the external intellectual and social impact on religious belief and ethnic behavior. This constituted the natural interaction of new and old. What reasoning person could protest this state of events, especially when the incipient antagonism of outer and inner world, over the duration, seemed evenly matched?

Beginning in the 1870s and continuing with unabated intensity until World War I, over 26 million new immigrants poured into the United States. Nathan Glazer and Daniel Moynihan have noted that this is the one critical example in history of a nation committing itself to a policy of cultural dilution.[2] They have wondered why this should have been the case. Obviously it was not a question intensely debated at the time. From all over Europe and Asia the immigrants came; they came to fill the mills and mines, to join the railroad gangs, to take jobs as urban day laborers, factory hands, garment workers, sodbusters, lumberjacks. The economic factor in this rapidly industrializing and expanding society was critical.[3] It may well be the key to the answer. But in another realm, the intellectual, there was real need for more manpower and the concomitant movement toward social modernization.

Ethnicity comes naturally to human beings. Its roots lie so deep

1. Horace Kallen, *Cultural Pluralism and the American Idea* (Philadelphia: University of Pennsylvania Press, 1956).
2. Nathan Glazer and Daniel Moynihan, *Beyond the Melting Pot* (Cambridge, Mass.: MIT Press, 1963).
3. William Greenbaum, "America in Search of a New Ideal," *Harvard Educational Review* 44, No. 3 (August 1974).

as to be accepted as a natural element in their makeup, perhaps as natural as the presence of a mother in the world of the child. *Homo sapiens* as a cultural animal invests the most mundane of social and physical relationships with symbolism and infuses them with meanings. These meanings are conventionally agreed upon between people. Sometimes, as in gestures and the singsong of conversation, one is not aware of this agreement. Cultural meanings are unique in the sense that they are not erected from specific and stereotyped genetic responses. Sound produced by the vocal apparatus is invested with significance in a myriad of ways and permutations. A smile, a slurp, an eyebrow lifted, all connote different meanings to different peoples.

But ethnicity, that expression of distinctiveness in people's informal domain, does not necessarily intrude itself into the social consciousness. Only when the Catholic bishops, for example, declare that they will not allow their Catholicism to be treated as if it were part of the gross social and material deprivation of the time does the minority problem come to the surface. In practice, one does not separate the cultural aspects of one's being from those aspects that would be normally attributed to material, economic, or social class. How often is "poor," "loud-mouthed," "Pole," or "Jew" considered irrelevant as an aspect of one's personality, integrity, or "being"? How often, indeed, have teachers fallen into the trap of attributing a variety of defects in a child that were caused by his economic and social condition to his ethnic, national, or religious heritage?

The problem did not arise significantly in the nineteenth century because, except for the Irish Catholics, most of the other immigrants accepted the Anglo-Protestant culture of the indigenous elite. They were eager to place their children into those educational hands that represented this authority. Of course, in the nineteenth century, the hand of government was not as overpowering as it is today. People fended for themselves in lonely prairie communities and in the heart of urban slums. They gave relatively little thought to the matter of how much ethnic purity they might be sacrificing if, in return for such a loss, the doors would be thereby opened through education to a better economic and social existence. Further, no one really questioned how deeply the institutional structure of the outside world could penetrate the private nighttime world of informal culture.[4]

4. See Kallen, *Cultural Pluralism and the American Idea.*

Minority Challenge to Education

It was some time before the impact of these new minorities was felt in the public mind. But toward the end of the century they began to arrive in greater numbers and, significantly, their progeny was abundant. The schools, as in the 1840s and '50s, were the major agency for acculturation. For the most part the minority groups did not fear the schools, although many a poignant conflict took place between parent and child over the problem of communication. There was tension between generations as well as between the old foreign culture and the new dynamic society. Parental attitudes toward education were generally receptive. The streets of the New World may not have been paved with gold, but the public schools would provide a means by which the young could attain unheard-of success and comfort.

Still, the sense of hope, the dream for the future, must mesh with the tangibles of everyday life. The hard present had to be coped with in terms of an ethnicity that was an irrefragible reality. Huddled together in urban or rural ghettoes, these minorities worked hard for economic sustenance at the same time as they lived out their lives in terms of their own special communal vision. While in some cities—such as New York City—at about 1900, nearly 80 percent of the population was foreign born, the majority of Americans in total numbers (83.4 percent in 1890), and certainly the economic and political power structure, were natives.

The American majority had less reason than the immigrants to look to the furture and the prospects of the melting pot. Manufacturers or union leaders could view the immigrants that came to the various power centers as potential sources for their own private good, but most citizens had no such raison d'être for welcoming the newcomers. The citizens could not envision that the assimilative forces that had been unleashed throughout America through the industrial machine would be powerful enough to dissipate minority tensions. This economic revolution was, however, a presence that transcended any one institution. It was perhaps the most pervasive cultural and philosophical trend the world had seen.

What the Americans saw was a frontier finally closed, millions of non-Anglo-Saxons, speaking foreign tongues and with foreign mannerisms, and packed into enclaves under conditions of near poverty. There was indeed a major clash of cultures. While the nation was an undeveloped fastness these differences were unimportant. What was important was to wrest control of the vast resources of this nation. Now, with communication and transportation bringing us ever closer together and with the cities and countryside filling up, the vision of national development seemed capable of completion. Yet there was fear.

The rapidity with which technologies and ways of living together had been transformed implied the ease with which science and technology would transform the cultural patterns of Americans into something new and at the same time absorb the diversity of the newcomers. As the twentieth century began, however, the absorptive capacity of America appeared limited for the first time. Even the schools seemed incapable of molding the teeming masses; these inchoate hordes were so different in culture and physical appearance! Is there any wonder at the rapid and apparently beneficent spread of laws for compulsory education at the beginning of this century?

THREE SOLUTIONS TO THE MINORITY PROBLEM

Anglo-Saxon Nationalism

Native-born Americans had to face the horrifying prospect of a national inner life that might be different from what they had idealized. The tide of immigration that had washed over America had not receded as yet. However, the changes that had occurred as a consequence of this thoughtless economic and social lapse aroused a new nativist hysteria. It was at this point that the so-called theory of Anglo-Saxon nationalism was applied to plug the dike. Soon there was agitation for a halt to unrestricted immigration and some determined efforts by the nationalists to shape various institutions, especially the public schools, in their own image. Characteristic of their views was a San Francisco segregationist's educational ruling of 1906 that depicted Orientals as "a lesser moral race." Segregation was therefore necessary to avoid contamination.[5]

The reasoning behind Anglo-Saxon nationalism was that even as the American people had made a political compact to live under certain rules of law, their traditions, though unwritten, were just as binding. American society had designed a Constitution that was flexible yet firm on the guidelines affecting the relationships of man

5. Gladys Wiggins, *Education and Nationalism* (New York: McGraw-Hill, 1962), p. 330.

to man, state, church, and society. Implicit in the compact was a commitment to Anglo-Saxon justice and to Anglo-Saxon culture. One could not sever the bond that united the people in the intimate, unspoken interrelationships of neighbor to neighbor, the altruistic love of community, the commitment to cleanliness, personal sobriety and morality, honesty—public and private—from the greater code of law that defined our nationhood. Anglo-Saxon culture and polity were essentially one.

While the newcomers during the earlier part of the nineteenth century (the Celts and Teutons) were different, the fact that they both had traditions of independence, dignity, and self-rule made their meshing with the culture established by our founding fathers a relatively smooth process. These new peoples, however, were from all over the world, from largely lower-class strata—in all, the greatest heterogeneity ever inflicted upon any nation. The old American reacted with dismay and perplexity at each new confrontation. His traditional image of the immigrant had been the sturdy, rustic clearer of the land—independent, hardworking, and clean. He had not dreamed that people existed who were so degraded socially and economically. He was shocked by the primitiveness of the conditions under which they were willing to live in the cities. That they tolerated such conditions not only reflected their origins but also hinted suspiciously at a future of crime, moral turpitude, and educational flaccidity.

There was fear. It would be arrogant hindsight to ridicule this concern.[6] Men such as educational historian Elwood Cubberley could not peer into the future. They were sensitive to the historic role of American society, its enhancement of values such as tolerance, social mobility, educational advancement, scientific and secular pragmatism, and its immunity to the worst sorts of political authoritarianism. The powerful, optimistic sense of destiny was an almost unique American characteristic. The nativists wanted a high public moral and social culture, and they identified this hope with the best in the traditions of the American past.

Unfortunately their vision was narrow and their sense of change in terms of the nonmaterial realm of culture unimaginative and static. Their pronouncements seemed hostile to those of non-Anglo-Saxon traditions. Coupled with their accrued economic advantage, their open hostility to the strange values and behaviors of the newcomers was extremely threatening. Their demand was

6. Lawrence Cremin, *Wonderful World of Elwood Patterson Cubberley* (New York: Teachers College Press, Columbia University, 1965).

simple: efface all cultural aspects of these new groups—language, social institutions, schools, and so forth. Transform them into true-blue Americans. The popularity of eugenics during this period can partly be traced to their realization that neither educational nor social pressure could readily ameliorate the alien ways of the newcomers. There was also a real possibility that a valid philosophical explanation of class differences could be derived from the scientific Darwinism (survival of the fittest) that might indeed identify inferior cultures with the moral and intellectual behavior of inferior individual beings.[7] Thus their cultural arrogance was not born merely of fear and ignorance.

If we choose to dispute the attitudes of the Anglo-Saxon nationalists on face value, i.e., if we disregard imputations that they argued solely from economic motives for advantage or that their psychological prejudices against "foreignness" stemmed from lack of confidence in their own sense of identity—or merely as a pathological manifestation—then a rationale can be found on their behalf worthy of discussion. First, they saw a strict relationship between the cultures of, say, Sicilians or Jews, and their political and economic abjectness. They feared that the difference between "we" and "they" was not merely a qualitative difference, but one which slipped over into the area of public behavior. They could not foresee that the chain of history might be broken, that a Sicilian peasant could be independent, self-sufficient, vote intelligently, and run for office or that a Jew could be a stock broker, a general, or an athlete and still retain his cultural identity.

Further, they could not envision a future in which these diverse cultural accents might leaven the traditional Anglo-Saxon dough, might even enhance Anglo-Saxon values. Perhaps they could not recognize that the American Anglo-Saxons of 1900 were vastly different individuals from those who inhabited the cities and towns of the colonies in 1700. When one considers the great ructions in attitude and behavior being wrought by the industrial revolution, it does not seem reasonable that the existence of a population of even 40 percent foreign-born and first-generation Americans could have altered significantly the direction of change in our culture. If they feared change in the quality of their life, they could have looked with far greater cause in the direction of the industrial system. It is important to consider here that the drive for a comprehensive public school system, which began in the 1870s, coincided with the high tide

7. Richard Hofstader, *Social Darwinism in American Thought* (New York: George Braziller, 1959).

of industrialism as well as immigration from non-Anglo-Saxon areas of the world.

The most obvious and regrettable aspect of the myopia of Anglo-Saxon nationalists was that they did not appreciate the practicability of absorbing such diversity into our society and its usefulness in creating more effective conditions for the sustenance of democracy. The various cultures that had been deposited on our shores might indeed provide a context for a richer life for the Anglo-Saxons themselves. Here was an opportunity to taste foreignness close at hand. Possibly they would return to their own communities wiser, more tolerant, and innovative to the benefit of their own life style.

As a time when the landscape was rich in variation and breathing room, the spector of homogeneity and its social impact could not be imagined. In 1900 America had about 76 million people, a vast continental territory, and an enormous diversity of people and life styles. The economy was yet balanced between farm and industry. Could any one predict that an infant born in that year would reach old age in the technological and cultural desert that has since enveloped us?

The Melting Pot

As noted, the Anglo-Saxon solution to the inundation of traditionalist America with millions of poor, socially undeveloped and culturally diverse people was simple: close the spigot of immigration and for those already here cut the cord of allegiance to the Old World by imposing a heavy dose of traditional Americanism in the schools. The schools would retain their assimilationist purpose. And the industrial system would continue to prosper on this source of cheap labor, until the unions put an end to its gross exploitations. Finally, in the early 1920s, at a time of temporarily renewed xenophobia in the United States, viz. *Pierce* v. *Society of Sisters* (Oregon decision) and the *Nebraska* decision, plus the fear of "Bolshevism," the flow of immigrants was staunched by a virtual ban on all non-Anglo-Saxon immigration. The absorptive process did henceforth make considerable headway.

The melting pot or assimilationist philosophy, given a great deal of national recognition at this time, was a contemporary version of the kind of integrationist sentiment we are experiencing today. What lacked at that time were the legal sanctions that we have today for forcibly moving people (children) around to achieve assimilation. The immigrants produced a cultural richness in the cities that had not existed before. Many of the earlier new Americans had already achieved middle-class status. This facilitated the later penetration into the United States by many from the cultural heartland of Europe. Artists and scientists from all over the world came to see what was happening here, from the Bohemian Antonin Dvorak in the 1890s to Sigmund Freud at Clark University a decade or so later, and to refugees like Albert Einstein in the 1930s. But for all the sentimentality of such as Emma Lazarus, Israel Zangwill, and Mary Antin, the ultimate aim of the melting pot was the same.

Still, its line of reasoning was fairly new in Western tradition. According to the melting-pot theory, there was an intrinsic relationship between political structure and ethnic identity (nationality). The state school was viewed as an institutional vehicle for the nationalizing, or in this case the homogenizing, of the existent diversity.

The melting-pot assimilationists saw America, as did the nationalists, as an integrity. But their instincts for the reality of contemporary cultural dynamics were more sure. They perceived, for example, in spite of what was a traditionally slower process of social evolution in Europe, that no culture remains unchanged or pristinely pure. In the America of the early twentieth century, with the tumult of industialism absorbing so much human as well as natural energy, the dynamics of change could easily assimilate even the unbelievable 8 million who entered the United States between 1900 and 1910 (the last full decade of immigration before the war and the restrictive legislation that was to follow).

The indigenous populace as well as the immigrants had to be persuaded that this social dynamic could utilize these people profitably and that, in contributing to the evolving American national scene, the newcomers could be inextricably embedded in its character. America was a great, beneficent haven and a beacon to the world. It would evolve in the physical as well as the cultural sense by the addition of these millions. Their sense was surer also in another way. As observed, the Anglo-Saxon nationalists were in the main neo-Darwinians of a conservative mind. They were deeply impressed by the possibility that the newcomers might be intractable to change. The assimilationists were environmentalists in terms of the possibility that the newcomers could become leaders and contributors on the highest levels. They had the traditionally American Horatio Alger myth on their side. The Jews already had a Brandeis and a Cardozo; the Italians were of the blood of Michelangelo, Marconi, and Verdi, if not of Caesar and Cicero. If one put one's foot down on the side of the geneticists (nationalists), how did one account for the denizens of English jails who were emptied out onto the shores of America during the eighteenth century? These gentle folk on their part were transformed in subsequent generations into the staunch and respected upholders of the Anglo-Saxon vision itself.

The melting-pot advocates were not worried. The intensely future-oriented leadership was willing to sacrifice the sensibilities of the older generations, who were torn by Old World loyalties and New World demands. The children and the school were the great hope. The informal traditions would settle down by themselves, while that great equalizer, the American public school, did its assigned job. All that was asked for was equality of opportunity, just the chance to show what could be done when political, religious, economic, and ethnic oppression was lifted from the shoulders of the unwanted.

In the end the assimilationists were anxious just to avoid making a minority problem from this tide of foreigners. That is the crux. They were willing to define the issue as one of absorption of the old into a new stew that would reflect no previous cultural valence whatsoever. Implicit in this attitude was the view that it would be impossible merely to shear off the old characteristics—the agricultural, feudal, subservient past—and keep the rich, human, colorful ethnicity, undeniably an ornament to any cosmopolitan society. But if the groups were able to preserve aspects of their heritage in process of becoming contributing members of modern America, it would be all to the good.[8] The expectation was that, given the evidence of the past, with the general rate of change and the uniqueness of modernity, a new culture would be created. No group, however, could predict the long-range future.

This intellectual movement was by and large correct in its assumptions and predictions. The malleability of the human being was there. Given opportunity, these repressed but intelligent and resourceful people entered into the spirit of the American enterprise and continued the Anglo-American linguistic tradition, but gave it wholly new dimensions.

In terms of a philosophy for the American educational system, it was also singularly successful. It presented a platform of beliefs upon which the formal educational system might rationalize the turbulent years of social and cultural change. Except in the case of

8. See I. B. Berkson, *Theories of Americanization* (New York: Teachers College Press, 1920).

the Catholic minority or the distinct language groups in the rural areas, the problem was never one of the content of the educational curriculum. What was important was that all knowledge be available in a common setting of equality. The fast-developing pace of scientific advance—an advance that was worldwide in its scope and application—the givenness of the English language, and finally the dawning awareness that the Iliad, Wagner, Balzac, Ibsen, and Leonardo were part of a great international tradition, however translated or communicated in the educational system, aided significantly the task of imparting knowledge to these minority young. As for the private differences, those could be handled in the inner sanctums of home and family.

Cultural Pluralism

"Cultural pluralism," a term coined by Horace Kallen at this time, was an approach to the minorities that was quite different from the previously described views. Certainly the most radical approach to the problem, it wholeheartedly accepted the reality of minority life and values on its own terms. The pluralist position was soon embraced by a number of noted intellectuals, including John Dewey.[9] These intellectuals took a jaundiced view of the entire perspective of homogeneity. With their intensely libertarian values, they saw in the ethnic minorities certain social dimensions which they felt were intrinsic to the basic rights of individuality. These behavioral and belief systems of the minorities were diverse in terms of traditional American patterns. But the diversities constituted a quality of reality that could be extinguished only by force and ultimately with dangerous consequences.

Thus, the two arguments which the pluralists pursued: (1) the rights of individuality derive from one's external and material conditions and also from one's cultural existence, and (2) it is the impossible for society to exist under a system of enforced cultural homogeneity.

As the pluralists interpreted the situation, the Anglo-Saxon nationalist groups, in attempting to cleanse the newcomers of their traditions, would be engaging in a vicious form of dehumanization. It would attempt not only to divest the newcomers of their sense of identity and meaning, but also to impose upon them the artificial garments of an alien and possibly dated culture.

9. See Clarence J. Karrier, "Liberal Ideology and the Quest for Orderly Change," in *Roots of Crisis* (Chicago: Rand McNally, 1973). Karrier challenges the view that Dewey was a pluralist.

While the melting-pot altruists saw the beauty and integrity of the new cultures, their ultimate solution was as debilitating to the immigrants as was this nationalist view. How were the various contributions of the minorities to be added to the melting pot so that it might produce a better America? The new America was to be an amalgam of the *many* old into a new *one*. The end result might be as foreign to the identity of any of the immigrant groups as if the goals of the nationalist groups were to prevail.

The only compensating factor in the melting-pot position was its beneficent attitude toward the new cultures. The assimilationists did not consider the newcomers to be intrinsically inferior or to exhibit a degenerate pattern of life. But these minorities still had no place in the new American scheme of things. Partial explanation of this attitude was the fear that the coexistence of differences entailed the risk of needless friction and hostility. Thus the newcomers must be gentled in the day-to-day interactions of life in the neighborhood, the city, the school, the economic marketplace. Possibly we could induce them to give up those jagged edges of behavioral idiosyncrasy that might ruffle the feathers of others or interfere with the smooth-running organizational timetable. In this way, they would learn the symbols of a new national life. But it was hoped that this new and multifarious generation of the semialien, in interacting with others, in sharing and arguing, in learning and working together, would thereafter transmit some characteristics that would be found superior to what were then existent. Gradually, the young would develop an awareness of their American identity and in a generation or two the melting pot would have worked its miracle of amalgamation.

Of all the pluralists, I. B. Berkson was perhaps the only one willing to take a chance on the natural laissez faire social trends exemplified in America's cultural makeup. He argued that the natural resiliency of the minority groups and their intense interest in their own cultural survival—as reflected in the enormous proliferation of newspapers, magazines, theaters, and fraternal groups—were vital to their perpetuation. After all, here in America, for the first time, at least in the recent history of the Jews (his own group), there existed no official hostility to the practice of their beliefs and traditions. They could not help but flourish. Where a group's cohesiveness was less effective, there would be a gradual dissolution into the larger society. There should be no official support, in the schools or elsewhere, to perpetuate what might not thrive on its own resources.[10]

10. Berkson, *Theories of Americanization.*

Many wrote in favor of the pluralistic theory. Some were minority-group members themselves; others, such as Randolph Bourne and even John Dewey, added their support on the basis of more philosophical and legal reasoning.[11] Dewey could see the inexorable erosion of diversity taking place through the aegis of the industrial and economic machine. For the culture of industry and technology hid more under its external physical cloak than might have appeared. It was enveloped in a host of behavioral nuances, work rules, and personal patterns between employees concerning language, dress, and personal deportment, etc., which demanded the fulfillment of more than only a narrow functional role in order to earn one's wage. Thus, for the most part, the pleas of the pluralists turned out to be poetical exhortations for the value of differences and the right of the individual and the community rather than practical blueprints for a truly intercultural society.

Those who were most liberal had to skirt the danger of associating their espousal of cultural pluralism, especially in the schools, with the demands of Catholics and other sectarian religious groups for official recognition of their own educational roles. Dewey used pluralism as an argument for breaking up the monolithic features of the growing urban environment into a more community centered structure.[12] With diversification, we would allow for a natural need for social identity in terms of face-to-face relationships and would also halt the totalitarian trend, even then foreseeable, toward the concentration of power, in both the economic and political sectors. Dewey's concerns for the integrity of minority cultures were more for the external structural strength of the society than the cultivation of the intrinsic value diversity of ethnic groups or their introduction of real differences into the heart of our national culture.

It was Horace Kallen who argued most persistently against the puerile qualities of a democracy whose pretensions did not extend beyond the external façade of political participation and economic opportunities. To him the vision of social integration was a nightmare that could never endure. Kallen could not completely explain why he felt that ultimately the drive for cultural expression and the need to maintain the integrity of one's own identity were indissoluble elements in our society that could be corroded only at great price. Kallen's expression was that blood is thicker than water and that

11. See S. W. Itzkoff, *Cultural Pluralism and American Education* (Scranton, Pa.: Intext, 1969), pp. 54–58.
12. See John Dewey, *The Public and Its Problems* (Chicago: Swallow Press, 1954; first published in 1926), p. 211.

those deep inner connections between people of like outlook would persist even as external workaday relationships faded away.[13]

Kallen was realist enough to recognize that the forces antithetical to the pluralist view were almost irresistible. And he was enough of a pragmatist (a student of William James) and follower of Dewey to accept for the most part the theory of scientific practicality in which people's external adaptation to problems of experience remained the desideratum of success or failure for their social needs. It was easy enough to see that the drive for Americanization, to forget the old and get on with the new, both in and out of the schools, was too forceful a carrot-and-stick combination to be resisted.

Kallen was famous for his prediction that were the assimilationist forces successful in structuring society so that there would be no functional room for ethnic minorities, the minorities would go underground. He predicted that they would live on in the private, quiet places, in the interstices of society. Our nation could not survive with an imposed homogeneity. The structure of nature itself is diversity. Witness the enormous cultural and physical diversification among this one species, *Homo sapiens.* Then how could one reasonably expect in a nation as large as ours, both in population and geography, that differentiation in terms of culture and personal value systems would not be the most natural mode of association.

> What is important, however, is the fact that the uniformity is superimposed, not inwardly generated. Under its regimentation the diversities persist; upon it and by means of it they grow. But instead of growing freely, and fusing by their own expansion into contact and learning with their peers, they grow distortedly, as reactions against and compensations for the superimposed unity. In the end they must win free, for Nature is naturally pluralistic; her unities are eventual, not primary; mutual adjustments not regimentations of superior force. Human institutions have the same character. Where there is no mutuality there may be "law and order" but there cannot be peace.[14]

It would follow that a truly democratic approach would be to help the existing minorities to retain their diversity and to create institutions and associations that would bridge the enormous social and economic gap that existed. A greater America would thus be a

13. See Horace Kallen, *Culture and Democracy in the United States* (New York: Boni & Liveright, 1924).
14. Ibid., pp. 178–79.

diverse America, in which people lived in equality in the daytime world of public work and explored the private realms of diverse values by night. Naturally, Kallen's chronological separation of day and night was only symbolic; life cannot be so neatly severed into distinct compartments.

Kallen could do no more than explain, in evocative and metaphysical terms, his deeply felt perceptions that what came to exist so naturally as part of people's social attributes—their sense of cultural identity—could not be so easily effaced either in terms of institutional pressure or philosophical prejudice. Yet he also saw very clearly the enormous gusto with which the young, the first-generation Americans, absorbed the American success ethic and strove mightily to transcend the conservatism and parochial huddling of the older folk. The young did opt for the openness and advance of the public world. Perhaps Kallen could also have predicted that the next generation, in regarding the accomplishments of their elders, the material and social freedoms that they had achieved, would go back to search among the values and traditions of their grandparents to find a historic cultural system of ideals with which they could identify.

In the years during which Kallen was writing and polemicizing, the inevitable course of events took place. The schools that served ethnic communities for the most part remained staunchly loyal to the traditional standardized curriculum. The teachers unvaryingly viewed the children as ripe for transformation to American standards of cleanliness, clothing, language, and behavior. The formal, vocationally oriented as well as academic curricula gave little or no attention to the inner world of meanings that was such an important part of their lives.

As observed, their private world was stained with imputations of lowliness, backwardness, and ultimately un-Americanism. The shame that was felt in many a child's heart at his parents' traditionalism when he was exposed to the public institutional world constituted an enormous alienating wrench for literally millions. Yet the old knew that justice lurked behind the lamented break between parent and child. It lay in the open-ended future that America provided for those who could make the shift. The power and authority of the great political and industrial systems dwarfed the understandable feelings of rage and dismay that these people felt toward a process that was coercive and philosophically questionable. But a dynamic social force moved in society. Science and the educational system supported it, as did the large majority of the American public.

A CONTEMPORARY DILEMMA

Another America

The lure of affluence held out to the traditional minorities by the educational and industrial systems was eventually fulfilled. In the years after 1945 virtually an entire economic group was shifted into the middle class. In terms of housing, automobiles, small and large appliances, entertainment and travel, higher education, the American people experienced an unprecedented material growth and prosperity.

But not all the Americans knew this sense of exhilaration. In 1963 Michael Harrington wrote *The Other America: Poverty in the United States*.[15] As noted earlier, he found that in terms of a governmentally defined level of poverty ($4,000 family income, 1960 purchasing power), 20 to 25 percent of the U.S population (35–40 million people) still lived in poverty. Further, Dwight Macdonald noted that in the twenty-five years between 1938 and 1963, the poverty level had been reduced from 68 percent of the population having 35 percent of the national income to 23 percent of the population in poverty but now having only 7 percent of the national income.[16]

This analysis came at the beginning of President Johnson's Great Society program. A nation as powerful and as wealthy as ours could not live with itself while so many citizens were denied the benefits of our newfound prosperity. A group of goals was set forth by which this national stain might be removed.

On close inspection, this group of poor constituted to a large extent wholly "new" and heretofore unrecognized groups of minorities: Negro, Mexican, Puerto Rican, and Indian. (Excluded from consideration at this point are the aged, the young married adults in graduate schools or young people "beginning" their adult lives, or those in isolated rural agricultural areas such as Appalachia.) It was slowly realized that the federal beneficence of the New Deal era, which aided poor blacks and whites generally and encouraged the entry of blacks with higher educational backgrounds into the federal and other civil service areas, had only postponed a confrontation with what now loomed as a national disgrace—segregation.

The contrast in circumstances of older ethnic minorities and

15. Michael Harrington, *The Other America: Poverty in the United States* (New York: Macmillan, 1963).
16. Dwight Macdonald, "Our Invisible Poor," *New Yorker*, 19 January 1963.

black people is revealing. For many ethnic groups, America was a place where one could strive toward middle-class status with some hope of achieving it, and at the same time develop a sense of identity and tradition.[17] They suffered some cultural attrition in the process, but the available alternative focus for their energies—educational, political, and economic—prepared them well for the upward surge of opportunity that occurred after World War II.

The formerly rural lower-class blacks who now resided in the decaying cities of the North were uneducated and inexperienced at dealing with a wholly new system of institutional life. In this they were no different from any other new minority group entering the cities. However, as they increased radically, demographically, they confronted the American social system with a challenge heretofore unique among the many minorities that had presented themselves before our national system.[18] The black middle class, on the other hand, whether in the segregated South or the North, was small in number and in percentage of the total black population and unfortunately did not reproduce itself.[19]

The Failure of Desegregation

The desegregation decision of 1954 *(Brown* v. *Board of Education)* nullified the older "separate but equal" view of *Plessy* v. *Ferguson* (1896). In effect it made race an illegal criterion of governmental action in both education and general affairs. It was a historic step forward. A second important milestone was the Civil Rights Act of 1964, which put the government on the side of legal equality and nondiscrimination. But the road toward economic, social, and cultural parity was rough. Faced by an intransigence that was obscure and frustrating, social theorists began to take a more active approach to the problem of equality of educational achievement than might have been warranted strictly on the basis of the mere existence of the concepts of nonsegregation or nondiscrimination.

As new schools in the cities were built, various compensatory programs were introduced and tried. What appeared to be easy solutions dissolved in failure. In the years after 1954, the issue

17. See Andrew Greeley, *Why Can't They Be Like Us?* (New York: E. P. Dutton, 1971).
18. See Daniel Moynihan, *The Negro Family* (Washington, D.C.: U.S. Department of Labor, 1965), pp. 25–27.
19. See Arthur Jensen, "Environment, Heredity and Intelligence" *Harvard Educational Review*, Report Series No. 2 (1969): 93–94; also Moynihan, *The Negro Family*, p. 29.

seemed increasingly clear: legal equality, while necessary, wa
sufficient to eradicate such a long accumulated deficit. With
earlier minorities, legal restrictions had been fought and eventua.
vanquished. The old minorities had only one basic demand: remov
all obstacles toward the achievement of the fundamental franchise,
equality of opportunity.

But the black people of America, and to a lesser extent the
Puerto Ricans and Mexicans, had experienced such unique circumstances that new conditions and new approaches were called
for. It was clear, however, that the possession of their statutory
freedoms had not gained for them their humanly rightful share of
the opportunities and fruits of citizenship. To paraphrase Lyndon
Johnson, too many years of having one's legs tied were poor preparation for embarking on the race of equality of opportunity.

Historical Causes

Before we could even begin to ameliorate this tragic deficit, we
had to have a full understanding of the problem. Certainly literature
on the subject was rich, but it did not seem possible to derive any
clear policy from it.

A commonly held view was based on the prima facie evidence:
blacks had begun their residency in this country as slaves. A great
discrepancy had existed between their cultural background and the
civilizational style of their master. Their few generations of freedom
were not enough to attain the necessary historical distance from the
past.

In addition to this, some put forth the view that the initial circumstances of black people were exacerbated by the fact that generally they did not struggle against their dehumanization. They had
no legal protections from church or state to establish even the
minimal conditions for the enjoyment of their most basic needs and
private rights. Traditional familial structure with regard to marriage
and children could be violated at a whim. Even murder was often
not proscribed. In sum, the preconditions for an independent social
or cultural existence were nonexistent. And without them, these
people had no preparation to go forward and compete in the outside
world.[20]

Recent research has questioned this latter view of extreme cultural deprivation and the traditional melioristic and gradualistic

20. Stanley Elkins, *Slavery* (New York: Grossett & Dunlap, 1963).

social policy that was implied, and also the inherently open-ended view of the problem. Was it simply a matter of wise environmental stimulation through progressive social policy that would eventually be realized in success? *Time On the Cross,* by two authoritative economic historians, seems to throw doubt on the thesis of inhumane exploitation as part of the Protestant slave establishment in the United States.[21] Blacks were relatively well treated socially and morally, but also, so these statisticians argue, the tacit cooperation of the slaves which was thereby enlisted made of the slave system an enormously efficient and economically profitable institution.

In an even more recent analysis, historian Eugene Genovese gives substance to this new perspective while concerning himself primarily with the inner realm of privacy and hope. It was essential that the slaves cultivate this realm to avoid becoming complicit in such an unjust system. Their faith in Christianity gave them the strength to retain their sense of integrity. Through it, they developed the unique religious and aesthetic sensibility that enabled them to counter the threat of "ultimate dehumanization." [22]

According to some of these later theories, black people left their condition of servitude with greater strengths than heretofore thought. Therefore, it is in the hundred years of segregation and social "obscurity" we must look to discover why such enormous disadvantages still inhere in a large segment of their lower class.

There is an interesting contrast in the role played in society by this earlier group of blacks and that played by West Indian blacks. Over the years, West Indian blacks have played a role disproportionate to their number in leadership positions in the United States.[23] If we understood the reason for it, we would have the kind of evidence we need to perceive how an elite black community develops those internal cultural resources that aid the entire minority community. The same kind of evidence concerning social structure could be derived from that remarkable group of West African blacks, the Ibos. The Ibos were one of the later Nigerian tribes to accept Western institutional patterns; and they took to these institutions, especially education, with great enthusiasm. They climbed to the pinnacle of Nigerian society before they met with at least temporary disaster in the civil wars between their own Biafra and the rest of Nigeria. What were the key social elements that

21. Robert W. Fogel and Stanley L. Engerman, *Time on the Cross: The Economics of American Slavery,* 2 vols. (Boston: Little, Brown, 1974).
22. Eugene Genovese, *Roll, Jordan, Roll: The World the Slaves Made* (New York: Pantheon Books, 1974).
23. Glazer and Moynihan, *Beyond the Melting Pot,* pp. 35–36.

stimulated the people so positively? It is to be hoped
enough left of their traditional tribal organization to t
relation to these issues.

Integration Programs

As noted, desegregation was essentially a legal position that
forbade any agency of government from so acting as to place a
racial criterion on any of its works—schools, transportation, drink-
ing fountains, etc. Government was to be color-blind. Implicitly in
this position, race constituted an irrational or unnatural criterion
upon which to base laws. The Civil Rights Act of 1964 extended this
principle to the private sector—all business or other ventures that
were subject to the interstate commerce clause of the Constitution
were enjoined from making any such discimatory actions.

To many liberals, this was not enough. This merely constituted a
laissez faire or a negative approach whereas circumstances cried out
for positive egalitarian actions. Thus the principle of integration
gradually evolved. In the field of education particularly, the idea of
integration recalled some of the attitudes of the Anglo-Saxon
nationalists. There was a determined effort to bring the black
American into the mainstream of American middle-class life. The
important difference was that the contemporary liberal accepted a
measure of responsibility for the deprivation of black persons and
facilitated their integration without the invidious comparisons, i.e.,
between native-born Anglo-Saxon Americans and Eastern and
Southern European immigrants, that characterized the nationalistic
rhetoric half a century earlier.

A variety of educational plans was proposed. Head Start (for
preschools) and open enrollment (placing black children in white
schools, where there was room for the children) are two examples.
Plans such as Head Start attempted to counteract the early deprivation that occurred in the black lower-class home. Family structure
was often disorganized because for a variety of historic and contemporary institutional reasons (welfare regulations) these homes
were often without a father. Social scientists have noted the traditional matriarchal character of Negro family life.

Daniel P. Moynihan, assistant secretary of labor in 1965, acting
on the behest of the Johnson administration's Great Society program, produced a study of the problem. In *The Negro Family,*
Moynihan pointed out that the problem of lack of self-image for the
male child and the inevitable disorderly conditions that derive from

the absence of a father in the home contrast vividly with the typical middle-class patriarchal orientation of the European tradition. Moynihan cites black social scientist E. Franklin Frazier's treatment of this problem as long ago as 1950:

> As the result of family disorganization a large percentage of Negro children and youth have not undergone the socialization which only the family can provide. The disorganized families have failed to provide for their emotional needs and have not provided the discipline and habits which are necessary for personality development. Because the disorganized family has failed in its function as a socializing agency, it has handicapped the children in their relations to the institutions in the community.[24]

By taking the child out of the home early enough and associating him with trained teachers in a highly stimulating social environment—such as Head Start—it was thought that the children's beginning handicap would be ameliorated. In those areas where such programs were not available, TV's "Sesame Street" proved immensely popular. The mass communication media in general committed themselves to a revision of some of the traditional prejudices that stereotyped blacks as perennially lower class. Periodicals such as *Ebony* could attribute much of their success with their black clientele to its vivid chronicling of the development of a self-respecting black middle class.[25]

The "Coleman Report," commissioned by the U.S. Office of Education in 1964, was published in 1966 (see pp. 339–40 on new Coleman Report). For it, 4,000 schools, 60,000 teachers, and over 600,000 students were surveyed in an attempt to locate both the source of black educational failures of the past and the institutional patterns that might point to ameliorative solutions.[26] The pattern of educational retardation that appeared among black students was consistent with past findings. In addition, the report cast doubts as to the ultimate success of Head Start programs, since the educational gap between black and white was found to widen with age. Even more significant, it was impossible to locate the souce for

24. E. Franklin Frazier, as quoted in Moynihan, *The Negro Family*, p. 48. See: *The Moynihan Report and the Politics of Controversy* by Lee Rainwater and William L. Yancy (Cambridge, Mass.: MIT Press, 1967), for a survey of the controversy and a number of insightful critiques of the Moynihan position.
25. See E. Franklin Frazier, *Black Bourgeoisie* (New York: Collier Books, 1962).
26. James Coleman, *Equality of Educational Opportunity* (Washington, D.C.: U.S. Office of Education, 1966).

this gap in the kinds of schools that existed for the two races—whether they were segregated, old and dilapidated, or integrated and new. The research made it clear that, at least for the white schoolchildren, external factors such as these had little to do with educational achievement. Slight improvement in the black child's achievement was, however, noted in those schools where he constituted a relatively small minority. A writer for *Science* summed up these implications by calling them "a spear pointed at the heart of the cherished belief that equality of educational opportunity will increase the equality of educational achievement." [27]

The causes for this, again, were highly hypothetical and controversial. This was true also of Moynihan's report, as evidenced by its widespread rejection by the black community. In the case of the Coleman Report, the implication seemed to be that the causes of the failures could be attributed to a highly obscure "cultural ambience" located in the home. However, the little glimmer of hope provided by the improvement in scholastic achievement by blacks in white schools did set off renewed and urgent advocacy of the "busing" method of achieving integration in the schools (see pp. 339–40).

Thomas F. Pettigrew, a Harvard psychologist, noting the increasingly critical state of black inhabitants of the urban ghetto, has argued that our transformation from a racist to an open society necessitates a strong admixture of integration. National social policy should be so oriented that among other strategies:

> . . . a major effort toward racial integration must be mounted in order to provide genuine choice to all Negro Americans in all realms of life. This effort should envisage complete attainment of the goal in smaller communities and cities by the late 1970's and a halting of separatist trends in major central cities, with a movement toward metropolitan cooperation.[28]

Black Nationalism

It may be helpful at this point in our discussion of black education to review the growth of an indigenous leadership movement among the black lower classes. Individuals such as H. Rap Brown, Huey Newton, Eldridge Cleaver, Stokely Carmichael, and Angela Davis became prominent and influential. Aside from the highly

---

27. Godfrey Hodgson, "Do Schools Make a Difference?" *Atlantic Monthly*, March 1973, pp. 35–46.
28. Thomas F. Pettigrew, "Radically Separate or Together," in *Cultural Pluralism*, ed. E. G. Epps (Berkeley, Calif.: McCutcheon, 1974), p. 25.

educated Carmichael and Davis, they represent a reaction against the integrationist movement. The Black Panthers, Congress of Racial Equality (CORE), and a variety of other groups met in Gary, Indiana, in 1971 and denounced both busing and integration in education. The heightening of black consciousness had been fed by the eruptive riots in the ghettoes of Newark, Los Angeles, Detroit, and other communities in the mid-1960s.

This new aggressive appeal to the nationalistic sentiments in the black communities only partially reflected the theory of cultural pluralism of the earlier generation. Along with "Afro" hairdos and a certain faddishness about Swahili in the schools and "soul food" in the cuisine was a serious attempt to acquaint children in "ghetto" schools with the distinctive background and circumstances of the black people. Interracial reading textbooks, black music, poetry, and history were introduced, and many colleges around the nation developed "black studies" departments.

While black nationalism did have its impact on developing an aggressive sense of identity among young blacks, it also exhibited elements of racial hatred of "whitey" and "honkie," some blatant anti-Semitism, and a violence within the movement which was echoed in renewed violence in the cities. The high incidence of drug taking and crime among black youngsters and an antiintellectualism and anti-middle-class rhetoric frightened many old-line integrationists as well as some white liberals.

It is precisely in the relative lack of real involvement by the black students in their own cultural resources plus the hatred of the white's culture that signaled the short-run demise of "black power" as an attractive cultural or even political movement. On the other hand, commercial film makers have capitalized with a series of crude "action thriller" movies, such as *Super Fly* and *Shaft,* which have been highly successful with the black young.

The most self-destructive aspect of the nationalistic surge in the black community has been the manner in which black studies has so often been linked to a blatant antiintellectualism, already in the wind among white radicals. Along with the attack on the middle class and the technological society came an attack on the schools and literacy. This was an attempt, self-defeating at best, to destroy the legitimacy of the school, standards of achievement, and merit as criteria for attaining the socioeconomic fruits of education.

One could thus argue in theory that even if the black child did fail academically, the failure was due to the inherently racist political structure. Neil Postman of New York University thus wrote:

The number of jobs that require reading skill much beyond what teachers call a "fifth grade level" is probably quite small and scarcely justifies the massive, compulsory, unrelenting reading programs that characterize most schools. . . . It is entirely possible that the main reason middle-class whites are so concerned to get lower-class blacks to read is that blacks will remain relatively inaccessible to standard-brand beliefs unless and until they are minimally literate.[29]

Those Who Remain

For almost one hundred and fifty years there has been a consistent American ethos with regard to minorities. According to this approach, minority rights are recognized insofar as they can be translated into private concerns. The First Amendment relegated religion to a status out of the public policy areas. The development of the common school in the nineteenth century forced religious and ethnic groups to found their own schools if they wanted institutional protection for their values. It became necessary to emphasize new forms of public truth and to cultivate forms of knowledge and intellectual skills that contributed directly to the larger public good.

In this way the individual was lured out of his protective sectarianism and into the secular society, from there to build a continental power. Robert Nisbet has shown that the process of changed allegiances that characterizes the building of the nation-state was one fraught with political dangers. The increased power of the state and the continued dislocation of millions of rootless individuals gave political centralism enormous impetus and the additional potentiality for totalitarian controls.[30] But while the formal educational system was relatively open and decentralized, this dangerous polarity of individual and state was buffered.

In this context the ethnic minorities exchanged a host of intrinsic symbolic values for almost unlimited opportunities in the economic and social sphere. Religion became increasingly nondenominational, and the cornucopia of wealth poured out for all. At first it seemed as if everyone had benefited but the masses of the black minority. The efforts at desegregation, the Great Society, and an unprecedented measure of goodwill and cooperation by the Amer-

29. Neil Postman, "The Politics of Reading," in *The Radical Papers*, ed. H. W. Sobel and A. E. Salz (New York: Harper & Row, 1972), pp. 53–54.
30. Robert Nisbet, *The Quest For Community* (New York: Oxford University Press, 1953).

ican people finally brought significant ameliorative results in the 1960s.

Ben Wattenberg, a statistically oriented political writer, analyzed thousands of government and other research documents to fathom the results of these economic and educational efforts.[31] His argument was that by the end of the 1960s a majority of black families had become middle class. In 1950 only 4 percent of black families earned over $6,000 (a rather high criterion of the middle class). By 1972, 34 percent earned more than $10,000. Black income had doubled in the 1960s. And young black families in which both members worked were doing exceptionally well.

With this general advance came a broad-based black political leadership—congressmen, a senator, a Supreme Court justice, and numerous mayors of large cities. The professions, entertainment, and sports can contribute their famous names. A business class began to be a significant component in the black middle class. All this progress, however, of a forward-looking portion of the black community could not obscure the even more hopeless condition of those who remained behind in the decaying ghettoes.

The deepening plight of this large segment of black citizens, in spite of the extraordinary social measures intended to raise them up socially, seems finally to have split the intellectual community into two wings. One group, of traditional integrationist sentiment, argued that the efforts had not been nearly great enough to achieve the hoped-for success. According to this view, the malleability of the individual was determined by social and historical circumstances. This view was met by an increasingly vocal counter.

The second group, comprising both psychologists and social scientists, saw the problem of social intractability as having deeper and more fundamental dimensions. Some, such as social scientist Edward Banfield, looked to the problem of social class. Those who constituted the lower classes had perceptions, interests, and social structure that made them incapable of coping with middle-class institutional life.[32] He argued that we ought to cease considering this as a problem of race. It was primarily a problem of social class, which transcended racial boundaries. Whatever the causes were, Banfield seemed to argue that these lower-class denizens would continue to resist the blandishments of upward mobility.

To the social perspectives of Banfield, Moynihan, and Glazer

31. Ben J. Wattenberg, *The Real America* (New York: Doubleday, 1974). Incomes corrected for inflation.
32. Edward Banfield, *The Unheavenly City* (Boston: Little, Brown, 1968).

was added a powerful reassertion of the hereditarian view of intelligence.[33] While the significance of this evidence for comparisons between races was clearly obscure, Arthur Jensen made an undeniably persuasive examination of the relationship of education, social competency, and intelligence to this problem of lower-class nonachievement. And while the support for Jensen's position was strong within his discipline and he was buttressed by the writings of Richard Herrnstein and the English psychologist Hans Eysenck, the uproar among intellectuals as well as among the students in the universities was deafening.[34]

Enforced Equality

While these conflicting arguments over the causes of educational failure in the ghetto continued to reverberate, the impetus toward integration and enforced busing continued. The Coleman Report, which was the statistical source of much of the pressure for busing, had indicated that the purely physical differences between educational plants for whites and blacks—schools, curricula, laboratories, teacher characteristics—appear to have little effect on performance. The only hint that the cause might be found in the environment and thus amenable to improvement was found when poor black children could associate with white classmates from affluent homes.[35]

> The finding is that students do better when they are in schools where their fellow students come from backgrounds strong in educational motivation and resources. The results might be paraphrased by the statement that the educational resources provided by a child's fellow students are more important for his achievement than the resources provided by the school board. This effect appears to be particularly great for students who themselves come from educationally-deprived backgrounds. For example, it is about twice as great for Negroes as for whites.

The problem of family structure is so serious that

> the task of increasing achievement of lower-class children cannot be fully implemented by school integration, even if integration were wholly achieved—and the magnitude of racial

33. Moynihan, *The Negro Family;* F. Mosteller and D. Moynihan, *On Equality of Educational Opportunity* (New York: Random House, 1972).
34. Richard J. Herrnstein, *I.Q. in the Meritocracy* (Boston: Little Brown, 1973); Hans J. Eysenck, *Race, Intelligence, and Education* (London: Temple Smith, 1971).
35. Hodgson, "Do Schools Make a Difference?"

and class concentrations in large cities indicates that it is not likely to be achieved soon.[36]

The scene thence shifted to the courts. How far would the Judiciary go toward neutralizing de facto segregation due to housing patterns? In April 1971 the Supreme Court upheld an intracity busing plan in Charlotte, North Carolina, which dissolved school zones that kept the races apart. The only stipulation in the law that allowed egress was a provision that exempted children or parents for whom a busing policy would incur hardship.

Massachusetts had already enacted a racial imbalance law. By this law, if local school districts or cities were found to include schools of more than 50 percent black children, they would be penalized by having their state funds withheld. In some cities, this would necessitate long-distance busing. Thus the percentage of black children in stipulated segregated schools was raised.

The effects of court-ordered integration in Boston (Fall 1974) was such as to precipitate first a boycott and then scattered violence. Here, busing had the effect of breaking up the long-established insularity of a predominantly working-class Irish community.

Intracity busing edicts in Richmond, Virginia, and in San Francisco were prelude to the most important of the recent Supreme Court decisions. In June 1974 the Supreme Court, by a 5–4 ruling, set back the hopes of the Detroit School Board for the integration of Detroit's virtually all-black schools with the predominantly white suburbs. The long-distance intercity integration of schools (black inner city and white suburbs) by busing seemed now to be out of the question. The long-standing traditions of independence of both city and suburban school districts could not be held culpable.

The Coleman Report had devoted but three pages on the impact on students when attending racially mixed schools. This constituted the admittedly scant evidence used to support the thesis that it benefited the black child. In a follow-up study published a year later, 1967, Thomas Pettigrew and David Cohen concluded that social class was more influential in its positive impact on the black child than random desegregation.[37] If the mere mixing of lower class with white was not beneficial, then a true integration, one in which race and class were not linked, would be needed.

36. James Coleman, quoted in Daniel Bell, "On Meritocracy and Equality," *Public Interest*, no. 29 (Fall 1972): 45.
37. Thomas F. Pettigrew and David Cohen, *Racial Isolation in the Public Schools* (Washington, D.C.: U.S. Government Printing Office, 1967).

A junior colleague of Pettigrew's at Harvard took on the job of studying in some detail the effect of busing on black students and white students. David Armor's study, entitled "The Evidence on Busing," came to diametrically opposite conclusions from Pettigrew's.[38] It again stimulated a short, acrimonious, but inconclusive debate. Armor argued that "induced integration" did not on evidence "enhance black achievement, self-esteem, race relations, and opportunities for higher education." Armor concluded, "the available evidence . . . indicates that busing is not an effective policy instrument for raising the achievements of blacks or for increasing interracial harmony.[39]

Pettigrew and his associates immediately rose to take issue with these conclusions.[40] The muddied complexities of the issue only served to underline the politically explosive character of this dilemma of minority equality and educational opportunity. As legislative, executive, and judicial branches of government ran for cover, academicians immersed themselves in ephemeral scientific investigations and prolonged polemics; the public became more and more confused, and college students increasingly politicized and agitated. The brunt fell, predictably, on the helpless schoolchildren and the lower- and working-class families who were supposed to be the ones to benefit by all this attention.

What could be considered an offshoot of Pettigrew's ultimate vision of the elimination of class lines was the issue of residential zoning. A controversial exemplification of this took place in New York under the mayorality of John V. Lindsay. The issue concerned the Queens residential area of Forest Hills, an old but upper-middle-class area close to Manhattan.

The proposal was to build a city-sponsored lower-income housing complex in the heart of Forest Hills. The high expectation of beneficial effects on the lower income groups, most likely blacks and Puerto Ricans, was countered by an outcry from the residents, who were fearful of the crime and alteration of their community that such a drastic change in residential character would entail.

Conflict promptly ensued. Questions were raised as to the extent to which government powers could be used to alter the private lives of citizens through such intervention. Replies to this argument cen-

38. David J. Armor, "The Evidence on Busing," *Public Interest,* no. 28 (Summer 1972): 90–126.
39. Ibid.
40. Thomas F. Pettigrew et al., "Busing: A Review of the Evidence," *Public Interest,* no. 30 (Winter 1973): 88–118; David J. Armor. "The Double Standard: A Reply," *The Public Interest,* no. 30 (Winter 1973): 119–131.

tered on the right of any class of people to engage in "snob" zoning and thereby avoid its social responsibilities to the poor. Resolution of the controversy came with a major alteration of the character of the housing development. A limit was set on the number of subsidized apartments that could be made available for welfare recipients and other lower-class tenants. The controversy did much to destroy John Lindsay's credibility to the middle class as a presidential candidate.

Quotas and Discrimination

Perhaps the most spectral turn that the minority question has taken is the attack on the principle of individual merit. Instead of merit, the principle of affirmative action, or quotas, has been substituted in education, civil service, and business. What makes this turn in social affairs so unusual is that the war against discrimination and quotas that has endured for so long at the behest of minorities culminated in the *Brown* decision (1954) and the Civil Rights Act (1964). Finally, a willingness was being shown to recognize the individual and to cease interfering with the full expression of his personality because of subsidiary and irrelevant characteristics, whether in commerce, education, or public life.

If indeed the public sector of life was to be widened and private and pluralistic enclaves reduced to the privacy of the hearth, then at least let us open up this public sector to a principle of the widest access, so the argument went. But wholly different conditions intruded. No longer did equality of access or opportunity yield increasing equality of result. The ethos of social and cultural uniformity had gone too far to back away from this new anomaly.

The various City Colleges in New York had developed a long and distinguished record for providing access to the talented children of the lower classes who were often barred from more prestigious institutions because of restrictive quotas. Entrance to the various colleges was gained by competetive examination or through high school grades. In this the City University was merely echoing another long civil-service tradition.

The spokesmen for the new minorities, black and Puerto Rican, felt that the rise in this constituency's enrollments was proceeding too slowly. The political pressures were such that in 1970 a system of open admissions was instituted that would allow every New York City high school graduate access to at least a community college education. To be sure, the free system of higher education had heretofore expanded too slowly. And the schools were certainly unprepared to accommodate such unprecedented increases in students. Standards declined almost immediately, followed soon after by administrative chaos.[41] Lack of preparation of a large proportion of students necessitated special tutorial and remedial efforts. What many observers regretted in the entire process was not the opening of the institution to more deserving minority students, but the blatant political attack on the principle of merit. The City Colleges had suffered a near-fatal blow. It could well be that they had lost their usefulness not only for those less well off, but also for talented members of all classes, races, and ethnic groups for whom they had for so long been a beacon of hope.

> The basic fact about higher education in New York City, prior to the controversy over open admissions, is that open admissions already existed. A high school student whose academic record did not entitle him to matriculation in one of the senior city colleges could register for night courses at those colleges, as a nonmatriculated student. If his course grades were subsequently good enough, he could then matriculate and either continue on to his B.A. or switch to being a full-time day student, if he so desired. If entering night school did not appeal to these students, they could enter one of the community colleges—where, if their grades were good, they could shift after two years to one of the senior colleges. . . .
>
> So what on earth was the controversy really about? The answer, alas, is clear and simple. The controversy was about equality—not equality of educational opportunity, but equality of a more substantial nature. The movement for open admissions was a movement to confer upon the black and Puerto Rican students of New York City, by administrative fiat, an equality of educational *status*—or at least the semblance thereof. That last qualification is important because, in this matter, appearances were and are more important than reality. Which is only another way of saying that open admissions had precious little to do with education itself, and almost everything to do with ethnic and racial politics.[42]

Not all institutions were able or willing to throw open their doors to all who wanted in. Prodded by an Executive Order of 1965 by

41. Martin Mayer "Higher Education for All? The Case of Open Admissions," *Commentary*, February 1973.
42. Irving Kristol, "The Pros and Cons," *Educational Record* 53, no. 4 (Fall 1972): 292.

President Lyndon Johnson, the federal government was ordered to ascertain whether all schools and businesses were taking steps to hire and promote members of minority groups. Indeed, some agencies were even obligated to draw up timetables by which given quotas would be achieved. The establishment of a new criterion of preferential selection by virtue of group ascription was under way.

Naturally, many minorities did not fit into the ascriptions, and so the protests began. As a member of one minority group pointed out to a beneficiary of this policy: "A quota for you is a quota against me." Others, pointing out that the principle of blood guilt was replacing the principle of individual culpability, the latter usually seen as one of the legal cornerstones in man's march toward civilization, wondered why their innocent children would have to suffer for the deeds of those who had gone before them.[43]

The question nearly came to a legal resolution in the DeFunis case. This concerned a candidate for admission to the University of Washington law school in Seattle. DeFunis was denied admission to the law school even though he had scored well on the qualifying examination. His place on the list had been taken by minority students, who actually had lower scores than he. After he filed suit, he was admitted to the law school. But his case did not reach the Supreme Court until after he had graduated. The Court majority found the issue moot and refused to rule on the question. Justice William Douglas in a separate opinion would have had the Court take up the case. His words are worthy of consideration:

> The equal protection clause commands the elimination of racial barriers, not their creation in order to satisfy our theory as to how society ought to be organized. The purpose of the University of Washington cannot be to produce Black lawyers for Blacks, Polish lawyers for Poles, Jewish lawyers for Jews, Irish lawyers for the Irish. It should be to produce good lawyers for Americans and not to place First Amendment barriers against anyone. . . .
>
> That is the point at the heart of all our school desegregation cases. . . .
>
> A segregated admission process creates suggestions of stigma and caste no less than a segregated classroom, and in the end may produce that result despite its contrary intentions. One other assumption must be clearly disproved, that Blacks or

43. See Alfred Zimmern, *The Greek Commonwealth* (London: Oxford University Press, 1961). The elimination of "blood guilt" and the institution of individual responsibility was adduced by the Greeks to be central in their transition to civilization.

Browns cannot make it on their individual merit. That is a stamp of inferiority that a state is not permitted to place on any lawyer.[44]

Additional legal tests are likely, since at the very least, criteria for establishing membership in the ascriptive group will demand the wisdom of a Solomon. For example, would a Sephardic Jew (a Jew of Spanish extraction) qualify as a member of the Spanish-speaking minority in Texas or California or ought he be considered, for purposes of preferential hiring, to be a Jew? Or what about a young black woman? According to some ascriptive criteria, such a person would be triply blessed.

The additional philosophical and moral issues that would arise from a general application of such guidelines strike at the very heart of what we once considered to be a democratic society. Daniel Bell has phrased the issue as follows:

> The historic irony in the demand for representation on the basis of an ascriptive principle is its complete reversal of radical and humanist values. *The liberal and radical attack on discrimination was based on its denial of a justly earned place to a person on the basis of an unjust group attribute.* That person was judged —and excluded—because he was a member of a particular group. But now it is being demanded that one must have a place primarily because one possesses a particular group attribute. The person himself has disappeared. Only attributes remain. The further irony in all this is that according to the radical critique of contemporary society, an individual is treated not as a person but as a multiple of roles that divide and fragment him and reduce him to a single dominant attribute of the major role or function he plays in society. Yet in the reversal of principle we now find that a person is to be given preference by virtue of a role, his group membership, and the person is once again "reduced" to a single overriding attribute as the prerequisite for a place in the society. That is the logic of the demand for quotas.[45]

CONCLUSION

In the nineteenth and early twentieth centuries the ethnic and religious minorities asked that the government cease their interfer-

44. *DeFunis* v. *Odegaard,* U.S. Supreme Court Reports, 40 Ed. 2d., 24 May 1974, pp. 183–84.
45. Bell, "On Meritocracy," pp. 38–39.

ence. They wished to be free of discriminatory policies in the distribution of governmental aid, especially to education. Above all, they wanted the freedom to enter—or not enter—the mainstream without inhibitory quotas or handicaps.

The emasculation of ethnic and religious life in the Great Society of the mid-twentieth century resulted in a precipitating individualism which sought a new locus of authority in ever more distant and powerful institutions. Preeminent, however, in the growth society model was an openness, not only in terms of its insistence on merit, but in the fluidity of individual participation in the national system. One must agree that while government power grew, those in charge were from diverse origins and were themselves subject to a variety of countervailing institutions.

The last decade has seen a shift in ethos that may be only a premonition of the change that is to come. Minorities once more enter our range of vision. But they are minorities to be dealt with in the abstract, not in terms of individual problems or value concerns, but by gross ameliorative policies. Quotas, the elimination of merit, percentile targets of persons with certain positive ascriptive characteristics were to be attained or the government would penalize recalcitrant institutions.

The ultimate goal was economic equality. But this was never targeted directly. By making entrance to institutions available to all, regardless of merit, it was supposed that individual competency and merit would follow automatically. Percentile equality by fiat would, it is now hoped, go a long way toward achieving a truly democratic, nonracist, nonsexist society.

In the process the old minorities have been pushed aside as we build an all-encompassing technological society. But now even individual merit, intelligence, effort, education, and creativity would no longer be rewarded. What had they achieved, then, in having traded off the old allegiances? What seems important to society is that the residual minorities be absorbed in this seamless social web. The irony is that our black minority has never had a chance to determine for itself whether it wished to cultivate that rich and historic realm that comprises its tradition. The black middle class has been quietly shunted into the suburbs. The remaining blacks, deprived of their most able members, are now being forcibly bused into hostile white areas, with little concern as to their own wishes in these matters.

The result of these policies seems to be that without minorities or social and cultural diversity, the "democracy" can finally get on with the business of the day. Its representatives would then be able to face an undifferentiated ocean of constituents. Can this kind of democracy succeed? Tocqueville had serious doubts:

> One must not blind himself to the fact that democratic institutions most successfully develop sentiments of envy in the human heart. This is not because they provide the means for everybody to rise to the level of everybody else but because these means are constantly proving inadequate in the hands of those using them. Democratic institutions awaken and flatter the passion for equality without ever being able to satisfy it entirely. This complete equality is always slipping through the people's fingers at the moment when they think to grasp it, fleeing, as Pascal says, in an eternal flight.[46]

---

46. Tocqueville, as quoted in Bell, "Meritocracy," p. 51.

10 Youth

No lion's whelp within thy precincts raise;
But, if it be there, bend thee to its ways!

—Aristophanes

THE PROBLEM

Ordinarily we deal with cultural phenomena—the interplay of institutions, styles of life, moral and political values—as historically unique. We see differences in historical development and can make some comparisons in conditions and perhaps learn in terms of the variations on a general theme. But given certain prior social conditions, no strict laws can predict a result merely by adding on a few years. The wisdom of those experienced in human foibles is usually a better guide than the equations or slide rules of the most brilliant scientist. Free will is an inevitable deterrent to optimistic determinants.

These observations hold true with regard to religion, professionalism, and ethnicity in education. On the issue of youth, we find that the force of culture, while still strongly enactive, is modified by the more general biological factors of immaturity. In every society, responsibilities and privileges are apportioned to the young according to certain age distinctions. This occurs in gradual degrees up until maturity. Even in our society, labeled by some as a juvenocracy because of its preoccupation with the wants, needs, attitudes, and values of the young, age eighteen will probably be the lower limit of the franchise. And in spite of the Kennedy youth charisma, there have been few demands for lowering the presidential age limit below thirty-five. After all, the beginning of the "criminal" age,

162

according to the radical young, is thirty. To reduce the presidential age limit to thirty would satisfy few in the youth cult.

How to educate the young—those who have passed beyond childhood into adolescence, where the physical blush of maturity is in evidence while the years of experience are yet to come—provides all civilized societies with a significant challenge. Youth can begin at twelve to fourteen years of age and be completed at twenty; or as occurs in our own time, not yet be fully completed by twenty-eight or twenty-nine. As Philippe Aries has noted, a period called "youth" hardly existed in the Middle Ages.[1] One passed almost directly from infancy into the adult world, with all its responsibilities, freedoms, and indecencies. But the Middle Ages were a transitional period, neither simple and primitive, yet still undeveloped institutionally and culturally. When in the fifteenth and sixteenth centuries national states had grown up and a tradition of new Western knowledge had been established, youth was taken off the highways, out of the university towns, and encapsuled in loco parentis in boarding colleges and academies.

At any one time, the youth of the society represents the future —the possibilities latent in the present which can accomplish the smooth evolutionary transition of complex, changing institutions. Schools provide the means by which the diverse talents of the young are molded to fit the various needs of the evolving civilization. Schools provide more than a vocational perspective; they provide the living embodiment of the philosophy of the society. They rationalize and stabilize the process of change.

To achieve this goal the schools do two things: (1) They must recognize which skills and allegiances constitute the core of functional behavior in the society as well as the set of meanings and beliefs that will allow the individual to adapt smoothly to the values of the day. (2) They must be sensitive to the new in terms of fact, philosophy, cultural and aesthetic trends, and new psychosocial styles (fads and trends) by which the educational experience hews to its social responsibilities and remains relevant. Schools should always be experimenting with new curricula, teaching methods, and organizational patterns.

What makes youth a problem is precisely that balance between maintenance of the basic structure of society, its emotional and intellectual commitment to its own existence, and the necessity to educate for inevitable change. For civilization means complexity

1. Philippe Aries, *Centuries of Childhood* (New York: Vintage Books, 1965).

and change. The old have the difficult job of planning and executing the institutional basis for their own obsolescence. They therefore have to plan for the young, the inexperienced and immature, to know what they will need in order to function in the unknown that lies ahead.

YOUTH IN SIMPLE SOCIETIES

In simple societies, where there is little change or complexity of structure, growing up is relatively easy. First, the sense of formal ideal, as in the image of the adult male or female, remains secure from generation to generation so that the elders can smoothly inaugurate the young into the values and attitudes of the earlier generations. The young learn early what informal values they must absorb. They identify readily with the old. The emphasis is on the wisdom that is the product of the accumulation of experience within an environment that is in stasis. In all the myriad of cultural environments, amid the vast diversity of personality nuances, sexual roles, hierarchical and class distinctions, simple societies, having essentially informal means of education, are able to effect the transition between youth and maturity most often accompanied by extraordinary panoply and ceremony with a smoothness and consistency that is both a wonder and a challenge to complex modern societies.

Not only modern society is afflicted with the dilemma of dealing with an exuberant population of youths. The ancient Greeks reflected in amazement on those bold youngsters—Achilles, Ajax, Hector—who precipitated the Trojan War; later, charismatic men like Alcibiades or Alexander fascinated as well as exacerbated the average Athenian. In the Parthenon frieze, in which the gods are depicted in various typical poses awaiting the completion of the great procession of the Panathanaea, it is virile but volatile Ares, god of war, who sits tense and impatient, his restless energies unnaturally contained. The antics and exercises of the university students of the Middle Ages are well chronicled in educational histories. Less known is the fact that in the 1640s even the Puritans had a mild juvenile deliquency problem, with the young intent on violating John Cotton's blue laws against bowling on Boston Common on Sundays. Sometimes the exacerbations are minor, petty violations of the regulations of elders. Sometimes they represent truly revolutionary upheavals in which youths and young adults become the wedge of a great new intellectual or social movement.

YOUTH AND FORMAL EDUCATION IN ADVANCED SOCIETIES

If we are to understand why higher civilizations have a youth problem and why simple societies traditionally have never faced up to this kind of social experience, we must return to our original educational model. In the earlier distinction between formal systems of education and the informal acculturational process lies some of the critical and conceptual tools for understanding the difference.

First, we must agree that neither "advanced" forms of society nor "simple" social structures have any theoretical priority. Both are examples of widespread social solutions to the conditions of humanity; neither has found *the* natural solution to the predicament of growing up as a human being. We cannot even accept the easier inference that because simple people have no significant ructions in the process of absorbing the young into adulthood that their patterns of education are significantly more basic than advanced social structures.

Three interconnected elements distinguish formal systems of education: (1) complexity of social structure, specialized vocationalism, and conscious exploitation of the material and ideational environment; (2) rapidity of change whereby the traditional interaction of one generation with the next is beset by great discontinuities in patterns and symbols of belief and action. As long as father and son speak the same language, love the same sports and music, have the same vocational bent, look upon the relationship between woman and man in the same way, the education of the young is relatively easy. As soon as rapid social change associated with a complex social structure occurs, the symmetry and stability of the process are disturbed and a new mode of balance and assimilation comes into being.

(3) This leads to the question of values. With the richness and complexity of civilizational life, something new is effected—tridimensionality of vision, which has inevitably led to the establishment of a conscious value system. No value system ever remains the same. It is subject to the same vicissitudes and modifications as any aspect of a culture. Because of its ineffable character and as an intangible reality that people must commit themselves to, it sometimes loses its effectiveness in demanding the intellectual and emotional loyalties of the young. In rapidly changing societies, this ideational bond

which the generations share—a bond which often incorporates room for change and a belief in "progress"—must be constantly renewed, altered, and reshaped in terms of experience. Sometimes the ideology of formal education atrophies through rigidity. If change is rapid, the process of formal education is endangered. The young thrash about wildly searching for new meaning, a sense of identity that will bind them into the future.

STABILITY AND CHANGE

Stable societies are not faced with such horrendous discontinuities. Two sets of circumstances have saved them from recurrent adventures with the young—place and time. In simple societies change and complexity are not at issue. The young can easily seize upon the implicit expectations and opportunities of adulthood and make a smooth transition. But this does not mean that this is a perfected model of social existence. The fact that there are no problems can lead one to expect that perhaps primitive societies are an ideal condition of humanity, somewhat along the lines of the early-nineteenth-century European image of Tahiti as a heaven on earth. The widespread ineptitude of these societies in dealing with change that comes from without ought to raise serious questions about their status in history. They have purchased millennia of stability, but face the prospect of experiencing a horrendous debacle of cultural dissolution when confronted by dynamic mainline civilizations.

Even in the case of such relatively stagnant classical societies as Egypt and China, their complexity and size were buffers which enabled them to absorb the shock of external force and social influence. They both became subject states until they learned the techniques of external modernity. Their complex civilizational, social, and intellectual structure allowed them the privilege of retaining their identity and at the same time coping with the challenge of modernization.

It is pleasant to conceive of a line of continuity and slow development as between father and son, teacher and pupil, or as the relay runner passing the baton back to his fast-advancing successor. However, there is a high price on forcing a culture into a mold so as to achieve this end with regularity. Basically, the thrust of innovation cannot be dammed up. The creative urge that is always concentrated in the youth of any culture shows itself in every society, even the most restrictive.

Who can say what new idioms societies have developed over the centuries in their rituals, dances, and festivals. These are only the surface manifestations of a boiling realm of potentiality. Either it erupts violently or it is forcibly suppressed, with resultant decay of the culture. We ought not idealize the primitive. He is the pursuer of a destiny of constraint that leads either to self-immolation or decadence and oblivion.

There is some evidence that stagnancy and primitiveness are relatively recent occurrences. The days of the *Völkerwanderung*—migrations of the people of the world—are not too far in the distant past. The people of the Pacific islands, of Africa, Australia, or the Americas have been locked into their geographies at the most for about two thousand years. In Africa, perhaps it has been even less. Thus we cannot say for sure that some of these people would not have created great and complex societies in those geographies such as eastern North America, where a fragment of contact with existing civilizations—the Mayan or Aztec—was possible.

It can be argued that informal educational techniques as the beginning and end of human development constitute a dead end. Simple societies either develop into civilizations or they become extinct by gradual hardening of the arteries. One can argue that the attempt to educate youth by rigidly shaping their creative surges through the machinery of social institutions subverts human nature. Ultimately it must work to the disadvantage of the society in critical ways.

All simple societies work in close balance with the environment around them. Understandably, any change is inherently a threat to a tenuous if long-achieved calm which connotes security. Each society creates a whole series of rituals, ceremonies, institutions, even myths, by which to drain off the innovative energies of the young.

We should not confuse the smoothness of what is achieved with the simplicity of the process. The complex set of institutional and symbolic procedures—rites of passage, totem affiliations—by which the young are inducted into the adult world are a well-traversed and intricately engineered social machine in which the rugged crevices of individuality and idiosyncrasy are honed smooth. True, no society is so undeveloped that it would not allow for some form of institutionalized deviancy, whether the individual becomes a shaman, half-man, half-woman, artist, or medicine man. Most simple societies have uncovered enough variance in personal traits within their own construction of social life as to necessitate some institutionalization of human variation. But in the main, little opportunity exists for the richness of possibility that has been expressed in (1) the diversity of personality types that have been realized across the spectrum of all cultures, and (2) the natural richness of diversity and individuality to be found in the cosmopolitan civilizations.

YOUTH AND FORMAL EDUCATION

We have argued that the development of advanced patterns of formal education is a natural, probably an inevitable product of cultural evolution. Formal education is a product of the society's awareness that the transition of the young into the old, the flow of successive generations, must be flexible yet institutionalized. Given the wide range of talents in the young, and the variegated roles and functions that must be played in the society, some intermediary institutions must exist to channel and shape this diversity, the raw and volatile youthful presence into responsible, committed, and productive maturity. This process has to take place within a society committed to evolving in a certain philosophical direction. The ideology or philosophy of the society is focused on the educational system that has the major responsibility for inaugurating the reasoned readjustment to the times.

Thus far we have discussed the role of youth and its education in terms of comparative forms of social structure, how simple and complex societies prepare the young to deal with the factor of change. In the main this discussion has concentrated on external and structural features. These are the historical variables in the life of the young, and while overwhelmingly powerful, they are also external to the unique qualities of the individual. The potentiality remains with the individual, but the social circumstances shape how and where it will manifest itself.

What we are concerned with here are those factors that remain the same in all segments of youth, in all places and at all times. The condition of partial maturity has been subject in recent years to a great deal of study. The theory of the developmental process of human beings tells us that there is a stage in life wherein, though the body is fully mature and the mind approaching full adult capacity, full adult development is yet to come. At this point in life, after puberty but before "maturity," the individual is suffused with enormous energies. He or she is malleable in terms of vocation and personality and is distinctly apart from that equable stage of calmly accepting the obligations of life that has been traditionally characteristic of full maturity.

We have tended, because our culture has always been supportive of the young—in spirit and ideas—to take seriously the idealism, drives, and values of the young. In a rapidly changing world, we have tended to interpret these enthusiasms as being the wave of the future. But as we mature as a society, come face to face with the historic errors of groups of young and youth movements, we become aware of the universality of the problems that this process presents to each civilization. It takes place in all kinds of cultures and in all historic epochs. Those, once young, must deal from a far different perspective with the newly young. And since being young is relatively a short interval on the road to maturity and age, the process will inevitably be described by the old. In all probability the description of the process will ultimately resolve itself into one of those transnational truths.

Obviously these truths are not as clear-cut as the knowledge we have gained in this century about the various medical, psychological, and social needs of infants and children to ensure healthy development. As children develop into adolescence and youth, they become ever more deeply involved with the psychosocial problems of their environment. These dynamics as yet elude us as concise principles. We are too close to the beginning of disciplined research in this area and too involved with the great social changes of the era to have a rich historical appreciation of the problem. Nevertheless, our educational task cannot be successful even in a changing social context unless we understand some of the basic features of a process that to say the least can be explosive.

BIOLOGICAL FACTORS

For our purposes we can leave aside other evolutionary considerations than those that can be directly assigned to human beings. The dominating fact of human biology is, of course, the human brain. This new morphological innovation in the history of life is responsible (although the functional mechanics are still unclear) for the creation of symbolic behavior. The gradual supplanting of the instinctive system of automatic responses and the domination of the cerebral cortex thus transferred practically all incoming information, except that dealing with gross motor responses, to perceptual processing and to the higher deliberative centers.

One of the most unusual factors contributing to this great transformation has been the process of foetalization, or neotony —the retention into the state of adulthood of characteristics of the young of the species. Thus many of the characteristics of young mammals—hairlessness, slow closing of the sutures of the skull, retarded maturity, reduced ratio of the snout and jaw to skull—have been retained by *Homo sapiens* into maturity. While this process seems to have taken place simultaneously with the evolution of *Homo sapiens* out of the forest of protohuman forms, it alone is not the key to understanding the uniqueness of the human being. Certainly the delay in the closing off of the skull bones so that the brain can expand explosively in those first few years of life, coincidental with the infantlike features of humans as compared with their anthropoid cousins, gives circumstantial evidence and meaning to the unique functioning of the "new" brain.

The changed nature of the human young is seen in the new status of play.[2] In the animal young, play serves a specific practical purpose—survival. Those higher orders of animal life that are capable of a large range of adaptations to the environment seem to be endowed with an extra capacity to explore the possibilities of the environment in the early stages of life. On the surface, the penchant for play is both human and impractical and even extremely precarious. For by going beyond what is soberly safe, the young can run into dangers that their more conservative elders do not have to face. On the other hand, nature has in all likelihood selected out favorably this characteristic of higher forms of life, especially mammals, for it allows the young to exploit a wide range of behavioral possibilities, some of which might be at the same time different from the patterns of the mature and even somewhat more adaptive to the intergenerational changes that have occurred in the environment.

For a moment in the ontogenetic development of life, there is a moratorium in the serious, practical business of existence. During this time, not only are the young bursting with energy, but they are also growing and malleable. It is a perfect time to try out the new; perhaps it will serve the practical exigencies of the changing present.

For various structural reasons that we cannot go into here, a series of huge genetic adjustments were made in the suborder *Hominidae* over the last two million to five million years. During this period many alterations were effected in the structure and functioning of this group of human forebears, foetalization among them.

2. See Lewis Mumford, *The Myth of the Machine* (New York: Harcourt, Brace, 1967), pp. 7–8. See also Johan Huizinga, *Homo Ludens: The Play Element in Culture* (Boston: Beacon Press, 1955); and Roger Caillois, *Man and the Sacred* (Glencoe, Ill.: Free Press, 1959).

Among the varying readjustments in behavior from the dominant motifs of the mammals, the role of play has undergone crucial changes. Play is now coextensive with human life. From the first rattle hung over the crib to an ancient's last pinochle hand, life is in essence a symbolic exploratory, creative game engaged in for its own intrinsic meanings.

Johann Huizinga was quite accurate when he labeled the human race *Homo ludens;* he extended this appellation from its usual meanings to a whole realm of seemingly practical endeavors—war, commerce, etc. But if humans play various games thoughout life, the question then intrudes: *Why* do they play these games? And this is the great deviation. Humans play these games for no practical reason. They are intrinsic to a search for symbolic meaning through the various paraphernalia of culture.

The gleeful playfulness of puppies and kittens is quickly subdued as the animal young attain sexual maturity. In their coming of age they become rigidified in their adult roles and the quest for survival. Human young engage in joyful games also, just as animals play, under the constraining supervision of the careful adult. In the symbolic worlds of human child rearing, however, no matter how lax parental discipline is, the child is still a product of the given state of things in the adult cultural world. In Freudian terms, the child has a parental and cultural superego attached to a budding sense of identity.

The state of dependency and the immersion of the child in a condition of unquestioning identification with the values of the adult societies begins to change with puberty. The drawn-out evolution of childhood and growth ends in a surge of development and surplus energy. The child's body and mind begin to be wracked by successive physiological, morphological, and psychological convulsions. The skills so painfully learned in childhood now become a prelude to a panorama of intellectual, artistic, and social possibilities. A sexual avalanche bursts outward to engulf the inexperienced youngster.

Social bars usually exist to restrain this flow of physical, sexual, and intellectual promise and channel it into social competencies. What the young need most is experience. In our own time the educational system has devised an even finer breakdown of the process to accommodate itself to these changes. The junior high school is an institution devoted to providing a few years of educational transition for those traversing the passage from childhood to young adulthood.

This passage is difficult in and of itself. And in many ways it is the most precarious; for during the years from twelve to fifteen, the child reaches full intellectual maturity. His brain comes of age. If it is trained well and the youngster remains receptive, its full utilization becomes a challenge as well as a self-satisfying means of playing the most exciting and enigmatic human game of all—intellectualization.

There is something prescient in ancient writers' casual disdain for childhood. It was depicted in sculpture and painting as a period of weakness and dependency to be gotten over with as soon as possible. Childhood was a precarious period in the life cycle. It was a time of limited powers. The joy was in adulthood or at least in manhood. Here the full flowering of the body's exuberant physical powers became manifest. Not only was the body a beautiful object, to be admired and artistically experienced, but it was suffused with sexual symbolism.

The surge of passion that constantly overwhelms the human being, so different from the abstract and impersonal drives of sexual periodicity in lower animals, is at first turned inward. As has been observed over and over again, this awful biological surge, in its authority over the individual's inner life, so contemptuous in its driving intensity of the authority of the outer world, partakes of an energy that is almost supernatural. All societies must surround this force with rules and attempt to tame it by prohibitions, rites, and moral admonitions. No society can resist the unleashed power latent in the combination of sexual excitation and physical exuberance that the young must know.

The raw nervous energy that is available to youth constitutes an element in explaining a variety of historically monstrous events: wars, crusades, revolutions, holocausts. These energies, geared to emotional symbols that destroy in the name of a cause, are representative of actions and enthusiasms that are often not fully under sober cognitive controls. In the more intimate neighborhood and familial setting, the young are often not fit to live with.

Yet it does not take deep perception to realize that these energies are not biologically aggressive in an instinctually destructive sense. True, youth is a time for bursting physical energies seeking symbolic social and cultural envisagement. These same energies are the stuff of creative socially responsible efforts, artistic production, the prodigious achievements and breakthroughs of young genius. So often we see these factors juxtaposed in one young person, passionately reckless and irresponsible at one moment, a demon of concentrated intellectual, athletic, or philanthropic efforts the next.

IDENTITY

During youth the mind expands and pulsates in newly found capacity and newly realized function. This period coincides with a qualitative transformation of the personality. Psychological identity, the capacity for introspection, a new creative dimension in one's interactions with the environment now evidences itself. The ego comes into being. It is a wrenching birth; accompanied as it is by intellectual, sexual, and physical powers heretofore not experienced or thought possible, the ego is turned and pulled by a diverse set of forces. The youngster attempts to cut loose from the childish past and make those necessary tentative steps in the direction of adulthood.

One of the classical conflicts of the young adult is an attempt to resolve the dilemma of the new "I" as against the older parental "I" of childhood. For the first time, the will to act is matched by the intellect's capacity to judge. Here, too, is the deep, almost bottomless awareness of the uniqueness of the self, where before there had existed only the inchoate and undeveloped "I" which aspired to adult support and sustenance.

It is important to emphasize that the new autonomy, self-awareness, and individual resoluteness that come out of the present ontogenetic stage are not impositions from the outside, not the stamp of an external form on a waxen tabula rasa. The creation of the sapient ego is a growth from within to be attributed structurally to those fundamental changes that our species has fallen heir to. And it is to this rather than to any other factor that we must locate the development of cultural and symbolic reality. Not only do human beings perceive and feel vast areas of significance, but they objectify what they perceive into a churning deluge of symbols, of words and dreams, of fantasies and aesthetic images, erotic and intellectual possibilities all externalized and presented to human consciousness in some symbolic image or word.

Identity presupposes the existence of a form of inner speech. The individual must, however, cope with external situations. This innerness translates itself into behaviors that we perceive as autonomous. In the interaction between that inner awareness of a unique self and the external means by which this self is expressed and molded by events evolves personality. There is thus a reciprocity between the individual, his or her inner subjectivity and the social world of language and institutional patterns of behavior. Without the external world the internal symbolic drives will fritter themselves away in chaotic physical and mental spasms.

No society takes the raw given of youth and absorbs it immediately into the adult society. To an extent all societies allow a time for the mellowing and shaping of this powerful innovative force. In advanced societies, where innovation is at a premium and is expected, space and time for experimentation are allowed. Here the forms which the society presents to the young in all their implacable rigidity will be subject to the enormously powerful transmuting impulses of the energetic young. No aspect of the culture—aesthetic, social, linguistic, or moral—is too persistent to withstand the surge of innovation of the young. The more naive and enthusiastic the generation, the more forceful the social results.

The buffer constituted by the peer group, which for a number of years will provide a psychosocial outlet for the individual, and personal expression by the young of their inner dreams and thoughts, can even constitute a means for making permanent these possible cultural changes. The peer group is both conservative and innovative. With their own age mates, the young begin to practice these adult virtues that they must one day put into play in the rough and tumble of multiaged society at large. The beginnings of sexual experimentation—friendship and individuality, competition and cooperation, leadership and social responsibility—all become vital factors in this intermediate period of learning, a period that transcends the boundaries of the school.

Erik Erikson, in *Identity and the Life Cycle,* has aptly summarized the importance of this period of apparent limbo for the young:

> . . . identity, in outbalancing at the conclusion of childhood the potentially malignant dominance of the infantile superego, permits the individual to forgo excessive self-repudiation and the diffused repudiation of otherness. Such freedom provides a necessary condition for the ego's power to integrate matured sexuality, ripened capacities, and adult commitments. The histories of our young patients illustrate the ways in which aggravated identity crises may result from special genetic causes and throw new light on those more or less institutionalized rites and rituals, associations, and movements through which societies and subsocieties grant youth a world between childhood and adulthood: a psycho-social moratorium during

which extremes of subjective experience, alternatives of ideological choice, and potentialities of realistic commitment can become the subject of social play and of joint mastery.[3]

Complex societies have created formal institutional means by which this moratorium can be observed while allowing the individual to maintain the dynamic tension that is the cornerstone of social change. Much of the paradox and perplexity of human existence is bound up in the attempted balancing of the deeply individualistic bent that resides in the heartland of ego identity (the self) and the social context in which individuation must flower in order even to become aware of itself. Between the recognition of the "I" and the realization that the "I" needs the outside world—if even to shut it out so as to become a recluse or a hermit—lies much of the mysterious ferment that besets the young in all complex, evolving cultures. Certainly simple socieites, having perfected the institutional means not for facilitating this social moratorium but for eliminating it, need to foreclose individual expression, so as to dry up any personal behavior that might create instability. An alternative route that the simple society plies is to channel innovative energies into highly stylized and stereotyped patterns of ritual behavior.

PERSONALITY

An interesting paradox lies at the heart of the general problem of personal identity. It relates to the widely recognized fact that individuation—personality—has been most highly developed in the Western world; indeed, it is a product of Western civilization. There seems to be a symbiotic relationship between the potentiality of realizing what is deeply embedded inside each individual, his or her capabilities for thinking and feeling and creating, and the character of the society within which the individual lives.

Even the awful anomie, aloneness, and psychological disorientation that arise in our own time as a widespread individual phenomenon are products of the interaction of individual persons and a certain kind of mass industrial society. We have liberated individuals from their embeddedness in society. As historic roots have been severed, the individual now drifts apart from society—and suffers as a consequence.

The depth of personal awareness, even consciousness, that hu-

3. Erik Erikson, *Identity and the Life Cycle* (New York: International Universities Press, 1959), p. 164.

man beings have attained cannot be effaced by any modern society. No totalitarianism, whether communist or fascist, can ever completely extinguish the flicker of private intuition and experience. As long as there is light somewhere, it gives off its glow to those denied their full measure of opportunity.

The primitive individual, however, is alone, cut off from this self-consciousness by a social system that reflects his or her own poorly realized capacities. The primitive's limited palette of social life is both cause and product of the lack of an identity that is dynamically charged with different facets and dimensions.

Even though he may be a product of a higher culture, the hermit or ascetic going off by himself to "contemplate his navel" falls short of what we would consider the development or expression of deep personality. Individuality is the product of the impact of one's uniqueness in the interaction with others in one's own culture. True, there are great strains in this dualism between person and society. One understandably rails against the fact that in order to be oneself to the fullest one must have an external life. And sometimes the world outside is not what we would prefer. This natural tension is also productive, as is shown by the lives and writings of such as Socrates, Buddha, Marcus Aurelius, Saint Augustine.

THE INDIVIDUAL AND SOCIAL COMMITMENT

A society rarely breaks down to the extent of losing the allegiance of its young. It is even rarer for a society that still functions to lose this support. As philosophically stagnant and as socially inert as is our society, a national dynamic still exists that allows it to draw the young into its tantalizing net, to challenge their energies even if to frustrate their idealism.

Mental or physical work allows us to explore our sense of mastery and competence. Often work can ameliorate the emptiness in our social and personal existence. Except for the zealous few who are consumed by revolutionary ardor, we find it necessary to come in from the cold and be as socially useful as possible.

Examining our welfare system, some wonder if the will to work exists. Yet it is surely merely the application of misguided philanthropy that makes it socially profitable to be on the dole rather than on the work force. The healthy personality needs and wants to be involved in a task that releases his or her intelligence and energies.

We would argue, agreeing with the existentialists, that while there is a core of individuation that makes each person intrinsically different from the next, this essence cannot be known abstractly. Within each of us is a kernel of various possibilities. Can a young man of eighteen know what he is and can do? Indeed, can he predict what the full flowering of his personality will produce as an acting individual given the various vocational choices he might make?

To youth, the sense of "I" is still undeveloped, even though there may be momentary heights of self-consciousness and intensity. One might see this period of life as a time when gates are opened for the realization of possibility. But no one can know where this ego will ultimately lead in a youth who does not have socially relevant responsibilities upon which to cast personal efforts and initiative. The powers of the mind and the imagination need acceptable social activity to find fruition. But work must be generative of human possibilities and not dull, stupefying, and unacceptable for objective moral or personal reasons, like that offered by much of the nineteenth-century factory system.

Again we emphasize how completely interwoven are those elements of individual uniqueness and social or external realization, elements which must forever be held in a dynamic balance. Otherwise the individual must face the possibility of dissolving into one or another of the extremes, losing the full flavor of what it means to be a whole human being.

No wonder societies have found it necessary in this elongated process of growth and maturity to give youth an extra measure of anonymity, privacy, a few years of experimentation out of the full glare of either parental or communal superego. In these unique ontogenetic moments the young can possibly find their diverse combinations and commitments.

IDEALITY

Arching over the entire educational and maturational process is a highly abstract yet nonetheless crucial dimension of coming of age. This is what has been called "ideality." The concept has been expressed as follows: "If one has not been at least for a moment, a communist, by the time one is 25, one has no heart. If one is still a communist by the time they are 35 they have no mind." The ubiquity with which the sense of the ideal is found in the young points to a factor that is hard to explain. There is a sense of global identity, an extreme sensitivity to the future in terms of perfectability as well as an easily engaged altruism. One might attribute this excitement to moral energy. At the same time it is worth noting that the greatest social excrescences have been generated by the zealous young.

Perhaps we have here the ideational side of that experimental coin, of which the other is physical play. It is possible that the powerful surge toward an altruistic ideal and a combination of intellectual fascination, moral-social commitment, and physical zest is the product of the human being's unique ontogeny of cultural renewal. Ideality is the concrete means by which the new bursts upon the scene with an inevitability that is the expression of generational renewal itself.

In its highest form the sense of ideality is also reflective of a philosophical bent, the human capacity to abstract, analyze, and synthesize experience into new interpretations. These constitute a means by which the evolving society can understand itself. Out of the dislocation of the present, philosophical thought can obtain for us a means by which we can understand, order, and stabilize the oncoming future. Philosophical thought brings into being for this purpose the social agencies, including formal education. It harmonizes with the drive of the young to accommodate themselves to the future. Often, philosophies are turned into simplistic ideologies by the young. Great youth communities such as the universities serve this function well. They become a direct means by which social change can be effected.

The function of philosophical thought and ideological activism is to bring society to a new level of stability and integration. The intellectual aspects are usually taken up by the young as a practical means of effecting the changes necessary in the existent state of society. The young can just as easily choose erroneous or vicious philosophies. Their sense of ideality is no test of the ultimate rationality inherent in their moral and philosophical choices. Great power for good or evil lies in the pragmatic efficacy of those historic institutions that have been established to cultivate reason. The young come to them at the very moment in the life cycle when their enthusiasms and passions run deepest.

CONCLUSION

We can note the factors that are critical in creating the "problem" and dilemmas of youth. Childhood and youth serve the higher forms of life by allowing the expression of a diverse set of behaviors that represent the wider possibilities of the species. This can be thought of as constituting a preadaptation for innovative and/or future responses. The behavior of youth symbolizes this cultural sense of possibility, since youthful experimentations are already suffused with the habits and patterns of their society. The infant even in the earliest months begins to laugh, loll, and babble; experimenting with sounds that in their full range provide the oral grist for every language that has existed, does or can exist. What happens is that each society reinforces certain sound combinations and ignores others. The infant gradually reproduces those sounds heard most often; the others fall into disuse and this spontaneous linguistic sense slowly diminishes. The residue is the conventional language.

What is natural to the human being in terms of youthful or adolescent awareness, creativity, and privacy does not have to find its expression in the culture. Any one society can ignore much of the possibilities in human nature. Thus the babbling infant is still to a great extent "with nature" and protected by its undeveloped state from the extreme social conditioning that the adolescent must undergo. The adolescent, on the other hand, is far more vulnerable to the blandishments of culture.

The fragility of primitive society is indicated by its rigidity of patterning, its isolation and lack of evolutionary gusto. This necessitates a wholly different approach to youth. No one would argue that the primitive pattern is, indeed, truly conscious and objectified, a set of decisions made in terms of logical necessity. Rather, it constitutes an implicit, a covert pattern taken in terms of cultural needs that lie below the surface of apprehension. The process of coming of age is tied securely into a nexus of social relationships by very specific and stereotyped rituals and institutions. These relationships are often clearly extended in time into maturity and after, much as are our college class homecomings.

The personal and value commitments that the primitive young make through their kinship associations at an early age are held throughout adult life. Those age-group institutions of tribal society serve to take youth from the years of turmoil and revolt safely onto the high road of adult responsibility. The result will be the stabilization of tribal society, securing it from possible revolutionary dislocations that might jar it from its precarious balance with nature as well as its neighbors.

But there is also a negative element. Much of the possible vitality, experimentation, and innovation that might have been exhibited by the young, were there a realm of second-chance experimentation, has been cauterized. The opportunities for the society to take advantage of situations for change and development have also been reduced significantly. It is the young who so often see new possibilities and have the initiative and passion to try to effect this change. The rigid social structure of tribal society binds the young tightly to institutionalized rituals of growing up. Beyond these associations they do not think to gaze.[4]

While the young in recent historic societies are never beyond the reins of the existing social order, the independence and special nature of the time of youth are recognized and accounted for. It is a period of potential renewal and growth for the society at large. In those deep reservoirs of personality and innovation which the growth of the adult ego makes possible lies a whole series of social, historical, and cultural renovations and allegiances. Indeed, one might argue that for many, the time of youth is a period when one learns the potentially unquenchable characteristics of the creative, ludic thrust which civilization itself makes possible: in athletics, politics, the arts, and scientific and intellectual creativity.

Illustrating this point is S. N. Eisenstadt:

> At the same time, however it is clear that such a system [differentiated, modern societies] involves a much stronger element of change, and perhaps even of instability, than those systems in which transmission of the social heritage is effected through rigid role prescriptions. Thus age groups also become foci of potential deviancy and change, and the borderline between change and instability is very fine. The lack of any rigid prescription of roles, of any clear definition of the roles of youth by adults in modern societies, necessarily makes youth groups one of the most important channels through which the numerous changes of modern societies take place and sometimes develops them into channels of outright rebellion and deviance. The crucial importance of age relations in all societies and of age groups in all universalistic societies is clearly seen in the fact that the smooth transmission of social heritage, various attempts at change and various manifestations of discontinuity are largely, even if not wholly, effected through them.[5]

4. See S. N. Eisenstadt, *From Generation to Generation* (Glencoe, Ill.: Free Press, 1956).
5. Ibid., pp. 322–23.

11 Youth and the Contemporary Educational Crisis

The "youth problem" as we perceive it today is in part a dimension of the larger cultural crisis, made poignant by the impact that this crisis makes on the young. In theory, as long as the lines of historical and social change are clearly delineated, there ought to be no disturbance or extraordinary ferment in the young. One can expect, however, that in periods of cloudy philosophical assumptions a disoriented generation of youngsters will transfer their malaise to that institutional setting most specifically responsible for the care of the future and the young—formal education.

Thus the travail is transferred from one aspect of society to another. In turn, the impact on the schools is cause for an increasing lack of confidence by the society in its institutions, values, and destiny. By our basic definition, formal education is that aspect of a civilization's institutional commitment to a philosophy of self-renewal, change, and idealization. When formal education fails to absorb the interests, ideals, and energies of the young, it is inevitable that the young will turn first to the educational institutions where their unhappiness is most concretely articulated and attempt to kick in the whole enterprise.

The young have had a decade of turmoil. There may be subsequent periods of quiescence, intervals of dispirited analysis and stock taking; still there is no general agreement upon a perspective that will explain the recent ferment. What does occur is the ready invoking of such value judgments as will make either society or the aged the villains, and the young, heroes. Or else the young will be labeled pampered and spoiled ingrates for rejecting a largesse, the extent of which no society heretofore has been able to present to any particular generation.

This type of approach, which is almost a synopsis of those perplexing contemporary events, does a disservice to understanding.

Our problem goes much deeper than the agitation of the young, right or wrong. As we have attempted to show, it is part of a process whereby our country has reached and now confronts a watershed in its evolution.

THE SENSE OF IDEAL

The United States and the other nations of the Western world entered into the process of industrialization and modernization 150 years ago. During this time of increasing social change, the cultural dynamics were such as to leave no room in the minds of the new generation for valuational ambiguity. Scientific truths were an unimpeachable source of knowledge; they stabilized our conception of truth. They undergirded the increasing scope and pace of industrialization and the social instability that was its consequence.

Contemporaneous with this process was the gradual withdrawal of the religious philosophies and institutions from their role in the forefront of directing the ideals and content of formal education. It was obvious that the necessities of modernization were dictated by scientific and empirical considerations that could not be touched by the religious beliefs of the past. Gradually we find organized religion playing its main role in the background realm of the informal culture: in the family and in community ritual in those cities and towns where the sense of tradition was still held to with nostalgic tenacity (see chapter 7).

At this point the young could still obtain a clear perspective of this world in the making. The systems of public elementary and secondary education and the growing college and university systems symbolized the institutional means by which the young of diverse backgrounds could acquire the knowledge, disciplines, and attitudes by which they could don the raiments of authority in the new society. Moving on in time, as the enfranchisements of blacks and of women and the protection of children and the laboring classes proceeded, great confidence was expressed in the unlimited potentiality for good in the democratic political forms. Equality of opportunity and the tangible educational institutional exemplification of this ideal plus the widening diffusion of new professions and vocations were exciting possibilities to each successive wave of American youngsters, native as well as foreign born.

The technological fallout from World War II effected an enormous expansion of the economy, which resulted in the middle classification of the majority of our population. These had their impact on our educational expectations–the burgeoning of the universities, the modernization of the public schools, and the geometric increase in spending for all aspects of the educational enterprise. Inevitably, as noted earlier, equality of opportunity was translated into a quest for equality of achievement. No longer was a high school diploma the ultimate aim. Now everyone had to go through the collegiate system to satisfy the credentialist ideals generated.

But as part of the mechanics of educational processing of these many millions, an ethos was created of American achievement, leadership, and altruism that drew both from the obvious and tangible successes of the system and from the reservoir of historic American goodwill that had accrued to our nation. In no small way, the American achievement in World War II was the capstone of its leadership role. We were the leading power in the world as a consequence of World War II. We were also the power that epitomized the spirit of the free world.

The crisis of institutions and morale that developed in the 1960s, both with regard to international and domestic affairs, shattered the euphoria. And it was more than a temporary mote in the eye of a giant who would drive invincibly forward. The problems were more basic: overpopulation, an unabsorbable lower class, pollution, an exhausted consumerism. All these factors seem to have transformed to dry grist the rhetorical ideals that had been taught to the young.

CONFLICT OF GENERATIONS?

There have been innumerable political, sociological, and moralistic explanations of the youth revolt. Of the more interesting, Lewis Feuer's *The Conflict of Generations* was an in-depth study of the concept of "de-authorization." Feuer's thesis was that, for a variety of reasons, the older generation had been contaminated by the general state of social disarray. The older generation had brought about the current and apparently insoluble problems and in doing so had revealed and exposed the perennial tensions underlying the conflict of generations. "As we have seen, a struggle of generations, in and of itself, however, will not give rise to a massive student movement. What is always required, in addition, is some signal event in which the de-authorization of the older generation as a collective whole, is vividly dramatized."[1]

1. Lewis Feuer, *The Conflict of Generations* (New York: Basic Books, 1969), p. 184.

The problem with the theory of "de-authorization," as Jack D. Douglas has noted, is that while it recognizes all the symptoms of generational hate and conflict, it does not clarify the process by which de-authorization takes place.[2] The revolts on the campus were directed at the most successful institutions and individuals. In theory, this process ought to be directed at those who had failed their children. Says Douglas:

> Yet it couldn't be their fathers in general, since Feuer knows as well as anyone else that their fathers were very generally successful men, not lonely failures skulking around skidrow. Their fathers were often significant participants in the machinery of the most powerful nation in the history of the world, men of financial success in the most wealthy nation in the world, men of power in a mighty nation that had won two world wars and innumerable little ones, men who could be heard in a nation that could destroy the world. What could these men or the faculty and administration at Berkeley possibly have in common in the way of collective "unmanliness," failure, "effeminancy," and "demeaning poverty." [3]

These factors were typical of generational conflict in older historical traditions. There is no question of the revolt of a segment of youth against the values and status of the older generation today—it is epitomized in the phrase "don't trust anyone over thirty." But the "why" of de-authorization remains unanswered. Douglas argues,

> ... the fundamental problem is precisely that of specifying why they no longer are willing to accept the authority of the older generation. Why, for example, do they choose one kind of group or standard in terms of which they judge their fathers and the collective older generation rather than another group or standard? Why do they see them as failures or successes? [4]

These are important questions which the theory of de-authorization does not illumine. Nevertheless, a disenchantment with the institutions of the adult culture has taken place. The clash between the rhetoric of liberalism and the reality that liberalism has brought about has to be confronted. But can we take at face value youth's overt expression of revulsion for their society?

2. J. D. Douglas, *Youth in Turmoil* (Rockville, Md.: National Institute of Mental Health Center for Studies of Crime and Delinquency, 1970).
3. Ibid., p. 122.
4. Ibid.

Charles Frankel saw the actuality of the youth revolt as the acting out of a long tradition in "liberal culture," which in looking forward to the future transformed the inevitable conflict of generations in dynamic periods into a philosophy of youthful rectitude. The liberal culture "would like to believe that if the old only did things right there would be no conflicts.[5]

> In our novels and plays, in our educational philosophy, in our psychoanalytic theories, the adult is regularly cast in the role of villain. He is always the enemy of youthful honesty and natural instincts, always the opponent of that process of purification and resurrection which it is the eternal role of youth to bring about. Even when he is presented sympathetically, it is in the role of slow-learner.[6]

It is natural to a society hurtling forward in social change to put all its emotional and intellectual eggs in the youth basket. The youth will inevitably inherit a world that is far different than their fathers'. Is it difficult to understand why the old ways and values should appear obsolete and reactionary and the attitudes of the young attuned to the "natural," the "honest?"

What has happened in our time has a new twist. The young have now come along just as the wave of progress has hit unexpected shoals. Instead of higher and faster, the entire élan of progress and change has encountered some realities that reveal the stark character of the path we have been following.

The person inured to a diet of a few bowlsful of rice per day will react with elation and anticipation at the prospect of the addition of a bit of fish and some vegetables. For the poor, a glimmer of improvement in the future is enough to elicit hope, striving, and altruism, as long as the results come near to fulfilling expectations. To those highly educated middle-class young who have seen their parents climb to unexpected pinnacles of success, and who are the pampered inheritors of this largesse, the future has a different cast. They are consigned to doing more of what has already been done. The unlimited horizons of their parents have been suddenly partially foreclosed.

But there is an even greater exacerbating factor. The very values by which one measures the ideals and canons of authority in our

---

5. Charles Frankel, *Education and the Barricades* (New York: W. W. Norton, 1968), pp. 16–17.
6. Ibid.

society have been called into question. One does not easily criticize that which is successful. Even in the not too distant past, one could find just as blatant examples of social irresponsibility and a corruption that pointed even into the educational establishment, where institution building and power brokering were not uncommon.

Today, when the dynamic of the society has been brought to a grinding halt, these failings are much more difficult to handle. Now we see the contours more clearly, not only of the society we have created but also of the problems of basic self-maintenance that face us in the future. The philosophy of growth, production and consumption, and profit, the assimilationist and centralist ideals which propelled us, have created a cultural miasma. The irony is that we have no alternative philosophical vision for which we have any realistic hope of countering it. Marxism has produced its own social cancer. The guerrilla philosophies of Che Guevara or simplistic Maoism constituted only momentary and dreamlike infatuations for the young.

Formal education, which has been implicated in our institutional structure, is now absorbed by the managerial ideals of growth, bigness, and "social service." It can offer little in the way of an alternative set of ideals or as a setting in which new philosophical visions can be created. The American educational system has inextricably implicated itself in the cultural trends of the last generation. Now that the "bridge" to the future has fallen short of its mark, it can offer no further guidance until a new integration of values gains enough consensus to mobilize our intellectual and social energies.

Thus the morale problems of the young cannot be attributed to an inherent failing in the young or in their tainted, if successful, fathers. The acts of agitation and outrage they have committed are the consequences of a more abstract, yet concrete, failure in our social and educational system. This system has jetted to its success on the ongoing élan of a social system that has outspanned every goal it has set for itself. The rising expectations of social success have been linked to intellectual and educational foundations that have fanned the fervor of achievement into our own day.

We have now run into obstacles and problems not external to our impetus, but dredged up out of the core of these spurious attainments. As a result our philosophical ideals now sound like empty slogans. There is no longer social payoff, only pain. The young have arrived on the scene at the height of our educational hubris, and they are disappointed. The ferment we see around us, even the inevitable apathy and inertia that must be its successor, constitutes the source of our difficulties. Formal education in America, by closely enmeshing itself in the ideals of the society at one stage in its evolution, has become mired in a past that appears to have no future. It has thereby failed the new generation.

SOCIAL COMPETENCY

Eventually everyone must work, even the young. In the past, nations geared themselves to developing the talents of the best and the brightest. The highest abilities and skills were needed not only for the competitive race within each nation but in the international arena as well. No nation could afford incompetency. In a period when the leading edge of change far outran the available pool of skilled manpower, there was an added premium on highly educated, flexible, and skilled individuals.

Until recently, there was a magic in education and one's chosen vocation or profession that was its consequence. No one could predict the outcome of any career, what with the changing rate of progress in knowledge and in social complexity. Each generation was brought to the starting gate, so to speak, brimming over with impatience and enthusiasm to show their mettle, to outdistance or outspan the achievements of their elders.

But what happens when progress slows down and society is "full up" with those skills that were once so necessary to have, and necessary in expanding degrees? This situation parallels the problem of idealization. As the society slows down, values tend to become muddled and paradoxical. Jobs are no longer as plentiful. It takes time for educational institutions to react to this fact. The process of population equilibration also takes time.

Even more confusing, many vocations have become tainted in the eyes of today's young. Lawyers are ambulance chasers and Watergate conspirators, medical doctors refuse to visit patients at night or treat the poor, chemists make napalm, professors engage in grantsmanship, teachers strike against the children.

Thus, on the simple criteria of unquestioned utility, emphasizing human capacities, and honor, there are not enough worthy jobs in our economy for average boys and adolescents to grow up toward. There are of course thousands of jobs that are worthy and self-satisfying, and thousands that can be made so by stubborn integrity, especially if one can work as an independent. Extraordinary intelligence or special talent, also, can often carve out a place for itself—conversely, their usual corruption and waste are all the more sickening. But by and large our economic society is *not* geared for the cultivation of its young or the attainment of important goals that they can work toward.[7]

The young face a work situation in society that is exacerbated by the current structure of formal education. Historically, extending the schooling period so far into the mature years is unprecedented. We think nothing of having individuals attend schools from age three to twenty-three, with perhaps another ten years tacked on for graduate study.

This process of extending schooling can be understood and accepted in the context of the recent increase in knowledge and the resulting discrepancy between the most advanced parts of our society, the professions (in terms of education), and the agricultural and urban poor in the populace. The schools needed more time to teach new skills. (One could not even predict what skills would be necessary or available from one decade to another.) The extension of time spent in formal schooling could be seen as a kind of institutional and educational readiness. Not too long ago, it was not unusual for individuals to change career objectives a number of times before actually committing themselves and with good success possibilities even in their late twenties or early thirties.

But that institutional situation is over. What was once an educational virtue carved out of social necessity is now a liability. James Coleman has stated it this way:

> This transformation of the schools in response to society has had a consequence that is important in considering the path to becoming adult. This is the massive enlargement of the "student" role of young persons to fill the vacuum that the changes in the family and work place created. The student role of young persons has become enlarged to the point where that role constitutes the major portion of their youth. But the student role is not a role of taking action and experiencing consequences. It is not a role by which one learns by hard knocks. It is a relatively passive role, always in preparation for action, but never acting. . . . The consequences of the expansion of the student role, and the action-poverty it implies for the young, has been an

7. Paul Goodman, *Growing Up Absurd* (New York: Random House, 1960), pp. 28-29.

increased restiveness among the young. They are shielded from responsibility, and they become irresponsible; they are held in a dependent status, and they come to act as dependents; they are kept away from productive work, and they become unproductive. . . .[8]

This extension of student life is not bad in and of itself, if long-range vocational goals are to be fulfilled and the young feel that they are preparing for a useful life and a solid measure of social competency. When formal education begins to fail in this endeavor, however, the schools begin to experience the turmoil that has been their fate recently.

Perhaps the most demoralizing aspect of the educational process and its relationship to achievement in the adult world has been the transformation of undergraduate education. American education, in expanding the base for undergraduate training, was pursuing a basically altruistic ideal. The benefits of a liberal arts education were to be extended to all who might be interested and able and who would profit themselves and society by undergoing such an experience. As an ideal it was good, but as a reality it evoked certain discontinuities. As the colleges opened their gates and the masses flooded in, the quality control inevitably suffered. And as students poured forth from the colleges and universities, the B.A. degree itself, representing good, bad, and indifferent training, began to be the basic coinage of a new credentialism that gradually supplanted the high school diploma as a key to civil-service, white-collar, or even semiskilled vocations.

The next step had to come. Whereas in the beginning many liberal arts colleges and universities attempted to maintain some standard of competency within their institutions, the pressures to let down all standards were inevitable. The need for the bachelor's degree as the admission ticket for a job began to transfer the old adage of "equality of opportunity" to "equality of achievement."

The net result of the dissolution of standards has been to make the young cynical of the entire collegiate process of certification and by implication that of the high schools below and the graduate schools above. In the case of the bachelor and graduate degrees, it is likely that as the easy flow into suitable jobs is increasingly impeded there will be greater self-selection by students attending appropriate

8. James Coleman, *What Is Career Education?* (Washington, D.C.: Council for Basic Education, 1973), p. 6.

institutions. Much depends on society's willingness to eliminate artificial academic criteria for job certification.[9]

It is probably healthier for the young, indeed for all of us, for there to be a shortage of positions. A certain amount of built-in competition, using "real" criteria, is necessary for society. It is more natural for human beings to have circumscribed limits on many of their actions in order for them to focus their energies on specific and economic goals. The indolent way students were able to move in and out of society in the recent past, taking and leaving jobs, always knowing that there would be a fourth chance, a sixth, maybe even a tenth, was psychologically and socially pathological.

It would be helpful if the positions in the world were clearly marked in terms of necessary skills. Further, those courses of study, e.g., certain specialized degrees, must be functional in terms of the objective. It is not a dysfunctional requirement for doctors, engineers, and teachers to be well versed in the historical, philosophical, and moral dimensions of their trades. In contrast, one can argue, for example, that it is fairly irrelevant that a teller in a bank have a master's degree in business administration or a telephone operator have a B.A.

Certainly in the future it will be necessary at some stage in the long educational hegira to introduce breaks in the purely classroom phrase. A society increasingly technologized and meritocratic in structure will hardly need fewer skills from its members. And merely shortening the process of education will not effectively free us from the current problems without adding new, if varying, difficulties. What will have to be planned is a closer correlation with life, more opportunities for service to the community, increasing respect by young and old for the complexities of decision making in the context of earning one's living. This can be done only by putting those "pampered ones" for a time in jobs that their background might ordinarily exclude from their experience. They might even learn to appreciate what it means to work with one's body. In some societies, e.g., Israel, the army serves to promote more adult and responsible behavior. In our society, a different stratagem might be necessary.

The current agitation and often sudden indifference among the young in terms of work, self-discipline, and commitment are probably passing phenomena. The situation has been brought to a head by the concurrence of a number of factors: (1) demographically

9. See Sheilla Huff, "Credentialing by Tests or Degrees: Title VII of the Civil Rights Act and Griggs v. Duke Power Company," *Harvard Educational Review* 44, no. 2 (May 1974).

disproportionate number of young; (2) sudden contraction of opportunities; (3) philosophical disenchantment with a great range of vocations and professions; (4) the slowing down of creative progress in a great variety of arts, sciences, and professions; and (5) a persisting state of affluence for many young.

The realization will soon come that vast and critical concerns in our world need attention. For the young to exhibit the élan, altruism, and commitment necessary to confront those concerns depends on the development of a real and positive set of ideals, of a philosophical envisagement of the future.

One can be persuaded to pick up the shattered remains of a destroyed edifice—the bricks, wood, and glass. But after one sweeps up and carts away the debris, the next step is critical. One needs a sense of future, a galvanizing of optimistic energies to go about the planning and construction of a new building.

There is much work to be done for which education is vital. But until one sees at least the faint outlines of a positive, even a utopian, future—beyond cleaning up the refuse of the past—it will take much persuading to generate the necessary energies.

IDENTITY AND INFORMAL EDUCATION

The themes of identity loss and the onset of alienation intrude repeatedly in the educational literature. Some see them as the key problem of modern, mass technological societies. Women, blacks, ethnics, and the young search to rediscover their identities. What is identity and why is it so important?

As we noted in chapter 10, the attainment of personal identity coincides with the maturation of the person and the individual's emancipation from the guidance of the parental superego. Henceforth, one feels one's own personal individuality in a way that is unique—distinct from one's peers. One is now free to choose and will be held responsible for those choices, a situation different from that when the child was under the absorptive hegemony of the family.

In the process of exploring our own personal depths, of discovering who we are and what we can do and think, we in essence attain that special capability that marks us as human beings. No other animal can feel as distinctly or think as widely and deeply, or experience in the way that each human creature is capable of doing. No external power, whether our biological needs or the coercions of a society, can henceforth claim suzerainty over our minds and hearts unless we so will it.

But we are social beings as well. We cannot express our individuality or our sense of personal identity unless we have the social means to do so. Our sense of person depends on language and the cultural symbols of the society in which we are nurtured. So what we are constitutes a lifelong dialogue between our special idiosyncratic personal identity and the various forms of education that attempt to bend us as much as possible to fit the norms of the culture in which we are bred.

In our own time the terms on which the identities of selfhood and society have interacted have undergone extraordinarily rapid alterations. In the nineteenth and early twentieth centuries, in spite of great social mobility, modernization, and alterations in living styles, a sense of place existed with which Americans could identify. Home, whether in a small town or on the farm, was a place where one could return. There one's history, community of friends and relations, religiosity, and even ethnicity could be seen and identified with. Even though one chose the city and startlingly new professions, an underlying sense of connectedness existed between past and present.

For a few decades, the school maintained and even symbolized this connectedness. Today, no one can argue that the recent cast of public education in the United States has been oriented to protect the values of historical tradition and local community life. On the contrary, formal education in the United States has been geared to the modernization and, implicitly, the homogenization of urban life in the context of a technology that is undergirded by huge trans-national corporate and governmental institutions and a consumer-ism upon which our prosperity depends and which seeps into and conditions every nook and cranny of our culture.

The enormously rapid growth of our economic and social structure and the changes attendant to the face of American life, the way we live, marry, and divorce, sleep in the suburbs, work in the cities, vacation and entertain ourselves, all point in one direction socially—toward transiency, impermanence, and novelty.[10] The young have absorbed this message in the baby food they eat and the diapers they wear. The past is no longer relevant in terms of personal identity. An entire generation of affluent middle-class Americans has soared out of this past and created for itself the life styles

10. Alvin Toffler, *Future Shock* (New York: Random House, 1970).

that substitute, for the moment, for those older personal meanings.[11]

Freedom from these traditional psychological encumbrances has proceeded apace, any sectarian or conservative resistance to modernity having been flattened by means of the law, whether the resistance consisted of literary or film censorship, blue laws, laws affecting sexual relationships, or even school practices that do not contain the principle of the lowest and widest common denominator—in curriculum, texts, holiday celebrations, etc. So rapidly have we been progressing that we simultaneously stand at the pinnacle of material affluence while before us gapes the abyss wherein all our outstanding bills will come due: pollution, ecological destruction, exhaustion of natural resources, psychosocial consequences of urbanization, overpopulation, etc. And all around us is the affluent revolution in personal morality and family structure. The consequences of these conflicting dynamics are at present as ambiguous as are our solutions.

That we cannot know the future is a generally accepted aspect of the ambiguity of life. Ordinarily we hope for the best. In times of decline or social stagnancy our anxieties are heightened to the degree that we plan conservatively for limited goals. The current concern for the fate of family and community life and for the mental health as well as the vocational future of the young is an outgrowth of our dilemma. We worry not so much because of an existential concern for our historical fate but because we feel impotent to act, to cast ourselves off dead center, and to become factors in pursuit of our destiny.

But we cannot hope to gain control over events until we understand our predicament. Rational control must precede social control. This lack of an intellectual center invites the young into nihilism and anarchy. A few of our recent educational radicals have now begun to recognize this situation. Writers such as Jonathan Kozol, in probing beyond the overt symptoms of our educational crisis and into the causes themselves, now see the responses of our revolutionary youth as an element and symptom of the crisis and not as a solution.

> . . . . [the young] read Ivan Illich or go off to Mexico to meet him; they come home and report to the parents of poor children that "school" as an effective concept is outdated, square, archaic. They read John Holt, and they report to the mothers

---

11. David Potter, *People of Plenty* (Chicago: University of Chicago Press, 1954).

and fathers of their students that you can't "teach" formal skills in any case, so we should not waste time even in trying. They read Charles Silberman and they report to their coworkers that "joy" and "joylessness" are the only words we need to think about or use in our discussions and our disputations. No need, to them, to be troubled about books or math materials or the building code. . . .[12]

CONCLUSION

The source of our identity crisis springs from the dissolution of the traditional relational bonds between formal and informal culture. A yawning gap exists in these private and intimate areas of social life where there ought to be a realm of rich, serene, and personally meaningful cultural symbolism. Formal education along with the larger apparatus of institutional America has been complicit in this trend. By making it impossible for the development of moral and cultural alternative value systems, both in education and community life, we have with premeditation undermined the religiosity, ethnicity, and cultural voluntarism upon which informal education rests.

The youth problem, in that it encompasses a crisis of intellect and idealism, work and vocationalism, as well as the perennial needs of identity, is thus only exacerbated by the immense gap in the informal area. Other nations that have gone through cataclysmic revolutions—France in 1789, Russia in 1917, China in 1949—had living and viable informal traditions that served not only as an area of succor, refuge, and continuity, but also as the root source of the hope for regeneration. A new formal ideal of education, in order to succeed, has not only to persuade people intellectually and philosophically, it must also exploit and release for use in their lives that rich lode of symbolic associations that lies closest to their intimate feelings.

The legitimacy of any political system rests on its ability to utilize and at the same time free the deepest dimensions of cultural life so that it can evolve in terms of its own intrinsic rhythms and pulsations. The Soviets used this factor against the German invaders in World War II when they appealed to the love of motherland and the echoes of history, tradition, and ethnicity to repel the outsider. Otherwise they have waged a continuous and

12. Jonathan Kozol, "Moving On to Nowhere," *Saturday Review,* 9 December 1972, p. 50.

unrelenting war of attrition against the older tradition. They have of course had important successes. But even more interesting and instructive has been the silent obstinacy to the continuous overt repression, an inner hostility and stagnancy in Soviet society that even the most externally patriotic citizens are not unaware of in themselves. For the young Russian, life is brutish and dulling. His mind is emasculated by inert educational propaganda. His inner life is entangled in impotent resentment.

Our own responsibility toward the future is to look for new and creative intellectual openings in education. At the same time we need to heal a wound and regenerate the forms of informal education. The healing and growth can take place naturally and without the need for external intrusions. For the society as a whole, the mark of improvement will be seen in our national optimism. As our people begin to see that it is possible through reason and will to affect their future, they will take it into their hands.

Our present world was created first by a unique philosophical and scientific vision of nature and humanity. It led to an epochal social transformation. In the process of achieving modernity many of the old meanings and cultural traditions that had been established through the contextual interactions of people were effaced. The old informal tradition has been swept aside with only the most superficial replacements—such as mass entertainments—substituting for humane and spiritual intercourse.

The contemporary social commitment to growth, expansion, and technology has stumbled; it has run out of gas. We need a new vision of external experience, a philosophy that is universal, rational, and responsible. Hopefully we can shape it so that it will produce a living context that is more of a whole and one that will blend the external with the internal, the formal and the informal. We desperately need to live a substantial part of our lives in contexts that are intimate, value-laden, and interpersonal.

Philippe Aries, recognizing this gap in our modern secular world, has contrasted our experience with that of the medieval. In his *Centuries of Childhood,* he describes an era when life was experienced as a unity of meaning.

> Modern man is divided between a professional life and a family life which are often in competition with each other, and all the rest is regarded as of secondary importance: religion and cultural activities, and even more so rest and amusement;

meeting with friends for a meal or drinks are considered as a mere relaxation, necessary to the organism like food which can be hurriedly swallowed, but not to be counted as part of the serious business of living—an extra, a luxury, which a man does not neglect, true, but whose importance he does not admit though he is not actually ashamed of it. But in the Middle Ages all these social activities which are today individualized and repressed, occupy an essential position in collective life. It does not matter to us that they had a religious origin in Mediterranean or Germanic rites of an orgiastic nature. What matters is that at that time people could not imagine a society that was not cemented by public recognition of a friendship—maintained by the common meal and "potacio," and sometimes sealed with intoxication. This rite was valued not only because it afforded sensual pleasure—men have never ceased to appreciate the joys of a good binge among friends!—but because this pleasure was transcended and became the perceptible, physical sign of a religious and legal engagement, of a sworn contract on which the whole of collective life rested, just as it rests today on our institutions of private and public law. The modern way of life is the result of the divorce between elements which had formerly been united: friendship, religion, profession.[13]

We cannot believe that this separation is integral to the modern condition. There must be patterns of education and social life that will make us whole yet contemporary beings. It is not a matter of merely waiting and hoping for a benign miracle to do the trick.

Part of our modernity is our commitment to the view that we have some rational control over our destiny. If we get into a jam, even one so fundamental as the desiccation of our cultural life, we are obliged to think the situation through and attempt to put into practice social policies that will relieve our perplexity. The crux is the kind of solution we opt for. First, we must light the candle and peer into the dimness.

13. Philippe Aries, *Centuries of Childhood* (New York: Vintage Books, 1965), pp. 245–46.

Part

4

**The
Problem
of
the
Future**

12 The Equilibrium Society

Population and capital are essentially stable, with the forces tending to increase or decrease therein in a careful controlled balance.

The Limits to Growth

Where does one discover the future for formal education? What social and intellectual concerns will dictate the course of educational research and practice? The future is never merely out there, that glimmer of light just beyond the horizon. It is entwined in an inextricable network of possibilities with the present and the past. Innumerable futures are within the compass of our reach today. What we end up with will in all probability be the consequence of the impact of our willpower and intellect. We have the capacity to choose and create the kind of world we want. And it is within our ken to develop wholly new intellectual conditions within which formal education can perform its civilizational function of bringing the future into being.

The question today is whether out of the chaos of the present, natural and social pathways might lead to a more enlightening and hopeful world in the future. Does the crisis that has affected our power-hungry world of huge institutional complexes, the mania of physical growth and expansion, give evidence of a popular awareness, a readiness for other solutions, that might free us from a social endeavor which now produces only a persistent pattern of diminishing returns?

HUMAN BEINGS AND THEIR WORLD

There is new hope. A movement is taking shape whose concerns and values arise from widely different disciplines and perceptions,

199

but whose meaning becomes increasingly clear. This new climate of opinion, still unfocused philosophically, has enough intellectual and social cohesiveness to generate a public attitude that has already had some political impact on our decisions. Today, due primarily to the depths of our moral disquietude, a surge of concern is the most hopeful trend we have had in generations.

It is not my function here to lay out all the contributing studies of our situation. Rather I attempt to outline the implications for the important educational questions for the future that inhere in this movement. For the sake of simplicity, I call this social vision of the future the "equilibrium society."

No one can predict the specifics of life in the equilibrium society. At the present moment, it entails a number of important values and attitudes that are directly antithetical to our commitments of the past, both educational and social. When these implications are spelled out, they may well entail striking changes in our social structure and in the content of our lives. The educational questions that will have to be posed and answered may well provoke the ferment and excitement in the discipline for which we have long searched.

The equilibrium society is not a mere slogan to generate emotional energies that might assist us in sorting out and clearing up the debris of the past and the present. It is not a pause or a rest stop on the highway of permanent growth, exploitations of nature, and the search for material palliatives for the dilemmas of human existence. Rather, it embodies a new view of the relationship of people to their world.

Heady with our power to alter relationships with nature through the scientific method, we have experimented with nature to the point of probing her limits. How far can nature be pushed to absorb our incursions? Are there any limits to what humans can do? If not, is there a human nature, with the limitations that this concept implies? The impact of our actions and the consequences that we begin to feel finally have begun to cause some general concern. In the realm of that most public domain, of the natural environment, where our mutual safety constitutes an immediate problem, René Dubos has succinctly expressed our present situation.

> Before long, all parts of the globe will have been colonized and the supply of many natural resources will have become critical. Careful husbandry, rather than exploitation will then be the key to survival. Developing stations in outer space or on the

bottom of oceans will not modify significantly, if at all, the limitations of human life. Man emerged on the earth, evolved under its influence, was shaped by it, and biologically he is bound to it forever. He may dream of stars and engage in casual flirtations with other worlds, but he will remain wedded to the earth, his sole source of sustenance.[1]

The new philosophy of man and society is predicated on the principle that there are inherent limits to the human manipulation and exploitation of nature. The precipitous squandering of the world's resources in the last one hundred and fifty years in the name of our achieved technological capacity may have been warranted historically. But it is now no longer possible to charge off this purported progress against nature or society. The gains are probably not profitable anymore.

Both physically and socially it has become necessary to live within the confines of nature's rhythms, much as we did in earlier centuries. We may well be able to move forward technologically here and there. And perhaps in certain aspects of our social system, growth will be possible. But it will be progress that is selective and thought out well in advance. The social and educational blunderbuss of growth and bigness with which we have recently been threatened will be relegated to the museums of social history.

In its place will come a new revolution in the nature of our social system. The equilibrium society will entail major alterations in both formal and informal education, in our social and economic structure, life styles, and cultural and moral values. These dislocations of habit will constitute a major preoccupation for thought. And it is because of our need to understand the possibilities of the future—if we are to hope to control events—that we must, even if only inchoately, envisage what the equilibrium society may be like.

THE LIMITS TO GROWTH

First, we should sketch some of the ineluctable factors that we must face if we project past and present trends into the future. Perhaps the single most important work dealing with the issues of the future is *The Limits to Growth,* a report written for the Club of Rome's project on the predicament of humanity.[2] The thesis of this

1. René Dubos, *So Human an Animal* (New York: Charles Scribner's, 1968), p. 235.
2. D. H. Meadows et al., *The Limits To Growth* (New York: Universe Books, 1972).

report concerns the inevitable results of the extrapolation into reality of the exponential growth rates today existing throughout the world in several critical physical variables. The report discusses the consequences that would result in the system were we to continue to increase at past and present rates—rates which are exponential in character—i.e., the doubling of factors over a delimited period of time.

An example of exponential growth is illustrated in the old French riddle. One is asked when the lazy boy will have to cut the lilies from his pond if he wished to cut them when they cover half the pond. It will take the lilies, which are doubling in size every day, thirty days to cover the pond entirely. The answer is, of course, he will have to cut the lilies on the twenty-ninth day. On that day he will have only one day before the pond is covered.[3]

Another example is given in the story of the Persian courtier who presents a handsome chessboard to his king and requests that the king give him one grain of rice for the first square, two for the second, four for the third, and sixteen for the fourth, and on up to the sixty-fourth square. This seems like a modest request at first until the king realizes that after even the twenty-first square he must produce over a million grains of rice.[4]

We are not facing water lilies or grains of rice but population increase. World population is expected to increase from 3.7 billion to over 7 billion by the year 2000. To accommodate for this, we must: (1) gear the worldwide industrial output necessary to maintain the living standards of the wealthy and keep pace with the needs of the poor; (2) maintain or increase food per capita, even as the amount of arable land may decrease (this may perhaps be offset by the increased use of fertilizer and insecticides); (3) deal with increased pollution that results from the effluent of exploding industrial production and vast increases in the use of insecticides and fertilizers; and (4) take into account the exponential depletion of nonrenewable resources (oil and coal), complicated by pollution and the increase in overall needs, yet tempered by possible new alternative mineral and energy sources and substitutes.

The computer analysis, which takes into account the most optimistic estimate of these variables as well as the partial control of some factors and the modification of crisis predictions in other factors, still leads to dismal forebodings as these elements all inter-

3. Ibid., p. 29.
4. Ibid.

act. Based on this analysis, the prediction is that our physical world system must collapse within one hundred years.

> We have shown that in the world model the application of technology to apparent problems of resource depletion or pollution or food shortage has no impact on the essential problem, which is exponential growth in a finite and complex system. Our attempts to use even the most optimistic estimates of the benefits of technology in the model did not prevent the ultimate decline of population and industry, and in fact did not in any case postpone the collapse beyond the year 2100.[5]

Of course, this physical model of growth does not include a discussion of the impact on the social, cultural, or psychic dimensions of human existence, those aspects that are necessarily more closely related to issues in education and society. But can there be any doubt that in a world expanding at present rates, given the social consequences that we have already experienced in our own lifetime from unrestrained economic and demographic growth, there would likewise be a social collapse? This cultural crisis could come far sooner than the physical collapse that Meadows and the other project members in *The Limits To Growth* predict.

But such predictions need not necessarily come true. Human beings, unlike lower forms of life, have the power to shape and reshape their destiny. That is what formal education is all about. People can study the past, learn from their mistakes, and teach their children not to repeat them.

Today we are witnessing what may be the first traumatic signs of the explicit disintegration of the growth paradigm of society. The rise in the cost of natural resources, the limited supplies of energy now causing social and political chaos and consternation in the West, food shortages, the dissolution of antipollution laws, and increased production costs are external manifestations of limitations that a few years back were inconceivable. But even before these occurrences, the loss of optimism, the explosive character of the social problems caused by economic and population growth and the consequent cultural indigestion, had erased much of our optimism and élan.

The recent decline in our birthrate is but a symptom, perhaps even

---

5. Ibid., p. 145. See also Carl Kaysen's critique of this book, "The Computer That Printed Out W*O*L*F*," *Foreign Affairs* 50 (July 1972): 662-68. One of his criticisms is the disregard and omission in *The Limits To Growth* of the increasing efficiency of technology in the use of available resources and in production.

a herald, of hard times to come. At the very least, it reflects a silent consensus that, at least for a time, limitation rather than expansion will be the rule in social life. The awareness of the inherent social irresponsibility that large families now connote in a society that has opted for the many social welfare benefits to be paid for from the general tax fund was produced to a large extent by those biologists and ecologists who first warned us about overexpansion and overpopulation.

At the time, Paul Ehrlich's concern that we might not live to see the twenty-first century was thought to be irresponsibly alarmist by many.[6] But even to pull back to a more conservative and realistic position about the threat of uncontrolled population expansion was to become aware of the elementary fact that ultimate survival was not compatible with unlimited expansion.

The equilibrium society connotes an international condition in which all the physical and material factors of civilizational life—food production and agricultural resources, pollution, population size, and social political destiny—are subject to the provision of international law and regulation. The basic consideration is to measure the needs of humanity today against the needs and possibilities of the future.

In this worldwide system, there are no sacrosanct and inviolable areas of private initiative and action where a consequence can be shown to have a public impact on others in the system, whether today or tomorrow. Even heat, that innocuous yet palpable residue of efficient pollution control, produced by reduction and degradation of energy resources, freely passing into our atmosphere inevitably affects our world system and must be considered for its impact. The mere fact that we might obtain 100 percent pollution control should never lull us into thinking that the ultimate consequences of geometrically increased numbers, energy production and use, etc., could be completely neutralized.

A philosophical principle is implicit in this discussion. It will ultimately be faced up to by people and adopted, albeit grudgingly. According to this principle, the resources of our planet earth, its seas and atmosphere, belong to no particular national group. And this applies to the resources that a nation, a culture, or a community may find beneath, around, and above the earth. These resources constitute a heritage from the past and a responsibility toward the future.

No country is completely self-sufficient. Nor is any country

6. Paul Ehrlich, *The Population Bomb* (New York: Ballantine Books, 1968).

completely independent of the consequences of its national actions, whether to the atmosphere, the land, or the seas, of an impact on its neighbors and humanity's future. It is responsible to those who will reside in its lands and in the world in general. At some point we will be forced to accept this truism. It is becoming more necessary to act on its assumptions every day. Hopefully we will soon be willing to sit down and draw up the guidelines for a self-imposed discipline with regard to those physical absolutes that we must all share: food, energy, water, air, and bring their use and development under some system of international controls.[7]

The result will be wholly new conceptions of what is mine and what is thine. Realms of freedom, privacy, individuality, and sociality will be redefined. And while many may balk at certain losses in freedom, the great educational problem will be to examine the meaning and character of the overall gains and losses that we have to choose from. Even as conservative an industrial giant as Exxon has published an article in its trade journal which, while arguing against zero economic growth, admits to certain limitations on its heretofore unassailable rights of free enterprise: "But rejecting a flat policy of zero growth does not mean that the only alternative is rigid adherence to the present system with its built-in bias towards continuous growth as the dominant indicator of a society's economic health. Much more likely, the dilemma posed by finite resources and growing demand will be resolved by a number of significant modifications in the present system. Thus, it is probable that although zero growth may not be the policy of the future, the future may be one of limited options." [8]

Taking into account the manner in which the educational institutions of our country have aped the methods and structural arrangements of the industrial trail-blazers, it is evident that there will be significant changes in the orientation of our schools and colleges. Today, for the first time, there is the beginning of a relative shortage of students, given the facilities available. Teachers are in surplus, classrooms partially empty.

First, the concrete situation will lead to practical changes in

7. Mihajlo Mesarovic and Eduard Pestel, *Mankind at the Turning Point: The Second Report of the Club of Rome* (New York: E. P. Dutton, 1974). This recent updating of the original Club of Rome report breaks the world system down into discrete ecological areas and extrapolates forward in terms of decades, 1975–2025, as to world possibilities. The prognosis is more explicit but hardly more optimistic, if we do not act immediately.
8. Jack Long, "The Great Growth Debate," *The Lamp*, Summer 1973, p. 10.

building programs, teacher training and selection, and the economics of the education industry. Then additional changes can be expected. New perceptions about education and its purposes inevitably will follow. A society that searches for rational choices amid limited material options engenders wholly new significant educational questions.

But these questions and attitudes about the external factors of social existence are only a small part of the new educational context. Our cultural and community life is bound to change. The interpersonal relationships of people, their values and commitments, all will be subtly and gradually reevaluated A wholly new context of social adaptation will evolve. Here, the deepest and most problematic educational concerns must be elicited and dealt with by committees of citizens and their schools.

Before we go too far here in suggesting the long-range educational ramifications, let us first pursue some of the most obvious and significant external issues that must become grist for the institution of education in the immediate future.

POPULATION CONTROL

The question of population as it will be formulated in the equilibrium society is only partially one of numbers. What level of human quality do we seek to maintain? How far can society intrude into heretofore sanctified areas of private choice? Will government be permitted to regulate the size of families? Does society have the right to establish eugenic standards in the population? Is it feasible even to begin to consider the possibility of an internationally enforcible policy of population parity among the nations of the world?

On the basis of the projected estimates of world population, it is difficult not to conclude that some kind of controls will be necessary, and soon. Eventually we will be forced to establish an international system that will balance a world population with existing productivity levels and that would strive toward the achievement of a decent standard of living for all. Into this calculus would come an evaluation of current natural resource availability; existing and future technological capability; and a variety of ecological, cultural, and social considerations. Into this systems analysis a final crucial element would be added: the interests of those humans yet to be born. Their rights, needs, and possibilities must be considered. We will thus have to act not only on the basis of what is, but also in terms of the probabilities of the conditions of life in the future.

Three basic issues get directly to the heart of the problem but at the same time will provide some stimulating controversy: (1) the right of society to intervene through either indirect or direct regulation to restrict or to encourage population expansion; (2) criteria for deciding the proper population any nation or geographical area could support given their own resources, ecology, industrial, and cultural contributions to the world community; (3) population quality, the means of assessing it, upgrading the general level in terms of local and international values, e.g., intelligence, creativity, industry, morality, lawfulness. Does humanity have the scientific resources necessary to evaluate these criteria? Should one attempt to intercede in favor of certain individual characteristics over others?

THE INDIVIDUAL AND THE STATE

When people were in short supply, it was easy to point ourselves in one direction. Progress was defined in terms of the steady fulfillment of our ideals of growth and physical mastery of the environment. For every momentary slippage in the birthrate, there was in the United States a ready supply of immigrant labor to fill the factories, mines, and lumber camps. Large families were smiled upon and fecundity encouraged, if not with medals and awards, as in certain nations, then through the gradual expansion of social-welfare programs that aided families regardless of economic status.

In fact, until recently, contraception and abortion were considered criminal acts. The nineteenth-century laws which leveled sanctions against such limitations were originally established by the then regnant Protestant establishment. In the twentieth century, the Catholic hierarchy waged a continuing battle against the "liberalization" of such statutes.

The federal income tax makes provision for deductions, which constitutes a de jure subsidization of families. Likewise, the great expansion of a variety of educational and welfare programs, even such diverse provisions as schools, libraries, hospital care, sanitation, police, drug rehabilitation, prison and reform schools, public housing, make it easier for poor or large (often both) families to survive through what is in fact a subsidy or bonus by the people for those who have children but not the economic wherewithal to pay for their cost to society.

In spite of the acknowledged press on our resources by the consumer population, especially that relatively small proportion of it that needs special state assistance to survive, we have not yet arrived at the point of eliminating our massive welfare programs. The thrust of much welfare legislation is to neutralize the sharp inequalities between people that would occur were the wealthy able to purchase or monopolize these social necessities.

There will be increasing emphasis, in the light of the fragile condition of the poor, on facilitating the voluntary regulation of family size. Hopefully, before legislation becomes necessary to enact more stringent sanctions, contraception or abortion will be utilized by all sectors of the populace. Even with voluntary family-planning practices, can we expect government not to place the economic responsibility for paying for social services on the family? We should eventually expect to have tax deductions for dependents modified, tuition increased in state higher educational institutions, as well as have limits set on the extent of society's subsidization of elementary and secondary education, health and social welfare services.

But this is only prologue to an even more fearful step. Suppose these indirect ways of raising the cost of bringing up children serve to limit the middle class but are ineffective with the rich, who can carry their own costs, or with the poor, whose social and economic incapacity is further exacerbated by their mobility, instability, or unwillingness to limit the number of children born to them?

Are there individually sacrosanct rights, such as the right to choose freely the number of children we will have, even to chance the personal consequences for parents and children which unlimited exercise of this right would entail? Does the government of our society have the legal power to interfere with the free exercise of this right, even if it deems that the free exercise by individuals of such choice would imperil other values that the majority may hold? If we grant society the right to inhibit the free exercise of choice with regard to the number of children a family may have, would we thereby render academic the recently acquired individual rights of contraception and abortion?

Could not the state at some future moment decide, if it so chooses, to encourage birth and discourage or even forbid certain forms of contraception and abortion, as it did in the nineteenth century? Would we not imperil the individual freedoms gained after such a long and protracted effort? On the other hand, does an individual have unlimited private freedoms even where society or the majority of its citizens decides that those private acts have serious consequences for the pursuit of other rights and values on the part of the majority?

THE INTERNATIONAL DIMENSION

Questions of individual rights when extrapolated to the international scene come dangerously close to the harsh edge of power politics. And soon we must expect that the gradual extension of international agreements on economic and monetary amalgamation, nonpollution of the atmosphere and the seas as well as economic, social, and technological assistance to the poorer countries will extend itself to a vast emergency operation. At current rates of expansion, from approximately 3.5 billion people in 1970, we expect 7 billion in the year 2000.

An entirely new balance of power may begin to intervene. Certain industrial states such as in Western Europe and Japan support populations far in excess of their indigenous natural resources. They import raw materials, which up to now have been either relatively cheap or obtainable from weaker states. As the value of raw materials rises, through demand and scarcity, these weaker or less-developed societies will obtain, in theory, the economic capacity to finance their own industrialization, with the consequent need to raise the quantitative level of their population. Previously wealthy and populous nations will have to choose whether to shrink in population or in standard of living.

However, they will probably argue that an international premium ought to be placed on their acquired skills, historical contributions to culture, the arts, and science and technology. They will demonstrate the existing efficiency and intelligence of their people, arguing that a developing society will make many errors and inevitably cause wastage of precious international resources. How does one calculate and evaluate the skills of the Japanese as against the incredible oil wealth of Arabia, when one must adjudicate each society's fair share of the resources of the world and the number of people it has a right to support on its own bit of terra firma?

We already hear new principles expressed. When the French set off their atomic bonbs in the Pacific, the people of the Pacific maintained that the atmosphere belongs to all people and that no one nation can take upon itself the right to pollute that which others must breathe. Soon we will hear arguments that the United States with its great agricultural resources ought to reduce its population level so that more of its productivity can go to support nations with less fertile lands. Counterarguments will be set forth maintaining that since one nation-culture has such poor ecological circum-

stances, it ought to reduce its population accordingly. The final
counterargument will be the one previously mentioned: We may
not have rich soil or minerals or geographical advantages, but our
intelligence and hard work have enabled us to develop technologically and we have contributed to the civilizational advance of
mankind. Is that not worth something in the judgment of our international polity?

Many of these issues will be resolved naturally simply through
the press of circumstances, much as international currencies adjust
to one another through national economic productivity and international demand. However, the force of population expansion and
the growth of demand to live the "middle-class" Western life style
will have to exert a revolutionary impact on our view of the internal
integrity of a nation's interests with regard to population levels, that
is, if we want to avoid another world war!

Nations will of necessity band together to discuss matters of total
world population as well as their own internal population levels, the
calculation of industrial productivity, sharing of available natural
resources—food and minerals, etc. This new principle will begin to
find itself expressed, perhaps, first in the overdeveloped democratic
nations of the West: the physical and material rights of any individual or nation have no unlimited validity as against the rights
and values of another person and nation.

Out of the steady realization, through harsh experience and the
consequences of this experience, all societies will eventually realize
that the general level of world population must be subject to societal
intervention. And that in order to reduce or expand populations,
people have the right to restrict such previously established private
rights in order to effect the greater public good.

THE QUALITY OF HUMAN BEINGS

Throughout the early and middle parts of the nineteenth century
in the United States, there was far more grazing land available than
there were cattle. A motley variety of animals browsed over the
plains, hybrids between the English shorthorn and the early Spanish
breeds. Later the longhorn cattle, which adapted to short grasses
and could travel the long distances to market, became an American
legend. As the land filled up, a more sophisticated populace back
East began to demand higher meat standards. New bloodlines were
introduced as well as new patterns of cattle raising. The new market
situation required an animal that met various standards not here-

tofore envisaged: a higher level of fat in the meat, fast weight gain, ability to forage far and wide, resistance to extreme weather conditions, docility. Those animals that showed these characteristics were maintained as breeding stock and the rest eliminated from the genetic pool.

The analogy to human populations is not too far-fetched. In the advanced nations, we need fewer broad backs for raw labor. Machines replace brute strength; people are expected to be supple, autonomous, and innovative in thought. The requirements of modernity place those who can offer only their bodies for unskilled labor at the bottom of the economic structure. The ultimate poor no longer support the leisure of the upper classes. They themselves are now the appendages.

Certain nations having the ready skills as well as resources have jumped into the lead in shaping the nation of the modern world. The patterns and life styles of today and the future have been created by this group of peoples. Their inherent conception of skills and abilities is the model of the adaptive man or woman at the end of the twentieth century. Whoever's abilities diverge and are unadaptable to the new age will inevitably be shunted aside.

Even among the successful people of the world, misfortunes of fate are suffered by practically all families. As biologists have long noted, any species well adapted to a niche in a bio-ecological system fights an often losing battle with genetic degradation (unfavorable mutations). Add to this the many social accidents that place us at the mercy of events, and we understand the need for every humanitarian culture to leave room in its social system to care for the less fortunate.

With the passage of time and the increased pressures for an equitable and efficient distribution of available wealth, no individual group will go unscrutinized. We will want to ensure that every family enjoy a minimal standard of living that we can classify in the best sense of the term as "middle class." In turn we will ask that the working members of each family be capable of contributing to the public good, at the very least, at an efficient and productive level in tune with the existing standards of the society: a fair day's wage for an honest day's work.

To what extent will we be able to subsidize indefinitely families who are not capable of bearing their share of the burden? Will we not have the responsibility of discouraging some from having children if we see that society is receiving less than it gives? Will families of greater intelligence, energy, altruism, and culture be so valued and admired that we will encourage them to bring more than the usual number of progeny into the world? The stock breeder accepts this course of action as the only sane way to stay in business. Will we want to encourage the mentally unstable, the criminal, the alcoholic or drug-addicted, the mentally lethargic to pass on their environmentally susceptible characteristics?

There will be even more difficult questions. For among the intelligent and talented there may also be disabilities, illnesses and weaknesses that are hereditable and for whose sustenance there is a cost to society. Recently we have had a spate of heart transplants, kidney grafts, etc. Medical technology is brilliant in saving lives. But will we be so wealthy and affluent that we can encourage those with congenital problems, especially those having some hereditary linkage, to pass on their tendencies? Indeed, will we be able to afford such extreme medical gifts in the future as in the present?

As our attitude toward the problems of population and industrial growth begins to change, issues concerned with the quality of our existence will emerge. For example, we have insufficiently considered the possible relationship between the characteristics of the particular individuals in a society, the sum total of their natural capacities and talents, the education they receive to develop these capabilities, the social and cultural milieu in which they live, and the resultant output for the character of the society. We have traditionally assumed that the quality of our national existence is a product of social and environmental factors. Individuals have been thought to be infinitely plastic.

It might also be important to give thought to the quality of the leadership in a society to understand its cultural tone. Concomitantly it is often the quality of the people—their talents, intelligence, independence, and altruism—that produces a leadership responsive to the appropriate national will. This raises an important question. Can democratic institutions survive in a sea of mediocrities?

Inevitably, these questions must be answered, not because of any logical assertion that intelligence leads to any one form of civilizational life rather than another, but because it is impossible not to believe that human beings tend to surround themselves with symbols and institutions that reflect their own perceptions of life. To deny that people create their own expectations is to deny personal individuality. Favorable preexisting social conditions and education are essential means to the enhancement of social life. But are we to disregard the variability among people and not to make an assumption that a society will reflect at its best the upper levels of its people's talents and interests?

When we first learn that all things are not possible, we learn to invoke a principle of selection. The population explosion and the efforts to halt expansion of the population and perhaps even to bring it back quantitatively to a better balance with our natural and social resources will dredge up a new class of educational and intellectual issues. Today, these concerns are largely latent, hidden through both existential indifference (they are not presently important) and through fear. The latter aspect should concern us, since our indifference is even now being rudely shaken.

The translation of an issue that lurks beneath the surface of our understanding because it is a cause of emotional involvement to an issue that can be objectively and rationally understood and confronted is a difficult process. But it is probably our key educational need at this moment. For the purpose of learning is to focus the powers of reason on as yet inchoately understood issues so that they can eventually become subject to social and political policy intervention. To that end the problem of population (in quantitative and qualitative terms) may be one of the key intellectual issues in the coming equilibrium society. We should be forewarned and forearmed.

ECONOMIC EQUALITY

"From each according to his abilities, to each according to his need." This traditional motto of communism has been a source of fear, hatred, revolutionary fervor, and conflict. In the century or so since the slogan was first uttered, enormous social and economic changes have accompanied the great political and ideological upheavals that brought Marxism to power in various parts of our globe.

The irony of the contemporary world is that democratic capitalism, in responding to the communist challenge, has done more to uplift the status of the industrial worker—the chosen agent of the proletarian revolution—than the communist nations. These societies are today so mired in psychosocially enervating systems of bureaucratic centralism, combined with the totalitarian suppression of rights of free expression and self-determination that the traditional philosophical issue of economic equality has become blurred in the minds of the world's peoples.

That this issue is not in the ascendancy at this point in history is not only due to the totalitarian political forms and the chaotic and still nonegalitarian economic patterns of the communist nations. It is due to a great extent to the ability of Western democracies to expand economically and redistribute much of the newly available wealth to the working classes who thence feed this wealth through their consumption back into the capital expansion of the economic base. While there is still grossly unequal distribution of the wealth in many parts of the developed noncommunist world, this is often due in part to the expansion of the demographic base, which has eaten up the accumulating surplus. In addition, the need to stimulate expansion at the top through business enterprise, ingenuity, and energy has necessitated giving a premium to profit and capital accumulation.

THE DECLINE OF PRIVATE WEALTH

The era of expansion is rapidly coming to a close. The negative impact of broad-based demographic, economic, and technological growth is well documented. Henceforth these themes, so supremely persuasive in the past as to make all other considerations appear secondary, will themselves be subject to a new calculus of values. In effect we will have entered a new historical era. Quantitative economic output will take its place among a large number of competing values. The rewards that accrued to those whose talents in business, finance, advertising and sales, and whose engineering and technological ingenuity gave them enormous premiums from society, will obviously change too.

Surely the day of technological innovation and development has not come to an end. But as the researchers in *The Limits To Growth* point out, a slow process of evaluation, testing, and sober consideration will have to take place before innovations will be widely adopted. Every new technological development would have to answer the following questions: (1) What will the physical and social side effects be if the development is introduced on a large scale? (2) What social changes will be necessary before the development is fully successful and removes some natural limit to growth, what limits will the growing system meet next? Will society prefer its pressure to the ones this development is designed to remove? [9]

The great revolutionary eras are periods of changing statuses, the upthrust of new classes and values, and in general a dissolution of the boundaries and traditions that hold individuals to account for their actions in order to retain their good names in established

9. Meadows, *The Limits To Growth*, pp. 154–55.

society and morality. The era of the "robber baron" saw the by-passing of the older vested classes; the adoption of the mantle of progress, rationality, even altruism; the assumption of a social stance of rightful privilege and inordinate wealth (social Darwin-ism—might makes right) that we are now finally beginning to question. No longer sure of the invincibility of economic growth, we will have limits imposed on random population growth. There will be a more general legitimization of meritocratic attitudes. The splitting of a society into the sometime socially productive haves and perennial productive have nots will not be tolerated.

Thus there will be a shift of power away from a class of the materially advantaged. The political challenge of the future is the means to achieve this goal without admitting through the back door that suffocating cloak of bureaucratic authoritarianism that de-scended over the communist world. Given a concomitant reduction in the economic and ecological pressures leading to a balance of decentralized local governments (cultural communities) with a sys-tem of national and international material controls, a world more committed to the pursuit of cultural, esthetic, and communitarian concerns, we may be able to achieve our ends.

It is difficult to conceive that those in whom wealth or power is concentrated will relinquish it voluntarily. Yet this must occur, if not at a revolutionary tempo. As long as we can retain our demo-cratic guarantees, the force of historical necessity, of having to live within an ever tighter, more disciplined economic budget, should itself establish conditions for economic and political equity.

This belief does not stem from any particular ideological com-mitment, socialistic or democratic capitalism. Nor does it assume the rightness of governmental or private ownership of important economic institutions. Rather it is predicated on the diminished philosophical capital of growth and exploitation. The privilege of wealth contrasts with the enhanced educational status and compe-tencies of the dominant middle classes. When certain heretofore privileged positions are held to be not crucial to society, when many individuals are capable of performing these jobs, inevitably the premium of wealth, prestige, and power extended by society at one point in history can be revoked at the next.

MERIT AND SOCIAL ADVANTAGE

No rational expositor of the traditional economic growth thesis disputes the need for a better balanced assessment of the factors involved in our ecosystem. Somewhere in our universe there is a finite limit on human numbers, earthly natural resources, physical space, and the capacity to tolerate pollution and environmental manipulation.

Within these limits we may be able to adjust some variable factors. If we raise production, per capita resource reserves may be reduced. By lowering population we may be able to work less and increase leisure time or expand economic consumption, but perhaps not both. In any case all such variations in the given equilibrium state will have to be evaluated judiciously to prevent the possible breakdown of the system.

Thus our lives will be lived in a context of limits. This is in contrast to an educational milieu of growth, affluence, and the sky's the limit, which itself has done so much to demoralize the young as well as the old. For a few generations we played dice with the future. Now we must learn to discipline ourselves in the material sense to enhance individual life as well as civilization to the highest degree. We will increasingly be concerned not only with the sharing of our resources equitably, but also with developing criteria, through the process of education and elsewhere, with regard to apportioning this wealth in terms of standards of merit designed to stimulate the best that is in man and society.

Without the cornucopia of unlimited affluence we have experienced in the past, everyone must now come under the scrutiny of everyone else. The rugged individualist of the past has long ago lost both ruggedness and individuality when it comes to economic factors. Those who have by right of privilege lived *la dolce vita* will ultimately be pressured by circumstance to abandon irresponsible luxury. On the other hand, will we have the surplus to support classes or groups of individuals who are incapable of coping with an increasingly complex and responsible social existence? Will the context of human existence that once supported those who could work on farms, mines, in factories (those of brawn and not of skill) find a place in the sun?

Obviously the cost to society of supporting individuals whose work can be done by machines is relatively too high. That is why machines are rapidly taking their place. On the other hand, will the equilibrium society, which demands that each individual carry his or her own weight, tend to exclude not only the less acute and intellectually capable, but more dangerously those of more subtle talents and personalities? Certainly no one could ever argue against allowing room in the economic structure for the care and support of those whom fate has dealt a sharp blow: the child with a sudden illness, the mother with a mental breakdown, the orphan and widow, etc.

But, of course, it will be argued that a society that does not allow the full flowering of talent, creative abilities, and less obvious forms of intelligence would not be a humane society. And in these cases, such individuals would be sanctioned to continue to carry on as best they could, their existence itself contributing to the moral well being of others.

We do know that for every species that is in dynamic equilibrium with its environment, survival necessitates the elimination of those naturally occurring mutations that tend to degrade the adaptive fit of the species. Thus, even within our own species, we face a constant battle against genetic deterioration, which must be confronted somewhat differently in an equilibrium society as compared to earlier expanding social contexts. In the latter, the process of social competition, which took place under constantly changing rules of social fairness, together with the general openness of social horizons, contributed to the larger dynamic fitness of the species. Now, in an environment of ecological stability, will conscious decision making, rather than random competition, be necessary to effectuate the cultivation of talent and the concomitant exclusions of physically and mentally less adaptable individuals?

From the standpoint of both the very succesful and the ultimate failures, there will be a continuing if gradual move to what Charles Frankel has called the tradition of "corrective egalitarianism:"

> "Equality," so conceived, is a principle for the distribution of hardships. Thus, traditional egalitarians did not oppose the situation in which the rich could go to their own universities, provided they paid enough in taxes to support adequate universities for others, and didn't steal all the best people away. . . .
> In this tradition, equality is to be understood, in other words, in relative terms. It is defined in relation to a specific imbalance, perceived to be dangerous to important values, and therefore to be prevented, reduced, or removed. So approached, there are no answers to the general questions, What is equality?, or, Why equality? There are only answers specific to definite problems. . . .
> What is the ethical outlook of egalitarianism as most of us grew up to recognize it? It was a conviction that there are people of power and feeling hidden away in all sectors of society, and that life would be richer if they were found. It was

the suspicion that there is nothing like being on top to make a
man a windbag, and that it does everybody a world of good to
see him slip on a banana peel. It was the knowledge that the
rich and powerful, not necessarily through malice but simply as
a reflex of who they were and what they had, would have a
natural tendency to try to form a closed club and keep others
out. A balanced distribution of power and resources was desirable, therefore, if the individual was to count for more than
social class.[10]

At the same time that we move toward correcting nonfunctional
social and economic inequalities between individuals, we ought to
be wary of an unconditional egalitarianism. Thus, John Rawls
argues that the nature of justice demands that even those social
advantages that accrue from the family hearth or more basically
from the fact of birth and natural disposition ought to be neutralized. The achievements and aspirations of those who are thus favored are "just" only if they concomitantly improve the expectations
of the least advantaged.[11]

Let us consider the problem of the least favored in the abstract.
Suppose we judge the separation between the most socially valuable
to the least socially valuable to necessitate no more than a 1:5
difference in economic reward (i.e., $10,000 base, $50,000 top). One
could argue that the base is sufficient for a modest life and the top is
stimulus for the most able and this apportionment of wealth constitutes the most efficient social distribution. But since the nature and
needs of society always change, one must examine constantly what
would constitute not only most valued performance, but also minimally functional contributions to warrant inclusion in our equilibrium society model and its various social-welfare protections and
subsidies.

Inevitably individuals will fall below the capability level, either
because of congenital social or mental defects or through sheer lack
of individual effort. In these cases we would have to decide whether
to include them for support, create a special temporary welfare
category, or even chance the possibility of creating a class of such
individuals and thus degrading the minimum work achievement
level.

To allow the latter situation to persist would inevitably erode the

10. Charles Frankel, "The New Egalitarianism and the Old," *Commentary* 56
(September 1973): 60–61.
11. John Rawls, *A Theory of Justice* (Cambridge, Mass.: Harvard University Press,
1971).

total economic wherewithal; it would certainly have to be taken out of the hide of those at the top or in the middle. It is hardly likely that over the years such a philanthropic but historically irresponsible social policy would be allowed to continue.

In reality, there would more likely be an effort by society to eliminate gradually from the gene pool those bio-socially less adaptive individuals or, if possible, to redraw the educational program to make it more efficient. In fact, as the distance between the less and the more able in terms of social capabilities is narrowed, the ratio of social and economic rewards might be redrawn to 1 : 4 or 1 : 3. Then decisions that both individual and society might make with regard to career choices would generally be based less on ability and skill than on individual preference.

The theory that the only reason individuals strive to self-actualize their talents is the lure of unlimited wealth is a myth. The drive for achievement activates a broad spectrum of personality concerns. The aspiration for wealth and power is not one of the more socially creative or desirable values. Humans seek to differentiate themselves as individuals. The range of rewards they seek to symbolize this fact of fulfillment and actualization is varied. Gross differences are probably less important to individuals than the perception of fine qualitative gradations. One might wonder whether, were economic differentiation kept within the 1–2 range ($10,000 to $19,000), people might strive even more mightily for a mere trophy, a ribbon, or a parchment reflective of some merited achievement from society.

Thus, in a world where material and economic resources will necessitate close husbanding, such economic differentiation will have to be kept at a minimum. The factor of minimal standards of social performance and remuneration will likewise become critical. The need for differentiation in this respect, for those rare but important talents, will continue to be necessary. But certainly, the gross inequalities and the unconscionable human and material waste which exist today (and to such small contemporary social benefit for mankind) will have to end.

FREEDOM AND MATERIAL CONTROL

Albert Camus wrote: "It is true that freedom, when it is made up principally of privileges, insults labor and separates it from culture. But freedom is not made up principally of privileges; it is made up especially of responsibilities. And the moment each tries to give freedom's responsibilities precedence over its privilege, freedom joins together labor and culture and sets in action the only force that can effectively serve justice." [12]

Camus' statement reflects on much of the dissatisfaction of contemporary man in the affluent Western societies. The growth of the economy, the superabundance of material goods, the freedom to travel, change jobs, be sexually emancipated, and develop affluent life styles have effectively disintegrated the traditional limitations, the sense of moral obligation, responsibility, and deference for tradition that were once part of our heritage. How else can one explain the recent cavalier rejection and disdain for priceless educational opportunities by our most affluent youthful beneficiaries? The lack of a national sense of responsibility goes far in explaining the consequent dissolution of our traditional informal culture and the educational desert that the young grow up in today.

This situation is changing rapidly. The world is imposing more and more limitations on our responsibility-less freedoms. We accept these limitations because they are happening gradually and seem part of the rhythm of change. But this gradualism may also quicken and an entirely new and urgent sense of the loss of freedom may come into being that could seem to usher in the various totalitarian predictions that so many writers (Orwell, Huxley, Skinner) have envisioned as our future.

Such developments as restrictions on burning of refuse; gasoline rationing; price, wage, and soon profit controls; limitation on the use of electricity; and skyrocketing prices on food, basic utilities, and other necessities will reveal to the average man the real extent of our crisis and the fact that impending are even greater limitations to our freedom than our schools have taught us to expect.

Today, many people, faced with the growing public awareness of the population explosion, recoil at the possibility that "the government will tell me how many children I can have." The enormously absorptive capacity of our society for population expansion, economic growth, and even the detritus of pollution and urban decay has given us a false sense of the absolute nature of our freedom, especially in the unlimited satisfying of our material wants.

In sadness perhaps, but certainly with sobriety, we can look forward to an era where such controls and legally imposed restrictions on our consumption and use of resources, the surplus wealth any individual has available, the kinds of carefree, unsacrificing

12. Albert Camus, *Resistance, Rebellion and Death* (New York: Knopf, 1961).

freedoms to move around in jobs, careers, or locations will all have diminished radically. Can we predict that a new and even more "absolute" philosophical principle will be discovered and undergird the equilibrium society? *Material existence, one's needs, use, and privileges in the physical realm can be totally restricted by law. The right of society to limit and regulate in any and every way the material and energic resources of this world for the general welfare is supreme. These resources are public and social, and affect the rights and freedoms of all. They are not private. They are not the inalienable provenance of the individual's freedom of action.*

Anthropologically, there is no such entity as freedom outside a culture within which freedom's rights and responsibilities are always delimited. We are made human by society. So, too, the specific act of acculturation or education inevitably acts to restrict alternative cultural and personality modes. Culture and formal education enhance and redirect that particular version of social reality that is our own heritage and that is to be our destiny.

It does not necessarily follow that as our traditional materialistic freedoms are circumscribed because of the real, concrete, and inevitable disciplines imposed by nature that all or even the most essential of our freedoms will be restricted. One could argue that the deepest elements of individuality and creativity will be left untouched. In earlier centuries economic and social limitations were imposed by blind political or environmental necessities. With each passing day, the discipline and social responsibilities of material control now demand self-imposition.

People were poor because they were ignorant, or because they were persecuted and exploited. We can now expect to be either rich—selfish, polluted, then ultimately destitute, without self-control—or else we can choose to be modestly well off but deeply enmeshed in a variety of regulations and controls. The critical question in this transitional period will be the extent to which we will have been able to preserve our democratic political structure. The great danger in not acting before the full impact of our dilemma is upon us lies in the political explosion that the shock of social and environmental disaster might set off. The deep resentment against those who have lulled the people to sleep in the face of such an impending crisis could very well prepare the ground for some form of fascistic tyranny exploiting the popular fears, both irrational and real.

The natural way out of such a situation lies in the educational confrontation of issues that today are ignored, feared, or even considered heretical. Probably only the advanced democratic nations have the schooling, communications, and political machinery that might develop communities of opinion able to face up to the hard social decisions that must be made. The law is only as good as the popular consensus behind it.

Something more important even than a consensus is necessary to face impending events. It is the capabilitiy of developing the foresight to see the consequences of actions long before they loom on the horizons. This important freedom not to be ruled by blind chance necessitates the development of a formal philosophy in education and society which sees social, environmental, and cultural problems as part of a larger historic movement. Then we can hope to muster the intelligence to become creators of events and not impotent reactors to the consequences of earlier actions decades before, for which we had no responsibility.

It is here that the educational method proposed by John Dewey and the pragmatic movement becomes particularly relevant. In their own era of great changes, the need for an educational method that would help to free us from the shibboleths of the past was seen as essential to being able to face new realities of the present and the future.

> Education takes the individual while he is relatively plastic, before he has become so indurated by isolated experiences as to be rendered hopelessly empirical in his habit of mind. The attitude of childhood is naive, wondering, experimental; the world of man and nature is new. Right methods of education preserve and perfect this attitude, and thereby short-circuit for the individual the slow progress of the race, eliminating the waste that comes from inert routine and lazy dependence on the past. Abstract thought is imagination seeing familiar objects in a new light and thus opening new vistas in experience. Experiment follows the road thus open and tests its permanent value.[13]

CONCLUSION

Our awareness of physical limits and the inevitable social controls to come is crucial to the educational command of the future. Yet, even as we accept it as a fact of life, we still recoil at its starkness, at the "brave new world" it seems to augur. It is too logical and demanding to be real. Is this a world that people will

13. John Dewey, *How We Think* (Boston: D. C. Heath, 1933), p. 202.

want to live in, even tolerate? Where is that minimal accommodations to the "divine madness" that inhabits the human soul, that at times escapes into social reality with such equivocal results—beauty and bestiality? So much of the misery of humankind has been due to the enormous and sometimes darkly irrational thrust of his psychic energies that we cannot hope or expect this demon to be exorcized easily.

Here we must return to the informal world of culture and education. For if our new sense of possibility in the formal world of material life must be held under severe educational and intellectual restraints, if we must cease making the world of matter, machines, politics, economics a glorious sports arena for our sense of competition and self-esteem, then we must provide alternative social areas for unrestricted creative enterprise. It will not be enough, as Konrad Lorenz and others have suggested, for people, in order to draw off their surplus aggressive energies, to have daily cold showers and vigorous physical exercise to dissipate their purported aggressive drives.[14] Aggressive and creative demands derive from extraphysical energies that are as much cognitive and symbolic as they are physical.

It is in the retention and development of informal education and the world that inhabits the intimate, the ethnic, the aesthetic, the religious and the cultural that we can hope to find a richness and openness to the creative and the unknown which the social restrictions on the conditions of our material existence will henceforth not give us. We may not be able to gasp in ecstasy at our new Thunderbird automobile with its tons of steel and chrome, its gasoline-gulping engine, and its annihilating exhaust. Our minds and imaginations will have to be far more inventive and ingenious. It will take finer sensibilities to appreciate sculpture in steel, chrome, or wood other than the assembly-line stereotyping of even a Thunderbird.

We will be required to find new relationships between informal, pluralistic forms of education and culture and the mainline universalism of the equilibrium world society. The possibilities here are intriguing. To develop this theme in our current educational dilemma as well as a concrete possibility for life in the future, we next turn to an analysis of the concept of the cultural community.

14. *On Aggression* (New York: Harcourt, Brace, 1966).

13 | The Cultural Community: The Depths of Thought

Civilization, therefore, obtains mastery over the individual's dangerous desire for aggression by weakening and disarming it and by setting up an agency within him to watch over it, like a garrison in a conquered city.

—Freud, *Civilization and Its Discontents*

THE LIMITS OF THE EQUILIBRIUM SOCIETY

The idea of the cultural community is based on several assumptions. First, the equilibrium society world model is essentially a negative social abstraction. It deals with humanity in terms of physical needs and restraints on behavior and policy that worldwide interdependence necessitates. By lawful restrictions on people's interaction with nature and with one another, the grossest social depredations are thus avoided. Life is made tolerable and the distribution of the necessities is maximized for all. But note, this does not give us any insights into the basic rationale and purpose of human life, and how we are to extract from this situation those intrinsic satisfactions that fulfill "human nature." It is no more than a scheme of international "shalt nots."

Second, there is a dimension of human existence that is vast and yet relatively unknown. It lies deep within the psychological structure of the individual. Where animal instinct and learned behavioral specifics leave off, this realm of subconscious forces and symbolic meanings begins. To think of society in terms of the physical model of the world is to omit the essential character of human motivation. Human beings need physical sustenance in order to dream, to love, to worship, to think and create. The origins of these powers lie deep within the consciousness. These forces erupt to the surface to permeate every human action and social need.

Third, human beings are not instinctively rooted to any particular ecological structure. The social forms that they can create are therefore almost limitless. Nevertheless, given certain criteria —accepted over the centuries as both rationally valid as well as historically truthful—we can make judicious comparisons and choices. Thus, certain contexts of social life are more humane, in which individuals have been freer, more productive, and have actualized more fully the potentials that were available. Because people can be saints as well as sinners, they have the capability to create social structures for good or ill. It is our claim that the cultural community embodies certain tangible criteria that can offer us a model for social living and education that is not reducible to the various anti-Utopias of the Orwells or Huxleys, and can save us from the starker social consequences of the world equilibrium society model.

The implications for formal education are clear. Technical competency in terms of scientific and academic skills will be necessary on a worldwide level. But this ought to constitute only a beginning. Schools must be so organized and rooted in their communities that they naturally elicit the assertive and dynamic capacities of individuals.

The union of thought and feeling that a formal educational regimen supposedly succeeds in developing arises out of the wholesome relationship between an individual and the community. The school is a mediator of this bond. The cultural community, by constituting the locus for the creation of a unique social being, tied to the values of a particular family and friends, can develop and exercise those rational powers of thought. In turn the individual can eventually serve the wider needs of the international community.

The next one hundred years should see an irrevocable trend toward the creation of the equilibrium society as the recognition of the interdependence of the world community. Our economic, ecological, and demographic concerns may even lead to progressive cooperative efforts in the political arena. Just as the nations of the European Economic Community are learning to subordinate small personal advantages for the greater good of corporate economic survival, so too will we all learn to accept the need for self-discipline and obedience to a more universal law of balance with nature and respect for the rights of the as yet unborn.

Increasingly, we should expect educational institutions, both in the United States as well as overseas, to entertain new curricula that widen our perspectives beyond our national borders in the scientific and social areas. To live in a context in which every decision affecting our material, technological, economic, or even social conditions has repercussions for people all over the world at present and in the future sets forth a wholly new educational challenge. Inevitably, our national interests will be diffused as an important educational focus. Our attention will be centered more on creating trained cadres that will perform skillfully for institutions, in organizations, and in bureaucracies, that will necessarily be worldwide in extent and allegiance.

We can see the new themes coming slowly but inexorably: law, self-discipline, egalitarianism, rationality, social responsibility, and forethought. Many idealists will be overjoyed at this prospect and will want the school more attuned to these values. Others will draw back in horror as they envision a creeping Orwellian nightmare of living regimented in perpetual gray twilight. Perhaps some will regret that the giddy materialistic "jag" we have been on will be ended. The question remains whether this vision of humanity, nature, and society that the equilibrium society of the future will bring is really an in-depth picture of people and culture.

We have already had a preview of what can happen in a democratic society when it has divested itself of the rich, informal culture of tradition to commit itself to building a vast and evolving technocracy whose great preoccupation is material acquisition and consumption. The barbarization: commercialization of high culture, erosion of community life, and gradual isolation and loss of identity by the individual has had its own set of social consequences.

Immense pressures and tensions will develop as we move out of the present transitional contexts into a world of constraint and limits, hopefully mediated through democratic political procedures. The peasants of the late eighteenth century were not so fortunate. Neither the luddites nor the *saboteurs* were able to turn back the march of industrialization that destroyed their peasant cultures, and consigned them to the machine. The equilibrium-society pill of total order is no easier to digest by its self-imposed ingestion.

Even now, hints are held out as to the potential resistance by our inner life. Our young, faced by the current monolithic institutionalism, have taken to drugs and a lethargic hedonism. The Russian young, satiated by propaganda and ideology, find their out in alcohol and apathy. In a sense, the active political and philosophic expression of revolt, as in our universities, is healthier in its tangible expression than the quiet but more alarming growth of religious cultism.

Merely setting forth on a social road of righting material and political wrongs of the past will not suffice as a core principle of educational endeavor. Like the building of our wealthy, powerful society, it may involve great energies of the young for a time. But in its essentially negative human aim, the equilibrium society will leave a large lacuna in human consiousness that will have to be filled from below.

Until recently we have been able to release these psychological elements onto the material and technological scene. Whether in the industrial, commercial, entertainment, or educational domains, the openness and expansiveness of opportunity for growth, innovation, even creativity, have been almost unlimited. While it has had sober tangible impact on our lives, the energies of a good proportion of our peoples have had a zestful, almost ludic, quality. In not knowing fully where our actions would lead us, we have had a sense of freedom and opportunity that was unique to our national history. The health of this psychological and physical interaction depended upon the assumption that the external expression of our energies would always redound to the good of all. Creativity and freedom are accompanied by optimism.

The deplorable contemporary historical situation lies in the very success of scientific and technological endeavors. With each thrust forward in our manipulation of the environment, the most subtle aesthetic and cultural skills have been pushed into the background. The blatant and crude skills of the robber barons have received their rewards. This has stimulated the whole society to emulate the élan of quantity and materiality that has produced our complex, if culturally primitive, civilization.

The passing historical scene will no longer allow for such values and freedoms. With more regulations, controls, and laws, even Wall Street may lose its psychological excitement. Computers and technocrats will no doubt displace the gambling urge of the financial speculators for the "big kill." But if the adventure of economic entrepreneurship is frustrated—an American instinct of many generations—what will replace it?

The educational challenge, then, goes far beyond the need to cultivate logical and technical skills that can be turned to good use in an industrialized society. Great libidinal forces need useful and creative social and cultural channeling of a type that we are inexperienced in handling in an educational or social context. If education in the equilibrium society is designed to save us from external disaster, then we must concomitantly plan a simultaneous educational task of staving off internal dissolution.

IRRATIONAL TRENDS

Our recent exposure to the counterculture is instructive, if only for negative reasons. This movement has reflected the disenchantment of the young with our massive institutionalism. Their attitudes toward knowledge, social life, and morality, however, represent a rebellion against the character and values of our society; at the same time, they embody this rebellion in a new life style. Little in the way of revolutionary philosophy would overturn the present social and political structure. Instead, the counterculture attempts to express in life within the interstices of a largely tolerant society (unlike the predicament of the early Christians in Rome) what the formal institutional modes of living have omitted.

The closest we get to an affirmation of a countercultural critique of the dominant culture and a philosophical statement of alternatives is in the rejection of the technocratic apparatus of our world and even the rationalism that created it. Theodore Roszak, a spokesman of this movement, wrote as follows:

> If there is to be an alternative to the technocracy, there "must" be an appeal from this reductive rationality which objective consciousness dictates. This, so I have argued, is the primary object of our counter-culture: to proclaim a new heaven and a new earth so vast, so marvelous that the inordinate claims of technical expertise must of necessity withdraw in the presence of such splendor to a subordinate and marginal status in the lives of man. To create and broadcast such a consciousness of life entails nothing less than the willingness to open ourselves to the visionary imagination on its own demanding terms.[1]

This vision of a new culture, Roszak conceives as one "in which the non-intellective capacities of the personality . . . those capacities that take fire from visionary splendor and the experience of human communion . . . become arbiters of the good, the true, and the beautiful." [2]

1. Theodore Roszak, *The Making of a Counter Culture* (Garden City, N.Y.: Doubleday, 1969), p. 240.
2. Ibid.

The concomitant exuberant growth of a wide variety of occult religions, bowdlerized versions of traditional religions, astrology, witchcraft, magic, "Jesus cults," reflect a dangerous reaction to the concrete and steel of our society. Do we have any assurance that the equilibrium society, certainly a benign and socially responsible world community, would be immune to such apparently irresponsible, even irrational trends? There is enough evidence to suggest that education will still have to deal with the informal elements of cultural existence if we have even a hope that the equilibrium society can be sustained over a long period of time.

What we are suggesting, then, is that even the most rationally and democratically planned society must build into itself a realm of the private and indeterminate in its social patterns—those areas of cultural life that do not bear on the essential surface physical and political questions of survival. Somewhere in our cultural lives there must be a place where what we do and how we live have no impact on the world-shaking decisions that must guide us in our external behaviors.

The complexity of the educational task must be evident, in dealing with factors that describe such subtle elements in man and culture. This difficulty is underscored when the pathological results of our contemporary world, the psychedelic as well as the violent behaviors of the young, must be bypassed to achieve a more general understanding of human motivations and needs. The complexity is deepened when we search for methods of self-understanding. No matter what social or psychological microscope or telescope we create, our ultimate instrument for understanding man is the human mind. As Ernst Cassirer once stated, "man cannot jump over his own shadow."

Perhaps we cannot have purely objective knowledge about human beings. We must, however, be open to all aspects of human behavior, to peer, however myopically, at that elusive creature that is the subject of our educational endeavors. At one time the goals and methods by which we might ameliorate the human condition were clear. Our ideologies of social redemption, the scientific and technological reshaping of the world, and finally, the work of formal education in raising up the young to live in this environment of opportunity, would presumably solve our most basic problems.

Unfortunately, with each advance, an almost equal setback was experienced. Deeper, unexpected currents kept rippling the surface. Our recent experience with youthful riot and revolution was merely a mild chill. The recurring horror of world wars and genocide seem to indicate that while social conditions do influence human behavior, people in turn create their own conditions. The most advanced cultures are not immune to being enveloped in barbarism. In fact the twentieth century, which has seen the development of unexpected power and physical capability by civilized people, may be concluded in a miasma of urban neuroses, psychoses, and social disorganization on a level that the world has yet to experience. Even in the urban heartlands of civilizational amenities and educational sophistication, the populace is today intimidated by criminality and terrorism. The old slogans about the environmental deprivation of individuals begin to pale in our dawning realization of ignorance before what seem to be primeval forces.

Can we accept the fact that we all live an important portion of our lives in terms of an inner psychological dimension in which there exist subconscious drives, aspirations for personal expression and symbolic meanings? Is it not likewise clear that these motivations are not merely the residue of simple drives for the satisfaction of our basic biological needs?

INNER MOTIVES

One need not agree with every detail of Sigmund Freud's structure of the human psyche, nor even with his views on basic human motivations. Yet his postulation of the existence of a tension between the individual and society has gained increasing credence simultaneously with our disillusionment with social ideologies and palliatives: [3]

> Civilization has to use its utmost efforts in order to set limits to man's aggressive instincts and to hold the manifestations of them in check by psychical reaction formations. Hence, therefore, the use of methods intended to incite people into identifications and aim-inhibited relationships of love, hence the restriction upon sexual life, and hence too the ideal's commandment to love one's neighbor as oneself—a commandment which is really justified by the fact that nothing else runs so strongly counter to the original nature of man. In spite of every effort, these endeavors of civilization have not so far achieved very much.[4]

3. Sigmund Freud, *Civilization and Its Discontents* (New York: W. W. Norton, 1962), p. 69.
4. Ibid., p. 59.

I think, the meaning of the evolution of civilization is no longer obscure to us. It must present the struggle between Eros and Death, between the instinct of life and the instinct of destruction, as it works itself out in the human species. This struggle is what all life essentially consists of, and the evolution of civilization may therefore be simply described as the struggle for life of the human species. And it is this battle of the giants that our nurse-maids try to appease with their lullaby about Heaven.[5]

Whether we agree or not as to Freud's interpretation of the nature of aggression, civilization, and to human existence in general, these views challenge us to rethink the relationship between an individual and society. It demands an analysis of those deeper urgings in all of us and the manner in which they can at the very least be channeled through all forms of education into life-enhancing qualities.

Philosopher Susanne Langer, who follows Freud and Ernst Cassirer on these matters, argued persuasively in her *Philosophy in a New Key* for a view that conceives of man's behavior not as biological reactions to the satisfaction of material needs useful in attaining evolutionary adaptation, but rather as a search for symbolic meaning.[6] She pointed to four factors which, among others, seemed to argue against the orthodox behaviorist or adaptational view of human nature. How could we explain the universality among people of such phenomena as dreaming, ritual, word magic, and art? It needed much imagination, she argued, to see in those phenomena practical and adaptive activities that would enhance the survival of the species.

Rather, they seemed to indicate a deep and pervasive tendency toward what she called "symbolic envisagement." This motivation rather than signifying an urge toward some practical behavior represented a basic urge to impute meaning and significance into all human activities. In every area of human action, we find the search for significance, an urge that wells up from the deepest ranges of the human mind.

As the new psycholinguistic tradition has demonstrated, an analysis of the surface features of the written or oral language is by no means sufficient to reveal the imputed meanings that lie within. This is what has bedeviled the attempt to devise computer trans-

5. Ibid., p. 69.
6. Susanne K. Langer, *Philosophy in a New Key* (Cambridge, Mass.: Harvard University Press, 1957), esp. Chap. 2.

lation programs. Only another mind from a similar culture can "see" the humor, metaphor, slang, play on words, hidden nuances that are inherent in language, and that are so imperfectly revealed in a surface analysis of grammar, syntax, and vocabulary (lexicality). One ought not view the "word magic" in primitive ritual or even in modern religious forms as delusory behavior. Their "practicality" is symbolic in that they communicate a wide range of mysterious and intimate meanings to the participants and the congregation.

The steady, inexplicable pumping of images into our dreams —that then return to haunt our daylight hours with their opaque significances—is another example of a dimension of our personality structure that defies simple materialistic explanations. And all of us know and participate in a variety of rituals that extend from morning ablutions to the most sacred and holy traditions of our religion. These rituals may not bake bread, but would life be meaningful without their regular, almost rhythmic, recurrence?

Art is the final symbolic dimension of human thought that seems so perplexingly antithetical to the biological model of behavior. All societies make of art one of their most intensely pursued preoccupations. Aesthetic perceptions, pursuits, and appreciations are powerful factors influencing the behavior of most human beings. And yet does that vast realm of human experience serve any apparent survivalistic purpose?

The range and intensity of the aesthetic experience in drama, music, or dance are immense. The kinds of objects that we transform from the practical to the artistic or the beautiful likewise seem to be unlimited. Such examples as a popular song, beauty of person, tantalizing cuisine, the aroma of flowers or romantic love, a painting or a poem, a collection of seashells or old guns, a jet airplane or a pickup truck indicate that few humans are immune to aesthetic fascination.

The earliest cave-dwelling humans painted dynamic and sensitive images of animal life on their darkened walls to symbolize and give visual expression to communal meanings that still baffle us.[7] All tribes design their tools of hunting, reaping, or war with a sense of aesthetic proportion and unity that complements functional utility but is not thereby limited aesthetically. Deep down in the basic structure of the human personality is a striving to transform the surface sensory experience we encounter into more meaningful symbolic structures.

7. Alexander Marshack, *The Roots of Civilization* (New York: McGraw-Hill, 1972).

Those people who have subordinated a preoccupation with commerce, militarism, and conspicuous accumulation to the cultivation of aesthetic form have won the admiration of all. Creative artists, whether they work with paint or in a scientific or industrial setting, elicit our accolades. In their receptivity to those deeper currents of sensibility and in their capacity to bring these forward into meaningful forms for others to appreciate, they represent a longing in each person. What they do, we would do, if we could.

Only when the freedom of creative experiment is contaminated or limited by extrinsic demands, commercial or political, does creativity suffer its greatest blockage. In our era the political power structure has learned that this creative force is dangerous; it must be kept in tow. In one society the artist will be threatened with imprisonment for not following politically motivated guidelines. In another society intrinsic forms and symbols are appropriated for commercial exploitation and cease to be serious vehicles for creative endeavors.

We still do not understand the origins or the significance of the symbolic urges of human beings. It is postulated that they came into being along with the development of the sapient brain. From a prosaic and endless seeker of physical satisfactions man has been transformed into what Loren Eisely has termed a "dream animal." The terra firma of the practical is not what motivates. Rather human urges spring from certain deeper tranformations of commonplace experiences.

Likewise we do not understand the unities in culture or the diversities that exist in the symbolic patterns of culture. Is there a principle of unity lurking somewhere waiting to be discovered or are our various interests and motives ulimately uncoordinated? Ernst Cassirer once pointed out that out of that primal force of what he called mythic feeling develop the great variety of symbolic forms of thought—the scientific, the aesthetic, the religious, the philosophical, and the poetic.

> Language and myth stand in an original and indissoluble correlation with one another, from which they both emerge but gradually as independent elements. They are two diverse shoots from the same parent stem, the same impulse of symbolic formulation, springing from the same basic mental activity, a concentration and heightening of simple sensory experience. In the vocables of speech and in the primitive mythic configurations the same inner process finds its consummation: they are both resolutions of an inner tension, the

representation of subjective impulses and excitations in definite objective forms and figures. . . .

Art like language, is originally bound up entirely with myth.[8]

And out of these root cultural expressions eventually come those highest qualities of civilization that combine both thought and emotion.

THE ROOTS OF BEHAVIOR

Feeling and emotion, the aggressive energies of the subconscious, achieve their realization in those social symbols that act to motivate us to go forward, to dream, desire, create, and believe. But they go beyond the individual, the family, the small community into the fabric of ordinary affairs of wider social experience. Usually these symbolic processes are attenuated by the practical necessities of the workaday world. True, we have our office parties, a ritualistic coffee break; we have company traditions, mottoes, even the gray flannel suit or, today, the instantaneously aged blue jeans, to identify us with the group. But the realities of making a living root our fancies to the work at hand.

These symbolic processes can sometimes go beyond the socially innocuous to become instrumentalities in powerful political mythologies that may unleash horrors, such as those that made the swastika a symbol of genocide and political madness, far from its once benign American Indian symbolism.

Johan Huizinga has written a gentle book about the "ludic" element in culture, the factor of play in relation to a wide variety of activities that one would ordinarily think of as being serious and practical endeavors. Huizinga shows that a significant range of these activities, from law and poetry to war itself, are infused with "agonistic" elements (contests and games) that not only lighten the boredom and the distasteful routine but endow the activity with special significance through rules, discipline, and controls reflective of the constant social need to master these deep and inchoate aggressive urgings at every point in the social compass.

Innumerable scholars have tried to understand the irresistible march of societies to war. The search for peace has been a long and persistent dream, but one whose success in distant past and for the

8. Ernst Cassirer, *Language and Myth* (New York: Harper & Brothers, 1946), pp. 88, 98.

future is illusory. The most that humans have been able to do is to discipline the activity, to order it through the agonistic principle as a competition subject to rules and regulations that might thereby mitigate its terrors. Huizinga writes:

> History and sociology tend to exaggerate the part played in the origin of wars, ancient or modern by immediate material interests and the lust for power. Though the statesmen who plan the war may themselves regard it as a question of power politics, in the great majority of cases the real motives are to be found less in the "necessities" of economic expansion, etc., than in pride and vain-glory, the desire for prestige and all the pomps of superiority. The great wars of aggression from antiquity down to our own times all find a far more essential explanation in the idea of glory, which everybody understands, than in any rational and intellectualist theory of economic forces and political dynamisms. The modern outbursts of glorifying war, so lamentably familiar to us, carry us back to the Babylonian and Assyrian conceptions of war as a divine injunction to exterminate foreign peoples to the greater glory of God.[9]

Only when the enemy is thus seen as beyond the pale—no longer subject to the game and its circumscribed rules—can total war begin with no limits set on the result. Huizinga wrote *Homo Ludens* before the full horror of World War II was manifested. His words were prophetic. Certainly the typical iconography—uniforms, medals, panoply of parades, the propaganda and emotionality—were evident as usual in World War II. Behind the usual symbols of the contest burned an unusually powerful demonic element, however, a myth of racial superiority and latent genocide that was unleashed to wreak havoc without limits. The dissolution of all law and regulations limiting the capacity of human beings for such uniquely human forms of debasement and savagery is again reflective of a force unlimited in its powers, but, it should be suggested, perhaps not necessarily evil or destructive.

As Freud and Cassirer have asserted, it is a power that, channeled constructively, can build and enrich civilization; or it can place people in a position to pervert life itself, below the level of all natural animalistic behavior.[10] But, if we do not study or even

9. Johan Huizinga, *Homo Ludens* (Boston: Beacon Press, 1955), pp. 190–91.
10. See E. Cassirer, *The Myth of the State* (New Haven: Yale University Press, 1946); Freud, *Civilization and Its Discontents.*

recognize these psychic forces, can we hope to use them constructively in educating the individual and his community?

One of the most interesting books in recent years probes the sources and significances of these subterranean drives. Few hidden human urges escape the scrutiny of Georges Bataille in his *Death and Sensuality*. Bataille is deeply influenced by the ideas of Freud. Yet he is an existentialist and thus suspicious of those reductive biological forces that Freud attributes to man's aggressive tendencies.

Bataille here reveals to us a human creature in whom basic biological drives as sexuality, eroticism, and death are intertwined in such contradictory psychological patterns as to do violence to any simple behavioral description. Bataille begins his book: "The human spirit is prey to the most astounding impulses. Man goes constantly in fear of himself. His erotic urges terrify him. The saint turns from the voluptuary in alarm; she does not know that his unacknowledgable passions and her own are really one. . . ."

> I do not think that man has much chance of throwing light on the things that terrify him before he has dominated them. Not that he should hope for a world in which there would be no cause for fear, where eroticism and death would be on the level of a mechanical process. But man can surmount the things that frighten him and face them squarely.[11]

He proceeds to set forth the enigmatic, paradoxical, yet strangely persuasive argument of his book:

> Sexual reproductive activity is common to sexual animals and men, but only men appear to have turned their sexual activity into erotic activity. Eroticism, unlike simple sexual activity, is a psychological quest independent of the natural goal: reproduction and the desire for children . . . eroticism is assenting to life even in death. Indeed, although erotic activity is in the first place an exuberance of life, the object of this psychological quest, independent as I say of any concern to reproduce life, is not alien to death.[12]

The implied argument in Bataille's contrast of the erotic principle in man versus the mundane work attitude of modern society is the implacable resistance to external domination offered by these

11. George Bataille, *Death and Sensuality* (New York: Walker & Co., 1962), p. 7.
12. Ibid., p. 11.

inner drives of man. For a short historical period it is possible for society, in the exhilaration of expansion, advance, and modernization, to discipline, organize, and bureaucratize society, to put people in factories and offices for hours of deadening daily routine. Indeed, it is possible to model the educational system to reflect the mechanized structure of the efficiency experts. We can build our educational parks or multiversities where we process thousands of youngsters through the credentializing machine.

Is it possible long to sustain institutional patterns that violate the inner rhythms of human behavior? Paradoxically, humankind creates that world of concrete and steel that so arrogantly flaunts its coercive power. There is a puzzling perversity here. Human beings create the institutions that thereupon provoke people to revolt, threatening them with annihilation by the machine or psychological castration, wherein they must conform like herded sheep. But it is all part of the circle of human folly. This dissidence and intractability prevent people from responding to even the most persuasive educational techniques. It constitutes the Achilles heel of the totalitarian solution.

The stubborn human soul revolts; the dam bursts. Often it takes place in unexpected and bizarre patterns, in ways that are least anticipated. In our recent experience, the most pampered and privileged of the young threw off their discipline and in the eyes of their parents strayed into the most embarrassing patterns of personal behavior. We would not wonder why if we understood the relationship between human psychocultural needs and the society within which we must live.

But just as the insect in the ecstasy of rapturous fulfillment satiates itself unto death in the flower's nectar, so too the human being is impelled to break from the machinelike regimentation of society and expend himself in the temptation of drug-induced self-annihilation, war, suicide, violent crime. They all share certain elements of the demonic, usually unrelated to such mundane causes as unemployment, territoriality, and economic poverty.

Bataille describes that perverse, yet so common, urging: the orgy:

> In the orgy the celebration progresses with the overwhelming force that usually brushes all bonds aside. In itself the feast is a denial of the limits set on life by work, but the orgy turns everything upside down. . . . The orgy is not associated with the dignity of religion, extracting from the underlying violence

something calm and majestic compatible with profane order; its potency is seen in its ill-omened aspects, bringing frenzy in its wake and a vertiginous loss of consciousness. The total personality is involved, reeling blindly towards annihilation, and this is the decisive moment of religious feeling ... the suspension of taboos sets free the exuberant surge of life and favours the unbounded orgiastic fusion of individuals. This fusion could in no way be limited to that attendant on the plethora of the genital organs. It is a religious effusion first and foremost; it is essentially the disorder of lost beings who oppose no further resistance to the frantic proliferation of life. That enormous unleashing of natural forces seems to be divine so high does it raise man above the condition to which he has condemned himself of his own accord. Wild cries, wild violence of gestures, wild dances, wild emotions as well, all in the grip of immeasurably convulsive turbulence.[13]

The orgy exists on the borders of socially sanctioned noncriminal behavior. In times of national celebration, religious rites of a Dionysian stamp, at carnival or Midsummer Night or even Sadie Hawkins Day, human behavior for one short moment can transgress the limits of normal decorum. But the moral control that society exercises so as to allow these transgressions to occur within temporal (a night or a day or two) and behavioral bounds is usually explicit. It is only when conditions are such—as in unlimited war against a despised adversary—that the sadistic and completely unbounded behavior of a Calley (Vietnam) or an Ilse Koch (the beast of Belsen in Nazi Germany) can occur. Such desecrations are permanently held to be excessive and under civilized conditions will be punished even by members of their own groups.

In this way society links itself with the secret forces within each person, to lead one forth into the open and through ritual, festivities, athletics, art, humor, and ribaldry, draw the web of culture around these powers and transmute them through informal education and through creative social works. In the higher civilization, new symbolic forms—science, philosophy, the fine arts, literature, even technology and commercial enterprises—are created so as to channel much of this energy into new expressive, even if practical, patterns of thought and action.

13. Ibid., pp. 112–13.

PERVERSE INSTITUTIONS

What happens to these psychological drives when huge impersonal institutions constitute an implacable barrier to the spontaneous flow of images, ideas, and impulses? The wily manipulation of the masses in modern totalitarian societies exemplifies some of the dangers. In our own society, the creation by the mass media of pseudo events—the mass entertainments and professional sports, the waves of hysterical enthusiasts for "rock festivals," the "Haight-Ashbury scene"—indicate the fragile balance we maintain today in fending off chaos and anarchy. The situation is reminiscent of that characterized by the late Middle Ages as the symbols and metaphors of that era began to break down as cores of meaning around which lives and institutions could be built.

The forces of centralization and interdependence are now so great that the immediate danger lies in the totalitarian solution, which can be succeeded only by chaos and dissolution. Yet the alternatives in the sphere of social reorganization and redirection are so opaque that we have instead tended to search for surcease within the individual. The recent wave of psychological retreats, Esalen institutes, etc., the sensitivity training, "T" groups, "Gestalt therapy," have been paralleled in the formal educational structure by a wave of hope focused on "humanistic education."

Educators who have promoted this movement have seen in it the possibility of developing programs for the cultivation of the affective domain—emotions, feelings, and innerness. The kind of society we have created, especially the educational institutions affecting adolescents and young adults in high schools and colleges, has been seen as the cause of the widespread alienation. Writers like Theodore Roszak and Charles Reich *(The Greening of America)* have been especially popular with the young for their condemnation of the aridity and meritocratic impersonality of educational institutions.

The humanistic movement has looked to individuals in the privacy of their being and in intimate relationships with like-afflicted people to emote, feel, express, and relate. Programs and curricula developed to counter the otherness of human relationships fostered by the technocracy have attempted to facilitate spontaneity in behavior, release repressed inhibitions, and break down the exteriority of interpersonal relationships. The fear of touching one another or of expressing a hidden thought or a secret emotion is expunged. The humanistic education movement has attempted to bring individuals, pupils and teachers, closer together in insight into common problems and relationships, to communicate on a level that heretofore was impossible in the traditional forms of educational organization.

The problem of humanistic education lies in the fact that even at the point of its greatest success, in awakening the individual to the reality of an inner emotional life and the capacity to contact others in intimacy of feeling, it constitutes a negative education. In merely reacting to the sterility of society and education it cuts itself off from important productive dimensions of life where those individual potencies can be expressed in real-life contexts. Intimacy, where it does not link itself with individuals in normal reciprocal relationships involving work and creation, becomes sterile.

You cannot manufacture emotions, feelings, or openness in artificial, often commercialized, settings, where individuals have few common bonds—of belief, religious or ethnic, or even neighborliness. Affect must in some manner be developed out of relationships that have continuity in time and contiguity in space. Humanistic education, then, as it conceives of one's inner psychic life as separable from one's social and intellectual life and attempts to release and activate it away from such normal contextual settings, cannot be other than dangerous. The preliminary excitation and stimulation of "humanistic" techniques having no productive fulfillments in work and life can only compound the sense of personal failure and frustration. At the least, they can be turned inward in apathy and hysteria; at the worst, outward, in dangerous projections.

In emphasizing the importance of the social dimension as a means of channeling, enriching, and symbolizing our inner drives, we do not mean to ignore the original tension between the person and the community. Freud was correct in noting the dichotomy in the human being between the "I" and the "not I." The problem is not only rooted in human aggressive energies but also in the fact that whereas animals are naturally restricted by the absolute character of their instinctual assertions and prohibitions, the human being has few specific instinctual patterns of behavior to fall back upon. To become a person one needs the primary informal educational sustenance of family, community, and culture. What kind of person and what kind of culture now constitutes our open-ended dilemma.

CONCLUSION

This discussion of the problems entailed in the education of people by the existence of an only dimly understood realm of drives, symbolic needs, and unconscious psychological processes has been presented to short-circuit any optimistic hopes that the planned Utopianism of an equilibrium society might give rise to.[14] The laws, universal principles, and disciplines of the equilibrium society may do well to account for the needs of the outer person. Indeed, there are those in politics and education who conceive of those material needs as being exhaustive of human motivations. But it is our contention that such a world is inherently unstable, as much if not more so than our present social system.

We will certainly be forced within a century to accept a set of social conditions that will roughly meet the requirements of the equilibrium society. At the same time we need to find room within this all-encompassing model for a structure of informal education that nurtures those less tangible motivations and concerns of the inner person. There must be a place in our lives where we and our communities are free to act at the least between the interstices of established regulations and guidelines.

So much in the human soul needs to be set free, to be unleashed, and yet guided and shaped in terms of evoking the powers of the mind and heart. Our knowledge of what these powers and needs are is still feeble. We have a responsibility at least to attempt to envision a structural counterbalance to the equilibrium society, a context drawn from the best source of knowledge about people, their own history. The successes and the acknowledged failures of the past will teach us that we can hope to perceive at least dimly the contexts for education that seem to retain the best and stave off the worst.

---

14. This entire utopian concern is reflected in the writings of Rudolph Klein of the Center for Social Policy Studies in London.

14 The Cultural Community: Historical Sources

To the size of states there is a limit, as there is to other things, plants, animals, implements; for none retain their natural power when they are too large or too small, but they either wholly lose their nature, or are spoiled . . . a state when composed of too few is not, as a state ought to be, self sufficing; when of too many, though self-sufficing in all mere necessaries, as a nation may be, it is not a state, being almost incapable of constitutional government. For who can be the general of such a vast multitude, or who the heralds, unless he have the voice of a Stentor? . . . A State, then, only begins to exist when it has attained a population sufficient for a good life in the political community. . . . Clearly then the best limit of the population of a State is the largest number which suffices for the purposes of life, and can be taken in at a single view.

—Aristotle, *Politics*

Is there a natural community that is appropriate for humanity? Are humans, like animals, fitted to live only in a restricted ecological context with nature, to be punished by nature if they transgress its limits? Aristotle, reflecting on the wisdom of his tradition, believed in such limits. Writing the above words over two thousand years ago and at a late period in his own maturity, he thus summed up his analysis of the lesson of the Greek experience.

In recent generations we have rarely looked back at human history to ask whether our own solutions to social life harmonize with either nature or human nature. So intent have we been on the process of modernization, social advance, and growth that we began to assume that nature was something we molded to our own contemporary needs. There was nothing we found impossible to accomplish. And of course formal education was empowered with the obligation to reshape man to a world that was always in process.

We are more sobered today. We have become frightened at the rapid degradation of our environment. Our social progress is impeded by enormous outstanding social debts (with interest), witness the excrescences of urban life. Many concerned citizens are more attuned to Aristotle's warnings. Unlike animals, we are without instincts to restrain our folly. Prudence, wisdom, and education have failed us as we have avoided critical questions about ourselves and our needs.

The purported short-term advantages of a few have created social monstrosities with problems so great they they blind us to the possibilities of creating more natural, human communities. But we must look to the time when people can live in a communal setting that will fulfill their ambiguous and ultimately unknown nature, in a manner potentially less devastating to their future prospects.

THE ARCHETYPE

Perhaps the fragility of our own social institutions has led archeologists to dissipate the mists of prehistory to probe that era of human existence between the time humans painted the walls of the caves of Altamira and Lescaux, 25,000 years ago, and the dawning of recorded history in Sumer and Egypt, 5,000 to 6,000 years ago.

The results of these recent excavations have altered our perspectives on the nature of prehistoric life and the communal structure under which humankind has lived for the major part of the existence of the species. As Graham Clark and Stuart Piggott report it, prehistoric people lived a more variegated existence than that which we usually attribute to recently analyzed primitive people.[1] The latter, usually frozen into an ecological and cultural niche, have developed a variety of extreme patterns of behavior that appear to be well off the main line of social and community advance that existed before the development of the great civilizations.

Prehistoric people apparently developed rich cultural resources; they traded and traveled over a wide territory. And while the pace of social and technological change was slow, it was steady enough to keep those communities constantly on the alert for new tools or items of trade. This ensured that they would not be stalled and shunted aside in the competition for survival. The limited technological skills available to them kept their tribal size down and in constant balance with the available ecology. Unstable climatic conditions in this postglacial era presumably were responsible for those migratory patterns that inhibited the development of such

1. Graham Clark and Stuart Piggott, *Prehistoric Societies* (New York: Knopf, 1967).

larger-scaled settlements as appeared in the late Neolithic, e.g., Jericho in Palestine, that subsequently could develop into settled towns and cities.

Clark and Piggott claim that these early settlements or villages were so well integrated in terms of social structure and balance with nature that they represent an archetypal social solution to which many higher civilizations reverted upon their collapse. We see some of these patterns retained even in development of the larger social forms as a model of community life. This is described as follows:

> By independent invention or by derivation, Indo-European and (in its later form) Celtic Europe shared in the simple social pattern in which a tribe or village is governed by the assembled free citizens and a council, and the office of king or chieftain, at least in the simpler societies, is elective. It was a stratified society, its component levels bound one to another by a system of obligations and privileges, with a ruler of greater or lesser power, an aristocracy which often also embodied a warrior corps d'elite, a priesthood, and a basic population of agricultural workers and craftsmen. This last category may have included poets of the oral tradition proper to such non-literate societies, who, if not themselves in the priesthood, may have had special status, as certain craftsmen and merchants may also have had. Caesar's "equites," "druides," and "plebes" reflect this in simplified form, and the early Irish literature, reflecting a prehistoric way of life, shows it to us in detail, sometimes idealized into complex legal fictions, but nevertheless recognizably a social structure which would have been familiar to Agamemnon or to a Sumerian of the fourth millennium B.C.[2]

And yet this simple structure, once penetrated by the various technological, literary, and military breakthroughs at the dawning of civilization, gave way before a series of great transnational civilizations—Egypt, Assyria, and Rome. Monolithic, expansionary, militaristic, these societies dissolved much of the individualistic and independent qualities of the earlier simpler societies. One can almost hear the collective groans of dismay that took place over the generations as independent communities were herded into the ironlike grip of the respective social machines.

We know no precise reason for this inevitable thrust toward bigness and away from the natural texture of informal education. The mystery devolves upon those same psychic sources as do our

2. Ibid., pp. 331–32.

creative and aesthetic urges, erotic and romantic drives, religious and ecstatic visions. The aggressive accumulation of social power is paralleled by the surge to know, to comprehend. Being without instinctual limits, we have no prima facie biological restraints to limit our excesses. Too often we have inadequate rational perspectives to inform us of the future results of our impetuous actions. Thus, as exemplified in the collapse of Egypt into feudalism following the tremendous human and material expenditures in building the pyramids, arrogance—*hubris*—in its social dimensions so often leads to the collapse of the great society into the simpler state.

Whether in its original prehistoric version or in the various reconstitutions since then, these societies contain within themselves the basic characteristics of what we might call the *cultural community*. The organic relationship between the whole community and its various personal and institutional parts, the awareness of identity and value as part of being a member of this community, all build that critical dimension of informal education which every human being needs to discover himself. Lewis Mumford has described an aspect of life in the cultural community which he calls the "neolithic community." [3]

> Wherever the seasons are marked by holiday festivals and ceremonies: where the stages of life are punctuated by family and communal rituals: where eating and drinking and sexual play constitute the central core of life: where work, even hard work, is rarely divorced from rhythm, song, human companionship, and esthetic delight: where vital activity is counted as great a reward of labor as the product: where neither power nor profit takes precedence of life: where the family and the neighbor and the friend are all part of a visible, tangible, face to face community: where everyone can perform as a man or woman any task that anyone else is qualified to do—there the neolithic culture, in its essentials, is still in existence, even though iron tools are used or a stuttering motor truck takes the goods to market.[4]

We do not have to equate the cultural community with the simple, undeveloped social unit described by Mumford. The rich human rewards that inhere in the cultural community can be reflected in a highly developed intellectual, economic, and technological setting. As Clark and Piggott point out, a relatively demo-

3. Lewis Mumford, *The Myth of the Machine* (New York: Harcourt, Brace, 1966).
4. Ibid., p. 158.

cratic society existed in Sumer and elsewhere at the same time that pharaonic Egypt dominated the upper and lower Nile Valley.

> The creation in Western Asia from Anatolia to Baluchistan of a social pattern which was individualistic and particularistic, rather than with any claims to universality, provided for elasticity and adaptability even if it also had in it the seeds of potential fragmentation unless its disparate units were welded together under autocratic rule. But the essential social unity, the autonomous village or town community that could become a city-state, despite the fact that the city god and the temple formed its centre of religious and economic organization in historical times, was based on concepts of local loyalties; it was organized and ruled by men whose service to the gods of the town was direct, and not conducted through the medium of a single god who as king ruled over all such towns within a realm which existed only in terms of his own divine person.[5]

If the lands of the Fertile Crescent (the Tigris and Euphrates valleys) were propitious areas for the development of civilized life, they were not well placed for the nurturing of small, independent clusters of urban life. Too many highways ran through this area over which migrating people wandered. With organization and intelligence, the people could produce great wealth on such land. But it was almost impossible, given the political and intellectual condition of these ancient times, to maintain diversified social units in the face of a strong unifying leader or an aggressive sociopolitical group.

THE GREEK COMMUNITY

While one cannot deny the cumulative civilizational impetus provided by the Near East, it was in the rock-strewn archipelago of Greece, a land with great ecological limitations, that the greatest burst of cultural, educational, and political achievement occurred. Here, in these small city-states, community life was so ordered that it released that rich variety of creative talents that has since been used as a social yardstick to judge and measure subsequent educational and cultural achievements.

The facts and names that constitute the Greek achievement are familiar, dawning in the Minoan and Mycenaean mists of about 1500 B.C., coming to a peak in Periclean Athens of fifth century B.C., experiencing a gradual political, though not cultural, subsidence in

5. Clark and Piggott, *Prehistoric Societies*, pp. 222-23.

the centuries that followed, then being absorbed under Roman hegemony. The problem that the Greeks present to us is that of understanding the special structural characteristics of their society that allowed them to release their creative and intellectual energies in such a positive manner. The Greeks were not a superpeople genetically. They had entered Greece through the same general migratory process that brought the Indo-Europeans into lands as disparate as Spain, England, and India.

Subsequent to their arrival in Greece, they underwent social and cultural transformations that lifted them from one plateau of human existence to the next. Ultimately, by balancing that delicate distillation of inner and outer man, they created a culture that we consider to be a peak in human history.

The historian Thucydides pondered the same question concerning the greatness of Athens. But he also contemplated the greatness in the context of the disastrous Peloponnesian War with Sparta. Why the rise, why the collapse? He attributed the cause of Athens' long tradition of internal peace and social integration (as compared with other Greek cities) to the relative barrenness of Attica, the peninsular homeland of the Athenians. Marauding people would always avoid Attica; it was too slim pickings. Thus the relative stability, ethnic, and social unity of the Athenians. This continuous inner texture of community life allowed them, as Alfred Zimmern has noted, to substitute a public code of justice for the law of vendetta.[6] The way was paved for the coming of the democratic political and social reforms of Solon and Pericles.

The early sixth century B.C. saw Athens as a small and relatively insignificant town scratching out its existence on the soil and through a mixed fishing, mining, and trading economy. Less than two hundred years later, in an era of few technological advances, it had become the preeminent city of Hellas. Hannah Arendt discusses this miracle of cultural creativity by comparing the Athenian concept of the public life with our own.[7]

Whereas today the creative, personal, fulfilling elements are maintained within private households and we concede as little as necessary to the corruptions and disappointments of the external world, the Athenians reversed this attitude.[8] They were fulfilled as

6. Alfred Zimmern, *The Greek Commonwealth* (London: Oxford University Press, 1961; first published in 1911).
7. Hannah Arendt, *The Human Condition* (Chicago: University of Chicago Press, 1958).
8. Ibid.

individuals out-of-doors among their fellows—in the marketplace, exercising at the gymnasium, in the Assembly where they met to resolve the great public issues that affected their city. The religious, ceremonial, and artistic work on the Acropolis, the Olympiads, the festivals and dramatic performances, indeed the entire city of Athens, as Werner Jaeger has noted, became an educational environment for young and old.[9] During the Periclean era, the Athenians themselves became conscious of this educational achievement, which they called *paideia*. Indeed, in his famous speech at the beginning of the Peloponnesian Wars, Thucydides has Pericles boast that Athens was the educator of the Greeks.

To what can one attribute this burst of cultural luminescence from such seemingly deprived natural and social sources and over such a few short generations? Obviously, the Athenians were a naturally gifted people. In addition, they shared with their fellow Greeks a rich, deep, and long-abiding informal culture from as far back as the pre-Homeric, Mycenaean era, almost a thousand years of cultural history on which to build. There was no great technological breakthrough that made possible the Parthenon, the plays of Sophocles, or the philosophy of Plato. It was their development of a public civic life that brought out the symbolic currents that heretofore had been held prisoner by the limited familial and tribal social structures.

There is, however, some evidence to show that the Athenians, through their educational forms, kept contact with their fund of creative symbols, kept in dynamic balance the connection between the emotions, memories, and traditions of their informal culture—a past that linked them with the ancient pantheon of gods and places and that increasingly present and active public world in which the shape of the creative act was being given tangible reality. It was in music and the dance, in the religious, dramatic, and civic festivals, that the inner life of Greek culture and thus of Greek education were being reinforced.

Let me quote a most reliable authority, Henri Marrou:

> In the Republic, Plato, describing the education of the "good old days," tells us that his was two-sided, comprising "gymnastics" for the body and "music" for the soul. From the beginning, as we have seen, Greek culture and hence Greek education had included, besides sport, an element that was spiritual, intellectual and artistic all at once. In Plato, music . . .

9. Werner Jaeger, *Paideia* (New York: Oxford University Press, 1945).

signifies the domain of the Muses in the widest sense; but in ancient education generally, music in the narrower sense of the word—i.e. vocal and instrumental music—came first in this category. . . . The historian has to stress this to correct an error in perspective: as they appear in our own classical culture the Greeks were primarily poets, philosophers and Mathematicians; and when we pay homage to their artistic genius we mean their architecture and sculpture. We never think of them as musicians. Our scholars and teachers pay less attention to their music than to their ceramics! And yet they looked upon themselves first and foremost as musicians.

Greek culture and education were artistic rather than scientific, and Greek art was musical before it became literary and plastic. It was "the lyre and sprightly dancing and singing" that summed up civilized life for Theognis . . . as Plato says bluntly: "Anyone who cannot take his place in a choir [i.e., as both singer and dancer] is not truly educated." [10]

It is ironic to compare our own vast society of hundreds of millions of people to the several hundred thousand Athenians. With all our wealth and talents, with the organizational power of many pharaohs, we have created an educational system awesome in its external attainment in literacy and technological capacity. The Athenians, on the other hand, paid relatively little heed to school organization and pedagogical problems of the three Rs. Their great pedagogical concern was with music and gymnastics, that delicate balance of inner soul and outer body which they saw as a central factor in the maintenance of their polis and public life. Yet can we say that in literacy or intellectual accomplishment they need take second place to us?

Stringfellow Barr describes this process of education during the "golden age" of Athens, the fifth century B.C.

An Athenian boy of Pericles' clan would spend his first seven years in the women's quarters with his mother. He was then schooled by men. First he learned to read and write and reckon, on his little wooden tablet covered with soft wax to take the stylus' mark. Then he studied music, which included not only melody, not only flute, the lyre, singing, and the dance, but the epic poets, Homer and Hesiod, and lyric poets like Solon,

10. Henri I. Marrou, *A History of Education in Antiquity*, tr. George Lamb (New York: Mentor, 1964), pp. 69–70. See pp. 192–93 and p. 197 on the decline of dancing, singing (chorus), music and gymnastics under the press of professionalization and a literary culture which is private.

Mimmermus, Theognis. Music and poetry were expected to
form his soul to gentle and to civilize him. Was not music the
lore of the muses of Olympus, daughters of Zeus, who danced
on soft feet about his altar on holy Helicon where Hesiod
shepherded his lambs? . . . The poems and melodies they could
teach to men must open the heart of the young Athenian to
things mere reasoning could not fathom; must bring his heart
into harmony with wiser minds and deeper knowledge than
any race of iron could hope to find without the muses' aid.[11]

Our system of education, by comparison, is more and more
geared to the needs of our great machinelike corporate institutions.
A transcontinental society presumably needs transcontinental
schools and a variety of legal compulsions to ensure those anonymous satisfactions. So we compel through law and taxation, attendance, school organization, curricula, certificates, diplomas and
degrees. It is a well-ordered system, but hollow. There can never be a
transcontinental community. Nor can public life be fulfilled through
the TV tube.

The core of human social life responds to more intimate urgings.
The public sharing of values, both of the heart and the mind, can be
facilitated only through interpersonal nuances, for people confront
each other directly with those matters which are of ultimate significance. The balance of factors that are directly public and affect the
political and the esthetic environment, and that also touch the hidden familial, personal, and even traditional concerns, is delicate. The
natural results of such a fortuitous educational melding can be that
momentary cultural exaltation of the human spirit that we saw in
Athens. Education will then have done its work unself-consciously,
but well.

THE HELLENISTIC AND ROMAN DECLINE

Soon the magic disappears and the disentangling proceeds
apace. Already Plato and Aristotle complain of the professionalism
in arts and sports that were beginning to infect this now comfortable
and sophisticated polity. Aristotle, writing about 330 B.C., still
affirms,

. . . . music has the power of modifying the character of the
soul: and if it has this power we must of course make use of it

11. Stringfellow Barr, *The Will of Zeus* (Philadelphia: Lippincott, 1961), pp.
122–23.

and educate the young by it. . . . Besides there seems to be a certain affinity between the soul and rhythm and scales, which accounts for the fact that many wise men say that the soul is or has a musical pitch.[12]

At the very time Aristotle was writing these words, Alexander was remaking the Greek culture. His far-reaching conquests served to establish Greek cities throughout the Mediterranean. In effect, he created an international Hellenic society. Literally dozens of semi-Hellenized states, distributed over the Mediterranean littoral, took up the themes of Greek culture in a diversity of modalities. Those were communities with a common cultural theme but a true plurality of variation. Whatever their political defects—and there were many—they were communities wherein a new message of Greek *paideia* was being broadcast.

Perhaps they did not achieve that acme of aesthetic, political, and philosophical attainment that the Athenians had achieved in their short burst of luminescence. But, as Rostovtzeff has noted, the intense competition (similar to the earlier period) evinced in these many diverse and scattered states in their attempts to recreate the Hellenic ideal, each within the bounds of their own particular communities, produced a profligacy of cultural attainment in every civilizational area we cherish today.[13]

In science alone, a burst of creativity was let loose that has rarely been matched. That it never generated technological momentum is due only to the special historical circumstances that ultimately displaced this most fascinating period. By 100 B.C. not only had the heliocentric theory been postulated, but also the circumference of the earth had been closely approximated mathematically, and the steam engine invented.

Slowly the atmosphere of educational fertility changed, and a new ethos began to take hold. Science, which had developed to a high state of theoretical grandeur and which could have altered the very structure of the classical world, advanced no further. It did not enter into the social fabric but remained in the academy and then disappeared as a creative force.

What could eventually have developed into a new technological emancipation, had this science been joined to practical invention, did not occur. The steam engine remained a plaything of religious and occult wizardry. In part the root of this failed revolution lay in

12. *Politics*, Book 8.
13. Michael Rostovtzeff, *Greece* (New York: Galaxy Oxford, 1963), chap. 17.

the rationalistic and nonmanipulative attitudes toward the uses of knowledge.

Ptolemy, a Greek astronomer, lived in a Roman era (A.D. 127–51) when scientific creativity was but a memory and when the great intellectual preoccupation was the codification of the past. The rationalistic and aesthetic attitude toward knowledge and education was still pervasive and typical. No experimental application would come from this persuasion:

> I know that I am mortal, a creature of a day; but when I search into the multitudinous revolving spirals of the stars, my feet no longer rest on the earth, but standing by Zeus himself, I take my fill of ambrosia, the food of the Gods.[14]

But there were even more important structural conditions that dampened creativity and progress in philosophy and the sciences. The roots of this weakness can be traced to the chaotic social conditions of the Hellenistic era—constant wars and revolutions in the various city-states. Ultimately Rome took advantage of these conditions of chaos to effect a state of political unification that could be achieved only through the military machine.

Just as prosaic Macedonia overcame the inspired but chaotic Hellenic Greeks, so too the sober political, economic, and military might of efficient and expansive Rome ground out the diversity of the Hellenistic world. Administrative order took its place. All roads now led to Rome; the educational and cultural preoccupations shifted. Roman civilization was not less bloody than the Hellenistic; it was more methodical and externally applied. The self-generated creative inspirations disappeared, while the schools and universities expanded institutionally to collate the knowledge of others into great encyclopedias.

Ludwig Edelstein has investigated the decline of science in the Roman Empire, noting that the great second-century scientists Ptolemy and Galen were systematizers rather than creators. It was not slavery, nor was it necessarily a practical lassitude toward nature, that dried up the wellsprings of thought. Rather, he argues, it was a shift in ideal, preoccupation, and ethos.[15] In short it was the supplantation of the cultural community by the mass society.

---

14. Ptolemy, *Anthologia Palatina*, ix, 577.
15. Ludwig Edelstein, "Recent Trends in the Interpretation of Ancient Science," in *Roots of Scientific Thought*, ed. Philip Wiener (New York: Basic Books, 1957).

This is not the place to inquire how far certain trends of eclecticism, noticeable even before the second century, or the Roman interest in encyclopedic summaries of knowledge prepared the way for work done by men like Galen, Ptolemy and others. One cannot help feeling that they were inspired by the practical unification of the world. It is surely of significance that Galen prided himself on having unified medicine, just as Trajan had unified Italy by means of the roads that he had built. At any rate, the ascendancy of the new vision of science was considerably aided by social factors. In the Roman empire the educational system as well as the attitude of society toward science underwent revolutionary changes. The state provided educational facilities. Public schools were founded, universities sprang up. Professorships were endowed, examinations for scholars were introduced. Instruction in the schools all over the empire became standardized. Alexandria, Rome, Massilia, Athens were all part of the same political structure, and consequently also represented the same science. The varied ancient democracies corresponded to the individualistic systems of science in the classical age; the various Hellenistic kingdoms corresponded to the several schools; the uniform Roman empire came to have one science only. . . .

Progress was retarded; there was a loss of fibre. The "sober drunkenness" which had inspired earlier investigations no longer prevailed; scientists became specialists and officials.[16]

The emperor Hadrian, ruling at the zenith of this era of centralization, spent his lifetime traveling through this ethnically disparate yet politically, economically, militarily, even culturally disciplined empire. The surge in prosperity and power epitomized in the efficiency and organizational ability of this great man resulted in an increase in progress and confidence reminiscent of our own recent national history. But it was only a superficial unity, a veneer of civilization.

In the arts, the process of decay was inevitable. Gymnastics, music, and dancing, the old tradition of the "chorus," gradually withered away. They were replaced by the more passive spectator entertainments, where professionals performed. Civic participation in the sense of the enhancement of individual skills as part of a public obligation passed away. Social controls and political power were too distant to make participation relevant—and in every walk of life.

16. Ibid., p. 121. See also S. Itzkoff, "The Cultural Community," *Notre Dame Journal of Education* 3 (Fall 1970): 225–35.

Gone were the days when a Socrates was said to have carved a muse on the Acropolis in only one of his variegated roles in Athenian life. What a difference between a typical Roman professional general and an Athenian officer chosen by lot! It is said that the Athenian general Themistocles, hero of the victory over the Persians at Salamis (480 B.C.), was shamed at a dinner party *(symposium)* because when his turn had come to play and sing with the lyre he had to admit that his "plebian" education had denied him these skills.

Henri Marrou describes this process of decline, even at the height of the "Greek revival" under Hadrian (A.D. 130):

> This growing paralysis of musical pedagogy, the ever-widening gap between school music and the living art, explains why the musical side of Greek education, which had been one of its really original and attractive features, gradually declined during Hellenistic times. The only places where it seems to have persisted were conservative regions like Laconia, Arcady, and Achaea, and here it was simply another sign of the ossification of these cities, which remained outside the main cultural stream. Here and there, of course, there were a few signs of its survival—as late as A.D. 163-164 we find the Athenian ephebes learning to sing hymns in honour of the divine Hadrian under the direction of a chorus master. Nevertheless, on the whole, it is true to say that music tended to disappear from liberal education. This does not mean to say that it disappeared from Greek culture; on the contrary it was more popular than ever; but it is one thing to listen to it, quite another thing to play it.[17]

Two generations later, Hadrian's adopted grandson, Marcus Aurelius, was forced to devote virtually his entire reign to personal supervision of the borders alongside his garrisons. If the external perimeters were not secured against the barbarian, the empire might totter. This military endeavor stretched well into the next century and eventually drained the empire of its life blood. It destroyed the middle class. What little local autonomy existed was eliminated. Christianity, Judaism, the many mystery religions spread a cloud of alienation and otherworldliness over the people. The desiccation from within, the brittleness of the external defences, ultimately allowed the barbarians to infiltrate and topple the monolith.

The Roman intellectual elite withdrew to their monasteries—rural fortresslike estates—carrying with them the echoes of ancient ideals. Here and there, through the amalgam of Greco-Roman and Judeo-

17. Marrou, *History of Education in Antiquity*, p. 197.

Christian elements, the message of civilization, of formal education, was quietly passed on from generation to generation. It became a bowdlerization of a once-great tradition. Its internal will and vitality had long collapsed.

Like Egypt, Assyria, and Persia before it, the great empire was unmanageable, uncreative, and incapable of generating a viable successor civilization. As the external formal culture dried up, as men such as Saint Augustine (ca. A.D. 400) denied the educational message of pagan Rome to search for another "superior" and supra-worldly vision, the Roman edifice died. It depended so much on force and power that it had sucked the inner vitality from that deeper and quieter sector of social life. It had smothered the very creative energies that must be continuously pumped into the public sector of every society to ensure its survival as an organized entity.

THE MEDIEVAL RENEWAL

As the Roman domination and influence waned, Europe returned to its communal past, to a cultural and community life that, as Clark and Piggott point out, it had lived with for thousands of years.[18] Now came agricultural independence, self-maintenance, even the linguistic differentiation that saw Latin splinter into the many Romance languages; an informal culture developed that was derived from interpersonal social contacts. It was not inspired and run by a disembodied ruling elite. The diverse civilization renewals in the later centuries of Gothic and Renaissance styles were all nourished by an indigenous, intrinsic communal culture, which yet retained here and there, especially through the church, the technological, intellectual, and institutional memories of the Greco-Roman era.

Eventually, as Friedrich Heer has detailed, the quiet germination of the informal culture would again produce that pervasive thrust toward civilization, a civilization that would not come into existence easily but in tension and conflict. For the superimposition of formal educational patterns upon the informal is not an easy process. Just as a child kicks and balks at the growing responsibilities of maturity, finding the gain of independence to be offset sometimes by the sacrifice of warm succoring dependence and embeddedness, so too the imposition of civilization's superego, which means building for the future and displacing the dark spontaneity of

18. Clark and Piggott, *Prehistoric Societies.*

peasant present-mindedness, was a slow and difficult constructive
effort:

> Archaic society was the substructure of European civilization.
> Western culture, technology and religion had roots in its great
> unities, connections, identities and relationships. It maintained
> itself down to the nineteenth century by a network of inter
> relationships. Visible and invisible threads tied folk-culture,
> the monasteries, the towns, the ancient nobility, the companies,
> fraternities and guilds together. . . . In the matter of fact popu-
> lar view of things this meant a system of unions and alliances
> which needed to be renewed, strengthened and reaffirmed
> through the ritual and rhythm of the cults of feast and holiday,
> of working life and of the dead. In the majority of cases,
> European popular speech (and for a long time the people's
> languages were, in a sense, only dialects of the one common
> language of archaic society and its people) had no words at all
> for these dualities and mental distinctions.[19]

The unity that enveloped European society in the informal cultural experience of the post-Roman, early medieval times was
eventually dissolved. Although much of the qualitative nuance of
this era is beyond recall, hidden behind an opaque veil, the unity
itself was unstable. The aggressive symbolic drives of men, even
though integrally accommodated in the folk culture, began to move
upwards. The vernacular poetry, the legends and epics, the songs
and jingles eventually had to be shaped into more powerful expressive forms. Just as the ignorant, illiterate clergy had to be educated,
so too did the emotional and energic thrust of mind need to be taken
into harness. But not without a battle.

By the end of the fourteenth century, the dissolution of this
seamless universe had begun. The monasteries, universities, academies, parliaments, curias all contributed to the organization of
society and the creation of this new European civilization. The
cultural communities were to be disciplined and structured. Friedrich Heer notes that the prohibitions and enactments from above, by
government and church, were countered from below by peasant
rebellions, schisms, heresies, and the spontaneous combustion of
war. The people resisted.

Gradually and inevitably accommodation occurred. Both the
formal and informal dimensions appear to have assimilated elements of the other:

19. Friedrich Heer, *The Intellectual History of Europe*, tr. J. Steinberg (Cleveland:
World Publishing, 1966), pp. 59–60.

The dress, fashions, architecture, music and dance of the aristocracy and the towns sank down to the level of the people, but so did thoughts, ideas and mental attitudes. Distortion of these ideas occurred frequently and produced bizarre responses among the people. Revolutions and heresies often arose out of misunderstandings of words, concepts, ideas and emotions. Mutilation of an idea often had a strange power to unleash explosive forces in the lower sphere. The migrations along the roads of Europe transmitted the ideas from group to group. The people scavenged in the palace of culture built by those who ruled them and picked up bits of theologies and ideologies and scraps of systems of thought and belief.... Within the great creative personalities a constant psychological dialogue went on between two worlds. Dreams, visions and childhood experiences of the lower culture fused with their philosophical and theological systems. At the same time, the personal underground of the subconscious mind fed their unconscious work from below. At its deepest level their intention was always reconciliation: reconciliation of the upper world, the world of order and government, with the lower world; reconciliation of time (something imposed from above) and eternity, which flows along in the time in flux, time asleep.[20]

   This fascinating and mysterious story that Heer tells is of course only part of the still murky picture of medieval life. For the struggle of the peasants against the higher culture was at the same time a struggle to retain their original prerogatives and freedoms that they had brought with them in the original *Völkerwanderung* (migration) during those centuries of conflict with Rome. Then they were free, equal members of small tribal units.
   And in the original settlements of the early Middle Ages, they were the strength of post-Latin society. Half a millennium later, they were being imposed upon by an elite, newly grown up around them, which was a blend of many cultural influences—Roman, Christian, and German. Serfdom, military conscription, social exploitation also beckoned behind the supposedly benign offering of culture set forward by church and nobility.
   Labor was turned into a commodity, culture valued in terms of material efficiency, luxury achieved through the surplus labor value produced by the downtrodden, and vast realms of real estate controlled from a centralized citadel at the cost of untold numbers of

20. Ibid.

sacrificed warrior flesh. These are also part of the price paid for the glories of the great society.

IS THE CULTURAL COMMUNITY POSSIBLE?

What is it that tempts people to leave the securities of the simple cultural community for the excitements of civilized life, to give their children over to institutions and values that will eventually sever their ties and allegiances with home and community? And again, can we understand the resistance that people offer to certain patterns of advanced institutional life, resisting the new and changing for that which is secure and comfortable?

The answer may be as simple as the character of civilizational advance. When the advantages, as perceived by the people, offer benefits to the individual and the community far outweighing the deficits, people will spring forward to actualize their powers in a life that formal educators altruistically attempt to develop. For they offer a richer and more humanly satisfying life than that in the static traditional community. The evidence from human experience is that people have seized those opportunities to build a life of rich cultural, symbolic, and intellectual meaning.

Several questions derive from the sterility of those vast transnational societies where centralized control limits human initiative and autonomy: What constitutes the most favorable context not only for the retention of individuality and community but also for creativity, richness, and change? Is there a paradigmatic model of a cultural community that releases the vast powers of the human psyche dynamically and creatively? Can a cultural community maintain itself without retreating into the stagnancy and primitiveness of the neolithic community, without becoming an impotent adjunct of a mass society where life and individuality are ground to powder in the drive to achieve mechanical uniformity and obedience to the standard?

Some intellectuals, such as Robert Dahl, believe that the problem of community life inevitably reduces to a question of human numbers:

> The idea that vast numbers of urban residents are needed to provide a center of creativity, innovation, and cultural amenities is unsupported by historical evidence. We ought never forget how very small the great cities of the Western world were when creativity flourished most. The ancient Greeks had only

three cities with more than 20,000 male citizens (equivalent to a total population of perhaps 100,000). Two of these were in Sicily. Athens, the largest of all Greek cities and the only mainland city over 20,000 may have had as many as 40,000 in Pericles' time and a total population not more than several hundred thousand at most. (The exact figure is unknown.) Throughout the Renaissance all the cities of Europe were comparatively small. Until 1600 there were only two cities (Naples and Paris) with populations over 200,000. Rome, Florence, and Venice each had less than 100,000 inhabitants. During the age of Elizabethan England, London had a population under 200,000. By the end of the sixteenth century, the inhabitants of Paris numbered a little over 200,000.[21]

Size is a critical element in defining the nature of a community. Size determines the character of human interaction. If the city is vast and shapeless, individuals have difficulty in placing themselves in a physical and political context; interpersonal relationships themselves are affected. A person cannot relate to a vast metropolitan community. Can someone share something of personal value in common with the literally millions of anonymous faces that surge past in the mobile contexts of urban life?

A human social context begins where nature interposes space between communities, where there are limits to numbers and size, where an individual can encompass the houses and streets of a neighborhood, the shopping centers and business areas, the public buildings and parks are all part of an organic structure of life over which the individual has some critical political controls.

CREATiVE COMMUNITIES

We accept the fact that creative expression is one of the hallmarks of a productive educational environment. And we attempt within our own contemporary social and educational institutional contexts to foster the creative elements in our cultural life. As we review the historical eras of great creative activity, we tend to view such luminescent periods as the Italian Renaissance as reflecting enormous creative bursts in spite of an environment that in our terms was regressive.

Thus, in Italy, the relatively decentralized and independent cities were constantly at war with one another, petty tyrants con-

21. Robert Dahl, *After the Revolution?* (New Haven: Yale University Press, 1970), pp. 156–57.

trolled the governments and/or the ruling oligarchies were consumed in bloody vendettas (the Montagues and the Capulets in
Verona, the Guelphs and Ghibellines). Overarching Renaissance
society was a venal papacy that extracted tribute from a secular life
that drained the people of their basic needs.

And yet it is not at all clear that the small population of north
and central Italy suffered unduly as compared with the masses in
other eras, even our own. The evidence, rather, seems to indicate
that widespread prosperity existed. People worked hard in agriculture, at the many crafts, in trade and industry; the basic legal
structure promoted stability, trustworthiness, and gave personal
achievement its due rewards.

The Italian Renaissance was not a period of utopian peace. Yet
it did avoid the horrors of mass urban industrial society and technological wars of genocide mustered by the so-called united "democratic" superpowers. More important, these Italians released the
creative powers dwelling in the human personality on a scale of
power, depth, and variety that rivaled the ancient Hellenic ideal.

The city of Florence may well have been preeminent. Close
behind were Siena, Rome, Venice, and many other towns that
overflowed with vigorous entrepreneurs of the mind, the arts, literature, even science and exploration. Over several hundred years
they created new cultural forms; these they cultivated in an abandon of intensity and enthusiasm, as a way of life and of livelihood.
They competed with one another, often displaced their rivals in
other cities in an attempt to surpass their achievements, to do the
finest work possible.

Smallness of scale was not an inhibitory factor because their
efforts depended not on the mass accumulation of materials and
people in order to produce industrial artifacts, as we do, but on the
labor and mind intensive efforts of a highly skilled populace. In
their allegiance to their local town, and in the autonomous coherence of their values and perspectives on life, each citizenry developed its own special vision and style in the various arts, crafts, and
technology.

We know how the painters, sculptors, philosophers, and scientists, working in these small cities, were crucially influential in the
awakening perceptions of modern Europe. Their efforts went far
beyond their expectations in influence, renown, and even in the
wealth that was produced. By merely mining the soil of local abilities and skills their educational impact was worldwide. The little-
known history of the violin is an excellent example of this.

TWO ITALIAN CITIES

By the early 1500s, the perceptions of educated Europeans were in a state of dynamic expectation. In every area of culture there was an insatiable curiosity about the world, which was not only expanding in geographical perspectives but also developing new cultural awareness and feelings. This new sensibility welded together with the technological innovativeness of the Italians had its impact in two towns of northern Italy (Lombardy)—Cremona and Brescia, long the centers of musical-instrument making. Many of the beautifully inlaid viols and gambas that had been the basic instruments of aristocratic households originated here. Naturally each town competed in terms of style, sound, and beauty of workmanship for the orders of the nobility, merchants, the church. It is not known exactly how the violin and its family were created—these great artist craftsmen had no public relations people to advertise their wares—but somewhere about 1550, the first violins were being produced in both towns and soon being eagerly bought up for use as far away as Paris for the court.[22]

The production of power and brilliance in the violin is not an accident of wood carving. It is a complex engineering and technological achievement and although there were precursors of the violin in the fiedle, rebec, and *Geige* of the Middle Ages, it constituted a great mechanical invention as well as an artistic creation. It was well over a hundred years before it was brought ultimately to the perfection that fitted the new classical musical esthetic circulating throughout Europe.

However, even today, the subtly different instruments of Cremona—of the Amati family—and of Brescia's Gasparo da Salò and Giovanni Maggini, of the period 1560–90, are still useful if in good repair. Most interesting, since they were designed along slightly different structural and thus acoustical principles, they are different to the eye and the ear to experienced musicians and connoisseurs. The competition to bring customers to their two towns was intense, though straightforward and ethical, and served only to enhance the progress of the art.

A plague spread through northern Italy about 1630, hurting Brescia more than Cremona and virtually wiping out the violin-

22. David D. Boyden, *The History of Violin Playing from Its Origins to 1761* (London: Oxford University Press, 1966); Emile Leipp, *The Violin* (Toronto: University of Toronto Press, 1969).

making community. In fact, it retarded its development there for about a century. The Cremonese instruments of this period, however, show consistent development in both mechanical efficiency as well as workmanship.

In the year 1637 the scientist Galileo Galilei wrote from near Florence to his former student, Father Fulgentio Micanzio, in Venice, then a wealthy musical center. He asked him to obtain a fine Brescian or Cremonese violin for his nephew.[23] Micanzio, on the advice of composer Claudio Monteverdi, the musical director of Saint Mark's in Venice and a native of Cremona, ordered a Cremonese violin at the cost of 12 ducats as against 4 ducats for the patently inferior Brescian product. (Today, we would still treasure these "inferior" productions.) The demand for these Cremonese violins was so great and the quality so carefully controlled that after six months of waiting, Father Micanzio had to settle for a more expensive (15 ducats), used Cremonese violin.

The violin came to its ultimate perfection in the early 1700s in Cremona in the hands of Antonio Stradivarius (1644–1737) and Giuseppi Guarnerius (1698–1744). Generation after generation of intense competitive discipline had created a form and a sound that fitted the evolving musical needs of Europe. From all over Europe they came to Stradivarius—wealthy merchants, nobility, clerics—waiting their turn as the master brought each of his approximately twelve hundred instruments to completion, each subtly different, yet each a masterpiece in its own right. By the mid-eighteenth century, new centers had grown up—in Naples, Milan, Venice, and Mittenwald in Bavaria—that competed in their own way with the Cremonese tradition. By the early nineteenth century, it was an international art form with France, Germany, and England having well developed schools of their own.

It should be emphasized that the impact of this musical (technological) invention was epochal. For, in that assemblage of wood, gut, and glue which is the violin, lies the heart of the development of the classical and symphonic tradition of Western music. It is no exaggeration to say that the invention and perfection of this family of instruments made possible the most aesthetically expressive as well as the geographically most pervasive form of musical expression the world has ever seen. And it is to those two small northern Italian cities, Cremona and Brescia, to their unique educational traditions

23. William Hill, Arthur Hill, and Alfred Hill, *Antonio Stradivari* (New York: Dover Publications, 1963; first published in 1902), pp. 240–43.

in these crafts, that one can point as the cradle of an art form whose impact has extended far beyond their borders.

The greatness of this tradition died with the end of the craft guilds and the beginning of the factory system of fabrication. Many of the skills and secrets have been subsequently lost; no violin makers of the nineteenth or twentieth century can honestly claim to rival the artistic and scientific principles that make preeminent the best seventeenth- and eighteenth-century Italian violins. It was the patient skills and training acquired over a period of 150 years by generation after generation of persevering intelligence, as well as a deep love and respect for the beauty that was a product of the craft that brought these communities of artists to the position where they could serve the entire Western musical tradition as it has since developed.

SCIENTISTS AND THEIR COMMUNITIES

We think of science as an objective, culturally neutral discipline. This is an area of research in which the personal nuances of cultural and national styles ordinarily might not be seen to be as crucial as in painting or music. Yet in the creative development of science, one can see parallel patterns not only with music but with all the arts. We do not see the sharp stylistic fluctuations as might the connoisseur of these other disciplines. However, we do see a shift in dominion and élan from one school to another.

The development of science can be seen as a process somewhat analogous to the passing of the baton in a relay race from the spent runner to the fresh and eager relay. Scientific communities reflect their broader affiliation with cultural communities. Their members are not disembodied intellects but share a variety of values, outlooks, languages, cultures, and social traditions.

When, for example, the Inquisition and Counter Reformation finally foreclosed the freedom of the Italian scientific community in the late seventeenth century, both England and Holland were primed to take up the initiative. The Dutch renaissance, and the great expansion overseas of this tiny nation, were part of a developing cultural and intellectual aggressiveness that made Holland an important factor in international society. The late 1600s saw it as the home of such figures as Rembrandt, Spinoza, Huyghens, and Comenius.

Across the Channel, the Royal Society established by Charles II in the mid-1660s produced a group of practical-minded experimental scientists, stimulated in part by the earlier outlook of Francis Bacon that "knowledge is power." One only has to travel to the Greenwich Observatory on the Thames River outside London to appreciate the enormous intellectual, political, and economic dynamic that emanated from England at the end of the seventeenth century and resulted in that small island nation becoming the dominant power for the two subsequent centuries.

In Isaac Newton (1642–1727), who taught mathematics at Cambridge, England produced one of the greatest theoretical minds of all times, a man who culminated two hundred years of searching scientific inquiry and who capped the domination of the scientific temper. It is interesting to note that these scientific personalities were by and large amateurs. They were members of the rising English middle class, humanistically educated at Oxford and Cambridge. Yet they rarely originated in these latter towns, but more frequently in London, towns in East Anglia, and the West country of South England. In this, they presumably reflected and were stimulated by their contiguity with Holland and Continental science.

Subsequent to Newton's death, the more usual practical bent of English scientific work is evident in a new community of minds, the so-called Lunar Society (1770–90). This group of entrepreneurs consisted of such personalities as Watt, Boulting, Wedgewood, and Priestley (scientists and businessmen).[24] Their center of activity was the Midlands, where coal and iron had begun to create an industrial empire. They came together monthly, in the evening, traveling over rutted and dangerous roads by the light of the moon to discuss new applications of science to technology and industry. The amateur had now been transformed into a unique English professional-gentleman-businessman-intellectual.

H. T. Pledge notes that after 1800 it is rare to find a great scientist who originated in London, in spite of its spiraling population and power. The shift is to northern England, southern Scotland, and northern Ireland, lands of new industrial progress, yet still small enough to have retained their sense of community. Well into the twentieth century, English community life was still in organic contact with the past, with strong regional ties and allegiances.[25]

Although English theoretical science moved somewhat into the

24. Jacob Bronowski and Bruce Mazlish, *The Western Intellectual Tradition* (New York: Harper & Brothers, 1960).
25. H. T. Pledge, *Science Since 1500* (New York: Harper & Brothers, 1959).

shadows following Newton, the thread was taken up by the French. Both preceding and following their Revolution, the French predilection for the abstract—perhaps following the lead of the great Descartes—resulted in one of the most significant advances in scientific education in European history.

Though founded in Paris, the Ecole Polytechnic, Ponts et Chausées, the Genie were institutions that attracted talent from all parts of France.[26] Through their mathematical brilliance, these thinkers gave their work a peculiar national slant. They luxuriated in this, especially as it contrasted with English science. As one more recent French scientist, Pierre Duhem, put it, the English scientific mind is broad but shallow (Newton excepted), the French is narrow but deep!

Throughout the eighteenth century, Pledge states, an inordinately high percentage of scientists in the various continental universities and scientific centers originated in Switzerland, southeastern France, and northwestern Italy.[27] Something about community life, educational and cultural attitudes, in this part of Europe seems to have acted as a catalyst of intellectual effort, transcended national borders, and disseminated its cultural results throughout the Continent and in a variety of intellectual contexts. The French domination in science lasted until about 1850, soon to be challenged by an English revival that would include Faraday and Maxwell. But more awesome was the arousal of the long nascent German scientific mentality.

Germany, which was slower to get started in science (Euler and Leibniz being important eighteenth-century exceptions), developed a great national scientific enterprise from the mid-nineteenth to the early twentieth century. While science was increasingly centralized and utilized by the Prussian state for its successive industrial and political ambitions, the roots of German scientific genius are to be located in the semiautonomous regional areas—in their cities, universities, and traditions. The fertility of German genius, which goes back in literature and music to the seventeenth century, is astounding, considering its dispersal in these regional centers. The lateness of scientific development and the manner in which the national state exploited and stimulated science should not eclipse the fact that for many German scientists, writers, and scholars, the small university

26. See John T. Merz, *History of European Thought in the Nineteenth Century* (London: W. Blackwood & Sons, 1907–14), vol. 1.
27. Pledge, *Science Since 1500*, pp. 94–95.

266 THE PROBLEM OF THE FUTURE

towns, such as Jena, Heidelberg, and Marburg, were a satisfying and creative context in which to work and live well into the end of the nineteenth century.[28]

History seems to tell us that educational and cultural creativity reflects the more general characteristics of society. Like scientific and artistic innovations, it needs autonomy and freedom from political and institutional restraints. It needs an environment sympathetic to its aims and a social context that is rich, diverse, and dynamic. The worst condition possible for the creative mind is to be cooped up in think tanks, as in Russian academic cities, or in university complexes where the creative person sees only the competitiveness of other professionals. Certainly scientists and artists have to see and know one another's work. But their lives ought to reflect allegiances broader and deeper than to the educational, scientific, or corporate institutions or, far worse, to governmental directives.

The more social diversity, differentiation of aims and styles, the better the cultural climate for creative work. Cities, when they begin to reflect a unique character and quality of their residents, historical traditions, vocational specialties, ethnic, religious, and cultural values, become settings for creative personalities and intrinsically serious work. The subject matter may be as universal and as abstract as mathematics or physics; still, the cultural community will be a source and an impetus for intellectual advance.

CONCLUSION

For the last one hundred years, modern education and culture have lived off the life symbols of the old cultural communities. These have gradually been eroded and displaced by the industrial society. The pathetic attempts of the young at communal living, the search for structural panaceas in the school, such as the open classroom and humanistic education, the nostalgia with country music and with their ersatz country people, are little glimpses of the search for those deeper sources long after the umbilical cord to our culture past has been severed.

Just the reverse of the process occurred when Rome gradually fell apart and the world returned to the agricultural communal life of prehistory. Today we have gone far out onto the limb of physical interdependency. There are few places where one is dependent on no one else for one's basic necessities. Thus we will probably have to

28. See Merz, *History of European Thought in the Nineteenth Century*, vol. 1.

invent a different structure of community life to fit in with the international society that is likely to dominate over the next several centuries.

But whatever necessities the coming of the equilibrium society will entail in the way of a truly universal system of law governing the relation of one person to another and people to nature, we will have to re-create additional conditions of social life. Should we not educate people so that these powerful psychic forces in our biocultural nature are channeled productively into socially and personally enriching endeavors? Can we avoid the costly errors of the massive machine societies in over-organizing, disciplining, and rationalizing every possible area of human fulfillment? If not, we will be even more vulnerable to those contagious political or religious mythologies that have infected the world with such devastation in our recent past.

We are now struggling to patch and retain a concept of formal education when we should be forging one anew. It must be an education that does not lay limp between the polarizing pressures of the hidden privacy of the home as against the spurious unifications effected by our mass society. Somewhere in between these two pressures are latent publics searching for an institutional core around which they can weave their own special vision of what it means to be an individual as well as a social being.

John Burnet, writing at the turn of the twentieth century from the standpoint of his own Scottish heritage and his training as a classical scholar, saw this need for social balance as perennial:

> It is easier for us than it was for the Greeks, or than it is for the French, to reconcile the claims of the family and the state, because we are perfectly willing to recognize the existence of many other communities and associations. We have learnt the lesson that the smaller community is the best school to prepare for the larger. We hold that family affection is the best preparation for loyalty to a school, that municipal and provincial feeling is the handmaid, and not the enemy, of national patriotism, as that is in turn of all healthy imperial sentiment. The very number of the communities to which we owe allegiance protects us against the danger of setting up an imaginary antagonism between them.[29]

29. John Burnet, trans. and ed., *Aristotle on Education* (Cambridge: Cambridge University Press, 1903), p. 133.

It is not enough to argue, as did the American educator Herbert Thelen, that students be given the opportunity to relate with adult members of their community in the normal contexts of day to day living.[30] That educational experts dominate the lives of the young is a fact. But it is also a natural result of the continuing impoverization of community life. The average American community lacks the core of beliefs, values, and traditions that give quiet substance to the intercourse of the young with the mature.

There is an important truth in the admonition of Matthew (22:21): "Render therefore unto Caesar the things which are Caesar's." If we retain for ourselves those important social areas of life necessary to the creative and personal expression of the deepest human throbbings, we will not, as Burnet points out, isolate ourselves from our larger national or international responsibilities. On the contrary, we will endow ourselves with a greater capacity to join in the democratic dialogue with other national communities, to establish international principles by which we all can thrive. By so acting, we remain free citizens, not manipulable pawns of distant czars.

Every intellectual aspiration needs its institutional first steps. Here formal education and the structure of our schools becomes central. For it is in the education of our children and the character of these schools that our cultural communities will take shape to be given flesh and substance. The young, infused with a sensibility of independence, creativity, and idiosyncrasy, will know what it means to value and treasure what may be unique to any community. But the community will be impotent if the young do not carry from these schools the knowledge and skills that will contribute to the larger whole, and by that act demonstrate the vitality of their own educational and cultural background.

30. Herbert Thelen, *Education and the Human Quest* (New York: Harper & Row, 1960).

Part

5

Redirecting
Educational
Policy

15 | A New System of Public Education

THE RIGHT OF SELF-DETERMINATION

This chapter argues for a new structure in public education. Reconstruction is necessary because of the special historical and social circumstances we are now experiencing. These circumstances are such as to have created a reservoir of unsatisfied needs in both the personal and the cultural dimensions of life. The exact coutours of a new system of public education that could more efficiently direct itself to the evolving character of American society cannot be detailed before the fact.

Only by allowing for far more freedom in the choice of schooling by the American people can the face of the new education be more clearly revealed. It is my presumption that the denial of the democratic right of social and cultural self-determination is at the core of the current frustration; future hopes for educational amelioration depend upon regaining this right.

What is needed is a move away from the domination of schooling by the stagnant, politicized, and bureaucratized state systems of education. Education must be given over to those who will be the ultimate beneficiaries of this social service and who are paying for it in the first place.

Rather than an educational system wholly operated by the state, I would hope to see a decentralized and semiindependent structure of state certification, supervision, regulation, and even inspection to ensure that minimal standards are being observed. Since all schools will be funded either through vouchers or other techniques, they will have to comply with minimal national levels of content and achievement as well as the usual health and safety requirements. But within these broad public safeguards, there ought to be allowed a wide range of educational freedoms in organization, method and content, cultural, moral, and philosophical values.

As part of this shift in the control of education by existing political and institutional elements to a more voluntary pattern it would be expected that private schools would be more carefully supervised in order to qualify for public support and that the sectarian and parochial sector of education, in order to survive, would agree to divest itself of church controls much in the manner that the sectarian college has altered its strictly religious nature so as to qualify for federal aid. The sole avenue of survival for those lower schools is to avoid the current Supreme Court interdict on aid to church-controlled lower schools (because of the religious establishment clause of the First Amendment).

The reconstruction suggested here addresses itself to a fundamental question as to what is constituted by a "public education." What kind of educational programs serve the interest of the people? Ought the people have choice in selecting the character of the educational environment within which their children will be educated? Have there been significant enough changes in our society over the past several decades to warrant a reconsideration of the nature of public schooling, an institution whose character and organization were originally *not* established by constitutional fiat?

THE NEED FOR PLURALISTIC EDUCATION

There are historic moments of opportunity. There are also periods when our ideals are impotent. In 1915 Horace Kallen began publishing a series of articles entitled "Democracy Versus the Melting Pot," which appeared in the *Nation.* In these articles he argued against the dominant melting-pot philosophy, which he saw assimilating and absorbing that precious ethnic and cultural diversity that was being contributed to our nation by the new immigrants.

In 1924 Kallen's views were elaborated and published as a book entitled *Culture and Democracy in the United States.*[1] While acknowledged as an eloquent and ground-breaking delineation of the philosophy of cultural pluralism, his argument fell on deaf institutional ears. The major social pathways had been well established. Our society was intent on completing its national homogeneous cultural destiny. Business and industry demanded it. And the schools acquiesced.

In 1927 John Dewey published *The Public and Its Problems,* the fruit of the same general observations and considerations that had moved Kallen.[2] Dewey's concern stemmed from his more typical

1. Horace H. Kallen. *Culture and Democracy in the United States.* (New York: Boni & Liveright. 1924).
2. John Dewey, *The Public and Its Problems* (Chicago: Swallow Press. 1954).

American experience as a small-town New Englander transferred to megalopolis and its violently changing social ethos. At the age of sixty-eight he could look back on his own experiences and those of his contemporaries to warn them about the dangers he perceived in the unlimited industrial and institutional expansion that had engulfed the traditional local community. It was this local community that had endowed our history with a special character of integrity, rationality, and responsibility. Now it was in danger.

> In its deepest and richest sense a community must always remain a matter of face-to-face intercourse. This is why the family and neighborhood, with all their deficiencies, have always been the chief agencies of nurture, the means by which dispositions are stably formed and ideas acquired which laid hold on roots of character. The Great Community, in the sense of free and full inter-communication, is conceivable. But it can never possess all the qualities which mark a local community. It will do its final work in ordering the relations and enriching the experience of local associations. The invasion and partial destruction of the life of the latter by outside uncontrolled agencies is the immediate source of the instability, disintegration and restlessness which characterize the present epoch. Evils which are uncritically and indiscriminantly laid at the door of industrialism and democracy might, with greater intelligence, be referred to the dislocation and unsettlement of local communities. Vital and thorough attachments are bred only in the intimacy of an intercourse which is of necessity restricted in range.[3]

These concerns of half a century ago were just as real then as they are today. The difference lies in the earlier effectiveness of the dominant values of minority assimilation, economic growth, and industrial priorities in serving as social and cultural values that motivated our populace and acted as symbols of commitment and cohesiveness. One could say that to the extent that these long-standing ideals have been consummated and absorbed into our social structure, to that extent they no longer function as ideals for future realization. It is a commonly accepted fact today that we are overinstitutionalized, too materialistic, and culturally homogenized.

Throughout the various levels of educational concern, there is an almost unconscious antagonism to the "edifice complex," to institution building and growth. The breakdown of large educational organizations and the sense of revulsion of the young to the inhumane

3. Ibid., pp. 211–12.

structures and relationships purveyed as education, are indicative of the exhaustion of our general educational trend.

The tragic aspect of this loss of respect and commitment for learning on the part of the young is that it has precipitated so many of them into an antiintellectual, antirational stance. The problem does not inhere in rationality per se, but in the heretofore accepted social uses for intelligence and action. What has happened among the young has been part of a more general realization that the era of supinely acquiescing to educational authority is at an end. The educational consumer is now an involved and outspoken evaluator and critic of the "goods" that were only recently so lightly dispensed and accepted.

The growing, if indeed hesitant, call is for an educational structure where value considerations and humane contexts loom as important as bigness and accommodating massive numbers of students reflects a trend in a positive direction. The ecology movement, which set itself squarely in front of the arrogant laissez faire attitude of the industrial community, has become a permanent dimension of our social and political scene. Clean-air legislation, auto-pollution devices, sewage-treatment plants all represent the encompassing social controls that the people are demanding for all segments of society.

We may have to balance values such as emission controls on autos with the scarcity of gasoline. And we are forced by rational necessities to build an oil pipeline through the Alaskan tundra or even drill in the offshore waters for oil. But this must take place in a context of rational discussions of the long-range public good.

As we impose these various restrictions upon ourselves, it will become increasingly clear that the sharing of scarce material necessities by our citizens requires a more equitable distribution of all the available wealth. The present level of disparities will not be tolerated in a society where every individual must put his shoulder to the wheel merely to maintain a minimal standard of life for all.

The changing world around us requires periodic revisions in our social contract. From a carefree attitude that allowed consumption at will, the call is now one of self-regulation, discipline, responsibility in local, national, and international affairs. Will we likewise take steps to ensure that the careful management and regulation required of us will not lead to greater concentrations of power at the top? Watergate should have warned us about the dangers implicit in the ongoing centralization of our governmental apparatus that has taken place over the years.

One cannot predict how this paradox of a need to regulate and need to defuse power concentrations can be resolved. The way out of the dilemma will come gradually, as we carefully question, scrutinize, and analyze every assumption of power and privilege. We will not have done ourselves good by substituting for the arrogance of private and corporate privilege the equally pernicious and amorphous public and bureaucratic forms of undisciplined power.

While on the one hand there can be, rightfully, suspicion and questioning of those who hold the reigns of power, there is at the same time a more positive face to our situation. Thus it is that, as we struggle for mutual interdependence in our quest for physical survival, there is a simultaneous movement among young and old, from all segments of society, for the cultivation of an almost forgotten domain of values. Community, individuality, cultural pluralism, and educational diversity are elements in a new and developing consensus about the character of freedom.

Especially in education, where value elements loom supreme, there is increasing resentment that the ideals invested in our historic commitment to public education have become embedded in an institutional structure that is decreasingly responsive to new community urgings and aspirations. One can generalize and argue that the public schools themselves, so central in the life of our people, constitute a paradigm example of institutional massiveness and rigidity at a time when our lives need to be lightened of as much surplus bureaucratic baggage as possible. Thus, the ultimate solution of our educational problems may illuminate for us a method of balancing national needs with diversity and community initiative.

Thomas Green several years ago wrote somewhat pessimistically about the movement toward greater community involvement in the urban schools. His view was that under present managerial conditions of administration, a true community of values in an urban educational setting could not exist.

> There is hardly anything local about either the power or the accountability of local school bureaucracies in such urban centers as New York City, Chicago, or San Francisco. At the level of the local school the relevant public, the local public, is virtually disenfranchised. Within the neighborhoods, or attendance districts of the local school, there is, it seems, precious little that parents, citizens, and friends of youth may do to influence, effectively, the way their children are educated. More often than not, it seems the local concerned public can

only appeal to the representatives of a larger and often unresponsive public to bring about change. And in the process, the efforts of the local public are deflected, dilated, and rendered inconsequential.[4]

Green postulated "value pluralism" as a way out of our morass. This would entail a society in which "the choices available to members of the society must be fundamental enough to produce significant differences between people in their attitudes and outlook on the world. On the other hand, those differences must not be so fundamental as to be divisive . . . . It seems to me impossible to maintain value pluralism in a society committed to mass education of a managerial type."[5]

His solution, albeit tentative in that he had little confidence in the possibility of realizing such idealistic hopes, reflects this disenchantment with the present structure.

> To alter this situation and create the value pluralism would require a massive commitment of our society to "humanistic education" a corresponding change in the allocation of resources to and within education, and a substantial shift in the structure of educational authority, the social roles of teachers, and the means of assessing the accomplishments and the purposes of schools. These changes, it seems to me, could come only by abandoning some aspects of the goal of mass education, by establishing genuinely pluralistic school systems instead of merely "comprehensive" schools, and by simultaneously redistributing the certification function of the schools to other institutions so as to permit free and random entry and exit from the educational system and to modify the functions of the schools.[6]

The general tenor of Green's exposition, especially in his added hope that state authorities would operate in competition with local school boards or that educational contracting wihh ecclesiastical or business groups could take place to foster competitive schools, supports a position that still accepts the general externalized structure of our school systems. His hopes for educational improvement through teacher militancy and corporate involvement in education contrast interestingly with a special appeal he makes for tuition support for the child rather than tax support for schools. Green's emphasis,

4. Thomas Green, "Schools and Committees: A Look Forward," *Harvard Educational Review* 3 (Spring 1969): 225.
   5. Ibid., p. 248.
   6. Ibid., p. 249.

however, still seems to be on changing the existing external structure through a new *system* of controls and directives.

But we should note his clear vision of the need for community involvement and his perception of the institutional problem. Out of this awareness may come a closer relationship between the school and its community. It is interesting to observe that while Green argues for value pluralism and its dependence on the life-giving support of a community and its schools, he does not push through to the ultimate consequence of value pluralism. Can this be other than a pluralism whose diversity runs deeply? Does he hesitate because he feels we are not yet ready or even brave enough to translate the philosophically ambiguous concept of "value pluralism" into its socially emblazoned concreteness of culture, ethnicity, and religion?

Perhaps we need to listen to one who has attempted to create an alternative to the educational system, to turn educational failures into functioning human beings. We need him to tell us the importance of radical structural changes in our school system. George Dennison saw his First Street School dissolve after two successful years because of a lack of funds. Apparently his established if struggling endeavor was not as interesting to the foundations as would have been a "scientific" study of the feasibility of a school such as he had already been running.[7]

His conclusions are as follows:

> Any solution which perpetuates the existing authoritarian bureaucracy is doomed to failure. And I have wanted very much to say that competence is impossible without love, for in this centralized, technological, expert-ridden age of ours it needs desperately to be said. To say it indicates, too, the direction of the essential change. We must place it where there is nothing in the environment which will "inevitably" destroy the vital breath of concern. Authority must reside in the community. It must be local, homely, modest, sensitive. And it must be tied once and for all, to the persons who not only do care, but will go on caring.[8]

BREAKING WITH THE PAST

The problematic character of many reforms of the public schools is exemplified by the fact that often the proposals are in reality merely old wine in new bottles. To cure us of one unsuc-

7. George Dennison, *The Lives of Children* (New York: Random House, 1969), pp. 271–72.
8. Ibid., pp. 279–80.

cessful system and its attendant institutional arteriosclerosis, we have proposed another institutional setup with its own nascent bureaucracy.

This is exemplified in a widely heralded "countercultural" educational tract. On the surface, Ivan Illich's *Deschooling Society* is such an antiinstitutional work.[9] It sees the current encrusted education establishment as constituting an implacable barrier to the free expression of the normal creative energies of the young and to the aspirations of the poor to take their rightful place in society, to receive an education that will allow them to grasp appropriate opportunities. This book has much of the spirit of Paul Goodman's writings in the latter's attempt to use the life and the environment of the young, the city streets themselves, as normal educational contexts.[10]

But Illich goes one step further. He too does not disdain technology, merely its suffocation of the natural man. He would use it, in the manner of Marshall McLuhan's new media, to supplant the old educational establishment and provide a new set of "learning webs" by which individuals could come together as teacher and student and exchange skills.[11]

> Fundamentally, the freedom of a universal skill exchange must be guaranteed by laws which permit discrimination only on the basis of tested skills and not on the basis of educational pedigree. Such a guarantee inevitably requires public control over tests which may be used to qualify persons for the job market. Otherwise, it would be possible to surreptitiously reintroduce complex batteries of tests at the work place itself which would serve for social selection. Much could be done to make skill-testing objective, e.g., allowing only the operation of specific machines or systems to be tested. Tests of typing (measured according to speed, number of errors, and whether or not the typist can work from dictation), operation of an accounting system or of a hydraulic crane, driving, coding, into COBOL, etc., can be easily made objective.[12]

Illich does not elaborate on the kind of world we would be creating in which humans qualify on the basis of such various "ob-

9. Ivan Illich, *Deschooling Society* (New York: Harper & Row, 1970).
10. Paul Goodman, *Compulsory Mis-education and the Community of Scholars* (New York: Vintage, 1964).
11. Marshall McLuhan, *Understanding Media: The Extensions of Man* (New York: McGraw-Hill, 1965).
12. Illich, *Deschooling Society*, p. 131.

jective" testing criteria. He seems to imply that one would always be judged on the basis of current achievement. Would we be forced to retire older employees whose speed and accuracy diminish over the years? On this he does not elaborate. For the matching of individuals who want to learn a skill with those who are able to teach such a skill, he proposes "peer matching."

> The operation of a peer matching network would be simple. The user would identify himself by name and address and describe the activity for which he sought a peer. A computer would send him back the names and addresses of all those who had inserted the same description. It is amazing that such a simple utility has never been used on a broad scale for a publicly valued activity.
>
> In its most rudimentary form, communication between client and computer could be established by return mail. In big cities typewriter terminals could provide instantaneous responses. The only way to retrieve a name and address from the computer would be to list an activity for which a peer was sought. People using the system would become known only to their potential peers.[13]

On the surface this system may be endowed with the charisma of the computer. Looked at more carefully, it raises many questions. How would we distinguish the level of the skill offered and needed through a computer match? Could we so easily and confidently assure ourselves of the competency of the person who offers the skill? Would it be feasible and economic to match individual and teacher on a one-to-one basis in this complex and populated world? Would not a newspaper want-ad column or a catalog of offered skills be more efficient if not as glamorous? Finally, when all the gloss is off, would we not probably wind up with that most practical and long-lived set of institutions: schools, buildings, graded classes, certified teachers, schedules, prerequisities, etc.?

The neutralization of the advantages of Illich's structure serves to highlight the retrogressive character of his "skill testing" suggestions. To reduce the variety of competencies we want in our world to a great system of skill testing to be run and measured by a super Educational Testing Service of Princeton, New Jersey, does not strike one as progress in freeing education from the more conservative and vested forms of institutional authority. Could any educational orthodoxy help but be potentially self-serving and inflexible

13. Ibid., p. 134.

in that they have the power to decide what are valid skills and what the criteria are that can be measured and therefore imposed as judgmental standards on those tested?

Too many educational reformers seek solutions that are often perverse images of the present system. The reason, perhaps, is that they fall into the rut of seeing education in the same way as one might the exploration, development, and distribution of a commodity. Americans are quite efficient at developing and distributing such economic goods. But it is clear that this model will not work in education.

No, sometimes the simplest is the best. The only way we can avoid becoming bogged down in bureaucracy is to return educational responsibility to the parents and children. This is not to suggest the wholesale dismantling of the current public educational system, but rather a gradual transformation of the voluntary area of education into a healthy rival of the state school system. Ultimately, there may be enough evidence to argue for a step-by-step shift to a wholly voluntary state of community-based schooling, in which individual choices and value commitments are maximized.

Through what method would the mechanics of the system function most efficiently? Would it be a graduated voucher system or a system of tax rebates or a combination of these, together with personal outlay of funds by parents, perhaps with state funds supplied for major building endeavors where needed? Needless to say, any system of education must have built into it some means of public accreditation and certification. This could be accomplished through voluntary regional organizations such as now exist in the independent school system and among the nation's colleges and universities. Probably, in addition, there would be a governmental inspection, such as now exists in Great Britain and France.

When we discuss the practicability of any set of proposals, it is not necessarily the specific technical mechanics by which we bring the proposals into reality which is critical. The important issue is the need, the will, and the popular consensus to venture down a road that will have many unseen traps and problems.

For example, in the not too distant past a consensus of authorities agreed that the theoretical possibility of a manned lunar exploration was possible. The necessary political support was soon mobilized for the venture. At that point the technological development, the actual realization of the means, was undertaken. It would be naive to believe that this or any similar developmental endeavor could have gone smoothly according to prior planning without delays, cost overruns, and unforeseen technical, material, and logistical problems. But with the theory well established and confirmed through prior experience in rocketry and in space exploration, and with enough money and determination mustered, the endeavor was eventually completed successfully.

The factors so critical in an endeavor as technically complex as a moon flight—planning for as many unexpected occurrences as is feasible—are not at all important in the restructuring of an educational system. Instead of foreclosing the possibility of the unexpected, what we need in education is the opposite—more innovation, new possibilities, the unexpected. Henry Steele Commager succinctly stated this need when he argued that the most essential area of private enterprise was "private enterprise in the intellectual and in the spiritual realm." [14] It has been our uncanny good fortune to have the natural resources and organizational acumen to be able to create the vast and efficient institutional systems that have contributed to our power. Now we need to muster initiative for a more complex, open-ended, but ultimately humane end.

There is a host of assumptions from the old existing educational structure that needs to be seriously questioned. In an earlier era (1870–1950), when even modestly educated and trained teachers were a significant notch above the average parent in education, there was understandably a need to develop a system that would elevate this population of peasants, proletarians, and immigrants. Indeed, the children of this era and their parents were almost wards of the public system, dependent on it for that marginal transformation that might open up so many new vistas.

But today a large part of the population is equally as well educated as the average public elementary and secondary school teacher. In some suburban districts, the public school teachers are distinctly lower in economic as well as in educational status than the families of the children they teach. Our present state of understanding the concrete practice of pedagogy and curriculum development is not so esoteric that it cannot be gained by parents interested in acquiring this knowledge and training so as to participate in the education of their children.

The involvement of parents in the schools that they choose for their children would add considerably to the life of the community, add much of the responsibility, intimacy, and authority that we want

14. H. S. Commager, "Education for American Freedom," in *The Conscience of Society* (Washington, D.C.: Association for Supervision and Curriculum Development, 1954), pp. 1–15.

to see in the schools, and, not unimportantly, lower the present astronomical costs of formal education. There are innumerable combinations using trained and certified teachers, part-time parent teachers (also certified), as well as parents in the role of teacher aides. A variety of skill areas could be thereby enriched including vocational education, languages, music and art, and the sciences.

With less concern for buildings, hardware, and material aspects, there would be greater opportunities for a richer curriculum—as for example in the arts—for travel and a variety of cultural experiences. Certain kinds of facilities could be shared by groups of schools: gymnasiums, language and science labs, etc. There is no reason why many of the facilities now duplicated in community and school might not become even more completely integrated into community life than they are today. We would thus break down the daylight-children, evening-adults separation with its artificial and even harmful encapsulation of young and old. Gymnasiums, pools, athletic facilities, libraries, theaters, assembly and concert halls ought to be places where young and old congregate, experience, and implicitly teach each other about the values of their community.

In an environment of cultural and community intimacy, which can emerge only in an atmosphere of voluntarism, people freely choosing a place to live and a school in which to educate their children, community interactions could be possible. It cannot happen in the present atmosphere, in which the public schools are the only educational option available to parents and where their choice of homes reflects a desire for safe anonymity in an environment of the most tenuous relations between neighbors.

It may very well be that the public schools are more efficient educationally than the current popular estimate. But while the system continues to constitute a state monopoly, there is no opportunity to run a reliable check. Even on a simple quantitative level of comparative achievement scores—the most schematic questionable manner of evaluating the relative accomplishments of schools—the public system itself constitutes the only criterion for measuring output. To be fair, it should be stated that the urban schools seem to show no clear relationship between expenditures, curriculum, pedagogy, and the net result. What *is* significant is what the child brings into the classroom from the home.[15]

15. Christopher Jencks, *Inequality* (New York: Basic Books, 1972); James Coleman, *Equality of Educational Opportunity* (Washington, D.C.: U.S. Government Printing Office, 1966); also see Daniel Bell, "On Meritocracy and Equality," *The Public Interest* (Fall 1972): 45–46.

In an atmosphere in which the objective evidence for the effectiveness of the state system is unclear, in which citizens are now more concerned that the education of their children take on some moral depth and substance and that the schooling process itself become richer, warmer, and more intimate, we must be willing to break with the institutional habits of the past. Citizens no longer feel they are wards of the state. They are intelligent and well educated; they are capable of making decisions crucial for the nurturing of the hearts and minds of their children. The democratic contract we have all made requires that they have this right to choose, initiate, and create in education.

PUBLIC SCHOOLING AND PARENTAL RIGHTS

We naturally tend to adjust to what is, to make the best of any given set of circumstances. We tend to reify our institutional structure. Only when these institutions begin to fail do we lurch about attempting to diagnose the situation. As of now, the cause has been diagnosed as technology, democracy, reason, schooling, and adulthood, in varying proportions or sequence. Only gradually are we recognizing that in part the organizational structure, which functioned so well for education over so long a historical span, may finally be succumbing to old age.

It is well to emphasize again that train of events, discussed in chapter 4, that eventually led to our present circumstances. The public school as we know it today is a product of historical need. It was created to transform a largely small-town agrarian populace, predominantly poor, into a society that could deal competently with the immense scientific, industrial, and social changes that began to transform the world in the early nineteenth century. Prior to this, two vastly different educational systems had developed. The church- and community-related township school of New England was the first. It started to develop in the mid-1630s and flourished well into the mid-eighteenth century. Education was supported by public taxation, schooling was compulsory, and education was deeply related to the religious values of the several congregations.

By the mid-eighteenth century, the gradual urbanization and secularization of the society brought about new values and attitudes. Scientific knowledge was ripe with possibilities. There was in addition great fear not only of theocratic government, but also of any type of political constraints over the voluntary acts of the people. It was a period of belief in the "diminished state." Further, this was a time of active private enterprise in education, as men strove to free themselves of the older values and knowledge and to cultivate, as did our paradigmatic intellectual, Benjamin Franklin, the secular power which the new knowledge promised for mankind.

For approximately seventy-five years, until well into the first decades of the nineteenth century, there was no effective state educational system. The Constitution reflects the lack of desire to build into its contents a provision for an institution of public education. Education was to be a delegated power reserved for the people and to their respective local and state governments. The Northwest Ordinance of 1787 did provide for the sale of certain public lands: "Religion, morality, and knowledge, being necessary to good government and the happiness of mankind, schools and the means of education shall forever be encouraged."

This act of Congress did much to support the establishment of public schools and colleges throughout the new states of the Union. But it placed the burden of carrying out this direction squarely on the initiative of the several states. Public school systems did not truly begin to expand until the 1830s and '40s. In the meantime, a flourishing and diverse system of private and parochial elementary and secondary school as well as colleges and universities had firmly taken hold in our nation.

Inevitably a certain tension arose, as when the state of New Hampshire's attempt to take control of Dartmouth College was declared unconstitutional by the Supreme Court in 1819 and when, almost a century later, Kentucky attempted to amend the charter of Berea College (211 U.S. 45) (1908). The Catholic school system, as noted earlier (chapter 7), evolved out of the fear that the public schools would adversely affect the religious values and commitments of Catholic children. Over the years, the church has waged a vigorous and sometimes desperate battle to obtain some entrée to the public treasury for the support of its schools.

On the other hand, a sporadic but continuous counter skirmish has been waged on the part of public authorities not only to regulate the private sector, but to control it rigorously and sometimes to have it dissolved. Presently the situation is at a legal standoff, with nonpublic education in an extremely steep decline because of the present state of educational economics.

The private and parochial sector has made some inroads in terms of the provisions in the general welfare clause of the Constitution, and the continuing requirements by the several states for compulsory attendance at an approved school, public or private.[16] Thus they can ask for bus transportation, school lunch funds, health services, and secular textbooks. They cannot use tax moneys for capital expenditures or ongoing budgetary costs such as teacher salaries, even if the teachers are lay teachers.

The attempt to control or dissolve the private sector was met with a firm denial by the Supreme Court in the early 1920s when the public system was riding its greatest crest of expansion and confidence. In *Meyer* v. *Nebraska* (1923) (as noted in earlier discussion, p. 96), Associate Supreme Court Justice McReynolds, speaking for the majority, put aside Nebraska's attempt to bar foreign-language teaching below eighth grade in any school in the state, whether private, parochial, or public. As part of this decision, he declared what were reasonable powers of the state in education in all schools, public or no:

> The power of the State to compel attendance at some school and to make reasonable regulations for all schools, including a requirement that they shall give instruction in English, is not questioned. Nor has challenge been made of the State's power to prescribe a curriculum for institutions which it supports. . . . No emergency has arisen which renders knowledge by a child of some language other than English so clearly harmful as to justify its inhibition with the consequent infringement of rights long freely enjoyed. We are constrained to conclude that the statute as applied is arbitrary and without reasonable relation to any end within the competency of the state.[17]

But perhaps the most critical decision allowing for the existence of nonpublic education was *Pierce* v. *Society of Sisters* (1925). Oregon in 1922 had required that every child between the age of eight and sixteen (with a few exceptions) attend a public school. Justice McReynolds again delivered the majority decision which turned this state law aside. The following section of the decision is as critical today as it was for those plaintiff schools then:

> Under the doctrine of *Meyer* v. *Nebraska,* 262 U.S. 390, we think it entirely plain that the act of 1922 unreasonably inter-

16. Art. 1, Sect. 8. First upheld in the *Cochran* case, 1930 (Louisiana Textbook law) and enunciated by Chief Justice Charles Evans Hughes. See also chap. 7 in this volume, pp. 99 ff.

17. Herbert M. Kliebard, ed., *Religion and Education in America: A Documentary History* (Sranton, Pa.: International Textbook, 1969), p. 120.

feres with the liberty of parents and guardians to direct the upbringing and education of children under their control. As often heretofore pointed out, rights guaranteed by the Constitution may not be abridged by legislation which has no reasonable relation to some purpose within the competency of the State. The fundamental theory of liberty upon which all governments in this Union repose excludes any general power of the State to standardize its children by forcing them to accept instruction from public teachers only. The child is not the mere creature of the State; those who nurture him and direct his destiny have the right, coupled with the high duty, to recognize and prepare him for additional obligations.[18]

The limit of state intervention in support of parochial schools has been clearly established to the advantage of the public schools. Concurrently limits exist, also established by the courts, as to how far a state can go in its attempts to dissolve or regulate the private sector. Presumably there is no further movement or "give" to be had. But is this standoff really so implacable? Let us examine the situation.

A RATIONALE FOR PUBLIC SUPPORT

At the conclusion of World War II, a massive federally sponsored program of educational training was awarded to veterans of this conflict under the GI Bill of Rights. Veterans were given funds to be expended for educational purposes whenever they could find an appropriately certified program of studies. Many religiously sponsored institutions, both secondary and collegiate, participated in such programs. But it became clear that this special grant of funds to ex-GIs was not to be a precedent for more general support of schools having religious sponsorship. This program of support was construed as a unique, "one time only" grant to the individual veteran and thus could be applied to all approved programs, secular or sectarian.

In subsequent years, especially following the onset of the cold war, there began again a series of federal bills supporting education, this time on a financial level unprecedented in history (see chapter 6). The Natonal Defense Education Act of 1957 was followed by several others. Especially important to higher education was the Higher Education Facilities Act of 1963 in which "up to three billion dollars could be generated for school construction throughout

18. Ibid., p. 125. See also chap. 7 in this volume, pp. 96–97.

the country" on a ratio of two dollars ($1.8 billion) private to every federal dollar ($1.2 billion) granted to the institution.[19]

The education housing bill of 1950, which earlier had provided long-term loans for dormitory construction, had been the first step in a process of federal involvement in higher education that attempted to deal with institutions on a strictly nondenominational basis and would include a variety of public, private, and church-related schools. The Higher Education Facilities Act deviated from the earlier bill in that it granted moneys to certain church-related schools for the construction of secular facilities—libraries, science, fine and performing arts buildings.

This federal act, together with a number of state attempts to aid private and parochial schools, instigated a flurry of court suits. In a historic series of three decisions set forth by the Supreme Court on June 28, 1971, and subsequently underlined by a successor set of decisions on June 25, 1973, the outline of a relationship of governmental support to religiously sponsored education was seemingly established.

In the 1971 decisions affecting the lower schools—*Lemon* v. *Kurtzman* (Pennsylvania) and *DiCenso* (Rhode Island)—the Court clearly forbade underwriting by any state of parochial school teachers' salaries or religious textbooks on the basis of governmental involvement (audits) in what is essentially in the lower schools a religious operation.[20]

These lower school rulings by the Supreme Court had been well within the guidelines laid down in earlier decisions concerning church-state educational relations. Where a seemingly new situation has developed was in the treatment of the Higher Education Facilities Act as here set down in *Tilton* v. *Richardson* (1971). The majority, led by Chief Justice Burger, argued that government grants for secular buildings in nominally sectarian colleges could be upheld: "Since religious indoctrination is not a substantial purpose or activity of these church-related colleges and universities, there is less likelihood than in primary or secondary schools that religion will permeate the area of secular education." [21]

The Court established that one could not judge the sectarian

19. Sidney W. Tiedt, *The Role of the Federal Government in Education* (New York: Oxford University Press, 1966), p. 157.
20. In the New York cases (June 25, 1973) the Court prohibited reimbursement for state-mandated testing and record keeping and other aid to schools or parents [72-269-270-271; 72-694-72-753-72-791] as well as a final prohibition in Pennsylvania for aid to parents of children in parochial schools [72-459; 72-620].
21. Chris A. De Young and R. Wynn, *American Education* (New York: McGraw-Hill, 1972), p. 53.

nature of an institution before the fact, merely by its identification with a sectarian tradition or value system. Each institution was to be judged individually as to the extent of its sectarian nature. Facts that would be relevant are its commitment to the American Association of University Professors' statement on academic freedom and tenure, the composition of the student body in terms of religious and ethnic background, and whether the faculty is drawn from a variety of religious groups or is made up of only one religious body. These factors are to be analyzed only in reference to the secular domain of the college and university and seem to override the objections of Justices Douglas, Black, and Brennan that moneys given by the federal government allow the institutions to divert their own funds into the sectarian theological areas.

In a related case of June 25, 1973 (71-1523) the Court supported the state of South Carolina in its attempt to aid all colleges in South Carolina, noting that there was no religious qualification for the faculty or the student body, which represented in a general way the normal percentage of Baptists in South Carolina.

One of the immediate outgrowths of these decisions was the reconstitution of many boards of trustees controlling heretofore sectarian institutions. Laymen began to replace clerics. Members of other denominations were invited to sit on boards in what had previously been a homogeneous religious control of the institution. Perhaps the single most telling statement to summarize the impact of the *Tilton* v. *Richardson* decision was a brief submitted by Edward Bennett Williams, who cited *Bradford* v. *Roberts* (175 U.S. 291 297-298) in support of the HEFA: "That the influence of any particular church may be powerful over the members of a non-sectarian and secular corporation, incorporated for a certain defined purpose and with clearly stated powers, is not sufficient to convert such a corporation into a religious or sectarian body." [22]

It is clear from these rulings that the Supreme Court holds that aid by government to sectarian parochial schools where religious sponsorship is fulfilled in the normal integration of academic and religious studies is not possible. There is little room in such settings for the separability of programs that there is in higher education, where sectarian sponsorship and academic and secular freedom are not incompatible within one institution.

That these rulings may be the fatal last straw for private and parochial education, except for the wealthy few, must be assumed unless a new element portends in the near future. It is no matter for

22. Briefs of Council, U.S. Supreme Court Report #29, p. 1101.

the Court that those who presently send their children to such institutions feel deeply that a previous human and social right is in process of being compromised. As William Ball put it in his brief of counsel to the Court on behalf of the Pennsylvania private schools in *Lemon* v. *Kurtzman,* and citing *Pierce* v. *Society of Sisters,* "Many citizens desire schooling for their children other than that afforded by the state—whether for religious, cultural, intellectual, disciplinary, ethnic, or other reasons. A choice of such schooling is a fundamental liberty." [23]

The erosion of such liberty can be seen in the fact that the Catholic parochial school system, expanding to a peak of 6.5 million students in 1965, has declined in every successive year. The steady inflation of educational costs, the inability of parents to support two school systems, one public, through taxation, and a second private, through tuition. By 1973 the total enrollment in Catholic schools had dipped to 3.8 million, and parochial schools were closing their doors almost weekly.

In the area of higher education, on the other hand, a wholly new era had been proclaimed. The gradual decline of religiously sponsored institutions had been arrested. They were enabled to enter the mainstream of American higher education not only because of their access to federal funds for the modernization of their plants but also because they had thereby been guided to enter more fully into the secular worlds of knowledge, the sciences, and the arts, diversify their faculties and student bodies, and broaden control over the institution to men and women from various walks of life and persuasions.

The solution to the dilemma of Catholic as well as private elementary and secondary education is thus simple, if stark. And it most likely will be acted out on the center stage of the Catholic parochial school system. For this system is the key to the future of private education, at least in the foreseeable future. Parochial schools will have to divest themselves of their sponsorship and control by their affiliated church. If they are to survive, they must do as Catholic colleges and universities have done, give over control of these schools to communities of laymen. The general orientation of the lower schools' curriculum and faculty must become secular in principle.

To the question of the role of nuns and priests in the schools, the courts will probably require not merely a fixed percentage of lay or non-Catholic teachers. They will inquire into the role of the clerical

23. Ibid., p. 1092.

faculty. Do the teachers determine the direction of the school? Is their religious commitment essential or incidental to their work as teachers? Is the clerical administration essentially religious or merely incidental to the direction of the school? What about the pupils? Are all non-Catholics barred in principle? Could a non-Catholic child attain an education in such a school, be accepted by staff and students?

A long history of Catholic polemical writings on education, which has argued that certain Catholic religious symbols and purely religious rituals and teachings are critically essential elements to Catholic education, will have to be put aside.[24] These arguments were adduced to show that the Catholic schools could not step backward theologically in order to receive general tax moneys and still remain Catholic. But having failed in the attempt to be supported publicly as they have traditionally been structured, and facing the threat of dissolution, they may be ready to rethink this issue and go the route of the colleges and universities. There is certainly an eagerness on the federal and state levels to grant them every conceivable type of support as long as they will meet the Supreme Court's test of Constitutionality.

What is required is a rethinking by all groups of the scope of their religiosity and the character of the school and community life that they want for their children in such educational settings. The values inherent in a religious education are certainly wider and richer than those purely theological beliefs and sectarian habits. The sense of moral values, the sharing of a heritage, a history of belief, the community of shared identity, the aesthetics involved in the religious traditions and symbols—all these factors root themselves deeply in the atmosphere and educational climate of a school, even if its actual teachings are secular. In an era in which the purely dogmatic or revealed truths of religion are looked upon increasingly from the standpoint of their symbolic significance rather than their literality, the broader facets of a religious commitment are developing importance for the perpetuation and survival of the community.

THE AMISH: A CASE FOR PRIVATISM

An additional lesson is to be learned in the educational experiences of the Amish religious sect in the United States over the last century.[25] As is well known, the "Old Order Amish" sect has re-

---

24. See Neil G. McCluskey, *Catholic Viewpoint on Education* (Garden City, N.Y.: Hanover House, 1959).

25. John A. Hostetler and Gertrude Enders Huntington, *Children in Amish Society* (New York: Holt, Rinehart, Winston, 1971).

jected much of the paraphernalia of modern technology—automobiles, telephones, electricity, etc.—in an attempt to retain their Anabaptist religious ideals and their agricultural way of life. In the earlier decades of the century, Amish children were sent to the public schools, especially as these schools were reflections of the agricultural economy and the level of education was simple and basic.[26] But as the era of centralization began, and the small rural schools were merged into larger districts, the curriculum took on a more cosmopolitan flavor. The Amish removed their children to their own schools and completed the education at eight-grade level, forbidding high school and collegiate education for fear of its effects on the values of their children and thence to the community.[27]

The Amish have subsequently been subject to intense harassment, at times the forcible attempt to wrest their children out of their own schools to be transported off to the public schools under the various state compulsory education laws and because the Amish schools, their facilities, teachers, and curricula, were considered noncertifiable. One argument of state officials has been that children receiving an Amish education might be permanently handicapped later on in life if they chose as adults to leave the Amish community. The Wisconsin State Supreme Court ruled in 1970 that "there is no such compelling state interest in two years of high school compulsory education as will justify the burden it places upon the appellants' free exercise of their religion. To force a worldly education on all Amish children, the majority of whom do not want or need it, in order to confer a dubious benefit on the few who might later reject their religion is not a compelling interest." [28]

The United States Supreme Court, *Wisconsin* v. *James Yoder* (406 U.S. 205), May 15, 1972, in upholding the Wisconsin court's decision, added that the right of religion was prior to the state's compulsory education law, especially in that the two additional years of schooling that one child lacked would not add or detract from citizenship or the ability to earn a living, given the factual evidence of Amish life. Justices Stewart, Brennan, and Douglas, in addition, noted that the parents did not prevent the children from attending the public school. Here the courts were establishing the child's decision as an important element in the priority of the exercise of religious freedom over the state's education laws.

It is interesting to speculate whether the courts would rule against the compulsory education laws of the state and for the

26. Ibid., p. 113.
27. Ibid., p. 4.
28. Ibid., p. 99.

parents were the words "culture" and "philosophy" substituted for the word "religion." Here may be the key to the limits of state control and nullification over families and communities that would have to be worked out in a larger system of public support for independent schools. One suspects that as radically separatist a sect as is the Amish, the fact that their schools do not reflect specific dogmatic religious beliefs and that they seem satisfied with traditional moralistic curricular materials—such as McGuffey's Readers—their schools might well in this respect qualify for support. Since the teachers are also laymen, albeit marginally educated from our standpoint (and thus certifiably suspect), their clerical role would not be at issue. Authors Hostetler and Huntington seem to feel that the critical issue on which the Amish had to break from the public school structure was the issue of values.

> Where the Amish were successful in their attempts to modify the public school system their children remained in the public school and thus continued to be taught by state-certified teachers. They were in an educational situation in which their distinctive culture was respected while they were at the same time introduced to aspects of middle-class American society. Where the state officials remained rigid and made little attempt to understand or work with the Amish, the Amish withdrew completely from the public schools and built and staffed their own schools. They withdrew because of changes in public school philosophy and organization that threatened their cultural identity, not because they wanted to teach religion in the schools. By Amish standards the public schools had become intolerable for their children.[29]

Those deep feelings of alienation which motivated the Amish to withdraw their children from the public schools are reflective of the value changes that took place within our century through the explosion of material plenty and technological sophistication. They reflect the distinct value choices accepted by the majority of Americans as necessary to the attainment of progress and modernity. The fact that most individuals acquiesced and disregarded the pluralistic value objectives of such as Horace Kallen and John Dewey (their doubts about the direction our society was taking) is evidence that this was a distinct choice in social and cultural orientation that we as a people were making.

In making these choices, the American people were giving evi-

29. Ibid., p. 113.

dence to a community of interest that had developed within the larger public. The goals laid out via secular and scientific modernism, however, were such that the Amish minority, and to a lesser extent the Catholics, could not approve. The public schools, on the other hand, flourished because of this general community of interest. They reflected the will of this large majority of citizens whose goals were roughly commensurable.

But now that this community of interests has lost its élan, the ideals of formal education have become opaque and begun to sag in vigor, it is hardly possible that this populace now represents a cohesive and unified whole. That it ever existed, as large as it was, as extended over so many thousands of square miles—in villages, cities, suburbs—is remarkable. One can understand the development and the longevity of the public school system as it has evolved over the last several generations only by reflecting on the equally far-reaching changes in our knowledge of the world, the enormous physical expansion of our society, and the unprecedented growth of the economy and the overall power of our nation, its scientific and industrial capabilities.

But diverse forms of public education are suitable for the differing demands of history. What we want from state or private education sanctioned by society is its contribution to the public good. For this reason, it behooves us to look far and wide for new elements, patterns, and ideas outside the bureaucratic structure that can give our educational and social system something of the optimism, dynamics, even altruism that were once assumed to be characteristics of its natural state.

Well over a hundred years ago Leo Tolstoy, reacting to an educational system developed by the Russian Ministry of Public Instruction, spoke about the ultimate public source of any long-lasting educational program. "To invent a Russian system of education such as would spring from the needs of the people, is a matter of impossibility for a committee or for anybody else in the world—one has to wait for it to grow out of the people." [30]

". . . for the educating class to know what is good and what bad, the classes which receive the education must have the full power to express their dissatisfaction, or, at least, to swerve from the education which instinctively does not satisfy them—that the criterion of pedagogics is only liberty." [31]

30. L. Wiener, trans., *Tolstoy on Education* (Chicago: University of Chicago Press, 1967), pp. 94–95.
31. Ibid., p. 29.

16 The Liberal Error

The liberal error in education is twofold. It derives from an extrapolation of successful visions, hopes, and ideals of the past into a present that has changed radically. First, the battle of scientific rationality against the parochial dogmatisms of the past has long been concluded. The hope to achieve unification of method and thought in our approach to social experience has been fulfilled and simultaneously found wanting.

An education method is no key for making correct social decisions or for holding off waves of irrationalism. The expectation that scientific consensus and educational uniformity would become links in an international network of rational cooperation has likewise been fraught with nationalistic dissensions. The ideal of consensus can be feared as the first step toward manipulation and authoritarianism by those who gain control of centralized power.

Second, the use of education as a facilitator of social equality has largely succeeded. It can be argued that historical industrial opportunities, leading toward a greater measure of economic equality, preceded and determined our advances, not public education. Nevertheless, the public schools contributed powerfully as an adjunct of the processes of acculturation and modernization during the past century and a half. A population now exists whose majority is middle class and who have taken advantage of the institutional availability for equality of opportunity. But outweighing this positive social development has been the growth of an increasingly intractable social residue at the bottom. The liberal, humanitarian concern for the depressed and the enormous power of government for programs of social intervention have created a wholly new situation in education.

Schools are less a reflection of local needs and concerns. They are more and more at the mercy of political and judicial manipulators who wish to achieve purported egalitarian ends concerning which they are basically ignorant. The failure of the schools to achieve such mandated goals has led to an increasing hysterical attempt by political forces to manipulate public education. The liberal who is persuaded to argue against equality of opportunity and for equality of achievement now is forced to rationalize the trampling of a new set of human rights by the state.

THE PROGRESSIVE EDUCATIONAL IDEAL

When Angelo Patri wrote in 1927 that "the schools of America are the temples of a living democracy," he was thinking of the public schools. He along with many Americans saw the school then and subsequently as an institution that would tangibly symbolize the cohesive values and goals of our nation. People who had been torn from their roots of place and tradition by the industrial upheaval, the millions of immigrants of diverse origins and beliefs, would be transformed through the public schools into members of a democratic polity.

The social wave we call modernity was composed of a number of seminal philosophical ideas and scientific discoveries, most of which were simple enough to be understood. They were greeted with enthusiasm at the time they first appeared. Their ultimate consequences, however, were delayed and surprising (as with the atomic bomb). The power of the new knowledge to redefine the conditions of social life, to bring nature and man under control, defied anything that had ever faced the human race. And it was in the newness and natural wealth of the United States where this new world was to be created.

The men at the leading edge of advancing knowledge saw the possibility for good in this ostensibly secular scientific and technological breakthrough. They also saw in the condition of the ordinary person and in traditional patterns a natural conservatism; it was a recalcitrance born of fear, ignorance, and personal privilege. This they sought to break down through that unique and fortuitously placed institution—the public school.

Such human progress had numerous enemies. They came in diverse forms. They were religious and sectarian irrationality and bigotry; vested economic and social privilege; and a variety of entrenched, know-nothing vestiges of a parochial and tradition-minded past. The force of liberal educational planning was to urge everyone into the state schools until this aim was permanently turned aside by the Oregon decision.[1] The compulsory education laws identified the child's interest with that of the new scientific knowledge needed in the modern world as against the agricultural or industrial exploitation of the young, or even occasional atavistic parental restrictions.[2] The general thrust of Progressivism and the pragmatic movement in education (1875-1945) was an unwieldy blend of fitting the child to function in our scientific and industrial society, catering to children's biological instincts and thus modifying the starkness of the industrial model in the schools.[3]

When we experienced the great economic failure of 1929-32, Progressive educators were quick to react. George Counts, who belonged to the political and economic reconstructionist wing of the movement, published *Dare the Schools Build a New Social Order.*[4] Stimulated by the apparent failure and collapse of the capitalistic model, he hoped that the schools could build into their programs attitudes and understandings that would bring about a cooperative effort of citizens to work for and with each other to dissolve the marks of privilege.

Following his retirement in 1930 from Columbia University, John Dewey, accompanied by a young colleague, R. Bruce Raup, visited the Soviet Union to investigate how a new social order based on equality, classlessness, and cooperation was faring. They were taken to Magnetogorsk, a city at the base of a vast mountain of iron ore. A new industrial community was being built here with American scientific assistance.

Dewey and Raup arrived in late afternoon just as one shift was ending. The workers, singing, in the cinematic tradition of Russian workers, instead of turning into the narrow street to go home to their barracks, crossed over into the factory on the opposite side of the road. They had volunteered, so their guide told the visitors, to work another shift. But to avoid the monotony of a full second shift at the same task, they would handle a different job in a new plant at the second round of work. Needless to say, Dewey and Raup were impressed by the workers' sense of altruism and commitment to

1. R. Freeman Butts regretted this decision and hoped that one day it would be reversed. See Butts, *The American Tradition in Religion and Education* (Boston: Beacon Press 1950), and R. F. Butts and Lawrence Cremin, *A History of Education in American Culture* (New York: Holt, Rinehart and Winston, 1953).

2. See Steven Selden, "Schools as Institutions: Goals," *Educational Psychology Today* (Del Mar, Calif.: CRM Books, 1972).

3. David Cohen and Marvin Lazerson, *Education and the Corporate Order* (Andover, Mass.: Warner Modular Publication, 1973).

4. George Counts, *Dare the Schools Build a New Social Order* (New York: John Day, 1932).

their nation. Deep in the recesses of Siberia, a new scientific and rational social system was being erected on the basis of equality and fraternity; across the seas in America, competition, inequality, and the materialistic residues of the past were consuming us.

Harold Rugg, also a colleague of Counts, Dewey, and Raup at Columbia, had come into education from engineering. He, too, was an enthusiast of the public schools and the new Progressive movement. As a leader in the social studies field, he hoped to infuse into this union of disciplines the new attitudes and ideals that were permeating the liberal mind.[5]

Rugg was responsible for a number of high school texts in his field sponsored by the National Council of Social Studies. His bias against organized religion and laissez faire capitalism was apparently too blatant; it dredged up a swell of opposition from "patriotic" groups. Bit by bit these texts were edged out of the public schools and eventually withdrawn by the publishers.

This, however, was merely a temporary defeat in the minds of liberal educators. It symbolized the intransigence of the reactionary elements in our society and how they played on the fears of the people. The New Deal did much in the following decade to effect reforms in society that the Progressives had dreamed about since the turn of the century. And certainly the American people were learning a lesson in the daily contexts of their lives about the social values of a welfare society. In addition, the public schools were still exposing children of immigrant parents to a unifying experience and preparing them at the same time to utilize the skills of modern knowledge.

As William H. Kilpatrick, another member of the Columbia group, reiterated, "people learn what they live." If they did not learn to mistrust and reject laissez faire capitalism in life and in the schools, they did experience the advantages of the welfare state as well as secular technology. The scientific power of the United States in World War II and the economic boom that subsequently lifted a great proportion of Americans into the middle class rendered academic much of the ideological impact of this movement. A totally new educational and social set of circumstances had been created.

There can be little doubt that the major liberal goals for education first promulgated in the early twentieth century have now been achieved. The respect for the procedures and the effectiveness of

5. Harold Rugg, *Changing Governments and Changing Cultures* (Boson: Ginn and Co., 1932).

science and a more egalitarian welfare society have been clearly established and are being extended even in our day. And religious dogmatism interferes less and less with our individual decisions as legislatures and courts increasingly abandon their moral caveats.

Certainly there is room for progress in our society. But it is not clear that the current social disaffection of the people is due to the incompleteness of the liberal "revolution." And this is precisely where it is becoming so difficult to promulgate solutions that will free us from our educational and social paralysis. The key to policy proposals lies in the diagnosis of our problem. In turn, the key to diagnosis lies in a set of philosophical values based upon sometimes unstated value commitments.

Liberals have a rather clear perspective of what they want. They view the twentieth-century revolution as incomplete, as blocked at every point by the residue of conservative opposition to the scientific and social amelioration of our problems. Liberals value scientific rationality both for its efficiency and for the intellectual, educational, and political results it will induce. They want equality furthered, and through the public school. They want fewer parochial, narrow-minded people controlling school boards or legislatures. They hope for more powerful governmental intervention in the political realm to further the equalization and unification trends set by the public schools.

RATIONALITY AND SCIENTIFIC METHOD

Over the generations, American education has expanded and prospered on the basis of its association with the profession's scientific wing. John Dewey's original conversion to the logic and import of science for our understanding of man and society date back to William James's publication, in 1890, of *Principles of Psychology*. Though James was skeptical of any direct, rigorous application of the science of psychology to the practice of education, a pervasive excitement ran throughout the social sciences over the impact of the scientific method on our procedures and goals in education.[6] Thus, when Dewey took up his position in the new University of Chicago in 1894, it was on condition of being appointed chairman of a new, unified department of philosophy, psychology, and pedagogy.

The rapidly expanding science of education movement that took

6. William James, *Talks to Teachers* (New York: W. W. Norton, 1958; first published in 1892).

hold in the discipline, led by men such as Thorndike and Terman, reflected this deep commitment to furthering the educational progress by measuring and testing and utilizing the results to set forth new policies that could improve human beings and society. Intelligence tests, child-development studies, scientifically graded curricula were only part of an optimism on behalf of reason.What came out of this, especially in the philosophical writings of Dewey and his educational followers, was something far more dramatic.[7] The expectation was that a new way of thinking about the social world could be accomplished. Scientific investigation, as applied to the world of physical entities and as later extended by Darwin to the world of biological phenomena, could as well be generalized into a method of thinking and acting in the social context. This method would be introduced into the public school; it could become a key means by which to expunge dogma, prejudice, and irrationality in a positive and educationally painless manner.

The scientific method as applied to education became the problem-solving and experience curriculum along with the project method, as developed by Kilpatrick. The dream of the educational Progressivists was to endow each child with the capabilities of meeting new problems with discriminatory intelligence. By subjecting "the new" to experiential tests of workability, the child would learn to evaluate ideas and proposals, to discard the old and worn and take up what passed critical inspection. Their dream was to enable each child to learn how to learn. The ultimate product of this public education was to create an educated citizenry able to take up its democratic responsibilities. By lifting the anchors of tradition and parochialism, the changing nature of social reality could be faced. If one set of solutions was unsatisfactory, new solutions could be proposed; and the ensuing results again subjected to the testing process.

Reflecting the importance given to this intellectual keystone of the scientific method as it could be universally applied through the public schools is this recent orthodox instrumentalist statement by Sidney Hook, one of John Dewey's faithful disciples:

> Method is central in a liberal philosophy as in science because it undercuts the absolutisms that would arrest the flow of new knowledge and new insights. Method should be central in

7. John Dewey, *Logic: The Theory of Inquiry* (New York: Henry Holt, 1933); John Dewey, *Human Nature and Conduct* (New York: Henry Holt, 1922).

educational activity because it not only evaluates the funded tradition of the past but enhances the capacity to enrich it.[8]

Hook's hope is tempting. One wishes that the teaching of the method of critical intelligence, either as logic for thought or in the context of a variety of factual situations, would have long enduring consequences for the behavior of individuals.

CAN THE PUBLIC SCHOOLS DEVELOP REASON?

This almost passionate commitment to the method of scientific thought in education, first set forth at the beginning of the century, was an essentially therapeutic vision. At that time men of secular temper could not envision the monstrous claims for scientific rationality in which fascism and communism would envelop themselves in order to accomplish their heinous ends. The scientific method in education and social policy was abstracted from the already prodigious achievements of science in its concrete disciplines.

By infusing into the public school child a respect for the practical, pragmatic approach to experience, as epitomized in the project method, it was hoped that more far-ranging attitudes would be engendered. Very simply, the use of the logic of scientific method in the public school classroom and the concomitant secularization of the public schools constituted the culminating battle against the theological attitude. By first breaking down rooted religious beliefs, a whole series of secondary adjustments would follow, dissolving the commitment to small-town provincialism, established hereditary privilege, and a suspicion of cultural progress.

Their expectations had a more positive side. This was the hope that the logic of scientific decision making would lead to wiser choices in social policy. After a respect for scientific fact had been inculcated through education, the matured product of our public schools would be better able to perceive the relationships between the contemporary problems and the prospective outcomes engendered by the several solutions to the problems. From these the individual would choose the solution that seemed to have the weight of rationality behind it: fact, theory, or historical precedent, etc.

On this critical positive set of expectations the educational hopes for the logical method of liberal pragmatism has foundered. Not

8. Cornelius J. Troost, ed., *Radical School Reform* (Boston: Little, Brown, 1973), p. 195.

merely have we been thwarted in our attempts to get the method into the schools by virtue of poor curricular materials, untrained teachers, or hostile school boards. More, it is impossible on the basis of the immediate factual evidence to make a prima facie decision that will be seen a decade hence as rational and in complete accord with the facts then and the outcome later on.

A case in point in the immediate past is the opting for the automobile instead of mass transport. Was this decision illogical on its face at that time? Could we have then foreseen and enlightened the American people about the long-term ecological, energy, and social problems that the commitment to the huge private car and superhighway has engendered? If we had been taught in advance a logical method of thinking with regard to this particular problem or any number of others, would it have helped us to make the right decision? A serious analysis of the consequences leading in both directions, the auto vs. mass transit, might have helped. However, behind any decision in this matter with regard to agreed upon existing facts, are deep values and commitments. Upon these our choice hinged. A logic of decision making would not have made a difference.

The method of inquiry itself, secular, experimental, extremely limited in its temporal expectations of what will be proved or not (if it works in the short run, will it work in the long?) is thus shallow in its perception of thought and human behavior. Can one teach individuals the logical conditions in all conceivable contexts to enable them to know when they have received enough information relative to the decision-making process?

It is meaningless to seek one logical method for thought, to be taught as a foundation of educational training. The desired ends of cultural experience are as diverse as the ends of human existence. Thus, a variety of logics is to be carved out of the contextual circumstances—the varied experiences that thought confronts, myriad structures of facts and theories, arts, humanities, social sciences. People's only possible hope in threading their way through them rationally or consistently is to commit themselves to a set of high-level philosophical or value assumptions. These are the mirrors in which our scientific decisions will be reflected. A logic of thought derives from values and beliefs; it cannot be derived from an abstract and mechanical method of behaving.

If one is committed deeply and irrevocably to a set of values, no raw factual data could interdict these beliefs. How many economic and social failures in Soviet Communism have to occur to cause doubt in the true believer? Or the other hand, can a person with no views on the larger aspects of life be anything but a whirling dervish? Will such a person not champion the always positive logic of the "new?" By its very reality, the new is here; it works. What criteria does the valueless person have for making decisions?

Thus it is with many who have in the past fought bravely and cogently for a better public school system of education. Our vision of thirty or forty years ago pointed to the continuous expansion and improvement of the schools. How can we persuade them that no longer can the slow, cumulative improvement of the existing public school structure be the aim of liberalism? Can any set of recent facts about American education and society prove logically to them that the entire structure has taken on a new character? No, they will continue to regard the same evidence differently than we, because their value assumptions have remained fast.

A quotation from a recent article by Fred Newman and Donald Oliver can exemplify this situation. Newman and Oliver are representatives of a new generation of educators to whom the entrance into education of great corporations—Time-Life, GE, Xerox, IBM, RCA, ITT—is symptomatic of a significant shift in the character of public education:

> We view with suspicion the emergence of national super-corporations venturing into educational production. It signifies most obviously the demise of any hope that education might be rooted in the concerns and pursuits of primary communities. It offers unprecedented possibilities for cultural uniformity, as the large coalitions begin to sketch long-range plans for the production of standardized educational kits to be marketed throughout the nation. The packages will be designed within professionalized and bureaucratized organizations, simple-mindedly devoted to educational "projects" as isolated goals. The great society evidently assumed that since the government-industry-unversity coalition seems to have solved problems of economic affluence and defense, it should therefore be able to solve educational problems.[9]

Is it possible to conceive that such a development is other than patently antithetical to the development of an individualistic and voluntaristic conception of rationality? One can claim that the dream of the Progressive followers of Dewey is even farther away

9. Fred Newman and Donald Oliver, "Education and Community," *Harvard Educational Review* 37 (Winter 1967): 88.

today than it was two generations ago. The method of scientific thought is difficult to attain because of the supposed social and cultural barriers raised to block it. Perhaps it cannot be attained. It is an *academic* goal. When we today evaluate the goals of secularism, scientism, and universalism (as evidenced by the entrance of the corporate giants), we have additional evidence, if indirect, that the methodological vision of a public school-induced rationality may itself be wide of the mark.

The question of the relationship between formal education and the development of a secular rationality, how by their utilization we are enabled to handle the complexities of modern life, however, ought not be turned aside so easily. It remains a crucial question, especially in our day, when periodic waves of emotional hysteria and mass cultural trends take hold of our people.[10] Thus far, its import on our society has been relatively benign. But, as noted earlier, dormant passions lay deeply within, awaiting release, to blind our capacity for reason. The weak, unstable, alienated masses in urban society are particularly susceptible.

THE ROLE OF VALUES

The solution is probably not methodological, as beautifully simple and as clear cut as is the "method of intelligence." It is probably one with a more subtle philosophical slant, one of the strengthening of values. When one faces great dangers, one must be able to handle these dangers rationally, in terms of possible solutions. One certainly must be capable of using the scientific method. But to use it, the individual must have the will, the strength that allows confrontation with danger. Will a person have that strength without a larger rational, philosophical understanding of the situation? The human ego's strength to use reason depends upon the values and understanding with which these threats from without or within are comprehended—in structures of ideas as well as deeply embedded assumptions and commitments. Irving Hallowell has phrased it this way:

> In *Homo sapiens,* unconscious mechanisms may be viewed as an adaptive means that permits some measure of compromise between conflicting forces. They relieve the individual of part of the burden not only forced upon him by the requirements of

10. William I. Thompson, *The Edge of History* (New York: Harper Colophon Books, 1972), pp. 170 ff.

a morally responsible existence but by the fact that the normative orientation of any human order permeates all aspects of living. A human level of existence requires an evolutionary price; man as a species has survived desperate proneness to conflict, anxiety, and psychopathology.[11]

The evolutionary price also necessitates a vigilance that is philosophical and value-oriented. Earlier we noted that the original purpose of formal education was precisely that: the inculcation in the next generation of the ideals and values of the adult sponsors of the school. There can therefore be no ready-made, sure-fire method for solving the educational problem of rationality away from the issue of the particular philosophical set of beliefs to which the young are being exposed. By not avoiding the question of what deeply held commitments are important for today, we can close that door through which the individual seeks egress from personal responsibility. There would then be less opportunity to envelop oneself in those unconscious and irrational symbols of nonresponsibility, by these social or personal pathologies.

The existence of diverse sets of philosophical and moral commitments among the people in any one society aids in the resistance to those terrible totalitarian social and political mythologies that have overcome even the greatest educational systems of the recent past. Ernst Cassirer, in one of his last published articles, argues for this point of view.

Cassirer tried to explain some of the underlying reasons for the unbelievably vicious hatred of the Nazis toward the Jews.[12] The Nazis saw the Jewish religion as a symbol of a commitment of this people to moral and intellectual standards rooted in a particularly impermeable historical tradition. The ethical imperatives of the Jews were likewise intellectual imperatives. Their respect for reason and their intransigence to any passing transgression against their own values made them a thorn in the side of political and ideological totalitarians.

It was not that Jews could not function with other people. It was that their use of reason, rooted in their own religious and communal tradition, had stood the test of centuries. As such, they could not be moved as easily as the more vulnerable, disoriented masses. Their intellectual and moral strength in the face of fascist mythologies

11. "Self, Society and Culture" in S. Tax, ed., *Evolution After Darwin* (Chicago: University of Chicago Press, 1960), 2:358.

12. Ernst Cassirer, "Judaism and the Modern Political Myths" *Contemporary Jewish Record* 12 (1944): 115–16.

virtually compelled the Nazis, in fury and hate, to seek that "final solution."

One might note that the Jews in the Soviet Union constitute a burr to that totalitarian state also. The Jews maintain certain values that resist the homogenization that such modern mass societies attempt to impose on their people. At its most benign level, in the United States such mass attempts at conformity have been used to ensure a secure and broad-based, consumer-oriented polity. The reason mass societies of all political colorations are so vulnerable educationally to the irrational is because of the seamless uniformity of social structure. This shallowness that is the result of its mass extendedness allows no resistance to the worst possible social and ideological developments.

The value neutrality in the scientific method of the Progressivists as extended to the mass constituency of the public schools now constitutes a *danger*. It can no longer be considered its salvation. The scientific method as such can validate as rational or pragmatically justifiable anything that happens to be politically or educationally expedient. A society in which diversity of values, ideals, or cultural patterns flourish is, on the contrary, able to build a structure of community life that has real depth of being; it cannot be easily coerced or enveloped. We ought not fear this diversity of philosophies or ideals. Rather, it constitutes the great hope, as Dewey himself finally came to believe, that it is in the interaction of one community's views with another's that those issues which touch on the unity of communities will be best and most rationally resolved. Indeed, this is what democracy ought to signify—a diversity of views being democratically hammered into a majority consensus—and not the docile, manipulated "yes" or "no" of masses of unrelated, isolated, and impotent human atoms.

IDENTITY AND RATIONALITY

In Erik Erikson's *Childhood and Society* is an important discussion of Freud's views on the relationship between rationality, ego strength, and the individual's awareness of ethnic and religious identity.

> The crowning value of what Freud called the "primacy of the intellect" was the cornerstone of the early psychoanalyst's identity, giving him a firm foothold in the era of the enlightenment, as well as the ripe intellectuality of his own race. Only once, in a letter to a Jewish lodge, did Freud acknowledge this

Heimlichkeit der gleichen inneren Konstruktion [the secret familiarity of identical psychological construction]. In this speech Freud discussed his relationship to Jewry and discarded religious faith and national pride as "the prime bonds." He then pointed, in poetic rather than scientific terms, to an unconscious as well as conscious attraction in Jewry: powerful unverbalized emotions *(viele dunkle Gefuhlsmächte)*, and the clear consciousness of an inner identity *(die klare Bewusstheit der inneren Identität)*. . . . Safely relying, then, on the basic premise of intellectual integrity, Freud could take certain fundamentals of morality for granted; and with morality, cultural identity. To him the ego stood like a cautious and sometimes shrewd patrician, not only between the anarchy of primeval instincts and the fury of the archaic conscience, but also between the pressure of upper class convention and the anarchy of mob spirit.[13]

The question as to why we have abandoned the local community, our ethnic and religious heritage as an educational source of personal strength has been alluded to earlier. Certainly the power of scientific reason and the expectation that a world of real objects, real truths existing outside our traditions and heritage in an objective reality, were partial causes. And while the external forces of science and technology were carrying us on to a new social level, education could identify with the logic of science. One can see the entire pragmatic and progressive tradition in education in the light of this dependence on external canons of rationality that would supplant the old-fashioned sectarian religious, moral, and social traditions.

To a large extent, a hope exists in liberal circles that in some miraculous manner, the secular homogenized public schools will still produce a religion of reason in the spirit expressed by Dewey in his *A Common Faith*.[14] Some feel that what is wrong with American education is not its basic structure but the current political locus of control. If we had more liberal school boards, progressive teachers, open-minded parents, and receptive children, we could still have our Utopia.

Mass America has produced a structure of social existence that is extremely vulnerable to that classic totalitarian phenomenon, the grab for power by those at the helm, usually aided by subtle manipulations of the popular mythologies of fear. The by now

13. Erik Erikson, *Childhood and Society* (Hammondsworth, England: Penguin Books, 1951), p. 273.
14. See Robert N. Bellah, "Civil Religion in America," in William G. McLoughlin and Robert N. Bellah, *Religion in America* (Boston: Houghton Mifflin, 1968).

classic example of Watergate with its façade of "internal security" masking the attempt to undermine the political opposition is reflective of the enormous stakes in power when a great society is so centralized. That the leadership itself, albeit cynically self-serving, was subject to paranoia in its own fears of opposition should merely warn us about the dangers inherent in the commitment of as vast a nation as ours to a "common faith."

The preeminent domination over the people of those vast transnational institutions such as the public school conditions us to accept greater and greater accumulations of power by persons whose use of this power is almost unlimited considering the symbols of nationhood which serve to mask and sanctify this power.[15]

It is time for the liberal to see reason and rationality not as emerging from some seamless pattern of external and objective truths but rather as welling up from the inner resources of individuals and the particular cultural community to which they have freely identified and committed themselves. Dewey himself never saw truth as existing apart from the concreteness of the experiential situation.

One would hope that the liberal educationist, taking into account this concreteness of factual and historical circumstances, will conclude that the greatest hope for developing socially responsible and rational attitudes in the young lies *not* in a school structure that receives its marching orders from the top. Reason cannot be produced by a bureaucracy reciting from an external methodological catechism, a daily lesson plan to produce scientific attitudes. For too long, we have only smiled in embarrassment at the various harmless NEA and state education department injunctions to inculcate moral and spiritual values in the classroom.

These critical elements of educational thought—the moral and spiritual—lie deep within our souls. Only in the intimacy of a voluntary school community can the freedom exist to treat of these intensely personal elements of human existence. A sober appraisal

---

15. See C. W. Mills, *The Power Elite* (New York: Oxford University Press, 1957). Robert Nisbet has written to this perennial issue: " 'More and more is it clear,' wrote J. N. Figgis in 1911, 'that the mere individual's freedom against an omnipotent state may be no better than slavery; more and more is it evident that the real question of freedom in our day is the freedom of smaller unions to live within the whole' . . . the most powerful resources of democracy lie in the cultural "allegiances" of citizens, and that these allegiances are nourished psychologically in the smaller, internal areas of the family, local community, and association. . . . When the small areas of association become sterile psychologically, as a result of loss of institutional significance, we find ourselves resorting to ever increasing dosages of indoctrination from above, an indoctrination that often becomes totalitarian in significance." Robert Nisbet, *The Quest for Community* (New York: Oxford University Press, 1953), pp. 255–66.

of our contemporary social circumstances can lead only to the conclusion that the best hope for an enlightened, rational society lies in the natural diversity and pluralism of communities and groups that have been given an opportunity and the wherewithal to develop schools of their own choice, a new but equally public educational system.

EQUALITY THROUGH EDUCATION

The vision of social equality, now as in the past, provides one of the most important pillars of support for the public school. It is an enduring ideal of our American tradition. In an era when there are few dreams and visions to inspire our tarnished national image, it is grasped even more tightly by those who espouse the cause of liberalism. In an era when the modern technological society needs so many variegated skills and competencies, we can agree that if not a similarity of educational results, then certainly a uniform level of general education is needed to realize our basic commitment to social equality.

It is critical that the old class barriers, fortunately for America always tenuous and rarely fixed, and also the barriers of race, ethnicity, religion, and sex, be eliminated so that each individual has the fullest opportunity for self-development. This dream goes back to the founders of the public schools themselves—to Horace Mann, James G. Carter, Henry Barnard, and Calvin Wiley—who envisaged a formal educational ideal that would transform the humble and ignorant into responsible, participating citizens. They saw an America with a destiny that was still vast and magnificent in its possibilities. The Common School was the institutional agent that would bring about the transformation. It could not have come into being without the powerful catalysts of scientific knowledge and technological know-how, which even during the first quarter of the nineteenth century was making itself felt in the United States.

This unique set of historical circumstances necessitated, even rewarded, those who were able to shift their line of social vision toward the future. The schools were a continuous focal point of this barometer of change. With every increment in knowledge, with important new inventions of technological application came social changes that were reflected in education. The perspective was that of an ever expanding, ever more comprehensive system of tax-supported schooling. The poor, the ignorant, the babble of immigrant tongues were never scarce. The school was an institution with almost unlimited possibilities for transformation.

The schools have by and large fulfilled this dream. Knowledge, education, and national wealth have complemented an aggressive, hard-driving, pragmatically oriented people who could look to the future with ease and confidence. But what about today? Why are we oppressed by so much turmoil and confusion? Why is it that this social ideal of equality through education, of upward, outward, and onward, still does not work?

Partially, we are out of historical phase. On the one hand we have reached a situation of majority plenty and middle-class achievement. The structural techniques that facilitated advance and were so successful over all these years for the majority poor do not now work. In a sense, we have reached that point in institutional senility where successive efforts have decreasing effects. The inner contradictions afflicting so many of our social institutions have affected formal education in America, both its public schools as well as its colleges and universities.

Yet an underclass of people still exists, partially black, but also of other and different ethnic backgrounds, including Latins and American Indians. A significant proportion of them have not yet been absorbed into the American dream. These people inhabit that unique never-never land of minority poor. Their progress in education relative to the sophisticated and successful middle class has been sketchy. This relative lack of success has caused a crisis in the liberal mind. The liberal is caught between two antithetical ideals.

On the one hand is the vanishing charisma of the public school, the feeling that it has all been said and done before, that it is a repeat of a tired and increasingly tarnished dream. And on the other hand is that committed belief that knowledge and competency constitute the surest path toward social equality. The public school still represents the single national institution committed to permanently dissolving the causes of deprivation. The liberal refuses to permit this educational failure to be placed at the feet of those who fail. Something must be wrong with the existing structure and pattern of the public schools to have allowed this unresolved problem to persist.

The liberal opts for a solution that is organizational in nature. It demands that the school obtain parity of achievement for the deprived. One of the ways this can be achieved is through busing, and the mixing of children of various ethnic, racial and social-class backgrounds. Thereupon the public schools must show cause (accountability) why any student has not attained parity of achievement. Whatever means can be found to fulfill this demand, including the lowering of standards to permit *all* to fall within the credentializing guidelines, will be acceptable. In their decline, the public schools may thereby gain a measure of historical justification, which presently eludes them.

The Old Equality

To understand the new direction which liberal thought and social action has taken with regard to this problem of intractable deprivation—and by which it is hoped a breath of idealism will be let into the stale middle-class-oriented public system of education—we ought briefly to discuss those traditional assumptions and practices.

In fairness it cannot be said that the early goals of the Common School were comparable with our recent vision of the educational race course: bring them all up to the starting line, set them off, and await the results and the winners. Throughout most of the nineteenth century, there was still a sense of fixedness in one's given occupation—farmer, storekeeper, factory worker. Social change occurred so slowly that education was ruled out as an important key to economic advance. If you were clever enough, the simplest of education would suffice in the pursuit of fortune. To the well born, education was more a matter of culture and class.

It is true that early workingmen's associations in the eastern cities saw the limits of such schooling, some of them went so far as to advocate boarding schools so as to reduce the advantages of money or background that would be obtained by the favored in their homes.[16] Yet there was a sincere attempt on the part of the nineteenth-century educational reformers to provide the best possible kinds of schooling depending on the particular circumstances. Boston Latin School was an example of a public secondary school that achieved extraordinary excellence during an era when public secondary schooling had not yet won its spurs. In the 1850s and '60s, many wealthy parents in the highly cultured atmosphere of Boston were moved by egalitarian ideals to remove their youngsters from private academies to send them to this particular institution.

But as the pace of social change steadily increased, as new sciences, inventions, and industries developed, it became clear that opportunities were beckoning for which education could be the key to a wholly new way of life. From the 1880s on, the number of high

16. Majorie B. Smiley and John S. Diekhoff, eds., "Public Education and Pauperism" (Philadelphia, 1829) and "Equality Only in Custody" (New York, 1830), in *Prologue to Teaching* (New York: Oxford University Press, 1959), pp. 177–81.

school students, as noted in chapter 5, doubled in each decade. The great public system was being assembled. The following comment of a Michigan educator in 1921 reflects the vision of equality of opportunity that had evolved from the simpler ideal of an educated and committed citizen:

> We can picture the educational system as having a very important function as a selecting agency, a means of selecting the men of best intelligence from the deficient and mediocre. All are poured into the system at the bottom; the incapable are soon rejected or drop out after repeating various grades and pass into the ranks of unskilled labor. . . . The more intelligent who are to be clerical workers pass into the high school; the most intelligent enter the universities, whence they are selected for the professions.[17]

Many educators and social thinkers recognized and clearly articulated the fact that equality of opportunity was indeed not too much more than a charismatic American slogan. After all, what the children brought with them from home and their neighborhoods often constituted a decisive handicap. Too often, the environmental deficiencies could not be made up, even with assiduous teachers and efficient schooling.

Yet so much general social progress could be seen from decade to decade that shortcomings in the ideal of equality of opportunity were not enough to precipitate any attempts to change the structure of things. The evidence was that many youngsters from extremely deprived backgrounds gained footholds in the power structure and succeeded well enough to give the Abraham Lincoln and Horatio Alger folklore some verisimilitude.[18] On a lower scale, immigrant factory workers saw their children become small merchants or clerks and their grandchildren professionals or corporate businessmen of note. Equality of opportunity was no mere slogan.

By the beginning of the twentieth century, there was a state university system for the energetic student of modest means. While William James may have been a Harvard graduate, John Dewey studied at the University of Vermont, a tiny institution in the 1870s. City College in New York prided itself on Bernard Baruch, its own Horatio Alger. In fact, though City College genuinely catered to

17. W. B. Pillsbury, "Selection—An Unnoticed Function of Education," *Scientific Monthly* 12 (January 1921): 71.

18. Selman Waksman, who later won a Nobel Prize for discovering streptomycine, was too poor to pay for his Phi Beta Kappa key and had to borrow the necessary $5 from his professor.

students of modest means, as a tuition-free institution, the number of students going on to obtain Ph.D.s and other professional skills compared well in the twentieth century with institutions for the wealthy, such as Harvard and Yale.

After World War II, a veritable revolution in the number of spaces available in colleges and universities was created. The California university system, the great midwestern state universities, and then the eastern university systems, such as those in New York and Massachusetts, demonstrated tangibly that equality of opportunity through education was an ongoing commitment to our society. There was no denying that the public university systems were in process of displacing and even inundating all but the most powerful private universities.

One more issue deserves mention in regard to our national quest for social equality. Until recently, the certification demands for a variety of jobs were only moderately encompassing. A high school and sometimes only an elementary education—plus intelligence and diligence—were all that was necessary for jobs that now require B.A.s. In addition to this, the growth of the unions steadily improved the lot of the working class. In the post-World War II period, the cooperation of unions and management have reduced strikes and increased both wages and prices so that a huge proportion of the population with lesser amounts of education in major industries, the trades, teamsters, miners, etc., earn salaries that vie with or surpass those of white-collar workers and professionals in many fields. One does not have to obtain parity of educational achievement in order to gain a significant amount of economic success and thus, in our society, social equality.

The New Equality

The *Brown* v. *Board of Education* decision of 1954 was in the tradition of extending the legal basis for equality of opportunity. It placed the factor of race beyond governmental actions. With respect to the law, race was now to be ignored. It soon became evident, however, that the deficit incurred by the black people was more than a legal one, heightened as it was by discrimination and prejudice.

Soon attempts were being made to alter the ideal of desegregation to integration (see chapter 9). In an era of practical ideals and fast-paced social change, the slow progress of amelioration seemed intolerable. To some, the ferment in the ghetto, caused in part by this sense of rising expectations, necessitated immediate and tangible equality. The variety of efforts aimed at integrated and compensatory education achieved indifferent results and now became doubly frustrating.

The Coleman Report (1966), which showed that money, improved facilities, modern curricula, and the like affect the black disadvantaged educationally surprisingly little, was an inherently depressing document. Yet for the liberal there was a ray of hope: when all other factors were neutralized, black students in majority white schools seemed to do better than black students in any other situations.

At this point, the surge toward forcible integration, the intercession of government, and the proliferation of quotas began to gain impetus. From 1963, when the Great Society programs expended $1.7 billion on new welfare programs, the expenditures rose 1,000 percent—to $35.7 billion in 1973.[19] And while there were real questions about the efficacy of this vast amount of wealth in alleviating the misery of those most desperately in need, we did see the movement of large numbers of minority young into positions of responsibility in both government and the private sector.

The ensuing years of legal battles to break down suburban school districts and housing zoning, the governmentally enforced quotas, affirmative action programs in jobs and education, the threatened dissolution of standards of admission to colleges—such as the open enrollment program in the City University of New York—were all part of a revolution initiated by a section of the liberal community to arrive at the method of achieving social equality. It was a revolution partially created by a startling educational state of affairs, the average low achievements of black students. But it owed much of its impetus to the general trend of our society to make use of the latent external power of our institutions.

The usual evolutionary expectations, that we ought to let things happen naturally—educational and social equality, cultural homogeneity or heterogeneity—were discarded.[20] If we could avoid an

19. Charles L. Schultze, Edward R. Fried, Alice M. Rivlin, and Nancy H. Teeters, *Setting National Priorities: The 1973 Budget* (Washington, D.C.: Brookings Institution, 1973), cited in N. Podhoretz, "A Call to Dubious Battle," *Commentary* 54, no. 1 (July 1972): 4.

20. I. B. Berkson, *Theories of Americanization* (New York: Teachers College Press, 1920), sets forth a laissez faire principle for cultural pluralism, arguing that human intentionality is the clearest indicator of the relative truth of our social ideals.

economic depression by government intervention, let us go full speed ahead; we could use the power of government, industry, and other institutions to effectuate our goals. The granting of money, the legal coercions, the equality of achievement by official fiat, the racial quotas and reverse discimination—now entering through the back door, in spite of the *Brown* decision of 1954, and the Civil Rights Act of 1964—all of these were attempts to create a new de facto social equality.

The rationale was evident. Centuries of slavery and generations of environmental deprivation and ghettoization made it unlikely that black people could rise quickly through their natural initiative. If only for a few years, all the power in our institutional armory could be expended toward creating tangible equality, even at the expense of invading the most sacrosanct private areas of individual initiative and freedom, it was morally justifiable. The mixed success of this endeavor and the ensuing social turmoil finally gave rise not only to a political reaction of the dominant middle class, but also to an intellectual reaction.

To critics of the new liberal orthodoxy, this trend was the prime exemplar of the theory that nature is infinitely manipulable at the hands of society and its political institutions. The despoliation of our environment, natural and cultural, was only part of an overall venture to eradicate the realm of private rights and values. There were those who saw no inviolable privacies or principles that were immune to governmental power, not if they hindered the cause of any altruistic ideals such as real social equality. As one educational opponent put it:

> It is the unbridled environmentalist who emphasizes the plasticity of the intellect, that tells us one can change both the general rate of development and the configuration of intellectual processes which can be referred to as the intellect, if we could only subject human beings to the proper technologies. In the educational realm this has spelled itself out in the use of panaceas, gadgets and gimmicks of the most questionable sort. It is the environmentalist who suggests to parents how easy it is to raise the child's I.Q. and who has prematurely led many to believe that the retarded could be made normal, and the normal made geniuses. It is the environmentalist who has argued for pressure-cooker schools, at what psychological cost, we do not yet know.[21]

21. E. Zigler, as quoted by Arthur Jenson, "Environment, Heredity, and Intelligence," *Harvard Educational Review*, Report Series #2, (1969): 29–30.

Three Educational Errors

The liberal's use of the public schools as their major attempt to realize parity of social equality has three factors working against its ultimate success:

1. *Equality by fiat.* The first, a typical American error, is not confined to our tampering with the public schools. It is rooted in some of our most basic intellectual assumptions and with that some of our most fundamental social conclusions. The awareness of this power of the human mind to create ideas that have tangible social consequences has been an intrinsic part of the modern consciousness now for at least three centuries. Increasingly, we have thought it within our power to remake the natural physical environment as well as man's social environment. At work here is a myth of human invincibility that decrees that each generation remake nature and society.

With great unwillingness we have begun to be aware of our human limitations and the apparent intractability of mother nature. The peasants and workers of Eastern Europe have gradually taught their Marxist commisars that ideological and political manipulation has limits. We also have begun to learn that our natural environment has limits to the kinds of ecological depredation that we have practiced so as to produce a "cheap" technological affluence. We have refused to live with nature, rather to subjugate her by exhaustive social demands.

Keynesian views of the role of government in economic affairs have reduced the pain of boom or bust economic development; they have had broader social implications as well. The democratic societies have increasingly explored the efficacy of governmental intervention in the laissez faire social system. But the character and extent of this intervention have not been examined philosophically and it has spread willy nilly as a social technique from the economic and industrial areas to the length and breadth of the social system. Only now are we becoming aware of the cultural and psychological price we pay for excessive governmental intercession and regulation in our lives.

This latest effort to put the full weight of the federal government behind the dissolution of school districts, forced busing, racial quotas, which is now being fought in the courts, brings with it the kind of social authoritarianism that has now caused the reaction in the ecological domain. The liberal counters that nothing must stand in the way of the primary social objective of our time—equality. Many observers ask when such effort—the billions of dollars, deeply moving altruism, unqualified human involvement—result in numerous program failures, if subsequent coercive efforts can succeed? Aaron Wildavsky, dean of the Graduate School of Public Policy at the University of California, Berkeley, comments:

> In the past, the clients of the New Deal had been the temporarily depressed but relatively stable lower and middle classes, people who were on the whole willing and able to work but who had been restrained by the economic situation; if a hand were extended to them or if the economic picture brightened, things improved for them right away. It hardly mattered one way or the other what government did or did not do in their behalf. Now, however, government policy was being designed to deal not with such people but with the severely deprived, those who actually needed not merely an opportunity but continuing long term assistance.... Or consider employment. There have basically been two objectives in this area of policy: employ the hard-core and create jobs at reasonable costs. It is very expensive to train the hard-core; that is why they are hard-core. It is also very discouraging, because many will not get jobs and many others will not keep them.... In the field of education, for example, no one had the faintest clue as to what amount of "input" would produce the desired result, and so vast amounts of enthusiasm were poured into various programs that ultimately ended in failure and bewilderment *(as it turns out, we have learned that variations in expenditures of almost four to one make absolutely no difference—or only slight difference—in student performance,* and that other variables, known and unknown, must be taken into account).[22]

What will be the ultimate outcome of this apparently futile attempt at external salvation? Will the courts continue to validate the programs currently in dispute? And if government intervention for purportedly benign social purposes are here legalized, then we must ask about the ultimate limits of the power of governmental agencies to interpose their rules into other voluntary cultural, religious, and community undertakings.

2. The economic road to equality. There is a serious aspect to the frontal attack on the principle of equality of opportunity and its resulting weakening of respect for talents and abilities of each indi-

22. "Government and the People," *Commentary* 56 (August 1973): 26–27. Emphasis added.

vidual regardless of race or class. These fundamental beliefs that have undergirded the democratic ideals of the public schools are being challenged in the erroneous belief that by muddying the waters of the credentializing machine, individual competencies will be blurred or made irrelevant. The implication is that in a system that has permitted gross injustices in economic power, a little injustice on the other side might help to balance the scales.

The net result is that the lower middle classes have revolted against liberal opinion because it is attacking the doctrine of equality of opportunity from which they have benefited, to whatever small extent. On the other hand, the great, powerful, and wealthy have not been touched at all, for they are well beyond the need to demand individual justice and equality of opportunity. And, of all the institutions of our society, it is education, the most fragile, that has been the butt of this quixotic crusade and the quickest to receive the mortal wounds.

For many the circle of poverty has not been broken, as noted above, even with massive external institutional interventions. In addition it has taken on an intergenerational aspect, one generation perpetuating itself into the next on the basis of governmental welfare programs. We must seriously consider the possibility that all societies may have segments that are not capable of moving even onto the ladder of a highly skilled and fast-moving technological society. And if indeed it is not possible for some to move slowly up the ladder of social success through merit, competition, effort, and self-sacrifice, no amount of external assistance will reduce the arduous labor or guarantee success. This is not to deny the urgent need for society consciously to make available opportunities for individuals to demonstrate their skills in a nondiscriminatory environment.

Families of the new working middle class live in great fear of liberal social policy. They have just attained a position where they see new vistas and possibilities for their children. But they see these gains threatened by the preoccupation of government with the lowest classes. The immense power of the state to intervene in people's lives results in increasing pressure on this new working middle class and minimizes values for which they live and under which they have gained so much.

Government-sponsored housing threatens to destroy their communities; welfare in the form of food stamps, medical assistance, reverse job discrimination, and open enrollment threaten to nullify their efforts and dissolve the meanings of their way of life by placing the welfare class in an advantaged position.

The City University of New York, recently committed to open enrollment, has virtually eliminated entrance requirements; it faces the possibility of a steady erosion of internal standards in order to fulfill its certification function. The truly powerful, including the intellectuals who have sponsored such programs, are not disadvantaged by the cauterization of such an institution since they no longer have recourse to Hunter College or C.C.N.Y.

The sudden affluence of so many middle Americans has left a residue of guilt about those left behind in the decaying ghettoes. But it is to no purpose to thrash around aimlessly, settling for solutions that have no theoretical or factual basis for social action, or to focus in on the schools in this redemptive manner merely because educational institutions are so vulnerable to pressure. Eventually, our policy failures will teach us that the world of our utopian dreams must be supplanted for the concrete if somewhat unsavory reality.

The wealthy can watch benignly as the have-nots carry on their internecine war. The wealthy send their children to private schools, the best universities, live well out of range of urban-suburban confrontations; they are only faintly touched by the rhetoric of fire and brimstone equality that emerges from the ultra-liberal.

If there are quotas on jobs, they affect the lower middle classes. If real estate taxes inflate or the economy goes into a tailspin, the little man suffers. It is he who takes the brunt of the social reform that some liberals wish to inflict on others. As one of the proverbial "silent majority" put it:

> People are thinking that after having slaved away for half one's life to be able to put a down payment on a house in the suburbs so as to get out of the slums, the government rewards them for their sacrifices by turning around and forcing their kids onto buses and then shipping them back down into the slums to go to school.

No reasonable liberal has ever argued that the purpose of democratic social policy is to institutionalize the dole or to perpetuate any one group as wards of the state. Thus, what we would want as national policy leading not only to social equality but to social equity is the maximization of individual talent and a just reward for its contribution to the public good. That talent takes many forms goes without saying. And the skills and abilities that a modern society needs are manifold. But one fact seems preeminent. Competency, whatever its character, is a quality that the individual manifests as a product of his own internal will and abilities. It cannot be programmed by an agency of the great society. Ultimately, the concern of both liberal and conservative must be with those individuals who will be fructified by exposure to the educational process, who are both willing and able.

From that point on, rational social policy demands equity in the rewards that society gives the able, contributing citizen. We must agree with Jenck's apparently radical statement:

> Americans are by no means universally committed to economic equality, but we doubt that most of them think the richest 5 percent of all families should have incomes 25 times as large as the poorest 5 percent. If income distribution were a political issue, and if Congress were forced to make explicit decisions about the degree of income inequality it wanted, some distribution will probably take place.[23]

3. Racism and class. Is the American society racist? Is it only bigots who would oppose forcible busing or the dissolution of suburban zoning and school districts? Are the new private schools in the south and the growing Jewish Day School movement educational refuges for the prejudiced? Many liberals would so contend. In an era of precious few moral values or religious truths in which to believe, there seems to exist a sense of intellectual and moral superiority in certain groups that reinforces their struggle for redemption. Seemingly the war of good against evil must be pursued zealously and relentlessly.

This is perhaps a misguided social crusade. The sad truth is that had the Court upheld the forced integration of ghetto and suburb —and fortunately it did not—it would in all likelihood have resulted in the destruction of the public schools. The ensuing turbulence, the hatred and resentments, and the educational chaos are what we can least afford in these tenuous times.

Of course there is a heritage of segregation and discrimination, and neither the *Brown* decision nor the Civil Rights Act of 1964 can easily or quickly efface this heritage. But in the meantime, with incredible rapidity a strong movement toward middle-class status has already been made by a large number of black citizens.[24] For those with the economic capability, the educational solution to be taken is not dissimilar to that of the white middle class. In the cities, the black middle class place their children in private schools or else

23. Christopher Jencks, *Inequality* (New York: Basic Books, 1972), p. 264.
24. See Ben J. Wattenberg, *The Real America* (New York: Doubleday, 1974), esp. chap. on "Black Progress and Liberal Rhetoric."

move to the suburbs, where their children are often integrated in a natural context of middle-class life.

Increasingly, ghetto schools have a residual population in which persists an atmosphere of violence or at the very least disciplinary coercion; it is a reflection of the inevitable tension produced by compulsory education for those who really want out. As one goes up the grades, the atmosphere in these schools is increasingly antithetical to middle-class values. Naturally, this is not universally true of all urban schools, or is it exclusively characteristic of predominantly black or Puerto Rican schools. If the schools are good, however, why are children brought in forcibly from the outside, or indeed bused out, to the suburbs, where they may easily suffer? An affluent atmosphere must wreak havoc with their own self-image; in addition it probably constitutes a disturbing element to the host school.

We quote Jencks,

> Our research suggests, however, that the characteristics of a school's output depends largely on a single input, namely the characteristics of the entering children. Everything else—the school budget, its policies, the characteristics of the teachers—is either secondary or completely irrelevant.[25]

We do not have the right to impute so lightly evil, race hatred, or prejudice to a large proportion of our population. Such accusations constitute acts of moral condescension that are illegitimate in themselves in the consideration of issues of great national import. But because these attitudes take on mythic and religious overtones, they can obscure the factual realities that could lead to pragmatic evaulation and remediation.

The great problems of the ghetto is the "why" of failure, failure that transcends the available opportunities for education, job training, community action, and welfare aid. Why are some incapable of taking hold and maintaining a niche in the middle-class structure? The sequence of family dissolution and neighborhood deterioration seems to lead on to an infinite regression of causes. While it remains a mystery unamenable to diagnosis or cure, is it wise policy to destroy that segment of the population—in all races and ethnic groups, which has so recently through dint of great personal effort established itself in the middle class?

Rather than undermine communities, we ought to help people

25. Jencks, *Inequality*, p. 256.

reinforce and strengthen their values, for the middle class constitutes a pillar of civilization. These values constitute a respect for family structure; stable and integral neighborhoods; a respect for law, work, and merit; an appreciation of tradition, and yet an openness to progress and opportunity.

There are incipient aspirants to the middle class among the poor even today. These are the people who need our aid, to emerge from the inferno, to build new lives and to contribute to the common good. These people need to become aware of the possibilities of choice, for jobs, neighborhoods, and schools that will respect their strivings. They need peace and time.

We submit that we here have an issue of social class, but with special contemporary overtones. Those who fight or flee the new programs of forced integration of their children into the decaying ghetto want to protect the right of their own children to develop in the best possible educational environment. They want to fit their children for the modern international, technically competent world that is coming to be. Such an education and the middle-class social status it connotes is what the poor of the world aspire to. They want the *opportunity* to rise out of their respective ghettoes, not be bused back into them.

17 Educational Choice: Vouchers

The objections which are urged with reason against State education do not apply to the enforcement of education by the State, but to the State's taking upon itself to direct that education; which is a totally different thing. That the whole or any large part of the education of the people should be in State hands, I go as far as anyone in deprecating. All that has been said of the importance of individuality of character, and diversity in opinions and modes of conduct, involves, as of the same unspeakable importance, diversity of education. A general State education is a mere contrivance for molding people to be exactly like one another; and as the mold in which it casts them is that which pleases the predominant power in the government—whether this be a monarch, a priesthood, an aristocracy, or the majority of the existing generation—in proportion as it is efficient and successful, it establishes a despotism over the mind, leading by natural tendency to one over the body. An education established and controlled by the State should only exist, if it exist at all, as one among many competing experiments, carried on for the purpose of example and stimulus to keep the others up to a certain standard of excellence.

Mill, *On Liberty*

These words, penned by John Stuart Mill in 1859—that fateful crossroads year—need careful consideration. For, while England hesitated to plunge into the building of a national educational system, most other Western nations proceeded to do so. And since the end of World War II, with the creation of so many new members of the Third World community, there has rarely been a society that has not provided for a national educational system in its constitution.

Mill, in this same work, argued that for certain special historical reasons, there could be a temporary exception to his caveat against a state monopoly in education. Americans can point to a unique historical condition in that era to argue that private education alone could not have met the dual challenges of the industrial revolution and the massive immigration of foreign peoples to our shores. Certainly, for a given period of time, a society can exempt itself from prudential action such as Mill advises, when faced with challenges far more immediate and pressing. But eventually, as conditions stabilize, the general principles upon which human liberty rests must assert themselves. We must then take heed.

What has taken place in our immediate past is the first stage of institutional arteriosclerosis in education. It was preceded by a period of unnecessarily exuberant institutional and bureaucratic growth that was made possible by our momentary affluence in the post-World War II generation. The years of steady, arduous construction of our national educational system, albeit a fairly loosely connected confederation of systems, was followed by an almost revolutionary revocation of limits. It was the story of the saber-toothed tiger and the Irish elk all over again, exuberant growth followed by rigidifying specialization and then a steady stultification of progress and gradual senility.

THE ILLUSION OF PROGRESS

Specifically, we today witness a system of education locked increasingly in the vise of political contestation and increasingly unrelated to educational value concerns except as they reflect the varying groups that vie for power and control over the entire system. The federal bureaucracy and the courts use racial, religious, and social egalitarian issues as means to exert their powers. The teachers' organizations attempt to maintain their tentative control over the purse strings while the educational establishment presents a never ending stream of "innovations" to maintain the illusion of educational progress from the top.

In spite of any scant progress we may have made, any alternative approaches to public education are nullified when we invoke the "democratic public school." The educational bureaucracies continue to argue for their irreplaceability with this steady barrage of new programs, changes in teacher certification, rules for state aid, new curricula, "special education" reforms, etc., that keep the entire system in a state of commotion. With much activity at the top, they are well able to stimulate the appearance of progress.

The latest reform is an especially significant example in that it has won widespread acceptance by the various states (but not by all of the teacher organizations) and many collegiate teacher-training programs. The philosophical and educational assumptions inherent in this development are typical of the culminating effects of "corporate" education. It has various dimensions and titles, including "behavior modification" and "performance- and competency-based teacher training and certification."

Whether they are concerned with the training of teachers or the evaluation of teacher performance on the job, those espousing performance-based criteria have attempted to utilize empirical, describable behavior changes in the students. The emphasis on performance both by teacher and pupil is undoubtedly a reaction against more ideational or intangible achievement criteria, such as understanding, comprehension, perception, growth, maturity, etc. Too often, so the argument goes, such nonobservable criteria of learning have been used to cover up poor educational achievement.

As one commentator described it, the objectives are to "write," "do," or "describe," and not to "understand" or "perceive." In training an apprentice teacher, it is further suggested, "the emphasis on performance reminds us that knowledge of content and teaching strategies are not sufficient in teaching—overt acting is important—but the essential element of a performance is emphasis on teaching the student [teacher] what he needs to do as a teacher in order to facilitate educational growth and change in youth."[1]

One can argue that this is an extremely narrow view of performance. In its short-run concern for immediate results in terms of changed behavior, it is reminiscent of training techniques used with animals rather than with humans. Where is the attempt to build on the individual's autonomous strengths, the ability to learn without constant external reinforcement? Focusing on the teacher in this mechanistic approach closely approximates the training of zoo keepers or assembly-line technicians. It is hardly in the traditional liberal humanistic view of the abilities that constitute the good teacher.

The limited scientism, which in this case is modeled on the behavioristic psychological tradition, is reflected in this comment arguing for the new method of teacher training. "The development of reliable, objective, valid measures of teacher behavior—a performance based teacher assessment system—will be discussed as the central focus of this research strategy. Without such a system, we cannot hope to learn what patterns of teacher behavior are related to student achievement; this knowledge is essential if performance based teacher education is to fulfill its promise."[2]

1. David Patten and Robert Houston, "Symposia and Abstracts," *AERA,* February 1973, p. 82.
2. Ibid.

The primary aim of such a teacher-education program is thus to maximize the growth of measurable competencies. In addition, a state that commits itself to these methods of certification has in mind the development of criteria by which either to grant teachers tenure or facilitate their dismissal.

Performance-based teacher education is inextricably linked with behavior-modification procedures in actual classroom work with children. Thus the curriculum and the work of the school will be closely tied to the teaching of easily measurable skills. One cannot object to this goal per se. But since it is linked to certain clearly identifiable teacher behaviors and procedures deemed proper and official by whatever prior evidence is used as a predictive and presumed measure of future success, it severs alternative experiments in both teaching and learning a variety of other skills. After all, who would want to put his career on the line in terms of a method or approach that might not fit the official criteria of measurable skill success?

The fence around teacher, school, and child is more constricted when we consider that measurability of achievement throughout twelve years of schooling usually works downward. Thus, given certain specified goals at the end of twelve years, we would extrapolate backward and calculate the official levels of achievement per grade. This is what is done today in achievement testing. But since these measures by and large are still informal and not used as an official weapon in terms of judging teacher success, such current guidelines can be relatively harmless in their impact on school policies.

Given an established method of purveying the competencies of successful teachers who have put these methodological and curricular procedures into practice, consider the impact on the child whose rates of development do not synchronize with the official estimates or whose talents and idiosyncracies are out of phase or latent. The school is forced to label that child early in education; the child is stigmatized by an inability to perform according to the official learning competencies that should have been elicited through behavior modification.

The massive homogeneous, bureaucratically controlled educational machine cannot do other than demand uniformity of result given uniformity of input. This humanoid replica of our industrial machine tools is thus geared to producing identically functioning and replaceable articles in a frightening educational environment.

Granted, the extension of state controls over the schools or massive attempts to improve the "quality" of education are never undertaken with purported malice against individuality, initiative, or innovation. Yet standardized goals inevitably cut down the options available to teacher, student, parent, and school.

Donald Arnstine, an educational philosopher, has phrased it in this way: "A bureaucratic form of organization is not appropriate for schools or school systems. . . . The open ended nature of educational goals does not lend itself to administrative treatment that aims at efficiency. . . . An educational system turns out no 'product' the utility or importance of which justifies the psychologically harmful impact that bureaucracies have on the people who work within them." [3]

One wonders why, under these artificial conditions, the continual manufacture of educational panaceas should be so heralded. To raise the question is almost to answer it. The bureaucracies in education survive by virtue of their new concoctions. The creations being fabricated to fit the needs of the bureaucracy take on a spurious scientific character to hide the reality that they constitute another link in renewed or expanding institutional controls.

At first, the "innovation" is a product of various forms of educational research, sometimes through foundations, sometimes through government grants, less ordinarily in the university departments themselves. Such self-sponsorship is then gradually touted in the teaching, administrative, and other professional conclaves where it is soon picked up by the mass media. With proper public relations treatment the ordinary layman can be duly coerced. Finally, the state boards officially mandate the "reforms" into practical operation in all state public schools. New teacher-certification requirements are soon instituted throughout the nation, and college curricula are revised to conform to the edict (else their teacher graduates may not be certifiable). Publishers are quick to take advantage of the "revolution" in education. As the heady scent of profit runs through the business world, the text and curriculum mill grinds out untold programs and books.

Do we carefully follow up the innovation to test the efficacy of what constitutes a massive financial investment in educational improvement? Rarely, and often with equivocal results. A few fallow years follow, the "revolution" is quietly forgotten, and shunted into the storeroom for inevitable discard. The old song will be heard again, albeit ground out in a new variation.

Recently a new compact has been formed among the states with

3. Donald Arnstine, "The Use of Coercion in Changing the Schools," *Philosophy of Education, 1973* (Edwardsville, Ill.: Southern Illinois University, 1973), p. 172.

regard to teacher education.[4] Now extended to over thirty states, this plan attempts to supersede college course requirements, which in certain states were made moderately flexible recently by an "approved program" plan. Instead of having students obtain certification through transcript approval (on the basis of college courses taken), the states undertook to investigate and approve individual programs developed by colleges for specific teaching areas.

While on the surface this may seem to allow for a variety of approaches, as it develops, given state involvement in certification programs, will not inspection teams have a specific model of teacher education in mind? It may or may not be competency-based or replete with behavioral objects. In the end it must bring the state more restrictively involved in the inner fabric of what colleges will offer to their students. For with program-approval certification in well over half the states, there will be persuasive arguments for conformity. Program approval means certification. Certification means an opportunity for a teaching job. Some may see this as quality control. Others will view it as intellectual coercion.

In Massachusetts, a new state law came into effect in 1974 that redefines the role of the regular classroom with regard to children having special needs (not the talented).[5] Depending upon their handicap, children will, whenever possible, be considered "innocent" until they are officially diagnosed handicapped by a "core evaluation team." The intent of this program is to give all children equality of educational opportunity and to avoid having children arbitrarily assigned to special classes in a school for "behavior problems" or placed in state schools.

These children with "special needs" now will be placed within the province of the local school district and presumably within the heterogeneous classroom whenever possible, as adjudicated by the core evaluation team. Deaf children and others with low incidence handicaps, heretofore given comparative freedom of choice with state subsidization in a school, residential or other, may now have to be returned to classes in the local district.

Parental choice is hereby rendered null. Instead, the core evaluation teams investigating the circumstances of thousands of children each year, using the 107 pages of administrative regulations in

---

4. *Standards for State Approval of Teacher Education* (1973 ed. rev.; Washington, D.C.: National Association of State Directors of Teacher Education and Certification, assisted by the U.S. Office of Education, 1973).

5. The Bartley-Daly Act, Chapter 766 of the Acts of 1972: *The Comprehensive Special Education Law Regulations for Implementation*, State of Massachusetts Department of Education, 28 May 1974.

this law, will serve as the final arbiters of the educational destiny of these children. It is not difficult to imagine the soaring costs of such an administrative spector. The weakness inherent in these procedural arrangements to handle the complex and unique factors presented by each child already adjudicated to have special needs and the daily occurring novelties that such teams will have to face are enough to predict ultimate paralysis and failure for this bureaucratic folly.

Why would experienced educators conjure up such a bizarre plan to replace a flexible parent-initiated program that can more easily deal with the uniqueness of each child? The answer is not too difficult to come by. Bureaucracies can show their usefulness only by creating conditions for their functioning. By periodically changing state curriculum requirements, certification programs for teachers, new financing procedures for state aid to local districts, etc., they seem to show purpose. But it is an artificial function in that it revolves around its own myth of the current public school structure. Parents, students, and communities are still purported to be incapable of defining their educational requirements and incapable of acting upon these needs through the free exercise of rational and intelligent choice.

EDUCATIONAL SENILITY

The general public response to the heavy hand of bureaucratic control of the schools has been a steadily increasing apathy to the process itself. Parents accept the public school as a given, something that has been written into the structure of social reality. One must live with it. The compulsory education laws continue to retain the academically unsuccessful within the gates. As long as the system continues to demand adherence to the certification process, diplomas and degrees, as keys to success, then the able will be likewise maintained.

Even such a dedicated and liberal adherent of the public school idea as Harry Broudy admits to the general failure of a quarter of a century of intense educational research. As concern actual improvements in classroom techniques or general educational procedures that might improve achievement, he is sceptical. The following consideration applies as much to the new competency approaches as it does to the past:

> Now it may be . . . and one devoutly hopes that it will be soon
> . . . that the behavioral sciences of empirical psychology, so-

ciology, anthropology and the like will provide educationists with extensive applicational theories from which rules of procedure can be derived. This would provide us with the methodology and technology. But as matters now stand, the applicational theory is scant and not very significant, whereas the interpretive, context building theory derived from the humanistic disciplines is plentiful but not applicational in the ordinary sense of the term.[6]

The search for applicational theory in pedagogy has come to naught in spite of the efforts of the last generation. The reason may lie in the fact that before our eyes the individual subject of redemption through the public school structure has changed. The context of formal education in the 1970s bears little similarity to that of the first quarter of the twentieth century. The social backgrounds and environments of the children of the two eras are totally dissimilar.

One can make a rough analogy with the astronauts atop a Saturn rocket. The rocket is computer programmed to blast the astronauts out into space on their way to the moon. In the initial stage, enormous force is necessary to lift them beyond the pull of gravity. At this time, they have little personal participation in the process. By the time they have reached the third stage, the astronauts need a delicate and sensitive set of instruments to direct them toward their objective. Here they come into their own. Their minds are far more effective than any computer in gauging and reacting to an almost infinite number of untoward eventualities. As they begin to approach their objective, their autonomous skills and judgments are central to the success of their mission.

It is reasonable to argue that for the majority of the population, modernization has effected an immense change in their conscious awareness of the world and their role in directing their own corporate destinies. What we need are different kinds of institutions to achieve ends that are different in kind than those of half a century ago. An institution designed for that earlier era, no matter how much modern research is poured into it, cannot achieve ends for which the institution is no longer fitted. Now that the tremendous pressure of numbers of children in the schools has waned, we can put those billions of dollars now being wasted on a senile institutional structure to far more effective use.

The changing circumstances of American life to which the schools have responded by developing their own refraction of insti-

6. Harry Broudy, *The Real World of the Public School* (New York: Harcourt Brace Jovanovich, 1972), p. 57.

tutional America has elicited a steady barrage of educational criticism. This criticism is quite different from that which was elicited during the 1930s and '40s when real philosophical concerns were expressed over the nature of progressivism and the intellectual future of the public schools.

More and more in recent years, the criticism has come to be directed at the very foundations of the public school movement.[7] One could argue that the gradual falling off of generalized criticisms of the public school on behalf of the middle-class child was due to the persistent success of these youngsters in avoiding the deterministic pressures that the bureaucratic structure directed at them. They were able to move into high-powered collegiate institutions. They were able to break away and join the counterculture or the radical Left, or even make the transition into the affluent professions. Whatever truth may have existed in Goodman's, Friedenberg's, and Holt's indictments of schooling, these youngsters remained alive and for the most part carried out mature careers that corresponded in no systematic way with the educational ethos they received in the schools. If there was a failing, it was that they were skewed to the extremes of conformity to the corporate system or propelled to extreme movements in culture and politics.

By the mid-1960s, the pattern of educational failure of the poor began to elicit the greater portion of concern. Internal reconstitution of the schools was abandoned as a goal in favor of breaking up the monolithic urban systems into a decentralized structure better able to respond to local needs. These communities, especially when constituted by minorities not equally represented on the larger school board, could thus be assured of a greater say in the schools. Here again, the decentralization plan often defeated its democratic purpose by creating new political entities through which a local political constituency within the city could embroil and manipulate education.

Some advocates of decentralization undoubtedly saw such political fragmentation as affording prime opportunities for exercising controls in a smaller domain, where it was not possible for them to do so in the city at large. The immediate politicalization that accompanied decentralization in New York City, exemplified by the Ocean Hill-Brownsville controversy in Brooklyn, argued the educational limitations of this highly touted public school reform.[8] For the

7. See Richard Pratte, *The Public School Movement* (New York: David McKay, 1973).

8. See Martin Mayer, *The Teachers Strike: New York 1968* (New York: Harper & Row, 1969); Marilyn Gittel, "Urban School Reform in the 1970's," *Education and*

ordinary parent and student, decentralization meant exchanging one set of masters for another.[9]

The free school movement that began to make an impact on the educational scene in the late 1960s was predicated on the possibility that young, enthusiastic, idealistic teachers might prefer to avoid the public school trap altogether. The free schools were in the main a heterogeneous lot. Often they were located in bucolic settings, determinedly apart from cities; in the main, they were variations of the upper-middle-class private school scene. Others were ad hoc experiments situated deep in the ghetto; George Dennison's First Street School is an example.

To the extent that a certain affluence existed in our culture, a little money and a great deal of voluntary enthusiasm went a long way. While many of these schools were short on expertise and long-range commitment, a good number provided an excellent alternative to the more rigid public school setting.

The gradual slowing down of the economy and the shortage of jobs began to make inroads on the movement in the early 1970s. The lack of long-term financing and their still variable academic success of the schools was eroding the rich variety of perspectives. Jonathan Kozol's indictment of the Boston public school system in *Death at an Early Age* earned him a leadership position in the free school movement.[10] He subsequently seemed to move away from the educational dimension of the free school and more into the political realm.

> This is, for me, the crucial question in regard to choice and freedom in the Free School: ferment, provocation, liberation or the sense of option does not "happen" by spontaneous combustion. It happens only if the teachers, parents, organizers, leaders, partisans, coworkers, are willing to stand up and defend a point of view, to introduce unusual kinds of catalytic possibilities, to risk the likelihood of error, sadness, anger, or upheaval by bringing into the context of the child's education visible and unexpected forms of provocation which he cannot independently discover.[11]

This view of the school might be a workable conception of creating an institutional base for political revolutionary action. But

---

Urban Society 1, no. 1 (November 1968): 9–20; Mario Fantini and Marilyn Gittel, *Decentralization: Achieving Reform* (New York: Praeger, 1973).

9. This is the conclusion of Michael B. Katz, a "radical" historian of education, in *Class, Bureaucracy, and Schools* (New York: Praeger, 1971), p. 146.

10. Jonathan Kozol, *Death at an Early Age* (Boston: Houghton Mifflin, 1967).

11. Jonathan Kozol, "Politics, Rage and Motivation in the Free Schools," *Harvard*

in so becoming, it loses its unique educational focus and becomes a means for specific inculcation of doctrines for specific social initiatives. The word that Kozol disseminates is not learning, it is *power.* Perhaps it reflects a realistic sense of frustration with the existing power structure in education. We must consider this trend to be a realistic manifestation of the current decay of educational thought.

Carl Bereiter best epitomizes the sad state of public education. In *Must We Educate?* he reflects on the fact that by 1973 the turmoil in education had largely abated, the state system had not been overturned, and the pressure for radical change had diminished.[12] This did not make the various constituencies happier, but certainly in this time of quiet, we gained a moment to evaluate our situation.

Bereiter is concerned with the basic moral position of public education, whereby children are shaped to a particular value modality of character and behavior by teachers and school. He objects to this assumption of power by the school:

> Education is a matter of purpose and focus. To educate a child is to act with the purpose of influencing the child's development as a whole person. What you do may vary. You may teach him, you may play with him, you may structure his environment, you may censor his television viewing, or you may pass laws to keep him out of bars. . . . The school teacher has a role . . . that does not merely supplement the role of the parents but competes with it and even, perhaps, usurps it. It is the role of "molder of citizens," and "shaper of the next generation"—a role that has been glorified in all the inspirational literature of education and taken for granted in educational philosophy and policy-making. But is it a necessary role and is it a morally acceptable one?[13]

Bereiter thinks not; he proposes as an alternative a system of skill training in the basics and child care that would not intrude on the area of moral self-determination and freedom. There is more to this set of proposals than an attempt to restore to the family important freedoms that are appropriated by the school. Bereiter implies that the recent revolt against the school was a valid expression of distrust. However, in spite of his opposition to the state school, to compulsory education, to credentializing and certificating by the schools as an

Educational Review (August 1972): 418; see also Jonathan Kozol, *Free Schools* (New York: Bantam Books, 1972).
12. (Englewood Cliffs, N.J.: Prentice-Hall, 1973), p. 5.
13. Ibid., pp. 6–7.

entrée to jobs, he backs away from the idea of the voucher. And that is because he sees no way out of the present public school structure with its varying vested interests. Instead, his proposals are geared to satisfy the basic structural needs of the present system by continuing to give it a function, i.e., skill training and child care, at least up to adolescence. For this age group, however, he eliminates compulsory schooling.

There is a hidden assumption in Bereiter's argument upon which he does not elaborate, but which is the key to his own positive suggestions. This ultimately weakens his highly radical perspective. This assumption is that the public schools have always violated the moral right of the parent and child to be free of state-induced indoctrination. This claim cannot go uncontested.

It is certainly true that at the peak of non-Anglo-Saxon immigration in the early part of the our century many raised their voices against the bias of the schools in dealing with the new minorities. To an extent, the theorists of the melting pot rejected the Anglo-Saxon model and proposed a more ecumenical culture scheme as a model. The cultural pluralists were quick to assert the legitimacy of the various ethnic prototypes as educational vehicles for those respective children.

Rarely was it argued that the school as an institution had no "educational rights" in this matter. The Catholics alone created their own schools because their deep sense of religious commitment was violated by the varying secular educational embodiments in the public school. But in building their own institutions, they did not hand back the educational and/or the moral function of building character to the family. They retained the school-family-community-church relationship, in which the value dimension of education was clearly related to the larger community structure within which the child was being reared.

Even during the height of the controversy over the relationship of the public school in the education of the immigrant, there was never a vestige of doubt about the legitimacy of the public school to "educate." Certainly, the Catholics argued that such an "education" as was given by the public school was merely not their particular choice. What they wanted were public subsidies for their own schools.

The traumas that the schools have recently undergone have arisen precisely because of our waning confidence in the school. The moral consensus that undergirded the public school for so many decades has dissolved. And in its absence the state schools have fallen prey to a host of political locusts. Drained of its integrity, public education has become an automatic target of every new political power grab. This has caused thoughtful people to abandon hope for the public school as a functioning national institution in its traditional moral as well as skill-training role.

THE VOUCHER

The coming of the voucher idea to education is the natural culmination of the social and educational events of the last several decades. As the great institutional monoliths of our nation have gobbled more and more psychic as well as cultural initiative, enormous tensions have been generated in that most value-sensitive area, formal education. The ferment has created a variety of unsuccessful revolutionary social trends. If in the main the educational embodiments of these trends have failed, the thoughtful search for change continues. Indeed, the voucher idea has had its proponents within a section of the bureaucracy itself, the Office of Economic Opportunity.

And while it is true that these public school voucher alternatives are still absorbed within the present educational structure, strong arguments continue to be made for a plan that will free education of its present structural paralysis. The stultification of the talented and the frustrations of the disadvantaged are exacerbated by a system that cannot be evaluated by any other yardstick than itself. As long as the present monopoly of state education exists, there will be no true measure of the educational failure of this system.

The private schools are usually much too specialized to give us a sense of comparison. And they are too few to be able to stand on their own feet educationally. The free schools, full of enthusiasm, come and go, unable to maintain themselves because they are without an economic base. Even defenders of the public school status quo must throw up their hands at our incapacity to fathom the true extent of the educational disaster in the public schools. "After a decade of intense concern about schools on the part of social scientists, it is still almost impossible to document the patterns of strength and weakness in school systems in terms that are policy-relevant. We have neither the data nor the conceptual models that would permit conclusions about relative achievement of school systems. If one takes into account their various socioeconomic and political contexts, who can say that the New York public school system is better or worse than those in Chicago, Los Angeles, or Atlanta." [14]

The voucher concept is not necessarily new, nor is it an untried educational pattern. Denmark, England, and France, among other advanced democratic societies, grant subsidies to independent schools and to parents who choose education for their children outside the mainstream of their national systems. [15] The basic rationale of the voucher is congruent with Mill's concern that schooling not be taken out of the jurisdiction of the state and therefore of the democratic process. Education is too important a function of society for the latter to relinquish all responsibility, control, and supervision. Rather, it is a matter of the society, deciding through the democratic means of the legislative process whether the ends of the educational process can be best served by a state run system or a voluntary system (where funds are assigned to the child, administered by the parent, and placed in schools that are supervised by the state).

We can apply a similar yardstick as that of public utilities, whether they be regulated or run by the state, to the problem of public or private support of cultural institutions such as museums, theaters, and symphony orchestras. In many cases, a reverse process occurs whereby private means no longer preserve essential public services, whether they be railroads or opera houses. In each case, the question of the capability of the institutions to operate efficiently in a particular context must be examined in the light of the changing dynamics of the society. Sometimes it is wise to allow certain industries or institutions to die a natural death. However, the natural historical process of institutional attrition is more likely to be circumvented when an institution is operated by the government than when it is merely subject to regulation established by the people's representatives. Dysfunctionality will be more clearly evidenced in voluntary institutions than would be the case given the ability of government to shift funds from healthy services to support those that are ailing.

In the case of the schools, the charismatic status of education has allowed a basically unhealthy structural situation to persevere to a

---

14. George R. LaNoue, ed. *Educational Vouchers: Concepts and Controversies* (New York: Teachers College Press, 1972), p. 130.
15. See Estelle Fuchs, "The Free Schools of Denmark," in *Educational Vouchers: From Theory to Alum Rock*, ed. James A. Mecklenburger and Richard Hostrop (Homewood, Ill.: Etc. Publications, 1972).

point that it is out of control. No one can estimate the actual economic support necessary to produce even a modestly comparable level of achievement were a more competitive, voluntary system allowed to develop. While this monopolistic situation exists, those who are the vested beneficiaries of this bloated institutional behemoth will loose a variety of smokescreens to obscure the real issues and prevent any such estimation.

In order even to consider the varying models of voucher plans —advantages or objections—one ought to place the idea in proper perspective. That the voucher idea has been a traumatic one to many sympathetic to the public school is understandable. We have invested the school, as Ivan Illich has suggested, with almost sacramental status. Instead of seeing it as an institutional receptacle to achieve far more fundamental social or cultural ends, we have looked upon the public school as an end in itself.

Thus, its senility has escaped many of us. And our pumping of unbelievable amounts of wealth without any measurable advances only testifies to our concern with myths and memories and not with the implacable present. The voucher represents only a functional alteration; it is intended to loosen up a sterile formal structure and allow a certain amount of fluidity, decentralization, and individual and community initiative. The voucher principle might even stimulate the flow of new creative juices into our formal educational patterns.

Indeed, it is not out of the question that we might at some point want to reverse some of the centrifugal dynamics the voucher idea would spark. And of course, the voucher structure even in its most laissez faire embodiment would not relinquish the reins of state supervision and regulation. Central to our thesis is that the voucher idea is not merely directed against the concept of a public school. Rather, the voucher is a positive approach to the attainment of fundamental democratic ends that increasingly elude us in the ever more inert state systems.

What are the main social ends inherent in the voucher idea? They can be given as follows:

Culture and conformity. A voluntary system of education would lead to the clustering of individuals with similar values, social concerns, and cultural ideals. These individuals would tend to group themselves as a community, with the school as one focus. This would inevitably enrich our community life. The fallout in terms of social benefits would be enormous. It is estimated that in 1974 schools in the United States lost $500 million through vandalism.

What kind of community life fosters such behavior in the young and not so young?

In addition, schools could become cultural centers where individuals could explore new and hidden depths of their creative potential in an atmosphere of mutuality and support, as distinct from the hostile "lowest common denominator" environment of the present public system.

It should be stated that the government would have the right to refuse certification to schools in which it can be proved that they foster ideologies or behaviors that are not in the public interest. But it should be pointed out that the burden of proof would be on the government. The present structure of education precludes any initiative to develop something truly new.

Educational achievement. The world has changed with extraordinary rapidity in the last decades. New perspectives in experience were released by changes in communication and transportation. The schools, especially after the challenge of the Russian Sputnik, attempted to upgrade curricular materials. Much was done through universities, foundations, and even governmental subsidies. In recent years, however, as the crisis of the educationally disadvantaged has worsened, the attention therein focused has been such that relatively little has been introduced in terms of upgrading or revising curricular materials at the highest achievement levels. Part of the inertia has been due to the fact that the counterculture revolt against the intellectual domain and against educational institutions took place at the highest levels of institutional education.

Nevertheless, innovation has probably been dampened to an extent because there is no longer the freedom and flexibility that once existed in education. From Regent's exams to College Boards, the system is increasingly lock-step. A voluntary system might tell us several things. We might discover how the epochal changes in our own time have speeded up the youngsters' environmental immersion in the materials of modern education. We might learn that much less time is necessary to attain relative efficiency of basic skills. A flexible system might also stimulate the production of wholly new curricular models that could challenge our existing conventions and be far more appropriate for the functional needs of our day.

Many years ago, it was thought that in order to attain proficiency in musical performance one had to have been a child prodigy. Later it was discovered that the rationalization of effective teaching methods made it possible for a musician to attain his peak somewhat later and still not limit his ultimate development. Had a state monopoly existed in this area, many a talent would have been turned away because he was not a full-fledged genius at eleven years of age.

How much of the frustration of the talented of the counterculture was due to our blunderbuss methods of instruction in the public schools, we will never know. What we do know is that we need real achievement in constantly new variety. And we need to thrust aside the irrelevant procedures and patterns of tradition so that we can keep what is always fresh. Only diversity and competition in education can do this.

Financial efficiency. One of the fears conjured up by the voucher idea is that it will promote duplications of facilities and thus lead to increased educational costs. One cannot easily turn this issue aside. The voucher idea involves a basic redirection in assigning an innovative role in education. It will be transferred from the school establishment to a parent-child-teacher association. It is impossible to test out this new relationship unless one allows the voucher idea to take place. As we will point out, the development of public school vouchers or alternative schools does not go even halfway toward the goal of the voucher plan, in that it limits itself to the present structure of education. The only innovation is that a variety of teaching and organizational styles are allowed to compete with each other.

The real question that the voucher idea embodies is the nature of the value ideals that citizens will choose for their children within the context of the unknown academic necessities of life in our technological society. We cannot tell in advance how efficient parents and schools will be when they personally have to squeeze the last bit of educational output from the dollar. One suspects that it would be unbelievably more economical, dollar for dollar, in bricks and mortar, in teaching personnel, and in curricular innovation.

There is no other potentially more inefficient model than the monopolistic one that we have. As each new difficulty or insoluble problem arises, we are asked to add more money, equipment, or personnel. Certainly, a dual system—voucher and public—might be more expensive in the beginning. But we cannot know for sure that this would be the case.

We would propose that in the beginning a modest voucher be given so that a large personal sacrifice would still have to be made. This would tend to develop schools in which highly responsible parental and community input would establish the best models, probably a mix of conservative and radical educational and value patterns. As the problems are observed and resolved, and if successful overall, the voucher subsidy would be expanded so that a variety of communities of various economic wherewithal, with suitable compensatory adjustments for the aspiring poor, would be included. Another alternative would be for one of the states or several adjacent counties within a state to be encouraged to take this step. Since a voucher decision is presently completely within the prerogatives of the people as expressed through their state governments, it could develop gradually.

Higher aspirations. Following the 1966 Coleman Report's suggestion that a pattern of higher achievement seemed to be evident in those black children who were integrated into predominantly white schools, a massive integration program was attempted. The entrance of the courts in an attempt to break down school districting lines, introduce compulsory busing, the wide variety of litigation that was attempted to break the patterns of ghettoization, soon convulsed the educational scene. The results were mostly negative —the flight of more middle-class people to the suburbs, where they still remain beyond the reach of the courts; the continued crisis of academic achievement in inner city schools; and the unlimited political infighting over who controls what in education.

A new Coleman report is in the offing. Commissioned by the Urban Institute of Washington, D.C., James S. Coleman, now of the University of Chicago, has been studying 70 urban school districts from 1968 to 1973 in an attempt to understand the dynamics of the changes that have occurred since his earlier study (1966) for the U.S. Office of Education.

Although final publication of these findings has not occurred as of this writing, Coleman has been interviewed widely about his research (see *Newsweek,* 24 June 1975, and the *New York Times,* 11 July 1975). He is now greatly concerned about the resegregation of the cities caused by the flight of the white middle class. The cause is more due to the search for educational quality and the avoidance of urban decay and its social consequences, and less due to racist fears. Coleman attributes much of this flight to the coercive actions of government, especially court rulings on compulsory busing.

He admits that the evidence from court-induced busing is fragmentary and inferential. Coleman believes that the great concern of parents is over class differences and not race. As such, he now backs away from a prime implication of his earlier report that the educational advancement of black students is dependent upon the presence of white students and the policy actions, compulsory busing for forced integration, which have been instituted as a consequence: "The general tendency is for middle-class families to move out to what they see as better schools for the money. That tendency is increased if their kids are suddenly being bused into ghetto areas for school with lower-class kids" (*Newsweek* interview).[16]

The voucher plan would have a significant impact on the forgotten poor. These are the hidden and exploited families who could make use of educational opportunity to rise beyond poverty and into the middle class. There is an assumption here that the massive indiscriminate attempt at racial mixing to achieve statistical quotas is counterproductive. The "quota view" of human beings has to perceive individuals not in terms of their intrinsic needs, but in terms of irrelevant ascriptive designations: race, sex, or ethnic group. These ought to be abandoned in education and law.

Many years ago, John Watson, the founder of behaviorism, thought he could condition an individual to be anything he wanted him to be. Watson would have presented before him "a dozen healthy infants, well formed, and my own specified world to bring them up in and I'll guarantee to take any one at random and train him to become any type of specialist I might select—doctor, lawyer, artist, merchant-chief and, yes, even beggarman and thief, regardless of his talents, penchants, tendencies, abilities, vocations, and race of his ancestors." [17]

In the half century since, we have experienced B. F. Skinner's work as well as other environmental conditioning techniques, to force us to come down to the complex reality of what it is that makes a highly educated human being. We can provide "optimal" circumstances but educational drive must develop inside the individual. It cannot be programmed into a person. Once we realize the essential voluntaristic character of human achievement, we must withdraw from arrogant attempts to make people over from the outside, a penchant of more totalitarian societies. We must allow them to exercise choice and will in developing whatever it is in their individual characters that will determine their lives for them.

16. Coleman's shift in perspective and his generally defensive posture (1975) have perhaps been influenced by the weight of recent research which seems to confirm David Armor's conclusion (see pp. 154–56) that busing effects no academic gains for black children and may cause a decline of self esteem. See: Nancy St. John, *School Desegregation: Outcomes for Children* (New York: John Wiley, 1975); also Diane Ravitch, "Busing: The Solution That Has Failed to Solve," *New York Times*, 21 December 1975.

On the political use of Coleman's earlier research see: B. W. Young and G. B. Bress, "Coleman's Retreat and the Politics of Good Intentions" and J. S. Coleman, "Social Research and Advocacy: A Response to Young and Bress," *Phi Delta Kappan*, November 1975, pp. 159–69.

17. John Watson, *Behaviorism* (New York: W. W. Norton, 1924), p. 82.

The voucher plan would help those poor who can muster the determination to find the education that will fit their needs and not what a flatulent bureaucracy decides they should have. Nor would it fit the momentary messianic visions of those itinerant enthusiasts who would purport to lead the poor against the power structure. By giving the poor the equivalent monetary value of what is now wasted on an unsuccessful education, one could not help but expect greater success than can presently be found.

Conservative economist Milton Friedman stated the issue squarely.[18] If a black family in the ghetto wishes to allocate more funds to culture, or a car, they can do so where they are. They have some choice with what they do with their funds. If they wish to make sacrifices for a child who shows some interest in academics, they now can exercise choice only by moving out of the city to the suburbs. This often represents a quantum economic leap which they cannot make. The child is condemned to the ghetto school. Were there to have been choice, his abilities would have been noted and a school found that would be compatible with the evolving economic possibilities of the family.

The right of all citizens of whatever race to equal opportunity should be asserted and facilitated. But we must accept the reality that not all human beings can ascend equally. From time immemorial, the test of the able has been their skill in utilizing opportunity and choice in carving out for themselves a place in the sun. The kind of massive state miseducation that we have today—to the extent that it treats individuals in the bureaucratic manner—discriminates against the able poor by grinding them down to the lowest common denominator of compulsion in education. A voucher system that recognizes the special economic disadvantages of the poor and yet combines special help with real choice is probably the only solution for an intransigent educational problem that has evaded every recent effort.

VOUCHER PLANS

The voucher idea has been in the educational wind for quite a while. Virgil Blum proposed it in the late 1950s as a suggestion to aid the parochial schools. But because of its linkage with the battle to gain public funds for Catholic schools, it was considered no more than another ploy to obtain money from the public till.

18. Milton Friedman, *Capitalism and Freedom* (Chicago: University of Chicago Press, 1962).

In 1962 Milton Friedman discussed the role of government and education.[19] He suggested moving to a system of education that would be independent of government control and would work out of a voucher system. But Friedman was seen as an arch conservative. (He was an adviser to Barry Goldwater.) And in 1962 we were still in an era of great demographic pressure in the schools; there was a great need for teachers and for intensive school building. The crises in the cities were still being met by new experiments in community control within the school.

In short, the voucher idea had not yet entered the liberal repertoire. There was still hope that the public school might be captured by progressive elements. The nature of the organizational beast had not been fathomed. By the early 1970s, such radicals as Jonathan Kozol, despairing over the steady attrition of the urban free schools, could now hope for a voucher plan that could rescue their voluntaristic alternative.[20]

In general, one must regret the absence of a significant liberal call for the voucher idea. That there was no such call may have been due to the somewhat uncomfortable sense of the abandonment of a sentimental ideal, one which was part of the liberal progressive movement of the John Dewey era. In addition, the voucher would free the school of the intense battle for political control. Giving the right of educational choice to the parent and child means accepting the possibility that given such liberty, they may make choices that might be quite different from those that liberals would envision for them.

In 1970, the Office of Economic Opportunity did yield to the growing call for vouchers by funding a public school voucher plan in Alum Rock, California.[21] In addition, through a U.S. Office of Education grant, the Center for the Study of Public Policy in Cambridge, Massachusetts, under the directorship of Harvard's Christopher Jencks, developed an elaborate proposal for a more far reaching system of regulated vouchers. This 220-page report was issued in March 1970.

The regulated voucher was in response to the growing call for more freedom of choice in education, which in the beginning tended to focus on the unregulated voucher Milton Friedman proposed.[22]

19. Ibid.
20. *Free Schools* (New York: Bantam Books, 1972), pp. 145–51.
21. In April 1975, such a public school voucher plan was announced for East Hartford, Connecticut.
22. See James Mecklenburger and Richard W. Hostrop, *Education Vouchers: From Theory to Alum Rock* (Homewood, Ill.: Etc. Publications, 1972).

And while there was a great variety of voucher proposals, they all seemed to group themselves into the two camps: (1) a system of unregulated vouchers, where children could take their vouchers wherever they would, and (2) those in which severe restrictions were set forth on the use of personal voucher moneys and on the right of schools to choose students.[23] The great issue stimulating the voucher plan is the extent to which an unregulated voucher would further encapsulate the poor and/or the black people in even more segregated educational environments. I deal with this issue below.

There are, it is true, other concerns with the unregulated voucher such that the financial costs of a voucher structure would be a great unknown. But, on the other hand, there is a consensus that the costs of education in the present structure are seriously incommensurate with the results. In addition, there is concern that the bureaucratic structure stimulated by the present system is highly inflated in terms of the proportion of moneys directly used for teaching.

There are other concerns, some valid, some not. How often have we heard the old saw that parents are too ignorant to choose wisely in education? As such, we need the state system to advise parents and children what is good for them. In terms of internal as well as external evidence as to what goes on in schools under monopolistic control, the answer to this charge is patent. In education, where the deepest human concerns over moral and cultural values, self-determination, and freedom lie, the primary initiative must be with the individual. If the state is to determine what in education is for the benefit of the individual, then we approach totalitarianism.

While we all would agree that the state has an obligation to regulate the content of manufactured foods to attest to the purity of the contents, in education we must freely determine the content and the structure of the values and ideals that constitute its contents. The future character of our society may be determined through schooling. The people, by their uncoerced choices, will here give tangible evidence of the direction in which they want their society to flow.

The extent to which the argument as to parental ignorance has been abandoned by the educational power structure is exemplified

23. Center for the Study of Public Policy, *Education Vouchers: A Report in Financing Education by Payments to Parents* (Cambridge, Mass., December 1970); John E. Coons, William H. Clune III, Stephen D. Sugarman, *Private Wealth and Public Education*, (Cambridge, Mass.: Belknap Press of Harvard University Press, 1970); John E. Coons and Stephen Sugarman, *Family Choice: A Model State System for Vouchers* (Berkeley: University of California Institute of Government Studies, 1971).

in a recent critique of the voucher idea by Albert Shanker, president of the American Federation of Teachers. Shanker now warns only against the flourishing of a variety of diploma mills in education, whose intent would be to take the voucher of the child, give nothing in return, and pocket the profits.[24]

This, of course, is a danger. But in the free market, were this fact to be discovered, the parent would have legal recourse. So would the state, if normal regulatory procedures were violated. The offending institutions would surely receive a fatal blow if the charges were upheld.

But what happens when the public schools do not fulfill their responsibilities? Those responsible for the educational failures can continue as before. There is no competing standard by which to measure their failure. In addition, they have a monopoly over the certification process and they have the backing of state laws mandating compulsory attendance. There is thus a triple cover ensuring that the public domain will never have to answer for the quality of its education.

REGULATED VOUCHERS

By far the most serious criticism of the unregulated voucher has been to the socioeconomic impact of this plan on the poor. Thus it is that Christopher Jencks, at first one of the few liberal adherents to the idea, retracted his endorsement. His shift to a qualified regulated voucher was made with the warning that unless special concern was given for the poor, an unregulated voucher "could be the most serious setback for the education of the disadvantaged children in the history of the United States." [25]

The significant issue is to what extent in an unregulated voucher plan will the poor be left behind and to what extent will racial segregation continue under the guise of freedom of choice.[26] The regulated voucher plan put forth by the Cambridge group has a number of features that they feel would neutralize these concerns and even bring voucher approved schools into the public school community. They foresee the current school structure as a continuing one, purifying itself through competition.

The several special features are (1) an approved school could

24. *The American Teacher* (AFT), April 1975.
25. George R. LaNoue, *Educational Vouchers: Concepts and Controversies* (New York: Teachers College Press, 1972) p. 54.
26. *Poindexter* v. *Louisiana*. See ibid., pp. 30–45.

charge only the value of the voucher, and no more; (2) it would have to admit all applicants for the available spaces (if there were more applicants than spaces, one-half would be chosen by lot, the rest chosen without discriminating because of ethnic background); (3) an approved school would have to accept uniform standards for suspension and expulsion of students. LaNoue gives as an example the 1969 Supreme Court decision in *Tinker* v. *Des Moines* (#393 U.S. 503), which ruled that public school students had the right to wear armbands protesting war if they did not otherwise disrupt the school. Thus, schools could not set up independent rules for student, or perhaps teacher behavior that deviated from official canon.

The concern in (1) is that schools that charged additional tuitions would effectively exclude the poor. In effect, they could become rich people's schools using the voucher to subsidize their exclusivity. In addition, by being able to use private moneys, they might seriously inflate the market, i.e., teacher salaries, equipment, and thus further depress the quality of the minimum voucher schools. Finally, as is the case in many areas where strong parochial systems exist, there develops an unwillingness to support increases in this basic voucher as costs rise, since the wealthy have the wherewithal to spend as they wish.

Of course, as John E. Coons, William H. Clune, and Stephen D. Sugarman have noted, wealthy school districts already use the public schools for this purpose. The Supreme Court has recently thrown the *Serrano* issue (of unequal tax support for school districts) back to the states for adjudication. The courts have maintained that the area of financial equity for each school child under the Fourteenth Amendment is still beyond its jurisdiction. In Illinois, in 1971, it "dismisses for lack of 'discoverable and manageable standards' a suit which asserted a duty of the state under the 14th Amendment to spend for each child according to his individual needs. The Supreme Court affirmed without argument or opinion, and with but one dissent." [27]

Thus, while the problem is not an insignificant one in public education, the aim of the Jencks plan is to keep the regulated voucher neutral with regard to this issue. And, of course, it serves to exclude patently private schools and at the same time gives each school community the freedom to use what it has in a competitively functional manner.

As to (2), the demand that schools certified by the "Educational

27. Coons, Sugarman, and Clune, "Education Vouchers," p. 63.

Voucher Authority" accept all students that apply stems from educational "market" considerations. Thus it is assumed that the school has a built-in advantage and that more students are searching for good schools than vice versa. However, an appraisal of our current educational situation, where a "pupil" shortage is fast approaching, with evidence that it will be a continuing phenomenon over the next several decades, this voucher stipulation is puzzling. It can only stem from a belief that "good" schools will always be in shorter supply than pupils. It also implies that schools would choose in ways that are socially inimical to the common good.

The thought obviously is aimed at preventing some schools from choosing all the best pupils and leaving the "dregs" to fend for themselves. It hopes not only to prevent racial and ethnic discrimination, but also to force all schools to accept a random proportion of those students educators would rather not have.

We have in stipulation (3) about suspensions and exclusions an attempt to prevent schools through internal rules of discipline or culture to become too exclusive in their internal organization. While there is certainly a consideration here for the civil rights of students, one suspects that the concern is more basic, that of personal values and social order. Schools could not suspend or expel for patent violation of school cultural rules. Thus, the 50 percent of the students who are chosen at random from those who apply will have had their rights safeguarded not to be squeezed out of the school through arbitrary regulation imposed by the school authorities.

Critique of Regulated Vouchers: The Limits of State Control

Few would question the right of the state to establish guidelines for education. The excerpt given at the beginning of the chapter by John Stuart Mill is certainly a classic assertion of the right of a people as represented by its government to ensure that the individual child's rights are protected not only in the school, but in the family as well.

Thus state involvement in establishing regulations on the use and application of vouchers is not questioned in principle but in terms of its social and philosophical impact on the character of education. The state does have a right to anticipate the long-range impact of any educational structure, or a particular school, on the society. Thus, a school devoting itself to the cultivation of ethnic or religious hatreds, or preaching the active revolutionary overthrow of the established system, might be excluded from voucher or other forms of public subsidy. Whether or not such schools ought to be forbidden to function is quite another issue.

It can be argued that any voucher plan must in addition to building into itself the usual health and safety standards that today apply to all schools must conform to the present constitutional injunctions concerning state aid to private education as well as those applying to the public sector.

Thus the First Amendment as it has recently been interpreted now enjoins any support for church-controlled lower schools. Until such schools divest themselves of affiliation, control, and operation by a religion, they would be unable to participate in a voucher program.

Similarly, the impact of the desegregation decision has been such as to render the state blind to the issue of race. This was certainly the thrust of Justice Harlan's dissent in *Plessey* v. *Ferguson* (1896). That race, but perhaps not religion or ethnic culture, ought to be irrelevant factors in the composition of school faculty and student bodies would have to be supported. Race connotes no value issues that rational people would find as a basis around which to organize educational ventures. Likewise, benign quotas or reverse discrimination of this sort ought to be firmly rejected.

From this point on, the regulated voucher plan begins to take on normative social and educational directives that a great many citizens might find onerous. They would see the various restrictions as not only impinging on certain basic voluntaristic rights but also contributing to potentially harmful educational implications.

Egalitarian vouchers. The so-called egalitarian vouchers approach, in which voucher-approved schools are not allowed to charge beyond the face value of the voucher, is an example of such a restriction. The ostensible reason for this proposal is to make sure that the better off do not gain too much of an advantage by pouring more funds into the education of their children. For the wealthy or even the upper middle class, there is no problem. They would send their children off to private schools where for good or ill they can spend on whatever they wish, whether dramatics or horseback riding.

This restriction would limit only those middle-class parents who would rather give to their children's education that portion of their income that might go for liquor or a vacation in the Bahamas. What this proposal does, then, is to punish those who prefer to engage in socially constructive behavior, e.g., educating the young.

In addition, it would encourage devious behavior. For example, what would prevent a school from having classes from 8:00 A.M. to 12:00 noon? And if their efficiency is such as to match in achievement other schools that operate from 8:00 to 3:00, would they be excluded from the plan? Promptly at 12:05, they could reopen as a club rented out to parents and children for cultural activities—music, art, drama, science labs—which the parents pay for out of their own pockets, much as they do today.

What would be wiser would be to give to lower-income families a compensatory voucher to be used in a school or schools as they decide. It might be as much as double the basic voucher for the poorest families with two children. There are socially persuasive reasons why it is not in the interest of society to subsidize an unlimited number of children per family with compensatory vouchers. Thus, a family with an income of $6,000 per year and five children would in getting a compensatory voucher for each child inevitably reduce the potential amount of the basic voucher that a family with two children and with an income of $12,000 per year could expect to get. The latter family is not that affluent that they can afford to spend the supplementary funds that the first family obtains free.

Thus, a limit on compensatory vouchers to two or three children per family would be equitable and socially progressive. For those who want more than two children and who are willing to accept the basic voucher for the rest, no penalty is advocated. They must be prepared to share the burden that they have voluntarily incurred. Whether the tax system could also be altered so as to benefit those who do not impose on the state for a variety of public tax-supported services is another issue. In an era when the burden must be more equitably borne, there are ample areas for legislation promoting this aspect of equality.

We ought not put exaggerated emphasis on the impact of money in elementary and secondary education. Let us establish a decent basic voucher. Beyond this, there will quickly be a point of diminishing returns. Except for snobbish and social-class concerns, the long-term impact of money in education is probably overrated. So, apparently, is the long-range implication of education for economic inequality. Both Christopher Jencks and Ivar Berg have argued that the direct correlation of education and wealth has not been established.[28] Why, thus, should there be imposed what would seem

28. *Inequality* (New York: Basic Books, 1972); Ivar E. Berg, *Education and Jobs: The Great Training Robbery* (New York: Praeger, 1970).

to be a malevolent barrier to parents making economic sacrifices for the educational enhancement of their children? *Accepting everyone.* The demand that schools accept anyone who applies is linked to the fear that irrational exclusions would occur, i.e., racial, and that there would be fewer good schools for students to choose from. Further, it assumes that there are some pupils that no school would want.

These assumptions are certainly linked to a belief that a school "is assumed guilty until proved otherwise." Certainly, the legal bar to racial exclusions ought to be maintained. However, it is by no means clear that lower-class students would find themselves excluded from excellent and devoted schooling, even if rejected by established elite schools. The recent surge of free schools in the ghetto argues against this presumption and so do demographic and teacher availability statistics.

One of the first developments in a voucher-supported public educational system will no doubt be the centrifugal differentiation of schools into interests, special talent, cultural and ethnic orientation schools. If 50 percent of the clientele of each school has to be taken by lot, there will inevitably be a divided constituency. Just imagine a school for the artistically gifted, or a Greek cultural school having to take half its students merely because they happened to live close by and applied for admission!

Just as it would destroy Harvard, such an open-enrollment plan would wreck any school that attempted for good educational reasons to select students who would benefit from its unique point of view. Its unworkability, as well as its basic controversion of the voucher idea, again labels such a limitation on free choice as a mischievous imputation of the moral turpitude of citizens. Indeed, there may be students who ought not be in ordinary schooling situations. Whether from heredity, family training, or the neighborhood environment, they suffer from severe personal and academic difficulties. Rather than being sloughed off into a coerced environment, they should be, and they would be, placed in specialized schools where they would get help. Indeed, if they are economically deprived and eligible for a compensatory voucher, this should make them more attractive for those schools prepared to handle such cases. This argument should apply for every "special needs" child, whether the special need happens to be for remedial or enriched schooling.

The myth of the incorrigible child and the chronic underachiever is due to the bureaucratic morass that restricts the natural give and take out of which functional educational environments are created for the almost infinite variability to be found in human beings. The scandal of a well-behaved, normally intelligent youngster who was passed through the San Francisco public schools without ever learning to read could not happen in a voluntary system.[29] The parent-school interaction would reveal problems far earlier than the twelve years it took San Francisco public educators to know that something was wrong. The malpractice syndrome can be avoided not only by giving parents and children choice of schooling, but also by giving the school the right to choose students whom they could benefit and thus help them accept full responsibility for their freely arrived at decisions.

Internal autonomy. The final important restriction in the regulated voucher plan developed for the Office of Educational Opportunity by the Center for the Study of Public Policy concerns uniform standards for student suspension and expulsion. In theory, this regulation is intended to prevent schools from quickly ridding themselves of students who exhibit stereotyped "lower class" forms of unruly behavior. Perhaps, in addition, it is aimed at preserving students' civil rights, such as in the *Tinker* v. *Des Moines* (1969) case, which validated the rights of students to wear armbands.

If one looks deeper into this restriction, it is perhaps the most subtle, if not the most pernicious, restriction on the right of school and value communities to develop. It purports to protect someone who cannot be protected, the incorrigible troublemaker, who should not be in an ordinary school. What it does do is lead the school right down the same path as does the lowest common denominator of value commitments in our present school system. In effect, it means we cannot form valuing educational communities.

For, if we demand admission to the school by lot, we invite a heterogeneous clientele. This heterogeneous clientele, even one person, can veto any of the internal rules, regulations, commitments, beliefs, standards that the community sets for itself. It is not as if the student has no other place to go. In theory, he would be able to choose another school. In fact, today in the public schools, both student and school are forced to the status quo. The student can not choose a *different* public school. So he now has recourse to the courts.

---

29. *Peter Doe* v. *San Francisco Unified School District;* see Stephen Sugarman, "Accountability Through the Courts," *School Review* 82, no. 2 (February 1974): 233–59; also G. Saretsky, "The Strangely Significant Case of Peter Doe," *Phi Delta Kappan,* May 1973, p. 589.

It is to be hoped that the voucher idea will eliminate the constant application to the courts for redress because of lack of choice and/or options for change. But, if we say that a school has to keep a dissident, then we throw the entire issue of student rights and behavior back into the courts for their decision as to what the voucher authority should set as minimum standards of behavior.

Here we have the key to the whole problem of compulsion, cultural homogeneity, and the bureaucratic impersonalism that are destroying our education in the United States. The contemporary view of the school and of the educational process is too narrow. It is not merely a system addressed to skill training or baby sitting—in this, Carl Bereiter has made a fundamental error, but not a wrongheaded one. These two options are the residual alternatives for the state school structure as presently constituted. The present result is a product of the destruction of that older voluntarism out of which commitment and belief were formed.

Education is a process of creating and shaping human values, of culture building. By giving citizens choice, a great measure of choice, we can begin to nurture those qualities of mind and soul that are intrinsic to the educational process. To choose, people also have to reject. By forcing student and school upon each other, we already limit choice. The next step is to sterilize the internal life of the school community so that the school cannot choose its educational life style. It might disturb a dissident minority. Rather, give the dissident minority its voucher. Let it form a school and persuade us of its merits. It can thereby gain the opportunity to become an incipient majority, and a shaper of our educational destinies.

PUBLIC SCHOOL VOUCHERS WILL FAIL

The widespread opposition to the voucher idea within the existing public school establishment, the reluctance, with the exception of Alum Rock, California, to accept an OEO grant to set up a modified voucher plan in the public schools, has led to a countermovement within the public schools. This is the trend, especially within larger school districts, of establishing schools with differing "learning styles."

The idea of alternatives within the public school, as a simpler variation on the Alum Rock voucher plan, was discussed by Mario Fantini in several articles published in 1971.[30] His recent book,

30. Mario Fantini, "Options for Students, Parents and Teachers: Public Schools of

Public Schools of Choice, argues for a trend that is estimated to encompass over two thousand examples of alternative education.[31] The basic antithesis here would probably be between advocates of open classrooms versus the more traditionally oriented 3 R's approach. In general, it is hoped that those elements of choice-lessness that have overwhelmed the schools with controversy will thereby be avoided. The Alum Rock experiment encompassed twenty-two possible programs for almost four thousand students in six variously structured grade schools (K–8). Naturally, in other settings the variety of learning-style schools, including those for the arts or academically talented, will be determined by the size and the particular character of the school district.

Now it may well satisfy many parents to have some choice. Certainly, the heady freedom here stimulated will dampen the fuse of discontent for a while. But if our analysis of the current malaise is correct, this new development will be merely the first phase in a process of rising expectations, which has consistently occurred in education and in society. The key element of failure in this new public school innovation will focus on that traditional educational *chez d'oeuvre* (specialty of the pedagogical house) that educators have cultivated—learning styles.

This skill is in the methodological area of teaching and learning techniques. Because of the inevitable cultural and value restrictions, teachers have been more and more forced to concentrate on "methods," "curriculum materials," and "school and classroom organization." Certainly, educators have presumed to teach "moral and spiritual values." But, as these issues have necessitated increasing resort to political controversy or to the courts, even the platitudes have been abandoned. It is no wonder the decline of the free school is followed by Bereiter's prosaic skill-training model.

But we are more than automatons. Eventually, the shallowness of the concept of "learning styles" will cause the same frustrations. The peripheral experiments will quickly be eliminated by the requirement for achievement. Those schools that are specialized in function, e.g., the performing arts or academically talented, will be accused of elitism and the admissions policy will be widened, thus further vitiating their uniqueness.

Eventually, since financial resources are not infinite for any school system, the more peripheral learning style programs must be absorbed by the major district-wide patterns. A minimum knowl-

---

Choice," *Phi Delta Kappan* 52 (May 1971): 53–54; "Public Schools of Choice and the Plurality of Publics," *Educational Leadership* 28 (March 1971): 585–91.

31. New York: Simon & Schuster, 1974.

edge of human beings should tell us that the so-called peripheral programs have a large clientele, percentage-wise. And these parents and children will be unhappy at not being able to secure their own particular educational interests.

Even the matter of real diversity of basic learning styles, such as between a conservative 3 Rs program and an open-classroom approach, should be questioned. Much will depend on the skill and temperament of the teacher. A comparison of achievement scores in the basic skills, as well as the happiness of average American children in each of these programs, should serve to bring the programs closer together in curricular emphasis and classroom atmosphere. Eventually people will notice that there are limits to pedagogical extremes, when similar academic and/or affective results are desired.

They will also realize that, as compared with the basic subject matter content of the curriculum, the value commitments that the school holds high, the purely technical aspects of pedagogical method or classroom organization constitute superficial elements. The public school voucher, which involves a reshuffling of pedagogical styles, now advertised as alternative schools, would constitute a mere sop to a public that demands fundamental change. Still standing in the way of this demand for social and cultural self-determination is an established if inchoate institutional self-interest.

George LaNoue argues that the voucher idea is not in the public's best interest. He worries about who will control the voucher idea.

> Those who advocate ideal or model vouchers don't seem to fully recognize the true nature of the voucher constituency. There is a latent coalition prepared to support vouchers, and it won't be led by the gentlemen scholars from Cambridge and Berkeley. The coalition is the one Kevin Phillips proposed in *The Emerging Republican Majority*. It is composed mainly of Southern Protestant nativists and Northern Catholic ethnics—plus, I would add, a touch of the far right and the far left. Aid to private schools was one of the ways Phillips suggested that coalitions might be brought together. The danger is, then, that while the intellectual debate focuses on ideal vouchers, the true voucher coalition will rise up to take command of the idea. Once united, that coalition might be able to bring about the kind of unregulated, non-compensatory, constitution-free vouchers that would lead to the social disaster Jencks himself warns about.[32]

32. *Educational Vouchers*, p. 143.

This is a typical argument of those who would limit the self-determination of any constituency: "These people don't know what is good for the general public. And, in addition, they don't agree with my view of things. Best don't introduce the extension of freedom because the bad guys might get the upper hand in the process of self-determination." There is no better argument against the present paternalistic, patently politically oriented use of schooling. There is also an assumption that those with whom LaNoue might agree are presently satisfied with the system. Certainly, the overwhelming voice of the black community is bitterly critical of the present structure.[33]

Indeed, a member of the staff of the Center for the Study of Public Policy, attorney Stephen Arons, had a quite different perception of our educational situation:

> The present situation in schooling and in the country generally is one in which we desperately need to let values and institutions develop from the people up. Continued top down efforts to cope with dissatisfaction by tightening the controls of existing institutions or making a few fine adjustments in the machine cannot be responsive to the basic changes in consciousness which are taking place. We need to give ourselves more space. We need to open up and in some cases even terminate institutions voluntarily. The voucher plan can be drawn so that it provides this needed space for development of new learning relationships, while at the same time guarding against the basic discriminations which we have been suffering.[34]

What the emphasis on learning styles in "alternative" public schools does not do is to provide for the free ranging experimentation by all groups. The misguided liberal view today that the underprivileged minorities need the liberals to take them in hand has in part been responsible for the tragic conditions of the schools in urban areas. The ensuing and nihilistic attempts to solve this ineffectuality has resulted in forced busing. The evidence is that these minorities merely aspire to educational self-determination. They want to rise in society and attain that competency that is a mark of middle-class status.[35]

33. See the various essays written by black educators in Edgar Epps, ed., *Cultural Pluralism* (Berkeley, Calif.: McCutcheon, 1974).
34. In LaNoue, *Educational Vouchers,* p. 96.
35. See Joseph P. Lyford, *The Airtight Cage: A Study of New York's West Side* (New York: Harper & Row, 1966); Henry S. Johnson and William J. Hernandez, ed.,

Without question some errors will take place under a new voluntary public education system. There will be trends that may horrify both liberal and conservative sensibilities. But these will be the errors made by the people themselves. Carl Bereiter has wisely noted that part of being free and adult is the right to make mistakes, to suffer thereby and thence personally to correct these errors. No self-appointed group that has gained power over the existing institutional system has the right to decide in this crucial area of education what are the orthodox values and methods of education.

At one time, a powerful consensus gave the developing public school system a mandate for expansion. But this was in a time when there was far more opportunity for self-determination. The education profession was still young and evolving. It had not hardened into a political force committed to protecting its hard won economic gains. The consensus is gone. The schools are by turns in chaos or inert. The national scepticism about education is pervasive. To a great extent the educational profession is complicit. The integrity and future of the profession have thus been undermined.

A RESPONSIVE PROFESSION

A little over one hundred years ago, Moses Woolson, a teacher of twelve-year-olds in a distinguished public school, the Boston Latin School, spoke to his students approximately as follows: "You are here as wards in my charge: I accept that charge as sacred: I accept the responsibility involved as a high exacting duty I owe myself and equally to you. I will give to you all that I have, you shall give to me all that you have." [36]

These words, absorbed by the young Louis Sullivan, eventually to become one of America's greatest architects, reverberated through his mind and soul. He regarded this man's teaching as a gift so heartfelt and profound that he recalled it with gratitude throughout his years.

Let us move forward to our own day and consider another description of the vocation of teaching. In this case, it is the carefully considered thoughts of a mature scholar in education, Harry Broudy. Here is his sense of the direction in which the profession

---

Educating the Mexican Americans (Valley Forge, Pa.: Judson Press, 1971); Francesco Cordasco and Eugene Buccheone, ed., *The Puerto Rican Community and Its Children on the Mainland* (Metuchen, N.J.: Scarecrow Press, 1972).

36. Louis Henri Sullivan, in Houston Peterson, ed., *Great Teachers* (New York: Vintage Books, 1946), p. 56.

will go: "paraprofessionals in all professional fields . . . medicine, law, education . . . are probable. In schooling the area most amenable to machine-like operation and therefore most easily assigned to paraprofessionals is didactics [basic skill teaching]. Hence we may have to settle for a relatively small cadre of, let us say, 300,000 to 350,000 teachers trained to the fully professional level, who will prescribe and monitor the work of the paraprofessionals." [37]

Here in a nutshell we have an insight into the present condition of the profession. At the very top, battling for control, are the power brokers. Whoever is victorious inherits the reins of power. Below are the hundreds of thousands, millions of functionaries whose fate is being decided from on high. They are being moved about the checkerboard, a vast army fulfilling its appointed task.

In the process of being tossed between the early glorious hopes and ideals of the American teaching profession, the soul has disappeared from the dream of being a teacher. We have so overregulated and stereotyped the function of the teacher that the sense of commitment and vocation has been submerged. What has happened is that the natural and flexible relationship between teacher and taught has been interdicted.

Whereas one can argue that in medicine or engineering, regulation and stereotyping of training and function insure uniform quality, the task of teaching is something else. It involves human values, and as such, concerns itself with producing a variety of skills and qualities of mind, attitude, and talent that will satisfy diverse constituencies.

By dissolving the artificial barriers that prevent a more flexible relationship between teacher, school, and child, the profession could obtain a new lease on life. Teachers are presently persuaded that their relative security derives from the present power of their professional organization, power directed as it is at boards of education, which are vulnerable to external pressure and ultimately not directly responsible to the parents and children for what they acquiesce to.

This is a spurious security. While the teacher continues to be the butt of discontent, subject to taxpayer and legislative revolts, his economic security is highly vulnerable. And yet the teacher, historically, has been invulnerable. His economic security has varied, but the universal condition of love and need between teacher and learner is perennial. Free choice is the key, the right to be taught by whom one chooses, and the right to teach only those one feels will

37. Harry Broudy, *The Real World of the Public Schools* (New York: Harcourt Brace Jovanovich, 1972), pp. 246–47.

benefit from one's skills. This is the natural first step. The present system makes this relationship impossible.

There is no question that the teaching profession in a voluntary system ought to have commensurable economic protections. Teachers ought to be licensed and certified. And the civil rights of teachers need to be secured. There is no clear evidence that the present system of private education, when one considers its precarious economic situation, is any less professional from this latter standpoint than the current public standard of civil liberties.[38] Ultimately, teachers will have to take their place with all other citizens in a structure of economic security and equity. The professional organizations in their total commitment to the economic side of things will then become moot.

What we would hope to see in a voluntary system is a more flexible approach to teacher training, one that is more directly influenced by the natural flow of innovation and need in diverse schools. With fewer rigid certification requirements, educational institutions would have to compete more directly to place high quality teachers in schools that have become highly selective. And of course there may be a wide variety of orientations in educational philosophy and cultural styles, thence leading to a heterogeneous approach to teacher training. This would be a progressive development.

The novice teachers will both choose and be chosen, and for real qualitative reasons. Standards of in-service training and further education will be held high. One's job security will in part be determined by how well a school meets the challenge to produce a quality education for its students. There is more than enough talent to meet the needs of every school—urban, suburban, or rural.

But there is also a need to keep personnel requirements imposed by the state more flexible. There may have to be certain regulations for the percentage of full-time certified teachers on a faculty. Beyond that, a varied complexion of the faculty, including part-time or temporary faculty with specialized community skills or other professional training—lawyers, doctors, ministers, volunteer mothers or fathers—ought to be encouraged. The richer the community mix, the more intimate and relevant the educational environment. It cannot but induce a deeper loyalty of teachers to their wards and reciprocally a deeper meaning to the educational ex-

38. Louis Fischer and David Shimmel, *The Civil Rights of Teachers* (New York: Harper & Row, 1973).

perience for the learner, than the cold, external nature of the relationships made necessary by the present structure.

A historically dangerous situation is building up in our public schools today. The concentration of legal hustling over noneducational factors, such as the statistics of race, the lobbying for power and more jobs, mandated state preschool programs, the growth of new teacher aide categories in the bureaucracy, all reflect a continuing move away from the free-flowing evolution of schooling. What is most serious is the lack of concern for quality and talent. We send forth too many teachers into the establishment with their certificates and little further reflection of their comparative abilities and little recognition for their in-service merit. This carelessness has to eventuate in a lack of concern of schools for the development of talented students.

We hear much of the need for compensatory programs and the fear that a voucher system of education would widen the gap between academic achievers and those who do not flourish scholastically. All reasonable people subscribe to the necessity of helping the disadvantaged to overcome their deficits. But one cannot expect to achieve the latter goal if it means that at the same time we impede the educational advance of the able.

It is an error to limit the growth of talent or ability in both learner and teacher, so that the spread between the ablest and the weakest might not thereby be increased. Our educational system now operates in such a way that the potential scholarly talents of an important segment of the young—teachers and pupils—are neutralized from the moment these young enter the present state system. The recent flourishing of free schools and the extent to which they did attract strong and dedicated young teachers is an indication that the desire and commitment to teach, even at personal sacrifice, still exists.

From the perspective of the demands of a complex modern society, the educational requirements are clear. A high general level of academic skill and an awareness of the structure of modern experience come first. An educational system also must be so structured that it feeds into the informal dimension of cultural and community life. There is, in addition, a need to ensure that individual talent both in teaching and learning has complete freedom to make itself manifest. Any structural impediment to this differentiation of skills can be a fatal neglect on the part of any society. The flowering of the best ought not be considered to redound to the potential disfavor of the weakest. Talent and ability are dimensions of social life that add rather than detract from their possible possession by others.

To the extent that the teaching profession would turn to put its weight behind a more open educational system, it could provide for its own advancement. More educational choice by individuals and communities can only lead to an explosion of innovation. This inherent and sometimes latent capacity of the profession to add to the advance of society is a factor of strength. New professional possibilities that might come forth could possibly weaken the present organizational powers-that-be in education. But it could ultimately add to the influence and stature of teaching.[39]

39. Two very important books which bear on the argument of this book have recently come to my attention. They are *Education and the State* (London: The Institute of Economic Affairs, 1970) and *Education and the Industrial Revolution* (New York: Harper & Row, 1975). Both books are written by E. G. West, an English economist interested in educational issues and now teaching at Carleton University in Ottawa, Canada.

West's research into English education in the nineteenth century leads him to conclude that private and voluntary education flourished throughout the century up until the education act of 1870. This bill fully established the state school system. West's view was that law was unnecessary and that literacy and economic development were well served as citizens from all classes expended personal funds on education.

In fact, his argument is that the virtual monopoly of education by the state schools has served to slow down educational progress. Without competition there has been inevitable loss of quality control. West even opposes the idea of the voucher, because no matter how minimal the base, and it could not be set too low for the poor, the voucher acts to buffer inefficiency.

Ultimately, the issue reduces to the question of maintaining a citizenry of quality with enough economic wherewithal to purchase the kind of education it sees fit. Perhaps the hope for educational freedom lies in the maintenance of a solid middle-class population capable of exercising choice.

Conclusion

In calling for a new public education one does not expect that a revolutionary razing of the existing structure will be enacted precipitously. Vast numbers of teachers will not be fired, administrators will live out their tenure, civil service rights will not be violated. Neither will storefronts and quonset huts blossom forth as schools, supervised by strangely garbed and youthful enthusiasts.

The primary need is for a reconsideration of what is most important in our evolving concept of the educated person. From this reconsideration we can go on to the problem of gradually reshaping institutional structures to effect our goals. The first step toward accomplishing such a goal would be to make available a wider range of educational choices for parents, students, and teachers. The opportunity to avail oneself of voluntaristic patterns of association through education ought not be the prerogative of only the rich. We will know far better what our basic national needs in education are when we allow people to choose, when they are not forced because of economic coercion into educational institutions established by the state.

Any proposals for educational change must take into account the historical purposes of formal education. A formal educational system acts as a bridge into the future established by the mature, to lead the young beyond the circumstances of today toward the eventualities they must face tomorrow. In a sense, society directs its philosophical ideals, cultural values, and social plans in the structure and character of the schools.

The schools are not the only educational institutions. In our own day powerful shaping forces exist in the political structures, local, national, and international, to which we are subject. Economic institutions of international scope and power, mass communication media which bring the world to us in a variety of forms—print and electronic—also act to give flesh to our hopes and ideals. Fast and relatively cheap transportation has broadened personal experiences and relationships far beyond the compass of schools, teachers, and books.

But there is in addition a perennial if subtle educational element in those informal and intimate relationships and experiences that evolve from family, neighborhoods, work patterns, and friendships. The quiet hours, the moments of leisure, all act to buttress or on the contrary to conflict with the more formal, institutional and external forces that form our overall attitudes and beliefs.

That there is great tension today in this nexus of educational forces and our basic human requirements goes without saying. No matter how we turn to resolve the strident and even critical institutional and emotional demands of our time, we will have to face the discipline of survival in a technological society. Though the current model of growth and affluent expansion is in disarray, perhaps in slow but agonizing decay, the technological and equilibrium society speaks to an educational modernity whose requirements will not disappear, even with great institutional changes in education.

We have traveled a long distance down the road from the simple neolithic cultural community. The need for highly refined and disciplined intelligence is worldwide in scope. There probably has never been such a vast educational spread between those at the apex of modernity, having the power and knowledge to alter the conditions of life for the masses, and those still living traditional agricultural lives in the byways of the world. Even the most hidden geographical contexts of traditional society are now being dissolved by the spread of modern forms of life. The simple peoples are being displaced and dumped into the shanty towns, the detritus of modern life. These hungry, miserable masses cannot return home. They have fondled the transistor radio.

As human beings, we are basically the same creatures who walked this earth fifteen thousand years ago. We have known the independence and the fears of walking the open plains and the primeval forests, of traversing the great unknown oceans. Humanity has known the throbbing creative excitements of life in small cities such as Athens and Florence. The need to think freely, to educate the young in accordance with reasoned conscience will remain, though we move into the physical and social constraints of an interdependent world.

There is a need, therefore, to plan out a new educational program that will accommodate itself to the requirements of material life in the tightly disciplined technological world of the future as well as one that succors those perennial personal and cultural needs of man. A society riven by class differences, economic or educational, is intolerable today. Nor can we return to the antiscientific medievalism of the theological tradition. Even that traditional working-class conception of education wherein the young acquire a rudimentary schooling as prelude to a life at work in factory, mine, or dock will be in decline. There is no need to prohibit these conceptions of education. The force of modern life will clearly demonstrate what is educationally required in a world of almost unlimited changes and readaptation.

To argue that intellectual, scientific, and academic competency is critical for life where brains count far more than brawn is to speak today of an educational context which at least for the United States and much of the Western world has already enveloped the horizon. The battle for a modern educational system was fought out in those early decades of the twentieth century. By the end of World War II the realities of modernity had etched themselves into the consciousness of the expanding American middle class with irrefutable indelibility.

The institutions of public education which evolved in the late nineteenth century to remake an ignorant immigrant and agricultural population has effected its goals well. In fulfilling the demands of modernization, in assisting in the development of an affluent efficient populace, they have paved the way for the next step in social modernization. The success of public schooling has in turn made the present institutional structure obsolete.

The efforts that now need to be undertaken in a school to make the average, middle-class child literate and academically competent in our modern world are quite different than those of half a century ago. The buttressing impact of all the adjuncts of modern life makes this effort less mechanical. We would argue that there would be few educational contexts and programs in a voluntary system of education that would long miss the mark academically. One can hardly argue this way for the efficiency of the compulsory state educational domain.

The major educational problem that faces us today is not a quantitative one, of merely developing the requisite skills in the largest number of students. Nor is it merely a matter of developing more flexibility in a bureaucratic system which would make wider opportunities available to those whose skills may vary from the norm, or to those whose pace and style of learning do not fit the established pattern. The greatest educational need is to create a whole human being in the context of the coming international corporate structure of life.

This new set of historical circumstances demands that we establish social contexts in which we can maximize personal and cultural autonomy. We need room for freedom of thought, intellectual and aesthetic experimentation, new patterns of community life, religious and ethnic commitments, that give scope for people to choose, decide, and make changes. Human beings as never before will need to sink their energies and talents into the rich inner soil of the human spirit, to mine the potentialities for creative effort in social and community areas, areas that need to be protected from the machine organizations of the corporate world.

Educational settings will be among the most important sources for the potential flourishing of cultural communities. It is significant and worth noting that formal education was not mentioned in the Constitution. Schooling exists among those residual rights reserved to the states, or to the people, as encompassed in the Tenth Amendment to the Constitution.

There is, therefore, nothing sacrosanct in the present establishment of public schooling that cannot be changed by the will of the people through their representatives. To argue for a new public education that respects the present needs of citizens and voluntary communities is not to argue for a return to apartheid and class distinctions in a world searching for equality and interrelatedness. We must always keep clearly in mind what each institution in society is designed to accomplish. Political and economic equality, ecological interdependence, a unification of mankind in the material and legal sphere in no way counters the need for cultural diversity and pluralism. Human beings are more than the sum of their political and economic parts.

On the contrary, in an age when decisions affecting the lives of all mankind will be made in distant parliaments, it is crucial that there be maintained as many areas as possible for decision making by individual citizens.

The hopes for a great system of world law, regulations disciplining the heretofore unplanned and chaotic behavior of billions of people, depend upon the creation of a system of international life that will have a stability at least approaching the best years of the Roman Empire. Any international social machine needs to elicit the long-term allegiance of this vast populace, or else it will inevitably break down.

The only way that this stability can be achieved is through an education that cultivates a two-tiered awareness of cultural experience, the spontaneous and creative autonomy of life in cultural communities, and the disciplined, rational sense of public responsibilities that must affect the fate of the entire human species. An education that inducts the individual into the process of decision making in his or her immediate life experiences releases productive energies in smaller social contexts that eventually make their way outward into the larger world society. In contrast, an education controlled from afar, only reflecting that austere and abstract structure of systemic life of the equilibrium society, must inevitably thwart and turn inward energies that are potentially destructive.

What a freely and flexibly evolving decentralized educational system can do for us today is to provide a variety of psychological and cultural settings within which life in the technological society can be given flesh and substance. Educational diversity implies a maximization of approaches to be developed within broad social guidelines established to ensure a basic public consensus. The impact of such a revised view of public education, in that it aims to succor people's inner life as well as their outer circumstances, would hopefully expand our historical options.

Index

DATE DUE

APR 2 7 1990		
NOV 1 6 1995		